# BIBLE STUDY NOTES

Volume 3

# BIBLE STUDY NOTES

MEMORIAL EDITION

By Anita S. Dole

Edited By Wm. R. Woofenden

AMERICAN NEW CHURCH
SUNDAY SCHOOL ASSOCIATION
1979

*Library of Congress Catalog Card Number: 76-24081*
*Complete set ISBN 0-917426-00-2*
*Volume 3 ISBN 0-917426-03-7*

Sales Agent:

Swedenborg Library
79 Newbury Street
Boston, Massachusetts 02116

*"Well done, good and faithful servant."*
*—Matthew 25:23*

Printed in U.S.A.

## TABLE OF CONTENTS

## INTRODUCTORY NOTES FOR TEACHERS

As we may see by the accompanying chart, this program was planned as a four-year Bible course, but it was originally arranged so that the whole Word was covered by periods each year, in order that the child might early realize that the Bible is one book–not only a continuous story but a completed one–and also that children might not so often enter the Sunday School for the first time in the middle of the Bible story with no idea of what has gone before. While this plan might in any one year seem to leave many important stories untouched, the retelling of the background of the successive periods from year to year in the context of different stories built up gradually in the child's mind both a surer knowledge and a better understanding of the whole letter of the Word. The plan insured that the beginning of the Bible story was not forgotten before the end was reached, and that the Old and New Testaments were seen in their proper relation and proportion. Although the lessons are now arranged in Bible sequence, it is still possible, by using the chart, to use the original four-year plan.

The notes for the various age groups are written with two purposes in view. It is *not* intended that the teacher should read them to the class. Neither is it intended that copies should be given out to the pupils in advance. Only the Bible reading should be done in advance. For the teacher, the notes are meant to suggest the points to be covered in the lesson, a possible order of presentation, and the general level of meaning which pupils in the particular age group may be expected to comprehend. For the pupil, if he has his own set of the books, they are meant to be taken home, read as a review during the week, and preserved for future reference.

It is very important that the teacher plan his use of the class time carefully. Five minutes or less at the beginning of the period are enough for review questions. Then give five minutes to a carefully thought-out covering of the background of the lesson for the day before going into the lesson proper. In the Old Testament build the background as far as possible about persons and places in order to fix these in their proper sequence in the pupils' minds. In the New Testament the background should be the factual story of the Lord's life on earth.

The writings of the church tell us that "generals" must be grasped before "particulars" can be understood in their proper context; so we may feel sure that our first object in the Sunday School should be to impress the general outline of the whole Bible story on the minds of our pupils. The covering of the whole story each year has this objective in view.

The two survey lessons (nos. 22 and 24 on the accompanying chart) are general lessons but are based on a different passage each year in order to give the pupils a wider variety in the study of the Prophets than has been possible in previous courses. They are also optional lessons, written in such a way that Sunday Schools with a school year of less than forty sessions may omit them without losing continuity. Each series also contains fifteen lessons from the New Testament. A different Gospel is studied each year. Two of the fifteen lessons are written as optional lessons; three are the special lessons for Christmas, Palm Sunday, and Easter; and three are from the book of Revelation.

# FOUR-YEAR LESSON COURSE FOR NEW CHURCH SUNDAY SCHOOLS

## Assignments in the Old Testament

| *Lesson* | *Subject* | *Series I* | *Series II* | *Series III* | *Series IV* |
|---|---|---|---|---|---|
| 1. | The Creation | General View | First Four Days | Days Five and Six | The Seventh Day |
| 2. | The Most Ancient Church | The Garden of Eden | Helpmeet for Adam | The Serpent | Cain and Abel |
| 3. | The Ancient Church | Noah Builds an Ark | End of the Flood | The Rainbow | Tower of Babel |
| 4. | Abraham | The Call of Abram | Abram and Lot | Birth of Ishmael | Abraham & the Angels |
| 5. | Isaac | Birth of Isaac | Sacrifice of Isaac | Isaac and Rebekah | Isaac & Abimelech |
| 6. | Jacob | Jacob & Esau | Jacob's Dream | Wives & Sons | Jacob's Return |
| 7. | Joseph | Joseph & Brothers | Joseph in Prison | Ruler of Egypt | Sons and Death |
| 8. | Moses | Birth of Moses | The Burning Bush | The Ten Plagues | The Passover |
| 9. | Escape from Egypt | Crossing Red Sea | Marah & Elim | Quails and Manna | Rephidim & Amalek |
| 10. | Mount Sinai | Ten Commandments | Ark of Covenant | The Tabernacle | The Golden Calf |
| 11. | Wilderness Wanderings | Nadab & Abihu | The Twelve Spies | Korah, Dathan, Abiram | Aaron's Rod |
| 12. | Entering the Holy Land | Balaam | Call of Joshua | Crossing the Jordan | Gilgal |
| 13. | Conquest of Holy Land | Jericho | Ai | The Gibeonites | Conquest & Division |
| 14. | The Judges | Deborah & Barak | Gideon | Jephthah | Samson |
| 15. | Samuel | Birth of Samuel | Lord Calls Samuel | Capture of the Ark | Asking for a King |
| 16. | Saul | Choosing of Saul | Saul's Impatience | Saul & Jonathan | Sparing Agag |
| 17. | David | Anointing of David | David & Goliath | Ark to Jerusalem | David & Bathsheba |
| 18. | Solomon | Wisdom of Solomon | Glory of Solomon | Building the Temple | Decline & Death |
| 19. | Kingdom of Israel | Elijah & Ahab | Elijah at Horeb | Elijah's Mantle | Elisha & Naaman |
| 20. | Kingdom of Judah | Reign of Asa | Hezekiah & Isaiah | Josiah | Zedekiah & Jeremiah |
| 21. | Book of Psalms | Psalm 1 | Psalm 19 | Psalm 91 | Psalm 119 |

| | | | | | |
|---|---|---|---|---|---|
| *22. | Major Prophets—Survey | Isaiah 6 | Jeremiah 1 | Ezekiel 47:1-12 | Daniel 5 |
| 23. | Major Prophets | Fiery Furnace | Ezekiel's Vision | Daniel & the Image | Daniel & the Lions |
| *24. | Minor Prophets—Survey | Micah 6 | Joel 3:9-21 | Amos 8 | Zechariah 4 |
| 25. | Minor Prophets | Haggai 1; 2 | Jonah & the Fish | Malachi 3; 4 | Jonah & the Gourd |

## Assignments in the New Testament

| *Lesson* | *Series I* | *Series II* | *Series III* | *Series IV* |
|---|---|---|---|---|
| 26. | Matthew 1:18-25; 2:13-23 | Mark 1 | Luke 1 | John 1 |
| 27. | Matthew 3 | Mark 2 | Luke 7:1-30 | John 2:1-11 |
| 28. | Matthew 4:1-11 | *Mark 3 | Luke 9:1-36 | *John 3:1-21 |
| 29. | *Matthew 4:12-25 | *Mark 4 | Luke 10:25-42 | John 4:1-42 |
| 30. | Matthew 5; 6; 7 | Mark 5 | *Luke 11 | John 5:1-16 |
| 31. | Matthew 8 | Mark 6 | Luke 14 | John 9 |
| 32. | *Matthew 13 | Mark 10 | Luke 15 | *John 10 |
| 33. | Matthew 17:1-13 | Mark 14 | *Luke 16 | John 11:1-46 |
| 34. | Matthew 26; 27 | Mark 15 | Luke 24:13-53 | John 15 |
| 35. | Revelation 1 | Revelation 4 | Revelation 6 | Revelation 12 |
| 36. | Revelation 2; 3 | Revelation 5 | Revelation 8; 9 | Revelation 13; 19:11-21 |
| 37. | Revelation 21; 22 | Revelation 20:11-15; 21:1-7 | Revelation 21:9-16 | Revelation 22:8-21 |
| *Special Lessons* | | | | |
| Christmas | Matthew 2:1-15 | Luke 2:1-20 | Matthew 2:1-15 | Luke 2:1-20 |
| Palm Sunday | Matthew 21:1-27 | Mark 11 | Luke 19 | John 12:12-50 |
| Easter | Matthew 28 | Mark 16 | Luke 24:1-12 | John 20; 21 |

*Optional Lessons

# BIBLE STUDY NOTES

## I SAMUEL - PSALMS

# THE BIRTH OF SAMUEL

*I Samuel 1; 2:1-11*

Review the general character of the period of the Judges and speak of Samuel as the last of the Judges and the only one recognized as leader by the whole land. The story of the child Samuel is so touching and so well known that the work of his later life is often overlooked in our Sunday school teaching.

---

## Doctrinal Points

*Our whole life needs to be organized around worship of the Lord.*

*We need to preserve or regain our childhood state of simple trust and obedience.*

---

## Notes for Parents

The story of the child Samuel is one of the most loved stories in the Old Testament. The longing of his mother for a son and her vow to devote him to the Lord can be understood by every woman, and the obedient, trustful nature of the child appeals to us all. It is a touching and beautiful story.

But often we fail to appreciate it fully because we do not so well know the dark background against which it stands out in the Bible. In our studies of the period of the Judges we saw how quickly the Israelites forgot their God, who had done so much for them, once they had gained the position in the world for which they had longed. The ark and the tabernacle are not once mentioned in the book of Judges. Before Joshua died, he had set up the tabernacle at Shiloh in the center of the land and the people had promised always to serve the Lord. In our chapter for today we find that the tabernacle is still at Shiloh, that there is still a high priest of the line of Aaron, and that at least some of the people still bring sacrifices to the tabernacle regularly. But most of the people have fallen away into the worship of the idols of the land, and even Eli's sons, the assistant priests, have become corrupt.

Can we not see in this a common experience? We are brought up to go to Sunday school and church, but when we leave the control of our parents and establish ourselves in homes of our own, we become absorbed in our daily tasks and responsibilities and drift away from the worship of the Lord from whom all that is good in our lives has come. We think we know enough to live good lives, and it is not until some serious trouble strikes that we realize our actual weakness and need of our Heavenly Father.

What shall we do? Our immediate resort is to the things we were taught and believed in our childhood and to an effort to recapture our simple faith. Samuel appears on the scene. He is not a warrior. He is first an obedient child and later a priest and a prophet. He is the last of the Judges and the only one recognized by the whole people as their appointed leader. It is obvious from the first that the Lord is with him and speaks through him.

So it must be with us. We must turn from our reliance on our own judgment and strength and acknowledge that our only salvation lies in simple trust in the Lord and obedience to His commandments. Hundreds of years after the time of Samuel, the Lord said to His disciples: "Except ye be converted, and become as little children, ye shall not enter into the kingdom of heaven."

Samuel was to live to old age and to anoint the first two kings of Israel.

---

### Primary

This is a simple story and easy to tell. The story of Hannah's prayer and vow should be told as an introduction. Then attention should be centered on the tabernacle at Shiloh—the fact that it was still there and that a descendant of Aaron (Eli) was high priest. The children will be interested in the two wives and their differences, and in Hannah's promise.

You remember the ark, don't you? It was the gold-covered chest made to hold the two tablets of stone on which the Lord had written the ten commandments with his own finger. And do you remember the tabernacle, or tent, which was made at Mount Sinai to hold the ark and to be the church of the children of Israel?

It is a long time since we have heard of the tabernacle.
At the time of our story today, the tabernacle is set up at Shiloh near the center of the Holy Land.

From the time the people left Mount Sinai, where the commandments were given, the ark and the tabernacle were always in the center of their camp or in the center of their line of march when they were traveling. After they conquered the Holy Land, and before they settled in their homes, Joshua set up the tabernacle at Shiloh, and there it stood for many years. The priests carried on the worship there, and the high priest was always a descendant of Aaron. You remember that Aaron, the brother of Moses, was the first high priest. At the time of our story for today the high priest was an old man named Eli.

The last and greatest of the Judges was Samuel.
He was the only one who was Judge over the whole land.
He was also the only one who was a prophet.
Who was Samuel's mother?
How did she happen to come to the tabernacle at Shiloh?
What did she ask the Lord to give her?
What did she promise if her prayer was granted?
Did she keep her promise?
After that, every year when they came to Shiloh to worship, Hannah brought Samuel a new little coat which she had made for him.
Because she kept her promise, the Lord gave her three more sons and two daughters.

Samuel grew up helping Eli in the tabernacle. When he was grown up, he became Judge over all the land; the Lord spoke to the people through him, so he was also a prophet. You should remember him as the last of the Judges.

---

## Junior

Remind the class of the construction and purpose of the tabernacle and have them look up and read Joshua 18:1. Review the general characteristics of the period of the Judges, and introduce Samuel as the last of the Judges. The class will remember the story of an earlier Judge, Samson, who was also a Nazarite, and should read first Hannah's vow (verse 11) and then the laws for the Nazarite in Numbers 6:1-5. Emphasize Samuel's later greatness.

What book follows the book of Joshua in the Bible?
Who were the Judges?
How was this period different from the earlier ones?

You will notice that we have passed over the book of Ruth. It is a beautiful story of something which happened in the time of the Judges, and you should read it some time, for it tells of the birth of the grandfather of David. But it has no internal meaning relating to the Lord and to our spiritual development; so we do not study it in Sunday school.

The characteristic of the period of the Judges was that "every man did that which was right in his own eyes" (Judges 17:6). This shows us the reason why the ark and the tabernacle are not once mentioned in the book of Judges. The people were looking to themselves for direction instead of to the Lord. When we think we are wise enough to decide for ourselves what is right and wrong, the Lord and the church seem to drop out of our minds. But they are there all the time hidden deep within our minds and hearts. So we find now that the ark and the tabernacle are still there in the center of the land. Look up Joshua 18:1.

Where had Joshua set up the tabernacle?
Who was the high priest at the time of Samuel's birth?
Who had been the first high priest?

Even though most of the people had turned to idol worship and forgotten the Lord, there were still some faithful ones who tried to keep the laws of Moses and who went regularly to the tabernacle to worship. Samuel's parents were such people.

What were their names?
What did Hannah ask of the Lord?
What did Eli think when he saw her praying?
What did Hannah promise to do if her prayer was granted?
How did she keep her promise?

We may well imagine that it was not easy for Hannah to give up the child for whom she had waited so long. Read chapter 2, verses

18-21 to see how she kept in touch with him and how the Lord rewarded her for her faithfulness.

In the book *On Holy Ground*, William L. Worcester helps to make the story of Samuel very real to us. He says in part:

> We must imagine ourselves in Shiloh, "the place of rest," in the tribe of Ephraim, on a little hill with a meadow about it, shut in by higher hills, a little off the line of travel. There are ruins on the hill. At the time of our story a town was here, and in a place by itself stood the tabernacle, the sacred tent which was made at Mount Sinai, according to the pattern shown to Moses in the mount, and was set up at Shiloh by Joshua when the land was conquered.
>
> We remember the tabernacle: its open court with the altar of burnt offering and the laver; its walls of upright planks and its coverings of curtains making the holy place for the table and lamp and altar of incense, and the most holy place for the ark of the commandments. The old priest Eli had care of the tabernacle. He was more than ninety years old and his eyes were dim. Some of the people still came each year to worship, perhaps especially in the spring, at the season of the Passover. But Eli's sons who were priests were not good men and robbed the people of their offerings.
>
> And a little boy helped the old priest at the tabernacle; his hair was long and he wore a linen ephod or vest like a priest. He helped at the altar, and went within the tabernacle to arrange the bread on the table, or to trim the lamp in the morning, or to light it in the evening, so that it would burn bright in the Lord's house all night. While the lamp was burning, Eli and Samuel slept near by, perhaps under the overhanging curtains of the tent. And in the morning Samuel opened the doors or the curtains of the tabernacle to the sunshine.

Samuel was to be a Nazarite. Read Numbers 6:1-5 to see what some of the laws for a Nazarite were. The hair, which is the outmost thing in the human body, pictures the letter of the Bible, which is the outmost of the Word of God. The Nazarites were commanded not to cut their hair or beards as a picture of the fact that anyone who is really devoted to the Lord's service will try to keep every bit of the Law as given in the commandments. Samuel grew up to be completely obedient to the Lord. He was the last and greatest of the Judges: not a warrior like the others, but a priest and a prophet.

### Intermediate

The necessity of going to the tabernacle should be stressed with this class, along with the fact that the disorganized state pictured by the book of Judges results in neglect and perversion of worship. Call attention to our reason for passing over the book of Ruth. This is our first opportunity to point out that some books of the Bible, while interesting and valuable, have no internal meaning.

The book of Judges appears as a series of almost unrelated stories. This is not hard to understand when we see it as a picture of the time in our lives when we are trying to go our own way without looking to the Lord for direction. Our lives then are just a series of incidents with no apparent pattern or orderly development.

We have passed by the short book which follows the book of Judges in our Bible—the book of Ruth, which is a picture of everyday life in the time of the Judges. It is a beautiful story and worth reading for itself, but our teachings tell us that it has no internal meaning.

With the book of I Samuel we suddenly return to the tabernacle. Joshua 18:1 tells us that the tabernacle was set up at Shiloh in the center of the Holy Land immediately after the completion of the conquest, but in the book of Judges the tabernacle is not once mentioned. In much the same way, people often forget about the church when they are absorbed in their own ideas and activities.

But the Lord, as we have often learned, always preserves deep within us the "remains" of good and truth which have been stored up in our childhood and youth. So in our lesson today we find that the tabernacle is still there at Shiloh in the center of the land. Eli, a descendant of Aaron, is high priest, and a few faithful people, like Elkanah and Hannah, still bring their offerings regularly.

The story of Samuel is a familiar one. It is in itself a beautiful picture of the orderly beginning and development of life. Every child should, like Samuel, be devoted to the Lord even before he is born and be brought early to the church and dedicated to the service of the church. He should be taught to perform willingly the little services of which he is capable. Then he is prepared to hear the voice of the Lord when it speaks to him, and to obey it. There are many things in the story of the little Samuel which remind us of the childhood of the Lord Himself. The Lord was taken to the temple when He was eight days old, "his parents went to Jerusalem every year at the feast of the Passover," and when at the age of twelve He went with them, He tarried behind in the temple and talked with the learned men there. Of course the whole story of Samuel, like the rest of the inspired Word, in its inmost sense speaks of the life of the Lord.

Hannah's vow (1:11) points to the fact that Samuel's life was grounded in obedience to the commandments in their letter, for the hair corresponds to the outmost and, in a prophet, to the letter of the Word. Samson's strength was in his hair and Samson was also a Nazarite. For the law of the Nazarite see Numbers 6:1-21. Because Samuel's use was in the tabernacle, his strength was spiritual strength and was constant, and produced results more important and far-reaching than did Samson's physical victories.

We may perhaps think of Samuel as the Lord speaking to us out of our childhood faith when as adults we finally come to acknowledge our own weakness and need of the Lord's direction. After the confused and disorganized period represented by the time of the Judges, it is this alone which can begin to unify our lives and bring them into order. Samuel was to be the last of the Judges, for he would anoint the first king and later the second, establishing the kingdom. It is the recognition of our need to obey the Lord in simple faith which leads us to adopt higher and higher principles for the guidance of our lives.

Samuel alone of the Judges was recognized by the whole people as the one who spoke for the Lord. The fact that he was devoted to the Lord's service even before his birth and that his call by the Lord came to him when he was very young also clearly indicates that he represents the Lord's voice speaking to us out of our early religious training. The Lord tells us, "Whosoever shall not receive the kingdom of God as a little child shall in no wise enter therein."

(Luke 18:17)

*Basic Correspondences*

| | | |
|---|---|---|
| Samuel | = | the Lord speaking to us as adults out of our childhood states of faith |
| the hair | = | the outmost, the letter of the Word |

## Senior

Emphasis here should be on the transition from the period of the Judges to the period of Kings, with Samuel—our childhood state of innocence and obedience—as the connecting link. Draw the parallel between Samuel's early life and that of the Lord, as suggested in the Adult notes.

Samuel was the last of the Judges. His life and work began a new period of unification and development, and it is significant that in the story of his birth we suddenly return to the tabernacle. The ark and the tabernacle are not mentioned once in the book of Judges, but we now find that they are still at Shiloh in the center of the land, where Joshua had set them up, that there is still a high priest of the line of Aaron, that the tabernacle rites are still being carried out, and that there are still some people in the land who come faithfully to the tabernacle to offer sacrifices and to worship the true God. This is true in our lives. So long as we are permitted by the Lord to remain in this world, the possibility of spiritual life is still not entirely dead in us; there are some remains through which we may be reached if we choose. As the Lord said to Elijah many years later, when he was in despair at Horeb (I Kings 19:18), "Yet I have left me seven thousand in Israel, all the knees which have not bowed unto Baal, and every mouth which hath not kissed him."

But the general face of the situation was that of neglect of the Lord. And even in the priesthood there was corruption. Eli, the high priest, was a good man but weak. His sons, Hophni and Phinehas, who assisted him and would supposedly succeed him, were evil men, robbing the Lord of the offerings brought by the people and committing other evils. The whole situation reminds us of the condition of the church hundreds of years later at the time of the Lord's birth, and there are many things in the story of the little Samuel which clearly image the Lord's childhood.

The two wives of Elkanah, Hannah and Peninnah, recall to us the story of Leah and Rachel, and the still earlier story of Sarah and Hagar. In each case the beloved wife is late in bearing children and the less beloved looks upon her with contempt. We have learned to see in this our own slowness in developing spiritual fruits, and the arrogance of the material part of us with its obvious productivity. But in each case the late fruit of the beloved wife becomes greater than the children who have preceded him in time.

We think of Samuel as representing the beginning of our mature consciousness of our own weakness and need of the Lord. The whole of the ancient Hebrew nation is present in our lives when we come to maturity—all the tendencies to materialism, to the worship of idols of one sort or another, to self-esteem and self-will, to profanation of holy things, to weak acquiescence in the sins of our times and companions. But Samuel is in us, too: the voice of the Lord speaking through our stored-up states of childhood trust and faith and obedience, through the Word planted in our memories in childhood. This is what we have to build on to begin the process of regeneration which is the work of our adult lives. Without this "Samuel state" the lamp of God would indeed go out in all of us (I Samuel 3:3).

---

## Adult

There are several good discussion topics here: the disastrous results of self-confidence, particularly upon our worship; the Lord's preservation in us of our good childhood states; the harm we do to others as well as to ourselves when we neglect or misuse our worship; the meaning of the Lord's words about becoming as a little child; and the difference between the innocence of ignorance and the innocence of wisdom.

With the first book of Samuel we come to a new stage in the history of the church or of the person who is trying to live the regenerate life. The wars in the book of Judges picture the various temptations which assail those who have found their home in the Holy Land—that is, who have become settled in the desire and practice of living according to divine laws—but who have allowed themselves to become overconfident and careless and to slip back somewhat into the ways of the world about them. These temptations are both external and internal and they take many forms. We yield to them almost unconsciously at first; they grow upon us until we find ourselves subject to them and find we must take active measures against them. In the book of Judges the state of the people becomes worse and worse until, in the last chapters, the tribe of Benjamin—which represents spiritual or interior truth—becomes perverted and is almost destroyed. So sometimes we allow ourselves to "backslide" through constant yielding to small or subtle temptations until we find ourselves in a bad spiritual state and almost robbed of the sense of the internal meaning of life which makes conjunction with the Lord possible. A new beginning must be made if we are to be saved. We must return for a time to a condition of simple trust and obedience and allow this to lead us to a new peak of spiritual living.

The story of the child Samuel has always been one of the best loved of the Bible stories. *The Sower* beautifully points out its lesson for parents and children of all time. Parents should realize that all children are loaned to them by the Lord to prepare for His service, and should dedicate them to that service as Hannah dedicated Samuel. Children should see in Samuel a beautiful picture of simple trust and obedience and willing service. There are many similarities also between the early life of Samuel and that of the Lord, even to the expression (I Samuel 2:26), "And the child Samuel grew on, and was in favor both with the Lord, and also with men." Compare this with Luke 2:52.

But the story has a wider application than that to physical childhood. Our childhood states of innocence, trust, and obedience are covered up as we grow older, but they are not lost. No matter how far we have wandered from them, if we realize the barrenness of our state and look to the Lord as Hannah did for a new birth, promising new consecration, the childhood states can be revived in us and lead us to new developments of spiritual living. This is very plainly told to us by the Lord when He says, "Verily, I say unto you, except ye be converted and become as little children, ye shall not enter the kingdom of heaven. Whosoever therefore shall humble himself as this little child, the same is greatest in the kingdom of heaven," (Matthew 18:3-4) Samuel's early ministry in the tabernacle is a picture of our return to a humble state of mind, in which we read the Word in simplicity, enter into the services of worship with genuine sincerity, and look to the church for guidance, as Samuel looked to Eli. Then we put ourselves in a state in which the Lord can speak to us and prepare the way for new growth. "And Samuel grew, and the Lord was with him" (I Samuel 3:19).

The picture of the little Samuel is so striking and so touching that the dark background against which it stands out is often overlooked. Eli, the high priest and descendant of Aaron, is an old man and his sight is dim. He has turned over the conduct of the tabernacle worship to his sons, Hophni and Phinehas, who are "sons of Belial" who "knew not the Lord." They profaned the sacrifices of the people by taking more than their due portion of the offerings and by taking it even before sacrifice was made to the Lord. "Wherefore the sin of the young men was very great before the Lord: for men abhorred the offering of the Lord." (I Samuel 2:17) Eli is warned by a "man of God" that the priesthood will be taken from his house. He has remonstrated with his sons, but has not exerted his authority to put a stop to their evil practices. He is judged "because his sons made themselves vile, and he restrained them not." This is a picture of a state in which worship is degraded by being used for self-interest and self-exaltation, and when the high priest in us—that inner dictate which relates us to the Lord—does not take steps to correct the evil, although it sees it.* It has

*This was also clearly the condition of the church when the Lord came into the world, and it is interesting to note that one of the two members of the Sanhedrin who accepted the Lord came from Samuel's birthplace. These

become dim of sight and is no longer able to receive directly the voice of the Lord. In I Samuel 2:17, quoted above, there is the suggestion of the harm which such a state does to others as well as to ourselves. Many people are turned against the church by the self-seeking and hypocrisy they see in some of its members. Our duty to keep our worship sincere and to live according to the teachings of the church is not for our own salvation alone. The Lord's service requires of us constant watchfulness and ever-renewed devotion. We must be on our guard against the thought that we are "saved" and cannot go astray as others may.

The Lord, in the letter of the Word, had promised the priesthood to Aaron, and his seed forever. Now He takes it from them. "I said indeed that thy house, and the house of thy father, should walk before me for ever; but now the Lord saith, Be it far from me; for them that honor me I will honor, and they that despise me shall be lightly esteemed." (I Samuel 2:30) This degenerate state of worship is contrasted directly with the simple obedient service of Samuel, to whom the Lord can speak. Samuel's parents, like Mary and Joseph, were among those who made the prescribed pilgrimages to the tabernacle regardless of the corruption of the priesthood. They represent in us the remains of the sincere desire to serve the Lord from which a new beginning must come. In comparison with our more sophisticated worldly attitudes toward the church they are ignorant; but they have the fundamentals of true religion, humility and obedience. In AC 9325[8] there is an interesting statement of this thought in reference to the church in connection with Hannah's prophecy (I Samuel 2:5): "By 'the barren' are also signified those who are not in good because not in truths, and yet long for truths that they may be in good; as is the case with the upright

---

two—Joseph of Arimathea and Nicodemus, who like Eli did not "for fear of the Jews" oppose their worldly associates—were simple in heart and able to recognize and cherish the Messiah (John 19:38-42). *Arimathea* is a later form of *Ramathaimzophim*. The word means "twin watchtowers," suggesting an ability to lift the thought above the level of the world because goodness is united to truth.

nations outside the church; as in [Isaiah 54:1, Psalm 113:7-9, I Samuel 2:5]. In the above passages by 'the barren' are meant the Gentiles who are summoned to the church, and to whom the church is transferred when the old church ceases, that is, when those who before had been of the church are no longer in faith, because in no charity . . . 'To bear seven' denotes to be regenerated to the full."

All the beautiful stories of children throughout the Bible teach this same lesson. Humility and obedience are the only means of conjunction with the Lord. "And the Lord appeared again in Shiloh: for the Lord revealed himself to Samuel in Shiloh by the word of the Lord."

## From the Writings of Swedenborg

*Arcana Coelestia*, n. 6148[5-6]: "As a representative church was instituted with the posterity of Jacob, therefore in one person conjointly was represented the Divine good and the Divine truth which proceed united from the Lord. But on account of the wars and of the idolatry of the people, these two offices were at first divided, and they who ruled over the people were called 'leaders,' and afterward 'judges'; while they who officiated in holy things were called 'priests,' and were of the seed of Aaron, and Levites. Yet afterward these two offices were joined together in one person, as in Eli and in Samuel. But because the people were of such a character that a representative church could not be instituted among them, but only the representative of a church, by reason of the idolatrous disposition which prevailed among them, therefore it was permitted that the two offices should be separated, and that the Lord as to Divine truth should be represented by kings, and as to Divine good by priests. That this was done at the will of the people, and not of the Lord's good pleasure, is manifest from the word of Jehovah to Samuel (I Samuel 8:7 ff.). The reason why these two offices were not to be separated, was that the Divine truth separated from the Divine good condemns everyone; whereas the Divine truth united to the Divine good saves."

## Suggested Questions on the Lesson

I. Why do we not study the book of Ruth? *no inner sense*

P. Who was the last of the Judges? *Samuel*

J. Who were Samuel's parents? *Elkanah and Hannah*

J. Where was the tabernacle at this time? *Shiloh*

P. Who was the high priest? *Eli*

P. What promise did Hannah make? *if she had a son, to give him to the Lord*

J. How did she keep it? *brought Samuel to live with Eli*

P. Where did Samuel grow up? *at Shiloh*

I. Why did the people get into so much trouble in the time of the Judges? *forgot the Lord*

S. What does Samuel represent in us? *the Lord's Word to us through our childhood remains*

# THE LORD CALLS SAMUEL

*I Samuel 3*

It is important that the children see the fallacy of thinking that we can lead and govern ourselves apart from regular worship of the Lord and obedience to Him. The sin of Eli's sons shows how even worship can be degraded by selfishness, self-satisfaction, and disobedience.

---

### Doctrinal Points

*The doctrine of "remains": the Lord's work in our childhood.*
*Memory knowledge of the letter of the Word is one of the essentials.*
*The book of Ruth does not have an inner sense.*

---

### Notes for Parents

The beautiful story of the child Samuel is one of the most familiar in the Bible. His mother's longing for a child led her to promise that if the Lord would only give her a son, she would devote him to the Lord's service. When her son was born, she named him Samuel, which means "God hath heard." And she kept her promise by bringing him to the tabernacle as soon as he was weaned and giving him to Eli, the high priest, to bring up in the service of the tabernacle. The Bible tells us that her faithfulness was rewarded, for the Lord afterward gave her three more sons and two daughters.

We think so much of little Samuel that we are likely to forget the dark things in the story. Eli was a good old man, but his two sons—to whom he had turned over the active conduct of the tabernacle worship—were using their high office for their own profit. Eli knew it and had remonstrated with them, but he did not exercise his authority as he might have done to put a stop to their evil practices. So the message that came to Eli through the child Samuel was that the high priesthood would be taken away from his house.

There are lessons here for all of us. Today we sometimes see ministers who appear to care more for their own glory than for the service of the Lord, and there are people who go to church because it is "good business" or so that they will be looked up to in the community, or because a community where there are churches is safer to live in. And the knowledge that there are such people in the church may turn some people away from it, just as it did in Samuel's time. But if we really want to follow the Lord, what other people do will not keep us from worship or from bringing up our children in the service of the Lord.

For our children do come to us from the Lord, and they really belong to Him. They are His children first. They are loaned to us for a time to love and care for and to bring to Him as soon as they are old enough to learn of Him. We should see to it that our children have every opportunity to hear the Lord's voice while they are young and open-minded, so that they may answer as Samuel did: "Speak, Lord; for thy servant heareth."

---

## Primary

The story of Samuel is a vivid one and easy to tell. The teacher should know the story of the first three chapters and tell it as one story. Review the history of the ark and the tabernacle, pointing out that in spite of the many enemies who had passed over the land in the time of the Judges, the tabernacle in the time of our lesson still stands at Shiloh where Joshua had set it up, a descendant of Aaron is still high priest, and some faithful people still come to the tabernacle to worship. Samuel's obedience and willing service should be stressed.

Near the end of the time of the Judges there lived a good woman named Hannah. Hannah had no children, and she wanted a child very much. At the time of one of the great Jewish feasts, Hannah and her husband went to Shiloh, the place where the tabernacle had been set up. There at the tabernacle Hannah prayed the Lord to give her a child, and she promised that if the Lord gave her a child, she would give him to the service of the Lord.

The Lord granted Hannah's prayer. She named her child Samuel, which means "God hath heard." And when Samuel was old enough, she brought him back to Shiloh and gave him to Eli, the high priest, to bring up in the service of the tabernacle. Eli taught him to do all the things a little boy could do to help him.

Eli was a good man but he was very old and growing blind, and he had to have his two sons do most of the things that the high priest usually did in the services and sacrifices of the tabernacle.

The two sons of Eli were also priests, but they were wicked men.
They took for themselves offerings which should have been given to the Lord.
The Lord had warned Eli about them, but Eli was not brave enough to stop them.
So the Lord gave Samuel a message for Eli.
How many times did the Lord speak to Samuel?
What did Samuel think at first?
What did Eli finally tell him to do?
What message did the Lord give him?
Now read verses 19 to 21 of the chapter.

The Lord speaks to us in the Word, and He wants each one of us to listen to Him and obey Him as Samuel did. Then He can always be with us and help us to do right. You may be glad, too, to know that because Hannah kept her promise to the Lord, He afterward gave her more children—three sons and two daughters.

After Samuel grew up, Eli's wicked sons were killed in a battle and Eli died when he heard the news. But Samuel became the leader of all the children of Israel. He was a priest, the last of the Judges, and a prophet.

---

### Junior

This is a good opportunity to see what the Juniors remember about the tabernacle and the ark. Remind them that the Lord promised to speak to the people from the mercy seat above the ark. Then read the first and last verses of our chapter for today, and use this as the basis for describing the condition into which worship had fallen in the time of the Judges and what Samuel accomplished for his people even as a small boy. Have them look up all the Bible references.

Do you remember what was the characteristic of the period of the Judges? If you have forgotten, read Judges 17:6. This shows us why the ark and the tabernacle are not mentioned once in the book of Judges. When we think we are wise enough to decide for ourselves what is right and wrong, the Lord and the church seem to drop out of our minds. But they are really there all the time, hidden deep within our lives. In the same way, the ark and the tabernacle were still there in the very center of the Holy Land.

Where was the tabernacle at this time?
Who was the first high priest?
The high priest was always to be one of his descendants.
Who was the high priest at the time of Samuel's birth?

Even though most of the people had turned to idol worship and forgotten the Lord, there were still some faithful ones who tried to keep the law of Moses and who went regularly to the tabernacle to worship. Samuel's parents were among these.

What were their names?

Their home was in Ramah, in the territory of Ephraim, to which tribe Elkanah belonged. In the first two chapters of I Samuel we learn that Hannah had no children and that, when they came up to the tabernacle for one of the feasts, she prayed the Lord for a child, and promised if she had one to give him to the service of the Lord. So, when Samuel was born she named him Samuel, which means "God hath heard," and as soon as he was old enough, she brought him to Eli to be brought up in the service of the tabernacle.

Eli at this time was an old man and becoming blind. His sons, Hophni and Phinehas, attended to the active duties of the priesthood. We learn how they profaned their high office by taking more than their fair shares of the offerings brought to the tabernacle and by taking the part allotted to them without consecrating it as they were supposed to do. Eli was told of their offenses and rebuked them, but he did not exercise his authority and put a stop to them. So he was warned by a prophet that he and his house should not continue to hold the priesthood. Eli was a good man, but weak.

Samuel was trained by Eli to do the things which a small boy could do to help around the tabernacle. Verse 15 of our chapter tells us one of his duties, and he also evidently waited upon Eli.

What was Samuel doing when the Lord called him?
What did he think at first?
How many times did the Lord call him?
What did Eli finally tell him to do?

Hearing pictures obedience. When your mother says, "Do you hear me?" you know that she means, "Mind!" Whenever in the Bible we read, "He that hath ears to hear, let him hear," we know that we are being urged to listen and obey.

What do you think it means when the Bible says, "Their ears they have stopped"?
Do we ever "stop" our ears when we do not want to obey?

Thus when Samuel said, "Speak; for thy servant heareth," it meant that he would obey the Lord, and we find that always did obey the Lord even to the end of his life.

What did the Lord tell Samuel to say to Eli?
How did Eli receive the message?

To see how this message was fulfilled, read I Samuel 4:10-18.

Verses 19 to 21 of our chapter tell us that the people soon learned that Samuel had been chosen to be a prophet of the Lord. The whole country came to recognize him as their leader and Judge, and he was the last of the Judges.

---

## Intermediate

The emphasis with this class should be on the correspondence of "hearing" and of the three calls. The necessity for obedience and sincerity in worship has an appeal for young people, and their thought should be directed along these lines. This story of Samuel is so familiar to most Christian children that its deeper lessons are likely to be neglected.

In the book of Judges the ark and the tabernacle are not once mentioned. This, too, is natural in a time when people were looking to themselves instead of to the Lord. But with Samuel, the last of the Judges, we suddenly return to the tabernacle.* And we find that it is still set up in Shiloh, that there is still a high priest of the line of Aaron, that the tabernacle rites are still being carried out, and that there are still some people in the land who come faithfully to the tabernacle to offer sacrifices and to worship the true God. This reminds us of the condition of the Jews hundreds of years later at the time of the Lord's birth, and there are a number of things in Samuel's story which remind us of the early years of the Lord's earthly life.

Read I Samuel 1:1-11. Verse 11 makes us think of an earlier Judge, Samson, for you remember that Samson also did not cut his hair and that his strength was in his hair. This part of Hannah's vow shows that Samuel, like Samson, was to be a Nazarite, one set apart for the service of God. In Numbers 6:1-21 we may read the laws governing one who had taken the vows of a Nazarite. Samson's strength pictures the power which comes from obedience to the commandments, for the hair represents the outmost or, in the case of a Judge or prophet, the letter of the Word. Samuel's power also came from obedience, but because his use was in the tabernacle, his strength was spiritual rather than physical, and was maintained to the end of his life; it produced results more important and far-reaching than those of Samson's physical victories. There is nothing in the story of Samson which indicates that he himself was impressed with his mission. But Samuel, even as a little child, heard the call of the Lord and gave willing obedience. To hear always means to obey.

The first high priest of the Jews was Aaron, and the high priesthood was always to go to one of his descendants. At this time the line of Aaron was being continued in Eli, and Eli himself was a

---

*There are many textual problems in the books of Samuel, not the least of which pertains to the worship structure. In both I Samuel 1:9 and 3:3 it is identified as a "temple" rather than a "tabernacle," whereas in I Samuel 2:22 it is clearly called a "tent." There are, indeed, so many glaring inconsistencies in the letter that the teacher would be ill-advised to overstress the literal details. —*Ed.*

good man. But his sons, Hophni and Phinehas, who should have been preparing to succeed him, were evil men, robbing the Lord of the offerings the people brought, and in this way discouraging the people from their worship of the Lord. Eli had been told of their misdeeds and had rebuked them, but had not the strength of mind to put a stop to their evil practices. In the same way, when we fall away from going to church and reading the Word, our religion becomes weakened and we do not take the firm steps necessary to restore it. Read the fourth chapter of I Samuel to see what happened to Eli and his sons.

Notice that in this time when the high priest was old and weak and his sons were corrupt and leading the people astray, the voice of the Lord came to a little child. Often in the Word we are told that we must become as little children. This means that when we have gone wrong through following our own ideas and desires, the first thing necessary is to return to a state of simple trust and obedience. Samuel was called three times before he recognized the voice of the Lord. The three calls picture hearing the Lord through our senses—that is, through reading the Word—with our minds, as we think about what we have read, and finally with our hearts, as we decide to obey the Lord.

Read the first verse of our chapter and then the last three verses. Samuel's simple obedience restored the connection between the Lord and the Israelites. He was the only one of the Judges to be recognized as leader by all the people, and this was because they saw that the Lord had chosen him to be a prophet. His life began a new period of unification and development for the nation.

*Basic Correspondences*

| | | |
|---|---|---|
| to hear | = | to obey |
| the hair | = | the outmost of life |
| the hair of a representative of the Lord | = | the letter of the Word |

## Senior

A very good lesson for the Seniors is found in the effect of the sins of Eli's sons on the people who came to worship. They need to know that what they do is important to the church as well as to themselves. They have something to uphold. And yet they should be reminded that the truly good people came to worship anyway, and that we should not let other people's weaknesses come between us and the Lord. Strength of character is in the ability to do right no matter what others around us do.

The story of Samuel is familiar to us all. It is a beautiful picture of the orderly development of life. Every child should, like Samuel, be "brought early to the tabernacle" and devoted to the service of the Lord. We do this when we bring our little children to be baptized and promise to bring them up in the Christian life. A child should be taught to perform willingly and faithfully the little services which are within his power. Then he is prepared to hear the voice of the Lord when it comes to him, and to obey it.

A number of verses in our lesson are especially noteworthy. "The word of the Lord was precious in those days; there was no open vision." Men had lost contact with the Lord through following their own ideas and desires. Eli's eyes "began to wax dim." The understanding of spiritual things was clouded. "Ere the lamp of God went out in the temple of the Lord, where the ark of God was." This would refer to the seven-branched lampstand in the Holy Place, which was supposed to be kept perpetually burning as a symbol of the presence of the Lord's truth in the mind. Its being nearly gone out pictures the fact that this connection with the Lord's truth was almost broken.

And then the Lord spoke to Samuel in the night, and Samuel, after the third call, replied, "Speak; for thy servant heareth." The three calls picture the appeal of the Lord to the three planes of our minds: the outer life, the intelligence, and finally the will. Hearing represents obedience. In the night-time of general indifference, the voice came to one willing to obey. "And Samuel lay until the morning, and opened the doors of the house of the Lord." Morning always pictures the beginning of a new spiritual state, and the opening of the doors of the house of the Lord represents the fact that through Samuel access to the Lord was once more given to the people.

We may think of Samuel as the beginning of our mature consciousness of our own weakness and need of the Lord. The first message given him was one of rebuke to Eli and his sons, which means that the first thing we must reform is our worship of the Lord. When, as young people, we have drifted away from the church and from reading the Word and praying, and have come to feel self-sufficient and to give ourselves credit for our good deeds—robbing the Lord as Hophni and Phinehas did—the Lord speaks to us through the remains of our childhood states of humility and innocence, showing us our folly and its inevitable consequences. We need to remember that the whole complex of thoughts and feelings represented by the ancient Hebrew people is present in us when we come to maturity—all the tendencies to materialism, to the worship of idols of one sort or another, to self-esteem and self-will, to profanation of holy things, to weak acquiescence in the sins of our times and companions. But Samuel is in us, too, as the voice of the Lord speaking through the Word planted in our memories in childhood. This is what we have to build on to begin the process of regeneration which is the work of our adult lives. Without this Samuel influence, the lamp of God would indeed go out in all of us.

Samuel was to be the last of the Judges, for he would anoint the first king and also the second. It is the recognition of our need to worship and obey the Lord in simple faith which leads us to adopt higher and higher principles for the guidance of our lives.

In several places in the Word Samuel is linked with Moses. Swedenborg tells us that they both represent the Word, as we know all the leaders and prophets in the Bible do. The Word is our leader, our judge, and our prophet, the voice of the Lord speaking to us. We recall that Moses in particular represents obedience to the Law in a period when obedience is a matter of duty, not of pleasure. Samuel also represents obedience, but the obedience to which we come back with all our hearts after an experience of the folly of trying to lead ourselves. Samuel was a prophet, the prophet of a transition period which introduced a development culminating in the glory of Solomon's kingdom.

---

## Adult

If there are parents of young children in the class, the first subject to be discussed should be the importance of bringing children up to serve the Lord. Then speak of the state into which the tabernacle worship had fallen, and call attention to its counterpart in the time of the Lord and in our own time. Finally the doctrine of remains and the necessity of simple obedience as a basis for all religious progress will make a good discussion topic. Our modern world is too much given to excusing the breaking of the commandments.

With the first book of Samuel we come to a new stage in the history of the church or of the man who is trying to live the regenerate life. The wars in the book of Judges picture various temptations which assail those who have found their homes in the Holy Land, that is, those who have become settled in the desire and practice of living according to divine law. These temptations are both external and internal and take many forms. We yield to them at first almost unconsciously and they grow upon us until we find ourselves subject to them and realize that we must ask the Lord's help in taking active measures against them. In the book of Judges the state of the people became worse and worse, until, for example, the tribe of Benjamin, which represents spiritual or interior truth, became perverted and was almost destroyed. So sometimes we allow ourselves to "backslide" through constant yielding to small or subtle temptations until we find ourselves in a bad spiritual state and almost robbed of the sense of the internal meaning of life which makes conjunction with the Lord possible. A new beginning must be made if we are to be saved. We must return for a time to a condition of simple trust and obedience and allow this to lead us to a new peak of spiritual living.

The story of the child Samuel has always been one of the best loved of the Bible stories. Parents should realize that all children are loaned to them by the Lord to prepare for His service, and should dedicate them to that service, as Hannah dedicated Samuel. And children should see in Samuel a beautiful example of simple trust and obedience and willing service. There are also many similarities between the early life of Samuel and that of the Lord, even to the expression, "And the child Samuel grew on, and was in favor both with the Lord and also with men." (I Samuel 2:26) Compare this with Luke 2:52.

But the story has a wider application than that to physical childhood. Our childhood states of innocence, trust, and obedience are covered up as we grow older, but they are not lost. The Lord stores them up deep within us as the "remains" of which we read in the writings. No matter how far we may have wandered from them, if we realize the barrenness of our state and look to the Lord for a new birth as Hannah did, promising new consecration, the childhood states can be revived in us and lead us to new and higher spiritual development. This is very plainly told us by the Lord when He says: "Verily, I say unto you, except ye be converted and become as little children, ye shall not enter into the kingdom of heaven. Whosoever therefore shall humble himself as this little child, the same is greatest in the kingdom of heaven." (Matthew 18:3, 4) Samuel's early ministry in the tabernacle is a picture of our return to a humble state of mind, in which we read the Word in simplicity, enter into the services of worship with genuine sincerity, and look to the church for guidance, as Samuel looked to Eli. Then we put ourselves in a state in which the Lord can speak to us, and prepare the way for new growth. "And Samuel grew, and the Lord was with him."

The picture of the little Samuel is so striking and so touching that the dark background against which it stands out is often overlooked. Eli, the high priest, the descendant of Aaron, is an old man and his sight is dim. He has turned over the conduct of the tabernacle worship to his sons, Hophni and Phinehas, who are "sons of Belial" and who "knew not the Lord." They profaned the sacrifices of the people by taking more than their due portion and by taking it even before the sacrifice was made to the Lord. "Wherefore the sin of the young men was very great before the Lord; for men abhorred the offering of the Lord." (I Samuel 2:17)

Eli is warned by a "man of God" that the priesthood shall be taken from his house. He has remonstrated with his sons, but has not exerted himself to put a stop to their evil practices. He is therefore judged "because his sons made themselves vile, and he restrained them not." This is a picture of a state in which worship is being degraded by being used for self-interest and self-exaltation. Although the high priest in us—the inner dictate which relates us to the Lord—sees the evil and condemns it, it does not take steps to correct it. It has become dim of sight and is no longer able to receive directly the voice of the Lord. In I Samuel 2:17, quoted above, there is the suggestion of the harm which such a state does to others as well as to ourselves. Sometimes people have been turned against the church by finding self-seeking and hypocrisy in some of its members. Our duty to keep our worship sincere and to live according to the teachings of the church is not for our own salvation alone. The Lord's service requires of us constant watchfulness and ever-renewed devotion. We must be on our guard against the thought that we are "saved" and cannot go astray as others may. The Lord, in the letter of the Word, had promised the priesthood to Aaron and his seed forever, but the descendants of either of Aaron's two sons, Eleazar and Ithamar, were eligible (cf. I Chronicles 24:1-3). Now the Lord takes it from the house of Eli: "I said indeed that thy house and the house of thy father, should walk before me for ever: but now the Lord saith, Be it far from me; for them that honor me I will honor, and they that despise me shall be lightly esteemed." (I Samuel 2:30)

This degenerate state of worship is contrasted directly with the simple, obedient service of Samuel, to whom the Lord can speak. The child Samuel is called by the Lord in the night three times. The night is the state of the church at that time. Three, as we know, represents a full state in which all three planes of life are conjoined. This teaches us an important lesson. We may read the Word and take in its literal meaning through our physical senses and stop there; this is the first call—we think the message is from men. But we may go on to meditate upon it and come to see it with our rational mind; this is the second call. We may still imagine we are merely hearing the voice of the church. It is not our will that is reached as yet. But if we hear the third call, we may then know we are hearing in the Word the voice of the Lord speaking directly to us, and that we should answer, as did Samuel, "Speak; for thy servant heareth."

Hearing represents obedience. In the story, Samuel was given his name because his mother felt that God had heard her prayer. The name Samuel means "God hath heard." Hearing–obedience–is the keynote of Samuel's whole life and work. We recall that Moses also represents obedience to the law, but he is obedience in its first aspects, when it is prompted somewhat by the desire for worldly honor and rewards, and at best by a sense of duty. The Israelites have come a long way since the time of Moses. They have gained the Holy Land. But in their satisfaction with their success they have allowed themselves to forget the fundamental requirement–obedience. They had to be brought back to obedience before they could progress further. It is a lesson we all need again and again.

## From the Writings of Swedenborg

*Apocalypse Explained*, n. 14: "To 'hear' is to obey and to live, because with celestial angels the things that are heard enter into the life; but as this is unknown, I would like to explain it briefly. There are two senses given to man which serve as means of receiving the things whereby the rational is formed, and also the things by which man is reformed; these are the sense of sight and the sense of hearing; the other senses are for other uses. The things that enter by the sense of sight enter into man's understanding and enlighten it, for which reason by 'sight' is signified the understanding enlightened, for the understanding corresponds to the sight of the eye, as the light of heaven corresponds to the light of the world. The things, however, that enter by the sense of hearing enter both into the understanding and into the will, and for this reason by 'the hearing' is signified perception and obedience. Consequently, in human language, to 'hear' anyone, and to 'give ear' to anyone, also to 'listen to,' and 'hearken to,' are common expressions; and by 'hearing any one' is meant to perceive, and by 'giving ear to,' as also by 'listening to' is meant to obey; while 'hearkening to' means either perceiving or obeying. These expressions flowed down into human language out of the spiritual world, where man's spirit is."

## Suggested Questions on the Lesson

P. Who was the last of the Judges? *Samuel*
P. Who was the high priest in his day? *Eli*
J. Why was Samuel brought to the tabernacle? *his mother's vow*
P. What did he do there? *served Eli*
J. What wrong things did Eli's sons do? *took offering for themselves*
J. Why did not Eli make them stop? *weak*
P. Where was Samuel when the Lord called him? *sleeping in tabernacle*
J. What did Samuel at first think? *Eli was calling*
P. How many times did the Lord call before Samuel learned who had called him? *three*
P. What message for Eli did the Lord give him? *sons to lose priesthood*
J. How did the people regard Samuel after this? *prophet*
I. To what does hearing correspond? *obeying*
S. Why did the Lord have to speak to Samuel three times? *appeal to three planes: outer life, intelligence, will*

## THE CAPTURE AND RETURN OF THE ARK

*I Samuel 4:1-11; 5; 6:1-16*

Review briefly the general character of the period of the Judges and the difference between them and the former great leaders who had been over all the people. The teachers should be prepared to give a brief review of Samuel's birth and call, first letting the pupils tell what they know about it.

---

### Doctrinal Points

*We should not ask the Lord to help us attain selfish ends.*
*The Word is a two-edged sword; it protects the good, but it also destroys those who do not wish to obey it.*
*Faith without love and good works ("faith alone") is dead.*
*When we have done wrong, we must acknowledge it and try to atone for it.*

---

### Notes for Parents

The ark, we remember, was a chest made to hold the two tables of stone on which the Lord wrote the ten commandments on Mount Sinai. It was the only article of furniture in the Holy of Holies of the tabernacle, and from between the two golden cherubim on the mercy seat—which was the cover of the ark—the Lord spoke to the high priest, we are told, "by a living voice" (Numbers 7:89). And we remember the wonderful things the ark had accomplished for the children of Israel: the parting of the waters of Jordan and the bringing down of the walls of Jericho.

All the stories in the Bible about the ark are given us by the Lord to teach us about the place the commandments should have in our lives and about the effect which our regard for the commandments has upon everything we think or do. They belong in our Holy of Holies: they should be "written on our hearts." We should keep them from love to the Lord and because we love to do what the Lord wants us to do. But in our story for today the Israelites took the ark out of the tabernacle and brought it down to the battlefield to give them victory over their enemies, the Philistines. And instead of winning the battle, they were defeated, and the ark was captured and carried off into the Philistine country. When we try to use the commandments to judge other people but are not keeping them ourselves, the Lord cannot give us the victory. Instead, we ourselves are judged.

The Philistines, in the story of the children of Israel, picture a certain kind of temptation. They worshiped the idol Dagon, which had the head and hands of a man but the body of a fish. We know what we mean when we say, "That sounds fishy to me." We mean that the thing is not what it professes to be. When we claim to be good people and talk about being good but are not trying to keep the commandments, the "Philistines" have carried off our "ark."

But the ark immediately began to show its power. When they put it in their temple beside the image of Dagon, Dagon fell down and its head and hands broke off, leaving it nothing but a fish. So the commandments show our professed righteousness to be nothing but a sham. And then a plague broke out among the people and mice began to destroy their crops, just as all our secret evils appear when we begin to compare our lives with what the commandments tell us they ought to be.

So the Philistines sent the ark back to its own country with a trespass offering. When we see that we have been only pretending to be good people, the thing to do is to put the commandments back where they belong, at the heart of everything we do. The trespass offering is our sincere repentance and intention to become really good, to be unselfish instead of selfish in our conduct.

---

### Primary

The details of the return of the ark make an interesting lesson. The simple moral lesson to be drawn is that the Lord cannot make us happy while we are doing wrong. The teacher should be prepared to fill in the story of the capture of the ark and the results of its presence among the Philistines, as the actual reading suggested for this class is only a brief part of the whole story. There are many details which will interest the children. The teacher might well read to the class I Samuel 5:1-11.

We have just studied the story of Samuel, whose mother brought him, when he was still a little boy, to the tabernacle at Shiloh to be a helper to Eli, the high priest, and of how the Lord called Samuel out of his sleep in the night and gave him a message for Eli. All the people knew that this meant that Samuel was to be a prophet of the Lord, and when Samuel grew up, he became the last of the Judges and was recognized by all the people instead of just by those in some one part of the country.

Before Samuel grew up, the people had a serious lesson which showed them how wicked they had grown through forgetting to worship the Lord. They were being attacked by a nation called the Philistines who lived in the Holy Land along the seacoast. The Philistines were a very strong nation and were getting the better of the Israelites. The Israelites knew that when they did right, the Lord always gave them victory over their enemies, but this time, instead of trying to find out what was wrong with themselves, they took the ark out of the tabernacle and brought it down to the battlefield, believing that it would give them the victory. And the Lord permitted the Philistines to capture the ark and carry it off to their own cities.

Then the Philistines learned a lesson, too. They put the ark in the temple of their god Dagon, and in the night the statue of Dagon fell off its pedestal, and its head and hands were broken off. Then a plague struck the people and many died, and mice began to destroy their crops. So the Philistines knew that they must send the ark back.

When they decided to send it back, who told them how this should be done?
What were they told to send with it?
How did they return it?
Where did the cattle take the ark?

Afterward Samuel called the Israelites together and they confessed their evils and promised to serve the Lord again.

## Junior

The Juniors are old enough to get the general lesson of what is meant by the misuse of the ark and also why it plagued the Philistines. Emphasize the fact that this story leads up to the acceptance of Samuel as Judge over the whole nation. This will help to lay the foundation for the story of the kings.

You remember that the Judges were men raised up by the Lord in different parts of the land to lead the people against particular enemies. None of them except the last was recognized by all the people as their head. And the people did not learn wisdom from their adversities. In spite of the Lord's willingness to help them they continued to go their own selfish way. Finally even the priests in the tabernacle were corrupt. The tabernacle had been set up by Joshua at Shiloh in the center of the land, and regular worship was still conducted there in spite of the fact that the people also worshiped the gods of the other nations. At the time of our story for today, Eli, the high priest, was a very old man and had allowed his two sons, Hophni and Phinehas, to take over his duties; and although he knew that they were profaning the tabernacle, he did nothing to stop their evil practices. Then, as you remember, the child Samuel was brought to the tabernacle to wait on Eli and the Lord called him in the middle of the night and gave him a message for Eli. Samuel became the last of the Judges, and the only one recognized by all the people as a man set over them by the Lord.

But before Samuel was grown up, the self-confidence of the people was broken by a great disaster, which is the subject of our lesson for today.

With what enemy were the Israelites fighting?

The Philistines were a people who lived on the plain along the seacoast. They were an active and wealthy people and had strong, walled cities. The most important of these were Gath, Ekron, Ashdod, Askelon, and Gaza. In the time of the Judges, the Philistines had grown very confident and were oppressing the Israelites. Always before, when their enemies have become too strong for them, the Israelites had turned to the Lord and asked Him what to do.

What did they do this time?

Was this the same as asking the Lord to help them?

Who brought the ark from Shiloh to the battlefield?
What happened to the ark?
What happened to Hophni and Phinehas?

The Israelites were expecting the Lord to save them without their changing their ways or looking to Him for direction. We sometimes do this ourselves. We do things we know are wrong, and then expect the Lord to save us from the consequences without even being sorry for what we have done.

Where did the Philistines first take the ark?
Where did they put it?
What happened to the statue of their god?

The Philistine idol, Dagon, had the body of a fish and the head and hands of a man. He was really a picture of what the Philistines were like in their minds. The breaking off of the human head and hands left him nothing but a fish.

Wherever the ark was taken in the Philistine country two plagues broke out. The people were afflicted with tumors, and mice infested the fields and destroyed the crops. These two plagues, like the plagues of Egypt, were pictures of the particular evils which were infesting the people.

When you are in a selfish state, does it make you happy to think of the commandments? No, the commandments are a trouble to those who do not want to obey them, and they want to get rid of them.

What was used to send the ark back to the Israelites?
How was the cart drawn?
What gifts were sent with it?
Who told the Philistines how to send it back?
Where did the cows take the ark?
What did the men of Bethshemesh do?

Every story in the Bible is really a parable, a picture of something which may happen in our souls. You will learn more about this story as you grow older, but you can see something of its meaning even now. In our lives our "ark" goes into "Philistine country" when we try to put the commandments away in the back of our minds because we don't want to obey them. It is "returned to Israel" when we make up our minds to put the commandments back where they belong, in the center of our lives.

The ark was never returned to Shiloh. It was taken from Bethshemesh to Kirjathjearim and set up in the house of a man named Abinadab, where it remained for twenty years. Both Bethshemesh and Kirjathjearim were "Levitical" cities. That means that they were among the forty-eight cities throughout the Holy Land which had been assigned to the Levites instead of a separate lot when the land was divided among the tribes. So the inhabitants of these cities were Levites and had the right to handle and care for the ark. The ark was finally brought to Jerusalem by King David, who pitched a new tabernacle there for it.

---

### Intermediate

The correspondence of the Philistines and of the details of the return of the ark are the most interesting lesson for this class. The general lesson in regard to the right place of the commandments in our lives is of course important.

When we, as the Israelites did in the time of the Judges, forget our duty to the Lord and begin to imagine that we are good enough to get along without Him, we not only get into one difficulty after another but we actually become worse and worse, and sometimes it takes a very serious setback to make us realize our condition and bring us back into our right relation with the Lord.

Our lesson today is again about Samuel, who was the last of the Judges and the one under whom the whole people was brought finally to a state of repentance. We all remember the beautiful story of the birth of Samuel—how he was dedicated to the Lord's service even before he was born and brought to Shiloh by his mother when he was still a young child to serve the old high priest Eli in the tabernacle. And we remember how the Lord called him in the night and gave him a message for Eli, rebuking Eli for permitting the evil deeds of his sons and telling him that the priesthood should be taken away from his family. The little Samuel represents the stirring in us of our childhood states of innocence and trust. This is the means the Lord uses to prepare us for the blow which must be dealt in order to shake us out of our self-satisfaction.

The enemy attacking the Israelites in our lesson is the Philistines, an enemy who had already gained considerable power over the Israelites. The Philistines picture the ever-present temptation to think that knowledge of spiritual things will save us without obedience. Many people think that because they belong to the church and have learned something about its teachings they have become good people and can do about as they please. If trouble comes to them, they blame the Lord for not saving them from it.

This is particularly true when we are starting out in the world for ourselves, when our worldly occupations and enjoyments are in the forefront of our consciousness and seem all-important. Our allegiance to the Lord comes to be something we take for granted without examining our actual thought and conduct to see whether or not we are living according to the Lord's teachings.

Israel, whose very worship had been profaned by the misdeeds of Hophni and Phinehas, the sons of Eli, fell an easy prey to the Philistines. This time, instead of seeking guidance from the Lord and being led to amend their ways, they sent for the ark to help them, as the superstitious sometimes rely on some amulet or charm. They took the ark out of the Holy of Holies and brought it down to the battlefield. But, although the Lord's power was still in the ark, it did not save Israel. We know that the commandments are given us to save us from evil, but it should not be hard to see that they cannot save us if we do not keep them.

The ark captured by the Philistines and taken into their country is a picture of the commandments held in our minds in a vague way as something holy but with no practical application to our lives. We should notice that after this the tabernacle, empty of the ark, still remained, just as people whose lives have lost their spiritual meaning often continue to go to church. But our spiritual life is bound up with our keeping the commandments; so the fortunes of Israel went with the ark.

The commandments in the mind of a person who does not want to keep them do not bring happiness. In the hands of the Philistines the ark caused three disasters. First it caused their idol Dagon to fall and lose its head and hands. Dagon had the body of a fish and the head and hands of a man. Fish, which swim in the water and are cold-blooded, represent the affection for mere knowledge. By adding the head and hands of a man to a fish body, this was made to appear human and fit for worship. But the mere presence of the ark was able to destroy this appearance. We cannot even read the commandments without recognizing that something more than mere knowledge is required of us.

Then appeared the plague of "emerods," or tumors. Skin eruptions are caused by the coming to the surface of impurities in the system. The commandments bring to light our hidden evils. The mice which destroyed the crops symbolize the many small evils in which we indulge when we are in the Philistine state, which destroy the good which we may try to do.

The return of the ark to Israel pictures in us a return to a state of obedience to the commandments. Our "new cart" is a new idea about the place of the commandments in life and the cows are our new affection for useful living. The calves which were left behind are the natural, selfish forms which our affections have been taking when we were in the Philistine state. The golden tumors and mice are our determination to replace our selfish habits with unselfish service to the Lord and the neighbor. The number five always pictures "a little but enough." It is used of the small beginnings of goodness. The lowing of the cows for their calves is our natural longing for our former selfish pleasures even while we are allowing obedience to the commandments to lead us into a better state. The sacrifice of the cows after they arrived at Bethshemesh is the consecration of our affections to the Lord.

The ark did not stay at its first stopping place. Bethshemesh was one of the forty-eight Levitical cities—cities which were given to the Levites for their possession when the land was divided by lot among the other tribes—but it was close to the Philistine country.

In our story it represents the first state of worship after the beginning of repentance. The ark was very soon moved to another Levitical city, Kirjathjearim, further inland and on higher ground, and there it remained for twenty years until King David carried it to Jerusalem.

*Basic Correspondences*

| | | |
|---|---|---|
| the Philistines | = | knowledge without obedience |
| Dagon | = | pride in one's own intelligence |
| "emerods" (tumors) | = | inner impurity appearing on the surface |
| mice | = | small evils, especially those connected with pleasures of the senses |
| cows | = | affections for useful activities |
| a cart | = | doctrine or a general idea of something |

## Senior

Again the lesson is one of warning for this age group against the temptations which will soon be coming to them as they go out to establish themselves in the world. We cannot say to them too often or too strongly, "Remember that the commandments are always to be kept, and that we need the Lord every step of our way through life."

The period of the Judges was a sort of interlude. Now this interlude has drawn to a close. The Israelites have reached a state of self-satisfaction and indifference to the Lord out of which they must be awakened or they will perish. The Lord prepared the way for this awakening by raising up Samuel, who was to be the last of the Judges, and calling him to deliver a warning to the high priest Eli, who had permitted his sons, Hophni and Phinehas, to desecrate the very worship of the tabernacle. The judgment on Eli and his house predicted through the child Samuel was promptly executed, and our lesson today is one of tragedy.

As a background for this lesson we need to have in mind the general outline of the history of Israel from the time at Sinai when they were given the commandments written by the finger of God on two tables of stone and were told to make an ark to hold them and a tabernacle in which to place the ark. From that time on their whole life had centered in the ark and the tabernacle. The ark had led them through the wilderness, across the Jordan, and around the walls of Jericho until they fell. It had been their protection and the source of their instruction. Finally the tabernacle had been set up by Joshua in the center of the land at Shiloh and their worship had been established there.

But once it was more or less permanently established, the people as a whole had apparently forgotten all about it. Some faithful ones still went to the tabernacle to worship, but most of the people were absorbed in their worldly occupations and had drifted into serving the idols of the nations among whom they lived.

Isn't this a true picture of what often happens to us? We are brought up in good homes, taken care of, instructed at home and in Sunday school. We accept the teachings of the church and join it, and believe that we are established as good Christians. Then we begin to earn our living and carry on our independent lives. Our days are busy with our work. We marry and settle in our own homes. We make friends in the community where we live and our pleasures are found in its social life. Some of us still go to church regularly and continue to study and to live the teachings of the church. But many, perhaps the majority, drift away from regular worship and begin to adopt the ideas and standards of the people with whom they associate.

Then the Philistines attack. The Philistines picture the temptation to be satisfied with knowing what is right without making any effort to live according to the truth we know. We get into difficulties. We suddenly find that we have lost our power of resistance to evil, and we remember the safety we had in our earlier lives and habits. The Israelites remembered the ark. But they did not go to the tabernacle to confess their sins and ask for guidance and help. They sent for the ark to be brought down to the battlefield for the sole purpose of saving their lives. We do the same sort of thing whenever we expect the Lord to support us regardless of our conduct, to save us from the consequences of our own wrong-doing without any effort on our part to repent and amend our ways.

The ark was captured by the Philistines. When the commandments are not kept, they have no power in our lives. They become merely knowledge held in the memory. Hophni and Phinehas were killed and Eli died when he heard that the ark had been taken. When we cease to believe that the commandments must be obeyed, all life goes out of our worship.

The tabernacle became an empty shell. Throughout the Old Testament the ark represents the heart of our worship. Its journeys tell the story of our changing states. When it is leading the Israelites it stands for those times when we are genuinely seeking to be led by the Lord. The various places in which it is set up mirror our considered attitudes toward divine law. When it is neglected, it pictures our states of preoccupation with worldly and selfish concerns. When it is captured by the Philistines it means we have consigned the keeping of the commandments to the realm of the impossible.

But we find that we are not happy in that state. The ark plagued the Philistines. The knowledge of the commandments, when we are making no effort to keep them, is a constant irritant. First the god Dagon was toppled over. Our worship of our own intelligence totters when the commandments enter our thoughts. We are forced to recognize the worldly and superficial nature of our thinking. Dagon had the body of a fish but the head and hands of a man. When, on the second morning, his head and hands were found to have broken off, he was only a fish. And the cold-blooded fish which swim in the sea picture our enjoyment of knowledges for their own sake. The commandments make us realize that such enjoyment does not measure up to our human capabilities. We have to "draw the fish out of the sea and eat them" to make them serve human needs. Then the Philistines were plagued by tumors, and their crops destroyed by mice. The thought of the commandments brings to our attention our hitherto unnoticed evils and shows us how our selfish indulgences take the wholesomeness out of even our good deeds.

We try by various reasonings to keep the ark in the Philistine country (that is, we try in spite of our troubles to continue to ignore the commandments). The Philistines sent it in turn to three of their great cities. But the plagues went with it. Finally we are brought to a recognition of the necessity of confession and repentance and the restoration of the commandments to their true place in our lives. The new cart pictures our new way of thinking about the commandments; and the two cows, our new determination to restore the commandments to their rightful control over our actions. The lowing of the cattle after their calves is the longing we have to go back to what seem easier and pleasanter habits. The golden images of the tumors and mice picture the replacing of selfish by unselfish motives. The number five signifies "a little but enough."

It is never easy to bring about such a reversal of the whole course of our thinking and living. The ark proceeded by stages, always welcomed at first but necessitating sacrifices. So the commandments, as they cause us to look more and more deeply into our hearts, take their inevitable toll of our selfish enjoyments.

---

## Adult

The "Philistine state" and the relation of the commandments to it should furnish an excellent basis for discussion, with the details of the story introduced by way of enlightenment and emphasis as you proceed. They are very forceful brought in this way rather than told in story form.

The first book of Samuel tells us about the end of the state of life pictured in the book of Judges and the beginning of a better ordered and directed life, beginning, as it does, with the birth of Samuel and continuing through the whole reign of Saul.

Samuel was the last of the Judges and the only one who came to be recognized by the whole nation as their divinely appointed mentor. In I Samuel 3:20 we read, "And all Israel from Dan even to Beersheba knew that Samuel was established to be a prophet of the Lord." We are all familiar with the story of the child Samuel and realize that he represents a calling forth in us of "remains"—states of innocence and trust from our own early childhood—to which we must return if we are ever to break away from our self-confidence and pride in our own intelligence and come again under the direction and protection of the Lord. Samuel's call carried with it a condemnation of the current high priest Eli because he had allowed corruption to creep into the very worship of the tabernacle.

In today's lesson the Lord's prophecy to Samuel is fulfilled and we have the culmination of the state which had been developing throughout the book of Judges. Eli and his sons die, and the ark is captured by the Philistines.

In AE 700 Swedenborg says: "The Philistines conquered when the sons of Israel departed from the statutes and precepts in not doing them." And in I Samuel 7:3 Samuel tells the Israelites how they can conquer: "If ye do return unto the Lord with all your hearts, then put away the strange gods and Ashtaroth from among you, and prepare your hearts unto the Lord, and serve Him only." The Israelites had thought to turn the tide of battle by invoking the power of the ark as a sort of fetish, without examing their conduct to see if it had been in accordance with the words written on the tables preserved in the ark. For this reason the ark did not save them. Its being captured by the Philistines was a symbol of what the Israelites had done to the commandments. They had kept the tables in the ark in the Holy of Holies but had not lived them out in their hearts and lives. This is exactly the Philistine state of knowledge separated from the good of life. The priesthood of Eli and his house perished because, while continuing the formal worship of the Lord, it permitted abuses to creep in, even to the setting up of other gods. It is the same with us whenever we continue going to church and taking our part in the Christian group to which we belong, yet at heart allow ourselves to be led astray into following worldly objectives and indulging in selfish practices: the commandments are still nominally our rules of life, but they are really only in our memories and have no vital connection with our thought and conduct. Our "ark" is captured by the "Philistines."

But our ark cannot remain with the Philistines. The very knowledge of the commandments, if we are doing things contrary to them, will plague us by showing us plainly the ugliness of what we are thinking and doing. The plagues of tumors and of mice were merely the manifestations of the evils into which the people had fallen, habits of sensual living which, as Swedenborg says, "eat up and consume all things of the church." The Philistines represent "those who are in the memory-knowledge of the knowledges of faith, and are not in a life of charity" (AC 8093). The Philistine state is the state into which we come when we stubbornly persist from day to day in doing what we find pleasant and convenient instead of looking to the Lord for guidance and applying His laws—which we know—in our thought and conduct. Dagon, the god of the Philistines, had the body of a fish and the head and hands of a man. We recall that fish represent affection for knowledges. So the breaking off of the head and hands of Dagon by the presence of the ark, leaving only his fish body, is an interesting picture of the effect of the commandments in showing us our own Philistinism.

How often also, when our knowledge of the commandments rebukes us and shows us our evils, we move them about from place to place in our minds (as the Philistines moved the ark from Ashdod to Gath and from Gath to Ekron) trying to find some abiding place for them where they will be quiescent and cause us no discomfort! But wherever they go, their power exerts itself to reveal hidden sins, until we realize that only by restoring them to their rightful place in our lives can we have peace.

Swedenborg gives us the correspondence of the return of the ark in considerable detail in several places: in TCR 203, DP 326[12], and especially in AE 700, as well as fragmentarily in other passages. When the Philistines determined to return the ark, they called for their diviners to tell them how to go about it. This recalls the story of Balak and Balaam. The fact that the diviners employed correspondences shows that the knowledge of these persisted in Philistia as well as in the eastern country. The golden emerods and the golden mice which were to be returned with the ark are symbols of the renunciation of the evils which the ark had exposed. They are called a trespass offering and involve the recognition of sin and the intention of putting love to the Lord and the neighbor in place of self-love as the motive of our outward conduct. The new cart is a "new but natural doctrine." *The Sower* suggests that it may be a new acknowledgment of the duty of carrying out the commandments in life. The milk cows on which no yokes had come are good natural affections "not yet defiled by falsities." It is not easy to separate these natural affections from the worldly objects upon which they have been fixed, and this reluctance is represented by the shutting up of the calves at home and the lowing of the cows. We may find an example of this in the difficulty we all find in learning to do good to others without any thought of the gratitude and praise we may receive, or to take our part in the work of our church without expecting everyone else to approve and follow our methods and example.

The cows, under the urging of the divine power of the ark, drew the cart on the road straight to Bethshemesh. Bethshemesh was the nearest of the Levitical towns, where the men had the right to lift the ark from the cart and to make the sacrifice of the cows with the wood from the cart. Spiritually this means that when we do acknowledge our evils and submit to the guidance of the commandments, they gradually resume their true place in our lives, and our natural affections and natural ways of thinking are consecrated to the Lord's service. We may note here that the ark never returned to Shiloh, but passed from city to city until David finally restored it to its place in the Holy of Holies in the new tabernacle which he set up for it in Jerusalem. When we have fallen into the Philistine state, we can never return to exactly the same simple attitude toward the commandments which we had in the period of our early zeal, but if we persist in submitting to their guidance, they will gradually be restored to the central position in our lives and again be written on our hearts, with a new understanding of their force and application.

## From the Writings of Swedenborg

*Apocalypse Explained*, n. 700: "By the advice of their priests and diviners they made golden images of the emerods and mice, and set them at the side of the ark upon a new cart, to which they tied two milch kine on which no yoke had come . . . The priests and diviners of the Philistines recommended this to be done because a knowledge of correspondences and representations was a common knowledge at that time, since it was their theology, known to the priests and diviners, who were their wise men. But because men at that time had become for the more part merely natural, they regarded these things in an idolatrous way, worshiping the externals, and giving no thought to the internals that the externals represented." (See also TCR 203.)

## Suggested Questions on the Lesson

P. Who was the last of the Judges? *Samuel*

J. What enemy attacked Israel while Samuel was still a child? *Philistia*

P. How did the Israelites try to win the victory? *took ark to battlefield*

P. What happened to the two priests who took the ark out of the tabernacle? *killed*

J. What happened to the ark? *captured*

P. What was its effect on the Philistines' god? *it fell and broke*

J. What was its effect on the Philistines themselves? *fear, plague*

P. What did the Philistines decide to do? *send it back*

J. Who told them how to send the ark back? *priests, diviners*

P. How was it sent back? *new cart*

P. What was sent with it? *five gold tumors, mice*

J. To what place did it come? *Bethshemesh*

I. What do the Philistines represent? *knowledge without obedience*

I. Why could they not keep the ark? *knowledge not obeyed plagues one*

S. What are pictured by the new cart and the milk cows? *new attitude, kindly affection*

S. How did the Philistine diviners know the way in which the ark should be returned to Israel? *knowledge of correspondences*

## ASKING FOR A KING

*I Samuel 8*

In all classes the difference between Samuel and all the Judges who preceded him should be made clear, and Samuel's birth and call should be covered briefly.

---

### Doctrinal Points

*The Lord adapts His treatment of us to our states.*

*The Word always shows us clearly the transition from one spiritual state to another.*

*It is natural and right for us to wish to understand the principles which the Lord gives to guide us, but we must be willing to recognize the difficulties if we are to enjoy the benefits of such knowledge.*

*When we try to have our own way in anything, it is always to some degree a rejection of the Lord.*

---

### Notes for Parents

We learned recently that it was said of the time of the Judges: "In those days there was no king in Israel: every man did that which was right in his own eyes." This led to weakness, to compromising with the enemies in the land, and often to defeat at their hands. Finally, however, a Judge was raised up who was devoted to the service of the Lord. Samuel was promised to the Lord by his mother before he was born, and was brought up in the tabernacle at Shiloh under the direction of the aged high priest Eli. While he was still a young boy, the Lord called him in the night and gave him a prophetic message for Eli. And as he grew, the Lord continued to be with him so obviously that "all Israel from Dan even to Beersheba knew that Samuel was established to be a prophet of the Lord." So Samuel, who was the last of the Judges, was a religious rather than a military leader, and was recognized throughout the land instead of in just one part of it, as his predecessors had been. He lived at Ramah in the center of the land, and from there went about from place to place much as our circuit court judges do today.

But our lesson for today tells us that when Samuel became old and had to delegate some of his duties to others, the people became restless under his direction and asked him to give them a king. They were never long satisfied with the government of their unseen God, but wanted to be like the people around them. Samuel quite naturally was displeased, but the Lord told him to let the people have their king, only first to tell them plainly how many sacrifices a king would require of them.

Most of us mean to be good people. We believe there is a God and that we ought to do right. And most of us believe that the Bible is in some way the Word of God. This is like the people's recognition of Samuel as the Lord's prophet. But this world and its demands seem very important to us, just as they did to the Israelites, and we cannot quite be satisfied to go on just obeying the commandments from day to day without seeing just what they are accomplishing for us. We want some big striking principle to follow which will make us powerful with those around us in the world. This is asking for a king. And the Lord never interferes with our freedom of choice. He understands all our weaknesses and does His best to lead us in the right direction, warning us of the difficulties ahead, and helping us to learn even by our own mistakes.

---

## Primary

Point out why the people wanted a king and, if you have time, read them verses 11 to 18. Be sure they make the distinction between the names *Samson* and *Samuel*. See how much they remember of the Samuel story. In the lesson itself, stress the Lord's words to Samuel.

Samuel was not only the last of the Judges, he was the greatest of them. The others had been leaders over one or two of the tribes, but Samuel was recognized as leader of the whole people. For by Samuel's time the Israelites were beginning to see that they were strong only when they looked to the Lord for guidance, and Samuel was a religious instead of a military leader.

Do you remember where he was brought up?

Do you remember the story of how the Lord spoke to him in the night?

Because of this all the people recognized Samuel as the one through whom the Lord would speak to them and direct them—a prophet of the Lord.

His home was at Ramah near the center of the land.

From there he went about hearing the people's problems and judging them.

When he was old, what did he do which displeased the people?

What did they ask him to do?

Was Samuel pleased?

What did the Lord tell him?

If you would like to find out what Samuel told the people their king would be like, read verses 11 to 18 of our chapter.

Did the people believe Samuel?

What reason did they give for wanting a king?

---

## Junior

This is a good opportunity to review briefly the history of the Israelites, with emphasis on their type of government, and it is also possible to relate this changing government to the life of the individual, as a preparation for later instruction in the spiritual sense of the Word. While we do not go deeply into the spiritual sense with the Juniors, foretastes of it can often be given.

The last of the Judges was Samuel, and he was very different from the others. He was not a military leader. By the time he was born the Israelites were beginning to realize that they could not get along without the Lord. Some of the people, of course, had been faithful all the time. There are always good, sensible people who remember that the Lord is wiser than men. So the worship had gone on in the tabernacle at Shiloh all through the centuries. At the time when Samuel was born, the high priest was a very old man named Eli. You have had part of the story of Samuel before and so you may remember how, before he was born, his mother promised that she would give him to the Lord, and how she brought him, when he was still a little boy, to Shiloh and gave him to Eli to bring up. And you remember how the Lord called Samuel in the night and gave him an important message for Eli.

I Samuel 3:19-20 tells us: "And Samuel grew, and the Lord was with him, and did let none of his words fall to the ground. And all Israel from Dan even to Beersheba knew that Samuel was established to be a prophet of the Lord." So Samuel came to be recognized as Judge not just in one part of the land but by all the people; He was a very good and just man. Read I Samuel 12:1-5. But in our lesson for today, which is in the time of Samuel's old age, we find that the people are becoming restless under his leadership. The last few verses of chapter 7 tell us that he lived at Ramah, which is a city not far from Jerusalem, and went regularly in circuit to Bethel and Gilgal and Mizpeh to judge the people, very much as our circuit court judges do today. But he could not cover the whole land in his own circuit.

Whom did he make judges under him?
Where did his sons judge?
What wrong things did they do?
What did the people ask Samuel to do?
Was Samuel willing to give them what they asked?
What did the Lord tell him?
What did Samuel tell the people a king would do to them?
Did the people change their minds?

Let us think back to the beginnings of the Hebrew nation. You remember that their first leader was Abraham. Abraham heard the voice of the Lord telling him to leave his home in Ur of the Chaldees and go to the land of Canaan and establish himself there. After him, Isaac and Jacob both received confirmation directly from the Lord of their right to govern their people. During the long sojourn in Egypt the Israelites had no leader of their own, but were under the rule of Pharaoh.

Who was their next leader?
How was he chosen?
Who followed Moses?
Did Joshua also have a call from the Lord?
How were the Judges chosen?
How was Samuel himself chosen?

You can see why Samuel was displeased at the people's request for a king, and also why the Lord says to him: "They have not rejected thee, but they have rejected me, that I should not reign over them." They wanted someone from among themselves, whom they might accept freely, to rule them instead of someone put over them by the Lord. They wanted to be like other people.

This long history is really a picture of your own life. All through your infancy and childhood and the time when you are growing up your life is controlled by others, by those chosen by God—your parents, guardians, and teachers. But there comes a time when you want to be ruled by your own judgment and not by someone else. This is like the time of the Judges. Then after a while you find that your own judgment often gets you into trouble and that it is safer to listen to the Lord. This is the time of Samuel. But after all you are not a little child anymore and you want to stand on your own feet and choose how to govern your own life. You mean to be good but you want to understand and choose the principles by which you will be led. This is asking for a king. Soon we shall see what kind of king the Israelites first chose to obey.

---

## Intermediate

The important lesson for this class is the meaning of the transition from the period of the Judges to that of the Kings, with Samuel as the connecting link. The teacher may draw on the Senior and Adult notes for material to illustrate the correspondence of a king.

You remember the story of Samuel. His parents were among the few faithful souls who still went regularly to worship at the tabernacle in Shiloh. Hannah, Samuel's mother, prayed there for a son and promised that if her prayer was granted, she would devote the child to the Lord. So when Samuel was still a little boy, she brought him to Shiloh and gave him to Eli, the old high priest, to bring up in the service of the tabernacle. Then in the night the Lord called Samuel, and gave him a prophetic message for Eli. And as Samuel grew up, the Lord continued to be with him, so that "all Israel from Dan even to Beersheba knew that Samuel was established to be a prophet of the Lord."

Samuel, therefore, unlike most of the Judges who had preceded him, was a religious and not a military leader and was accepted by the whole nation. You remember that the Judges represent particular truths recalled to our minds by the Lord to meet particular temptations. But this last Judge, Samuel, represents the Word as a whole. We may go along for some time turning to the Lord for help only when we find ourselves in real trouble, but the troubles pile up, and we must finally come to see that we can have no safety and peace unless every part of our life looks to the Lord for direction. Under Samuel the life of the nation became centered again in the tabernacle at Shiloh.

Samuel ends one period and begins another. His life ties the two together. The Lord is always at work in our lives preparing us for the changes He sees are coming. It was necessary for the Israelites to go back for a time to dependence upon an individual who obviously spoke for the Lord just as Abraham, Isaac, Jacob, Joseph, Moses, and Joshua had done. So when we, after the period of indifference pictured by the time of the Judges, come back to wholehearted worship of the Lord, we at first are satisfied with the simple dependence and obedience which we knew as children. But this satisfaction does not last. We are grown up now, and, although we are willing to admit that we need the Lord's constant direction, we want to understand and adopt that direction in our own way. This is asking Samuel for a king.

A king represents truth ruling—not a single truth but a great general principle under which everything in our lives can be organized. The Israelites told Samuel the reason why they wanted a king: "That we also may be like all the nations; and that our king may judge us, and go out before us, and fight our battles." All the other nations had kings. Everyone has some general principle which rules his life. It may be a selfish principle such as, "Everyone must take care of himself first," or even, "The world owes me a living." Such principles are represented by the kings of the enemies of Israel in the Holy Land. The Israelites wanted a king who could put up a strong opposition to their enemies. They were not content just to obey the Lord's commands from day to day as they received them from the lips of Samuel. That was why the Lord told Samuel, "they have not rejected thee, but they have rejected me." If we are faithful, the time comes when we are satisfied to look to the Lord as little children look to a wise and loving parent for daily guidance, but this state does not often come in our youth.

The Lord understands us all the way and does the best He can for us from state to state. He told Samuel to let the people have a king, but we shall see that, all unknown to them, He directed their choice so that they would finally learn by experience what kind of ruler they really should have. One of the cardinal teachings of the New Church is that the Lord never interferes with our freedom of choice. He tells us plainly what is right and He warns us of all the things we should avoid, and then He leaves us free to choose His way or ours. So He told Samuel to tell the people "the manner of the king" that should reign over them, and Samuel did tell them just how much the king would demand of them. When we choose a certain principle—no matter how good—to rule our lives, we must expect to have to give up many things we have enjoyed. Truth is a hard taskmaster until we have learned to love it. We may have to make over our whole way of life. And then we may find that our first understanding of the truth was faulty and that we have made mistakes which add to our problems. We shall study this possibility further in future lessons.

*Basic Correspondences*

Samuel = the Word of the Lord as a whole
a king = a ruling principle

---

## Senior

The meaning of asking for a king comes close to the thinking of the Seniors. Stress the correspondence of the leadership of truth separated from good and the hardships it imposes. Prepare the way for later lessons by suggesting that we may find that our first understanding of truth is not altogether reliable. Be sure they understand the continuing function of Samuel.

Samuel was dedicated to the Lord even before he was born, and while still a small boy was brought by his mother Hannah to Shiloh to be brought up in the service of the tabernacle under the direction of the old high priest Eli. When the Lord called Samuel in the night and gave him a prophetic message for Eli, Eli recognized that Samuel was the Lord's messenger, and we are told that as Samuel grew up, "all Israel from Dan even to Beersheba knew that Samuel was established to be a prophet of the Lord." So he came to be Judge over all the nation instead of over one tribe or another, as his predecessors had been. His home was in the central part of the land at Ramah, about midway between Shiloh and the city which was later to be Jerusalem, and like some of our judges today he went about in a circuit to hear and judge the people.

For a time under Samuel the Israelites went back to simple acceptance of the Lord's direction as it came to them through the individual chosen by the Lord to lead them. The earlier Judges represented particular truths needed to meet particular temptations. Samuel represents the Word as a whole. When we, after trying out our own spiritual judgment and strength and finding them inadequate, return to dependence upon the Lord, we are content for a time to accept His direction from day to day as in childhood we accepted the direction of our parents. This is, of course, the ideal attitude and the one which we must eventually adopt. "Whosoever shall not receive the kingdom of God as a little child, he shall not enter therein." But when we are in the full strength of our young manhood and womanhood, our natural disposition is not satisfied to obey the Lord as if we were children. We want to participate actively in the determination of our spiritual as well as of our worldly destiny. This is pictured in the Bible story by the Israelites asking for a king.

Swedenborg tells us that the office of divine good in our lives is represented by a priest and the office of divine truth by a king. Good and truth are one in the Lord and proceed from Him as one. They are meant to be received by us as one, as they were united in the person of Samuel. But because of our tendency to exalt self and to think in terms of this world, we will not steadily receive them in this way. Truth is not always what we want it to be. We do not always love to do as truth teaches, even though we think we want the truth. Again we have to learn by experience.

The Lord knows our nature and makes provision for it. So, although the people's rejection of Samuel—the Lord's prophet—was really a rejection of the Lord, as our chapter tells us, the Lord told Samuel to let the people have their king, and we shall find that He knew the kind of king the people would first be willing to obey.

The separation of the office of king from that of priest marks the beginning of another period in the history of the Jews, and you remember that in each period we have seen a representative of this same separation of good and truth or charity and faith. The Lord recognizes that because of our nature we must be led by truth until we come to love it. And truth is a hard master. So the Lord told Samuel to tell the people what treatment they must expect from a king. Whatever principle—good or bad—we may choose as governor of our life, we have to make many sacrifices in its service. All the things which Samuel mentions in verses 11 to 18 of our chapter represent such sacrifices—unwilling adjustments which we shall have to make in our feelings and thoughts and conduct to meet the demands of principle. For truth is hard and unbending, and condemns what is contrary to it. Read Matthew 19: 24-26.

Samuel lived possibly another thirty years after he anointed the first king of Israel and anointed the second king also. He continued to be the religious leader of the nation through whom the Lord spoke to the people. This was a provision of divine providence over the Israelites, and it represents the provision which the Lord makes for our protection and guidance through the difficult years when we are finding our way to a true understanding of our religious principles. Samuel is the hold which the simple trust of our innocent childhood retains upon us after we come to adult years.

## Adult

The quotations given with the Adult notes should provide ample discussion material. We shall continue our consideration of Samuel in lessons which follow, but his relation to the proposed king—the fact that he continued to be the Lord's prophet, so recognized by all the people—should be stressed.

Our spiritual life advances in cycles. Our lesson for today marks another beginning—a transition from one cycle to another—characterized by the familiar choice of truth rather than good. In this story we do not have the simple picture of the older and younger brothers. The choice is more subtle and complex, for Samuel retains his actual control even though the king apparently supplants him.

We are all very familiar with the story of Samuel's birth and call, but we do not always stop to think of his actual position in the Bible story. Because his story does not begin in the book of Judges, we are likely to forget that he was actually the last Judge. And because we think of the period of the Kings as immediately following that of the Judges, we forget that Samuel overlapped the period of Kings, that he lived to anoint the second King, David, and that the second book of Samuel takes us almost to the end of David's reign. This is an illustration of the fact that changes are never sudden either in the Word or in life. They may sometimes seem sudden to us, but on the Lord's part there is always foresight and preparation, and the Lord helps us to adjust to new conditions.

It is rather curious that, in spite of the fact that two books of the Word bear Samuel's name, there are only a few brief mentions of Samuel in the writings. We are told in AE 750[21] that Moses and Samuel "in the representative sense signify the Word." This confirms a point which seems obvious from the letter, since Samuel was Judge over the whole nation, whereas his predecessors—who, as we remember, represent particular truths—were local Judges. We also recognize easily from the letter that Samuel's influence was religious rather than military, although he was the spokesman of the Lord in the battles fought during his lifetime.

The writings do give us, however, in two places a clear picture of Samuel's function. In AC 6148 we read: "The Divine good was represented by priests, and the Divine truth by kings . . . In the Ancient Representative Church the priesthood and the royalty were joined together in one person, because the good and truth which proceed from the Lord are united, and in heaven with the angels are also joined together . . . Moreover as a representative church was instituted with the posterity of Jacob, therefore in one person conjointly was represented the Divine good and the Divine truth which proceed united from the Lord. But on account of the wars and of the idolatry of that people, these two offices were at first divided, and they who ruled over the people were called 'leaders', and afterward 'judges'; while they who officiated in holy things were called 'priests', and were of the seed of Aaron, and Levites. Yet afterward these two offices were joined together in one person, as in Eli and in Samuel." It is evident, therefore, that Samuel, although not a Levite, was considered a priest as well as a Judge. We know from I Samuel 3:20 that he was early recognized by all the people to be a "prophet of the Lord."

The period of the Judges culminated in Samuel. The people, after a bitter experience during about two hundred years of trying to get along without divine leadership, had finally come back to united worship of the Lord. Samuel, as we know, was brought up in the tabernacle at Shiloh, and his later home was at Ramah, also in the center of the land. From there he went out to other towns in a circuit to judge the people. Yet we recall that in Samuel's childhood the ark had been taken out of the tabernacle and had been captured by the Philistines in battle; and that although it had been returned to Israel, it had never been replaced in the tabernacle. This suggests the hollowness of the worship which the people now offered. This is confirmed in the continuation of AC 6148[5]: "But because the people were of such a character that a representative church could not be instituted among them, but only the representative of a church, by reason of the idolatrous disposition which prevailed among them, therefore it was permitted that the two offices should be separated, and that the Lord as to Divine truth should be represented by kings, and as to Divine good by priests. That this was done at the will of the people, and not of the Lord's good pleasure, is manifest from the word of Jehovah unto Samuel (I Samuel 8:7 ff. and 12:19, 20)." The people wanted to worship the Lord not in childlike trust and obedience—which the sole leadership of Samuel represented—but in order that they might be "like all the nations" and overcome their enemies by their armed strength.

AC 6148[6] gives us further light on our chapter: "Divine truth separated from Divine good condemns every one; whereas Divine truth united to Divine good saves. For from Divine truth man is condemned to hell, but by the Divine good he is taken out therefrom, and is elevated into heaven. Salvation is of mercy, thus from the Divine good; but damnation is when man refuses mercy, and thus rejects from himself the Divine good; wherefore he is left to judgment from truth." And AC 2015[11] (see below) uses this same thought to explain why the Lord told Samuel to tell the people "the manner of a king" they would have if they persisted in their desire. All the demands which are mentioned in verses 11 to 18 of our chapter picture the demands which truth separated from good makes upon us.

The explanation of this chapter given us in these passages from the writings is given as to the internal historical sense, showing the application of the chapter to the history of the Jewish Church, but it is not difficult to transfer this explanation to our individual lives. We have seen that the period of the Judges pictures the time in our lives when we believe ourselves to be established in the regenerate life and think we can rest on our oars and enjoy ourselves without further struggle against temptation. The results are disastrous and in time we have to return to the admission of our own evils and weakness and our dependence upon the Lord. This admission, in its first form, takes on the appearance of a return to our childhood state of simple trust and obedience. Samuel, the Lord's prophet, becomes our leader. But we are not actually children. The time of the innocence of ignorance is long past and we still have a long way to go before we attain the innocence of wisdom. We want to see and understand for ourselves the religious principle we shall follow. And the Lord never interferes with our freedom of choice. He adapts His unseen government to our wayward state and lets us have our king, but with a clear warning of the sacrifices which will be required of us by the principle He foresees we will adopt.

---

## From the Writings of Swedenborg

*Arcana Coelestia*, n. 2015[10-11]: "As 'a king' signifies truth, it may be seen what is meant in the internal sense when the Lord is called a King and also a Priest; and also what it was in the Lord that was represented by kings, and what by priests. Kings represented His Divine truth, and priests His Divine good . . . government from truths alone would condemn everyone to hell; but government from goods lifts every one out thence and uplifts him into heaven . . . But as the kings represented truths, which ought not to have command, for the reason, as before said, that they condemn, therefore the desire to have kings was so displeasing as to call for rebuke, and the nature of truth as regarded in itself was described by the rights of the king (I Samuel 8:11-18); and at an earlier day it was commanded by Moses (Deuteronomy 17:14-18) that they should choose genuine truth which is from good, and not spurious; and that they should not defile it by reasonings and memory-knowledges. This is what is involved in the directions concerning a king, given in Moses in the place just cited; which no one can possibly see from the sense of the letter, but yet is evident from the several points contained in the internal sense; so that 'king' and 'kingship' evidently represented and signified nothing else than truth."

---

## Suggested Questions on the Lesson

P. Who was the last of the Judges? *Samuel*
J. Where was he brought up? *Shiloh*
J. Who was the high priest when Samuel was a child? *Eli*
J. How did he and all the people learn that Samuel was to be a prophet? *Lord spoke to Samuel*
J. What was the difference between Samuel and all the earlier Judges? *religious leader, accepted by all*
J. Where was Samuel's home? *Ramah*
J. In his old age what did he do which made the people dissatisfied? *let his sons judge*

P. What did they ask him to give them? *a king*
P. Was Samuel willing? *no*
P. What did the Lord tell him? *give them a king*
J. What did Samuel tell the people a king would be like? *harsh*
J. Did they change their minds? *no*
I. What does a king represent? *truth ruling in our lives*
S. What does Samuel represent? *the Word as a whole restoring order to our lives*

## THE CHOOSING OF SAUL

*I Samuel 9; 10*

All but the youngest children should be able to tell about the characteristics of the period of the Judges and why the people were always getting into trouble in that period. The teacher in his preparation for the lesson should reread I Samuel 8 and be able to give the class this background for the lesson. Be sure the children understand that Samuel is now an old man and a very great man, who speaks to the people for the Lord—a prophet or "seer."

---

### Doctrinal Points

*The first principle under which we organize our adult lives in the Lord's service is limited by our superficial judgment.*

---

### Notes for Parents

We have studied the history of Israel under several types of government. First they looked for direction to the patriarchs—Abraham, Isaac, and Jacob. Then for a long time they were slaves in Egypt. Then they followed the two great leaders Moses and Joshua. During the period of the Judges we saw that they had no single ruler or leader, but looked to themselves and sought leadership only when they were in trouble. Most of the Judges were local and temporary leaders. Then came the last Judge—Samuel—who, because he proved to be the Lord's chosen prophet, was eventually looked to for direction by all the people.

Samuel judged the land for many years and was always wise and just and wholly faithful to the Lord. But when he grew old, he turned over some of his duties to his sons, who abused their power. Then, as we learned in chapter 8, the people became dissatisfied and asked Samuel to give them a king so that they might be like other nations.

Samuel was unhappy, for he felt that the people were forgetting all that he had done for them, but the Lord told him to let them have their king and that, because Samuel was known to be the Lord's prophet, it was really the Lord whom the people had rejected. And the Lord promised to show Samuel who should be king. Our lesson this time tells us how Saul was brought to Samuel, how Samuel first proved to Saul that the Lord had really chosen him, and then how the people were led to recognize and accept Saul as their first king.

We need to notice the reason why the people accepted Saul so willingly: "he was higher than any of the people from his shoulders and upward." In other words, they judged him by his appearance. Is not this the common experience of all of us when we first look for a general principle to direct our lives? We judge by appearances. We know that young adults sometimes feel that they have the answers to everything: if only other people would do as they think they should, the world would be all right. They see only the surface of things and have not enough experience to recognize the deeper issues and forces involved and to take account of them. They are "well-meaning," eager, and energetic, but they are not yet wise.

Older people, however, should have patience with this state. There is a lesson for us all in our story. The Lord chose Saul. He knew that the people were not ready to accept and follow a really wise leader. They had proved it by turning against Samuel. They had to be allowed to learn by experience. So do our young people when they reject wise advice.

---

## Primary

Tell the whole story very simply, explaining what "anointing" means, and then point out why the people liked Saul and were glad to have him for their king. Even little children need to be taught that we cannot always judge things by their appearance.

When Samuel grew old, he let his sons do some of the governing for him, and his sons were not good men. They did not govern the people fairly, and so the people came to Samuel and asked him to give them a king to rule them as the other nations were ruled. Samuel was unhappy about it, but the Lord told him to let the people have what they asked for, and the Lord promised to show Samuel who should be king.

Who did the Lord show Samuel was to be the first king?
What tribe was Saul from?
What did he look like?
Saul was out looking for some lost asses of his father's when Samuel found him.
Samuel told him that the asses were found, and then that he was to be king.
A little later he "anointed" him.
This means that he poured olive oil on his head as a sign that the Lord was with him.
Then Samuel sent Saul home and called the people together at Mizpeh.
How did it seem to the people that their king was chosen?
Who really governed the way in which the lots fell?
Why were the people pleased with Saul?

---

## Junior

The Juniors may like to trace on a map the wanderings of Saul and his servant in search of the asses. Stress the humility of Saul at the start, and the Lord's way of reassuring him and leading him to accept his office. Discuss the casting of lots and the part the Lord played in the choice of Saul. The Juniors also need the lesson concerning Saul's appearance.

Samuel was recognized as the Lord's prophet, and when he grew up, he was accepted as Judge by all the people. He served faithfully for many years, always obeying the Lord. But when he was old, he turned over some of his duties to his sons. They were not good men, but were greedy for money, and took bribes and did not judge the people justly. So finally the people asked Samuel to give them a king who would rule them as the other nations were ruled. Samuel was reluctant, but the Lord told him to let the people have their way, and that He would show Samuel who was to be their first king.

Who was this first king of Israel?

From what tribe was he?
What did he look like?
What was Saul doing when he first met Samuel?

We can see that the Lord was directing Saul's life. But Saul had to have some preparation before he was openly proclaimed king. He was very humble at first, for when Samuel told him he had been chosen, he answered that his tribe was the smallest in Israel and he himself the least in his tribe. After Samuel anointed him, the Lord gave him several unusual experiences to prove to him that he had really been chosen. We read about these in the first part of chapter 10. The Lord's providence is over each one of us just as much as it was over Saul. Each one of us was created to fill a particular place and to do some special work for the Lord, and nothing happens to us which cannot in some way help to prepare us for this work, if we use our experiences rightly.

Where did Samuel call the people together?
How was Saul chosen this time?

Samuel, of course, knew on whom the lot would fall, but all the people had to see for themselves that the Lord's choice was Saul. Saul knew also, and the fact that he hid himself showed that he was still in a humble frame of mind and thought himself unworthy of so high an office.

Why were the people pleased with Saul?

We shall find, however, that Saul was not as big a man inside as he was on the outside, and that his humility did not last; but the people did not know this. Do we ever, like the Israelites, judge things by their outward appearance without making the effort to look into them more deeply?

Even today kings are still consecrated by anointing, that is, by pouring oil on their heads. It is a very old custom and it comes from the knowledge of correspondence which the ancient peoples had from the Ancient Word. Oil is the symbol of love, and Samuel's act was a sign that Saul must rule from a love of serving the Lord and the neighbor. If everyone who had power used it with this love in his heart, the world would be a different kind of place.

---

### Intermediate

This class will be interested in the correspondence of the ass (remind them of the lesson on Balaam) and will be able to see what is meant by Saul's being called while he was hunting for his father's asses. Nothing in the Word is there by chance. Everything fits in when we see the internal meaning. The general meaning of Saul is not hard to teach to young people of this age.

In chapter 8 of I Samuel we learned that when Samuel was old, his sons—just as Eli's had done—became corrupt, and that the people became dissatisfied. So they came to Samuel, whose home was still at Ramah, and asked him to give them a king. They said they wanted a king so that they might be like all the other nations. A king represents truth ruling. A priest represents love. Samuel was a judge, but he was also a priest, so Samuel's government of the land pictures a state in which we are directed primarily by love to the Lord. If you think of this, you will understand what is meant by I Samuel 8:6-9. The Lord always leaves us free to choose our own way, but He does everything He can to protect and direct us.

Israel's desire for a king pictures our desire to choose our own ruling principle. We want to do right, but we want to understand why it is right and not merely to do as someone else—even the Lord—tells us to do. We think we are quite capable of judging. But the truth is that it takes many years of experience to become really wise. At first we judge according to appearances. The way which looks best on the face of it we believe to be best. We don't like to wait for results. We don't like to study a problem more deeply to see what really will be the best solution in the long run.

Saul pictures this first superficial standard of judgment. When he first came to Samuel, he was looking for his father's asses which had been lost. The ass pictures our "natural" reason, our common sense. It is a very sure-footed animal but very stubborn, and not at all willing to be guided. Saul's search for his father's asses pictures our attempts to find a "common-sense" solution of our problems, one which will bring some immediate change in things, without waiting to see whether or not the change will really be for the better.

The people liked Saul for his apparent strength and size—they could "look up" to him literally, for he stood head and shoulders above everyone else. This is the way our own reason looks to us when we are young. We simply can't see how the world could fail to improve if others would do what we think they should.

The Lord really chose Saul, first by telling Samuel to anoint him, and then by governing the lots which the people cast. The Lord knew Saul's weaknesses, but he knew that Saul was the only kind of king the people would accept and follow until they had had more experience. In the same way He lets us try out our own judgment and do the things that seem to us right when we are young men and women, even though He knows our judgment is faulty.

The anointing of Saul by Samuel pictures the fact that in this first effort to set up a ruling principle there is a genuine desire to do right. Oil represents love. Any principle which is worthy to govern our lives even for a time must have love in it. If it has not, it is merely the old selfish desire to have our own way. Saul represents a genuine desire to serve the Lord and the neighbor, although not a wholly wise one. In all our first attempts to work out our lives for ourselves, we must be sure that our basic wish is to do good.

Most young people do want to do right. Their ideals are high. They want to do great things in the world for others as well as for themselves. And they mean to serve the Lord. Their ideals and enthusiasm are needed, and can be a great help to everyone so long as they do not assume that they are wise enough to direct affairs. So do not hesitate to offer your help and to try to "get into things" in your church as well as in other fields of activity. But try to be willing to listen to advice, remembering that real wisdom is acquired only by long and patient effort. Saul's reign is a picture of the time of eager and impetuous youth, and we shall see that he won some victories but also made some very serious mistakes.

*Basic Correspondences*

| | | |
|---|---|---|
| oil | = | love |
| a king | = | truth ruling |
| a priest | = | love directing |
| Saul | = | the rule of truth as we judge it to be from external observation |

## Senior

In this class dwell especially on the meaning of the people's asking for a king and read Samuel's description of what a king would be like (I Samuel 8:10-18). This is a picture of what truth as a ruler does to our lives if we leave out love. The discussion of this and of the meaning of Saul as the first king will bring out questions and illustrations.

The story of Saul contains a lesson which is much needed both by us as individuals and by the world. We often hear it said that youth is the hope of the world, and of course in one sense it is. Those who are young now are the ones who will later control the destiny of the world. This is true of every new generation. But there sometimes seems to be a tendency to imagine that it is the young people who should be in control now. People—especially young people—say, "Look what a mess the older people have made of things! Youth has ideals; youth has energy. Let the young people take over the reins, and everything will be better." The story of Saul's reign over Israel is the Lord's answer to this mistaken idea.

In our individual lives we all go through the stage—from twenty to thirty perhaps—when we think we know how everything should be done. It seems to us so simple. If everyone would do as we suggest, the world's problems would be solved. The Lord knows, as wise parents and older leaders know, that young people must go through this period, must have this experience. And the ideals and energy and dissatisfaction of youth are needed to keep things stirred up, to keep us from settling down in old ways, to keep our minds open to change. But the judgment of youth is hasty and superficial. It is apt to ignore the deep problems presented by human nature in every situation, individual or social. It assumes that conditions can be corrected quickly by one or another external method, without the long, slow process of regenerating individuals.

That is, the first ruler we choose as young adults is chosen on the basis of external appearance—it is apparent rather than genuine truth, truth as our "natural rational" sees it. This is Saul as king of Israel. When Saul first came to Samuel, he was hunting for his father's asses, which had been lost. The ass, sure-footed but stubborn, represents the natural reason, sometimes called "common sense." When we are young, we exalt common sense—as we see it—and look for what we consider the obvious solutions for our problems. We jump at any solution which seems to make sense. We have no patience with anyone who suggests that our solutions may not in the long run prove really practical. They promise quick results; so they look good to us. The people welcomed Saul as king because of his appearance—he stood head and shoulders above everyone else.

Saul "meant well." Samuel, at the Lord's command, anointed him. Anointing oil is a symbol of consecration by divine love. Saul entered upon the kingship knowing that he was dedicated to the Lord's service and under obligation to obey the Lord's commands. Youth also means well and intends to serve the Lord. (There are vicious young people as there are vicious adults, but they are a very small percentage of the whole.) The Lord chose Saul as Israel's first king because He knew the state of the people and that they were not prepared to recognize and follow a wiser leader at this time. We shall find that Saul was to lose his humility very soon—with his first victory—and was to make many mistakes and lose his right to rule because he came to think he knew better than Samuel, the Lord's prophet. In much the same way young people, if given control, often make mistakes and learn by hard experience that lasting leadership must be based on deeper principles and more wisdom. And wisdom comes only slowly.

## Adult

This lesson with the Adults may well be geared to improving the underlying attitude of the older people in the church toward the younger people. In many even of our own societies there is a cleavage between the two groups which is damaging to both and to the church as a whole, and which need not exist if the older people have understanding and patience.

With this lesson we enter a new phase of ancient Hebrew history, and we should have the general outline of the history to this point in mind, beginning with the patriarchal leadership of Abraham, Isaac, and Jacob which in the individual life pictures the period of infancy, childhood, and early youth, when we are under the control of our parents albeit with ever-increasing understanding and initiative of our own. After the sojourn in Egypt a new type of leadership is introduced in Moses, who represents the Law. This is a period of self-compulsion which lasts until, by experience, we are so convinced of the effectiveness of an orderly life and the disastrous results of disobedience that external obedience to the commandments has become a matter of course in all ordinary affairs. Then we are ready to take the next step and attack the evils in our inner lives. Joshua comes to the fore—the truth fighting—and we follow him until we feel that we are really established in the good life—until the Holy Land is conquered.

But the book of Judges shows us that the conquest is not complete. As soon as we cease to examine ourselves and to fight temptation, our enemies both within and without begin to gain strength again and our lives become a series of battles waged under the leadership of one or another truth, represented by the various Judges, with periods of rest between. Throughout all the time from Moses to the end of the book of Judges the office of priest is separate from the office of leader, the priest representing good and the leader truth. So far as they work together the leadership of the people is sound, but if they are out of harmony—if either is corrupt—disorganization and disaster result. In Samuel the two offices are for a time united, but presently we read: "It came to pass, when Samuel was old, that he made his sons judges over

Israel." And his sons were corrupt. Here we have the lesson of the necessity of constant watchfulness; our own ideas creep in and corrupt the divine order in which we think we are established. A new beginning must be made.

The desire for a king can be most easily illustrated from the experience of young people. They are often genuinely perplexed by their parents' reaction to their conduct. "Why should my mother allow this thing and forbid that? I can't see that there is more harm in the one than in the other. How can I tell what I ought to do?" It is the demand for a constant principle of action which will apply to all cases. They have reached the point where they wish to be able to judge for themselves what they ought and ought not to do. They do not want to be always asking permission. This is a natural development. The Lord foresaw its expression in the history of Israel. In Deuteronomy 17:14-20 it is foretold that Israel will demand a king, and the people are commanded to take the king whom the Lord shall choose.

There is an element of loss in this desire for independence from priestly authority. The celestial state desires nothing else than to look to the Lord as a little child to his parent. Self-dependence, even when the desire is to obey the truth, involves ignorance, mistakes, and disasters. Loving and wise parents often sigh when their children reach this stage, as Samuel disliked and feared the change. Yet it is a natural stage, and the Lord has provided for it. The Lord told Samuel to let the people have their way but to warn them that life under a king would not be easy. A king represents truth judging, apart from good, and truth apart from good is always a hard master. In AC 8770[2] Swedenborg makes an interesting distinction; he says that the kingdom of the judges represents the rule of divine truth from divine good; the kingdom of priests who were also judges (Eli and Samuel), the rule of divine good from which is divine truth; but the kingdom of kings, the rule of divine truth without divine good. In AC 1672, in making the distinction between the meanings of "nation" and "people," he says: "Before the sons of Israel sought for kings, they were a nation, and represented good, or the celestial; but after they desired a king, and received one, they became a people, and did not represent good or the celestial, but truth or the spiritual; which was the reason why this was imputed to them as a fault." See also AC 2015[11] (below). The Lord tells Samuel, "Hearken unto the voice of the people in all that they say unto thee; for they have not rejected thee, but they have rejected me, that I should not reign over them." The desire for independent judgment goes deeper than mere rebellion against parental authority; it is rebellion against all authority which is not felt to be self-derived. Parents cannot prevent it; they can only point out the dangers and try to give their children principles in accordance with divine order—the king whom the Lord shall choose.

Saul was the Lord's choice as king. Not only did the Lord tell Samuel to anoint Saul, but the lot taken at Mizpeh fell upon Saul. Yet Saul's time of favor with God was to last only a short time. His victories would be few, and he would prove wholly inadequate to save Israel from most of their enemies. Why did the Lord choose Saul? Why did He not at once choose a David or a Solomon? Because the people were not ready. They would have rejected a wiser leader, while, except for a few "sons of Belial," they accepted Saul gladly. We have said that what young people demand is a consistent principle of action. There is only one such principle—the law of love—but they are not ready for it. We begin to understand and appreciate the law of love only after a lifetime of effort and experience. This may not seem to be so. We like to think we are acting from the law of love when we follow our natural good impulses, and many never outgrow this superficial idea of goodness. But the law of love is the law of divine love, which cannot be separated from divine wisdom. It has nothing to do with our natural impulses or with the outward appearance of things. The people accepted Saul gladly because of his external appearance of superiority. He stood head and shoulders above all the people. They had to learn by experience that he was not adequate to their needs.

Yet Saul had a measure of fitness for his office. He was to conquer some enemies. We cannot expect of young people the wisdom of experience. We can expect them to recognize the Lord and to try to do the Lord's will as they see it. They will inevitably at first judge by appearances. They will often be misled by specious arguments and apparent results. They do not like to wait for their results. Saul's size and power appeal to them. They must learn by experience—their own experience—in many cases. But we can help to prepare our children for states and experiences beyond their present knowledge, especially by means of these stories from the Word. The Lord did this with His disciples: "And now I have told you before it come to pass, that when it is come to pass, ye might believe." Saul represents divine truth in a natural and external form, suited to the needs and comprehension of certain states through which we all pass in youth and in which we sometimes remain long after we should have grown wiser. "By a king, or by the royalty which belonged to Saul, is signified Divine truth in respect to protection and judgment." (AC 10540[7]).

---

## From the Writings of Swedenborg

*Arcana Coelestia*, n. 2015[11]: "As the kings represented truths, which ought not to have command, for the reason . . . that they condemn, therefore the desire to have kings was so displeasing as to call for rebuke, and the nature of truth as regarded in itself was described by the rights [*jus*] of the king (I Samuel 8:11-18); and at an earlier day it was commanded by Moses (Deut. 17:14-16) that they should choose genuine truth which is from good, and not spurious; and that they should not defile it by reasonings and memory-knowledges [*scientifica*]. This is what is involved in the directions concerning a king, given in Moses in the place just cited; which no one can possibly see from the sense of the letter, but yet is evident from the several points contained in the internal sense; so that 'king' and 'kingship' evidently represented and signified nothing else than truth."

*Arcana Coelestia*, n. 8770[2]: "In the representative church among the posterity of Jacob, there was first a kingdom of judges, afterward a kingdom of priests, and lastly a kingdom of kings; and by the kindgom of judges was represented Divine truth from Divine good; by the kingdom of priests, who were also judges, was represented Divine good from which is Divine truth; and by the kingdom of kings was represented Divine truth without Divine good."

## Suggested Questions on the Lesson

I. Why, when Samuel was old, did the Israelites ask for a king? *his sons were evil*

I. How did Samuel feel about it? *rejected*

I. What did the Lord tell him? *they were rejecting Him*

P. Who was the first king the Lord chose? *Saul*

J. What was Saul doing when he first met Samuel? *seeking lost asses*

J. How did Samuel prove to him that the Lord had chosen him? *anointed him (see also I Samuel 10:2-6)*

J. What does anointing mean? *pouring oil on head*

J. Where did the Lord call the people together? *Mizpah*

J. How was Saul chosen there? *by casting lots*

P. Who really governed the choice by lot? *the Lord*

P. Why were the people pleased to have Saul for their king? *tall and strong*

I. What does a king represent? *truth ruling*

S. What does the rule of Saul represent, and why? *rule of truth as understood at "common-sense" level*

## SAUL'S IMPATIENCE

*I Samuel 13*

Samuel, his character and office, forms the link between the period of the judges and that of the kings. The difference between the time of the judges and the time of the kings can be brought out, and the children should get clearly in mind the difference in office between Samuel and Saul and the reason why Samuel really stood above the king and why he had to continue through Saul's reign and until David had gained the confidence of the people. The reason for the people's desire for a king should be pointed out, as well as Samuel's reaction to it and the reason for the Lord's permitting them to have a king even though it was in a sense a rejection of both Samuel and the Lord. In the older classes this should be discussed especially, as it brings out the necessity for our freedom of choice.

---

### Doctrinal Points

*Trust in the Lord instead of in self is the basis of spiritual progress.*

---

### Notes for Parents

Our lesson for today is about the first king of Israel. This, we recall, was a new kind of leadership. The first leaders were the patriarchs, Abraham, Isaac, and Jacob. The Jews then were really just a family, growing in numbers and developing several "collateral" branches, but still living together and recognizing as the head of their family its oldest male member. Then followed the period in Egypt when they had no leader, but were first protected and then enslaved by the ruler of Egypt. Then Moses was raised up to lead them out of Egypt and through the wilderness and to give them at Sinai the commandments and laws he received from the Lord for their guidance. Moses was the lawgiver. He died when they reached the border of the Holy Land, at which point Joshua, the military leader, took command and led them in the conquest of the Holy Land. Then followed the period of the Judges, a series of local leaders, whom the Lord raised up to conquer particular enemies. This was a time of disorganization when "every man did that which was right in his own eyes."

The last of the Judges was Samuel. Samuel was the only one of the Judges who was recognized by all the people, and this was because he was seen to be a prophet also, and they had not had a prophet for a long time. But Samuel was not a military leader, and the people wanted a king who would gather an army and lead them against their enemies. Samuel did not lose his position when the first king was chosen. He represented the Lord to the people all his life, and the Lord gave him the duty of anointing the second as well as the first king.

The first king was Saul. The people were delighted with him because he stood head and shoulders above all of them and they felt that surely he would be a leader whom their enemies would respect. But like many strong, brave young people, Saul was more energetic than wise. He won his first battle against the Ammonites and that made him self-confident. So when he was to fight against the Philistines, who had become the virtual rulers of the land, he did not wait for Samuel's help as he had been told to do. Samuel was to come and offer sacrifices, but Saul became impatient and offered them himself, afterward excusing himself to Samuel on the ground that his men were getting nervous and deserting, and he did not dare to wait. Most of us have had times when we were not willing to "wait on the Lord." We really know that the Lord's way is best, but in the stress of some difficulty we trust ourselves instead of the Lord. Saul was told by Samuel that his kingdom would not continue. We have to have a wiser leader than our own judgment. We have to learn patience and trust.

## Primary

See what the children can remember of the story of Samuel's call. Then remind them why the people wanted a king and go on to the story for the day.

There will be no difficulty here in teaching the whole story, and the lesson of Saul's impatience and its result can be understood even at this age. The children will also be interested in verses 19-22.

Who was the last of the Judges?
He was the last because the people decided they wanted a king, so that they could be like the other nations.
But Samuel would still be the Lord's prophet, the one who spoke for the Lord.

So the Lord told Samuel to anoint a man named Saul to be their king. The people were pleased with Saul because he was taller than any of the other men. The Bible says: "He was higher than any of the people from his shoulders and upward." So the fighting men were glad to have him for their leader, and he easily gathered an army.

But Saul did not turn out to be as good a king as they expected. You know we can't always judge things by their looks. Saul was big and strong and brave, but he was not very wise. Samuel was still the Lord's prophet and Saul knew that he ought to do what Samuel told him to do.

So Saul easily gathered an army, and he won a great victory over an enemy called the Ammonites.
Then a very strong enemy, the Philistines, prepared to attack Israel.
What had made them angry?
Jonathan was Saul's son.
Samuel had told Saul to go to Gilgal and wait for him seven days and he would then come and offer sacrifices.
Saul knew that Samuel spoke for the Lord and that he ought to obey.
So he waited seven days at Gilgal for Samuel to come.
What did he do on the seventh day when Samuel had not arrived?
Are you ever in such a hurry to do something that you forget to obey?
Saul had hardly finished his sacrifice when Samuel came.
What excuse did Saul give?
What did Samuel tell him?
What king of man would the next king be?
Why did the Israelites not have swords and spears to fight with?

---

## Junior

The Juniors will be interested in studying Israel's position in relation to the

Philistines, the relative size of the armies, and the reasons why the people wanted a king and were pleased with Saul. They should look up the Bible references and study the map. Saul's strength and weakness make excellent lesson material for this age.

For a time the people were satisfied to have no leader except Samuel. Read I Samuel 7:15-17, and find on your map Ramah, Samuel's home, and the three places where he went to hold court. Samuel was a great judge, but he was not a fighting man, and the enemies of Israel were troubling the people. So they asked Samuel to give them a king. They saw that the other nations had kings who led them in battle, and they wanted one to lead them against their enemies. Samuel did not like the idea—he knew they should have been satisfied to let the Lord lead them—but the Lord told him to do as the people asked, and he told him whom to anoint as the first king. It was Saul.

Why were the people so pleased with Saul?

In chapter 11 we learn that Saul won his first battle, which was against the Ammonites. The people were delighted, and went to Gilgal and "renewed" Saul's kingship there. Then (chapter 12) Samuel made a solemn address to the people at Gilgal. He reminded them how he had served the Lord from his childhood, and asked them to say if he had ever done a wrong to any man. The people agreed that he never had. Not many people could win this reputation, could they? Then Samuel told them that if they hoped to prosper, they must obey the Lord, and he called down a storm of thunder and rain as a testimony to the people's wickedness. The people were very much frightened and begged him to pray for them. He promised to do this, but charged them solemnly that both they and their king must obey the Lord.

What enemy now rises against them?
What had made the Philistines angry?

Jonathan was Saul's son. The Philistines were camped at Michmash and Saul's army was gathered around him at Gilgal. Samuel had told Saul (I Samuel 10:8) to wait for him at Gilgal seven days, and not to go into battle until Samuel had come and offered sacrifices.

What did Saul do?
What excuse did Saul give?

We have seen before that people in the Bible are sometimes punished very severely for faults which seem to us not very great. But these faults always involve direct disobedience to the Lord, and that is never a small fault.

What did Samuel tell Saul?

In the Bible a king always pictures the principle, good or bad, which rules in our lives. A bad king is the principle that everybody else should do what pleases us; a good king is the principle that we should obey the Lord and help our neighbor. Saul, Israel's first king, was chosen for his looks. He meant well, but he was not very wise. Young people generally mean well, but like Saul they are sometimes in too much of a hurry. They do what seems right to them without taking time to think whether or not it is really right. It seemed to Saul that his men were leaving him and that if he did not hurry into battle, he would not be strong enough to conquer. Can you think of any stories in the Bible so far, that were in the history of Israel which Saul knew, which should have taught him better?

The Lord had often showed Israel that it was not their own strength which gave them victory. They could conquer only by means of the Lord's strength, as they obeyed Him. This is just as true of us. Whenever we think we know better than the Lord, we are headed for disaster. We have to make obedience to the Lord the first of our ruling principles. This was why Samuel told Saul that his kingdom would not continue.

What kind of man did Samuel say the next king would be?

Verses 19 to 22 tell us one of the ways in which the Philistines had been able to keep Israel in subjection.

What occupation did the Philistines keep in their own hands?
What was the result?

### Intermediate

The relative correspondence of the earlier judges, of Samuel, and of the kings is the important study for this class. The correspondence of the Philistines should be touched upon and the reason why Saul was more successful against the Ammonites. The correspondence of weapons should especially be noted, as it will be important in later lessons.

Samuel was the only Judge whom all the people recognized as their leader. What do you think this means? It means that Samuel represents a truth which is meant to apply to every part of our lives. It is the truth that in every problem we have as the first thing to remember that we ought to trust and obey the Lord's commands, because our Heavenly Father is wiser than we can ever be.

The people should have been satisfied to obey Samuel, but they were not. The armies of their enemies seemed to them so strong that they could not quite believe in the Lord's power to save them. They wanted a king such as the other nations had, a king who would raise an army and lead them in battle. Samuel was displeased that the people wanted a king, because he felt they were rejecting him, but the Lord told him to let them have their way, and that the first king should be Saul. Samuel found Saul and anointed him and then, so that the people would be satisfied with the choice, he called them all together to cast lots, and the lot fell upon Saul. The people liked Saul as their king because of his appearance.

Saul was strong and brave, but he was not very wise. He meant well, but you know that people who mean well can make very serious mistakes if they act without thinking. Saul needed Samuel to guide him. Without Samuel he might have led the people into serious trouble. So Samuel lived and continued to be the Judge and the Lord's prophet almost to the end of Saul's reign.

The kings of Israel represent principles that rule our lives. They all represent the Lord's truth ruling, but we know that we see the truth in different ways at different times. For instance, when you read in the Sermon on the Mount (Matthew 5:39), "But I say unto you, That ye resist not evil: but whosoever shall smite thee on thy right cheek, turn to him the other also," your first thought is that the Lord is giving you a command to be obeyed literally, and this is the way the early Christians took it. But presently you find that there are other statements in the Bible which show that we are certainly meant to resist evil, and you begin to try to find out what the Lord really does mean by this command. If you try hard enough, you will find that the word translated "resist" really means, in the Greek, to set something against itself, so that the thought is rather "oppose not evil with evil," and what the Lord is telling us is that we should not try to "pay back" wrongs that are done to us by doing wrong in return. So even the Lord's truth can be misunderstood by hasty and superficial judgment, and yet we have to read and learn the literal statement before we can try to understand it.

Saul represents the truth as it first appears to us. He won his first battle and that made him self-confident. So when Samuel did not come to Gilgal just as soon as Saul expected him, Saul went ahead and offered sacrifices himself. Read verses 11 and 12 to see how he tried to excuse himself. He was like the thing he represents. He judged by external appearance and did not wait to be sure he was doing the right thing. So Samuel had to tell him his kingdom would not continue. Whenever we make decisions hastily without taking time to be sure we are right, we are heading for trouble. We have to learn to think carefully and to wait until we are sure.

The enemy attacking Israel this time was the Philistines. They were a very strong and prosperous people who lived in the Holy Land along the Mediterranean seacoast. They had caused the Israelites much trouble, and at the time of our lesson were really ruling over them. We can see this in verses 19 to 22 of our chapter. Agricultural tools picture truths used in developing the mind and character. In the parable of the Sower the development of plants is explained by the Lord Himself as teaching about the growth of truth and goodness in our lives. Weapons picture truths used to overcome our weaknesses and bad habits, the spiritual enemies we all have. The Philistines are one of the most dangerous of these enemies—our tendency to be satisfied with knowing what is right without doing it. Do you see how true it is that this enemy keeps us from possessing and using effectively our spiritual weapons? Even in the literal story this was a serious handicap. It meant that Saul not only had a much smaller army than the Philistines, but that his men did not have proper weapons. Saul should have known that his army was helpless by itself, and that his strength was not in his army but in the Lord. He did really know it, for he felt that he must make sacrifices to the Lord before he went into battle; but his fear made him forget that he and his people had been solemnly warned by Samuel (I Samuel 12:20-25) that they must obey the Lord in all things.

The story of Saul is given us in the Bible to teach us that we must never set up our own judgment above the Lord's command.

*Basic Correspondences*

| | | |
|---|---|---|
| the Philistines | = | the temptation to be satisfied with knowing what is right without doing it |
| Saul | = | truth from the Word understood in its letter only |
| Samuel | = | childlike trust and obedience to the Lord |
| weapons | = | truths used to defend us in our temptations or falsities used against truth |
| agricultural tools | = | truths used to develop character |

## Senior

The correspondence of Samuel and Saul, their relation to each other, and Saul's weakness and its results are particularly important for this age. The recollection of this lesson may save them from making serious mistakes after they leave home. They will meet the Philistine temptation very soon and need to recognize it for what it is and to be armed against it.

Samuel was the last of the Judges and the only one of them to be recognized by the whole nation as its Judge. The other Judges represent particular truths drawn up by the Lord from our memories to help us overcome particular faults that are bothering us.

When the fault is overcome, the particular truth drops back into our general knowledge. But Samuel represents a general truth which our experience with our faults and weaknesses finally leads us to recognize. It is the truth that in relation to the Lord we are always little children, weak and ignorant, and that we ought to look to Him as our Father and trust and obey Him whether we understand His commands or not.

This does not mean that we should not go on trying to understand. The Lord has given us our brains and He expects us to use them, even though He knows we shall make mistakes. So long as we try to do right and recognize Samuel as our Judge, the Lord can help us to profit by our mistakes and to understand more and more. This is what is meant by the fact that Samuel lived to anoint the first two kings of Israel, Saul and David, and that he continued to judge Israel even while Saul was king. Read I Samuel 7:15-17. Saul is believed to have reigned nearly forty years, although the exact time is not stated in the Bible, and Samuel lived until about four years before Saul's death.

The three great kings of Israel represent successive ruling principles, the Lord's truth understood in three different ways. Saul represents a natural understanding of the truth, such as younger people are apt to have. It desires to serve the Lord and is eager for action but impatient under delays and, reasoning from appearances, is liable to set itself up as a better judge of what should be done than even the Lord. Saul was able to overcome the Ammonites, but not the Philistines. Chapter 11 tells about his first great victory. The Ammonites were descendants of Lot and picture external evils. Even a superficial understanding of the truth is able to show us that we must live outwardly moral and useful lives.

But the Philistine temptation is of a different kind. It is possible for a person to lead a very upright external life and still be inwardly selfish and self-satisfied and proud of his own intelligence. The Philistines represent the temptation to think that such an external knowledge and acceptance of the truth is all that is necessary. The only way in which Saul could have been successful against the

Philistines was by keeping constantly before him the remembrance that his power came from the Lord and that only as he obeyed implicitly the Lord's directions as they came to him through Samuel, the Lord's prophet, could he hope for victory. Saul did not have this kind of wisdom and courage. His real trust was in external strength and not in the Lord. So when he saw his army deserting him, he thought he must take things into his own hands. This is just what our first understanding does. It wants quick results. When things do not seem to be going well, it wants to hurry into some new course. It is not willing to trust the ultimate wisdom of simple obedience to the Lord.

Saul's punishment seems severe, but it simply means that our early understanding of the truth is not an adequate guide. It lacks depth of insight and patience. It must be superseded by another ruler, "a man after the Lord's own heart." Notice verses 19 to 22. Israel's dependence upon the Philistines at this period for all its weapons and tools is a clear picture of bondage to self-intelligence. This comes out in young men and women in their tendency to exalt the findings of natural science and humanistic reasoning and to think religion impractical.

Saul as king does represent the rule of truth, but it is truth seen and understood in an external and natural way. This understanding has definite weaknesses and limitations; so it is to be superseded by a deeper and more spiritual understanding. But it wins some victories, and it produces some genuine truth or doctrine. This true doctrine to which our natural reason can lead us is represented by Saul's son Jonathan, about whom we shall study later.

---

## Adult

Here again the Philistine temptation is an important topic, as well as the various aspects of truth presented in the lesson: the Judges, Samuel, the kings, the weapons, and the agricultural implements. The note on verse 21 can well be tied in with the discussion of the meaning of the Philistines.

In I Samuel 7:15-17 we learn that Samuel judged Israel "all the days of his life," holding court in a circuit of three towns near the center of the land. Samuel, we recall, represents a necessary return to a childlike state of trust and obedience after we have experienced the unhappy results of trying to direct ourselves. Samuel lived to anoint David as the second king of Israel. His death (I Samuel 25:1) came before that of Saul but after David had risen to popularity. Samuel, as prophet and judge, represents the Word of the Lord, accepted in childlike faith, instructing and judging us as we pass from a state of reliance on our own ideas of right to one of intelligent acceptance of the Lord's guidance. Just as Moses had to remain in the land of Midian for forty years before he was prepared for his call to lead the children of Israel out of Egypt, so Samuel had to retain the actual power in the Holy Land until the people had reached the point when they would accept as king a man "after the Lord's own heart."

Throughout the Word a king represents truth (or falsity) ruling. Recall the Lord's answer to Pilate in John 18:37. The three kings of Israel all represent the Lord's truth ruling in our lives, but they represent that truth seen by us in three different ways, at three different levels of understanding. All three of these levels are adult states and they are necessary stages in our regeneration. Ideally we might live out our lives under Samuel's direction, and some few people do. We recall that when the people asked for a king, Samuel was displeased because he felt himself rejected, but the Lord told him that the people, in rejecting him, were really rejecting the Lord. The Lord then told him to do as the people asked. We are not in an ideal state and we must choose our leaders in freedom, but the Lord provides that with each person who truly wants to do right, the childlike trust represented by Samuel shall remain in control until he has come by the way of experience into the recognition of the higher rational as his leader. David would not have been accepted by Israel at first. Only their experience with the results of Saul's weakness made them see David's strength.

Saul was accepted immediately because of his appearance, because "when he stood among the people, he was higher than any of the people from his shoulders and upward." The shoulder corresponds to power. The people were looking for a strong man to lead them against their enemies. Saul as king represents divine truth in its hard, external aspect, untempered by mercy, as it appears to those who have not yet gained any depth of experience and wisdom; to young adults, for example, who are just beginning to form their own independent judgments as to conduct. Saul was completely victorious in his battles with the Ammonites (I Samuel 11) when they attacked Jabesh-gilead, because Gilead, in the territory of Gad across the Jordan, represents good works, and even a superficial understanding of the truth is able to recognize and repel the false arguments which would blind and enslave the affection for doing external good works.

But the Philistines, who are the attackers in our lesson today, were an enemy of a different and more subtle character, an internal enemy, the ever-present and powerful temptation to rest satisfied with knowing what is right without making the effort to do it. It is obvious that truth understood only superficially cannot overcome this enemy. Samuel had told Saul to wait at Gilgal seven days, until he should come and sacrifice to the Lord and assure victory. But Saul was impatient. It appeared to him that his men were leaving him, that the delay was weakening his military strength, and finally he took matters into his own hands and offered the sacrifice himself without waiting for Samuel. Young people almost always feel a good deal of sympathy for Saul in his impatience, which is good evidence of the truth of the correspondence. When we are young and active, we do not like to wait for the right time and way of doing what we believe ought to be done. We may know that we ought to wait, as Saul did, but things seem to be going from bad to worse. We judge by appearances and act before our remains of childlike trust have had time to fulfill their true mission. Actually we put our own judgment before the Lord's. The failure which inevitably results shows us that the principle on which we have been depending is not adequate, that if our good intentions are to have good results they must have a new principle of a different degree from the mere external judgment, something which goes deeper. The kingdom is to be rent from Saul and given to another. "The Lord hath sought him a man after his own heart, and the Lord hath commanded him to be captain over his people, because thou hast not kept that which the Lord commanded thee."

Judgment from mere appearances fails, and the first lesson learned is: "Wait on the Lord; be of good courage, and he shall strengthen thine heart: wait, I say, on the Lord." (Psalm 27:14) The strengthening of the heart is what the Lord is waiting for. Parience is a virtue which is developed only through trial. Saul was impatient. Young people are impatient, for example, with the slow advance of reforms. To them any action seems better than no action. They must learn by experience to wait as well as to work. Saul's whole strength was in the Lord's help. When he set his own judgment before the Lord's command through Samuel, his efforts were doomed to failure. So it is with us whenever we judge by appearances only and imagine that the Lord's providence is failing and that our own way will bring success. Whenever we act contrary to the Lord's commandments, even though we tell ourselves that we are doing it to hasten the accomplishment of a good purpose, we cut ourselves off from the only power that can bring about good. For our only real strength is the Lord's strength in us. The Lord knows best. "A little one shall become a thousand, and a small one a strong nation: I the Lord will hasten it in his time. (Isaiah 60:22)

Saul's accomplishments were sufficient to accustom the people to the rule of a king, to arouse their loyalty, to establish their courage, to teach them to meet the demands made upon them; and Saul was able to overcome external enemies and partially to overcome more internal ones. But Saul was impatient and self-assertive, superficial in his judgments, and prone to place these judgments above the explicit commands of the Lord. In the same way, the external understanding of truth is sufficient to accustom us to accept the truth as our leader and to develop our ability to stand up for it bravely as occasion requires. But is is not sufficient to show us the necessity for delays or to get to the root of evils within ourselves and in the world. Verses 19 to 22 add an interesting thought. Tools of all kinds represent truths. Weapons of war are truths of use in fighting evils. Farm implements are truths necessary for developing and preparing uses, the "fruits and grains" to be made part of the life. The Philistines are those who like to know truths but have no desire to live them. In this passage they suggest the people who enjoy intellectual discussion—the sharpening of the mind—but are anxious to keep the "religious" people from doing the same thing except under their direction and control, and especially unwilling to have arguments developed which might expose their own weaknesses and selfish motives.

---

## From the Writings of Swedenborg

*Apocalypse Explained*, n. 700[20]: "The Philistines represented, and thus signified, those who make no account of good of love and charity, and thus no account of good of life, placing everything of religion in knowledge . . . therefore they were like those at the present day who make faith alone, that is, faith separated from charity, the essential of the church and the essential of salvation. This is why they were called 'the uncircumcised,' for to be uncircumcised signifies to be destitute of spiritual love, thus of good. . . . This makes evident why the Philistines conquered, and sometimes the sons of Israel. The Philistines conquered when the sons of Israel departed from the statutes and precepts in not doing them; but when the sons of Israel lived according to these they conquered. To live according to the precepts and statutes was their good of love and good of life. At this time the sons of Israel had been conquered by the Philistines because they had gone away from the worship of Jehovah to the worship of other gods, especially to the worship of Ashtaroth, as can be seen from what Samuel said to them (I Samuel 7:3)."

---

## Suggested Questions on the Lesson

P. Why did the people want a king? *to lead them in war*
P. Whom did the Lord choose as the first king? *Saul*
I. How did the people know that the Lord had chosen Saul? *drew lots*
P. Why were they pleased to have Saul as their king? *tall, strong*
J. What enemy did Saul first conquer? *Ammonites*

P. What enemy then attacked them? *Philistines*

J. What was the relation at this time between the Philistines and Israel? *Philistines in power*

P. What had made the Philistines angry? *Jonathan's attack at Geba*

J. How were the Philistines trying to keep Israel from making war? *allowed them no blacksmiths*

J. Where was Saul's army gathered? *Gilgal*

P. What had Samuel told Saul to do? *wait for him seven days*

P. What did Saul do that was wrong? *offered sacrifice himself*

J. What excuse did he give Samuel? *people were scattering*

J. What did Samuel tell him? *he would lose kingdom*

I. To what do the kings correspond? *divine truth ruling*

S. To what particularly does Saul correspond? *natural understanding of truth*

S. What is the correspondence of the Philistines? *faith alone*

I. What were Saul's weaknesses? *impatience, lack of faith*

## SAUL AND JONATHAN

*I Samuel 14:1-46*

Stress the fact that the people liked Saul because of his appearance, but that physical strength and prowess do not imply wisdom. Draw the distinction between Saul and Jonathan, which will form part of the background in a future lesson.

---

### Doctrinal Points

*It is God's intent for us to enjoy the good things of this world; it is shortsighted automatically to place evil in such enjoyment.*

*If we will trust in the Lord's power, attacking our evils with the strength we have, the Lord will help give us the victory.*

*A king represents the principle that we should obey the Lord's truth.*

*Even our first idea of truth—imperfect as it is—will produce some good.*

---

### Notes for Parents

Jonathan's fine character makes him one of the favorite Bible heroes. His father Saul, the first king of Israel, was a brave man, but he was hasty and self-confident, not willing to wait for Samuel, the Lord's prophet, to give him the word to attack and not careful to obey fully the commands the Lord gave him through Samuel. So the Lord could not always give him the victory.

Jonathan was equally brave but he did not rely on his own judgment and strength. He trusted in the Lord. When the rest of the Israelites were deserting Saul and hiding themselves for fear of the Philistines, Jonathan, with only his armorbearer to support him, went boldly forward and attacked the enemy—waiting only for a favorable sign from the Lord—relying upon the proved fact that "there is no restraint to the Lord to save by many or by few." And his small initial victory was enough to throw the host of the

Philistines into confusion and enable Saul's army to drive them back into their own territory. So our temptations often seem too great for us to hope to conquer, but if we will only trust in the Lord's power and attack them boldly as soon as we are tempted, we shall find our enemy is not invincible, as it seemed.

The rest of our chapter has something to teach us, too. Saul's foolish command to his men not to taste food until they had completed the conquest reminds us of the way some good people afflict themselves and others, imagining that it is impossible to enjoy life and be good at the same time. But the Lord created all the good things of this world for our use and enjoyment, only telling us not to misuse them. Jonathan found the honey on his way and when he had tasted it, "his eyes were enlightened." We remember how the Lord gave the Israelites the quail in the wilderness and how He provided the manna every morning, the manna which tasted "like wafers made with honey." The Lord is a God of love and mercy—not a hard taskmaster.

---

## Primary

A simple lesson which can be drawn from this story is that it is not size or physical strength that counts and that the Lord always helps those who try to learn what is right and do it. The teacher, in pointing out the difference between Saul and Jonathan, should use as an illustration the story of the rest of the chapter. The people's support of Jonathan against Saul prepares the way for the fact of their later admiration of David.

We find that the Philistines, after they had returned the ark, went right on trying to conquer the Israelites. Samuel, you remember, was recognized as Judge by all the people, but Samuel had been brought up in the tabernacle and he was not a fighting man. So the people had asked him to give them a king who could lead them in battle against their enemies, and the Lord told Samuel to grant their request. The Lord also showed Samuel whom to anoint as the first king, the powerful young man named Saul, who stood head and shoulders taller than all the other men. The people thought he would make them a fine leader; so they accepted him as their first king.

But you know we cannot always judge things or people by their appearance.

Saul was brave, but he was not wise.

He very soon won a victory over the Ammonites, and this made him self-confident.

He did not fully trust the Lord; so the Lord could not always be with him.

But he had a son named Jonathan who did trust the Lord.

First Jonathan and part of the army captured a city from the Philistines.

But Jonathan was not depending upon the army.

What did he tell his armorbearer about the Lord?

What did the Lord enable the two young men to do?

The rest of the chapter tells us how Jonathan's victory threw the army of the Philistines into confusion so that they attacked each other.

Then Saul and his army overcame them.

---

## Junior

The Juniors are old enough to understand something of the meaning of the change from the Judges to the kings and also of the difference between Saul and Jonathan and of the effect of Jonathan's victory on the host of the Philistines.

Who was the last of the Judges?

Samuel was a different kind of Judge. He was brought up in the tabernacle and was not a fighting man. But he had a greater power than physical strength. He was a prophet as well as a Judge. The Lord spoke through him and all the people recognized that he had been appointed by the Lord to tell them what they ought to do. He had a regular circuit, as some of our judges do today, going around each year to certain appointed towns to judge all the cases that were brought before him (I Samuel 7:15-17). He called the people to repent and promised them that if they would obey the Lord, the Lord would save them from their enemies.

The enemies were still there, however, and the people could not get over their fear or quite trust the Lord They wanted to fight their enemies and they wanted someone to lead them in battle. They saw that every other nation had a king and asked Samuel to give them one. Samuel was very much disappointed by their lack of trust, but the Lord told him to let them have a king and showed him what king to choose. The Lord always does the best He can for us. When we make mistakes and refuse to obey Him fully, He finds some other way to teach us—some way which we will understand. The king He told Samuel to anoint was Saul, a young man who stood head and shoulders taller than all the others. As this was just the kind of man the people thought they wanted, they willingly accepted Saul as their king.

Saul was a brave and bold young man, and he very soon won a victory over the Ammonites—the same enemy whom Jephthah had overcome, you remember. But Saul, like most people who depend on physical strength, was inclined to be self-confident and hasty. He knew that Samuel was appointed by the Lord to be his advisor, but he was not always willing to wait for Samuel's advice or to follow it exactly. So the Lord could not continue to be with him, any more than He could be with the Israelites when they brought the ark out of the tabernacle without asking Him.

But Saul had a son who was of a different character.

Who was this son?
What enemy was attacking again?
What did Jonathan decide to do?
Who went with him?
What did Jonathan say to his armorbearer about the Lord?
What sign did he ask of the Lord?

William Worcester tells us in *The Sower* some interesting things about the place where Jonathan won his victory. The two great rocks are still there, one on either side of a narrow gorge with a brook at the bottom. The gorge runs east and west. The rock on the north side is always in full sunlight, and was called *Bozez*, which means "shining." *Seneh* is the name of a thorny shrub which probably grew on the other rock. It is the same word that is used of the burning bush from which the Lord spoke to Moses.

How many men did Jonathan and his armorbearer kill?
What was the effect on the rest of the army?

There are several instances in the Bible in which a small victory causes the enemy's army to start fighting each other, making them easy to overcome. I wonder if you can see what this means. You know that you have little temptations every day. If you trust the Lord and have the courage to do right in these small battles, you will be surprised at how much weaker the big temptations will seem afterward. Saul and his army were able to attack the Philistines, who had seemed so strong before, and to drive them back into their own part of the country. But Saul never really overcame the Philistines, as the last verse of chapter 14 tells us.

Saul showed his lack of wisdom in another way in our lesson.

What order did Saul give to his men when they started to pursue the Philistines?
Who disobeyed through ignorance?
What did Jonathan eat?
What did he say about Saul's order when he heard of it?
What did he try to do to Jonathan?
Who saved Jonathan?

---

## Intermediate

The general correspondence of the story is the lesson for this class. They can see its application to their own problems and temptations even though at their age these are external rather than spiritual.

When Samuel grew old and his sons, as the sons of Eli had done, did not uphold the high standards of their father, the people began again to be afraid of the Philistines and wanted a strong man to lead them against their enemies. So they asked Samuel to give them a king. We are often weak in this way. We know with our minds that the Lord will be with us if we do right, but we allow ourselves to get to worrying and we feel the need of some special practical teaching to help us in our problems, something which comes right down to the plane on which we are living.

A king always represents a ruling principle. Samuel as leader represents a simple, childlike trust in the Lord. This is an ideal state to which, if we are regenerating, we may come back in our old age. Samuel himself was very much disappointed that the people were not satisfied with just his leadership, but the Lord told him to give them a king. The Lord, as we have seen before, knows our weaknesses and leads us by whatever means He sees will best reach us. The first king—pointed out to Samuel by the Lord—was not an ideal king, but was the only kind the people were prepared to accept at that time. He was Saul, a powerful and brave young man who stood head and shoulders above all those around him.

The three kings who ruled over Israel while it was a united country all represent the principle that we should obey the Lord's truth, but our idea of that truth changes as we grow in experience. Saul, the first of the three, is the first idea we have of it, when we judge things by their appearance and jump to conclusions on the basis of only partial understanding. Saul was hasty and self-confident. He won a victory almost immediately over the Ammonites, the same external temptations we considered in the story of Jephthah. But the real enemy whom the people feared was the Philistines, the temptation to think we are good just because we know what is right, without always trying to do right. This is an inner temptation, and the self-confident kind of thinking which Saul represents cannot meet it.

In our lesson today Saul and his army are camped at Gibeah opposite the encampment of the Philistines, but they are not sure how to proceed and many of the people are deserting Saul and trying to save themselves by hiding. But in the reign of Saul there is one element that makes for real spiritual progress. Our first or natural reasoning, with all its shortcomings, is able to acknowledge the lessons learned from experience. Saul's son Jonathan represents this kind of knowledge of the truth. Jonathan was familiar with the history of his people. He knew how often in the past the Lord had helped them and that even a small number who obeyed the Lord completely had been able to conquer an enemy of apparently overwhelming might. He said to his armorbearer, "there is no restraint to the Lord to save by many or by few." So, once he had received the sign he had asked of the Lord, he did not hesitate to attack, even though the way was hard. They had to go down one steep rock and up another to make the attack, which is a good picture of coming down from our self-satisfaction and climbing up in the way pointed out by the Lord.

Jonathan's victory was the opening wedge which enabled Saul and his army to put the enemy to rout. But Saul's victory was due chiefly to the "trembling" which the Lord sent upon the Philistines, which caused them in their confusion to fall upon each other. This was a kind of help the Lord gave several times in the course of the history of the Israelites. It pictures the fact that when we trust the Lord and in obedience to Him attack our weaknesses bravely right where we find them, we very soon discover that our temptation is not so strong as we thought it and that the arguments which supported it are conflicting—they really don't make sense.

Then Saul made another hasty and foolish decision. He told his army not to taste food until they had finished the pursuit. So they became weary and finally were driven to eating to excess and without preparing their food properly. We have seen before that the Lord never drives us in this way. He gives us our spiritual food a little at a time and gives us our times of enjoyment and personal satisfaction to help us continue. This is what is represented by the honey which Jonathan stopped to eat. Jonathan was wiser than his father, but his father would have killed him for his disobedience if the people had not prevented it. We often see illustrations of the meaning of this story. People who think they are serving the Lord sometimes drive themselves and others beyond endurance because they think they must always be fighting and never stop to rest and enjoy the good gifts the Lord gives us all along the way. Sometimes for this mistaken idea they would destroy the best qualities they have.

Saul never wholly conquered the Philistines because he trusted in himself more than in the Lord.

*Basic Correspondences*

a king = a ruling principle

Jonathan = knowledge gained from experience
honey = enjoyment

## Senior

The Seniors have not yet reached the period pictured by the kings, but their thinking is already similar to that of Saul in that their decisions as to what is right are apt to be hasty and based on a superficial understanding of the truth. So this lesson can easily be made practical and helpful to them.

The period of the Judges, when the people were being brought to realize that there is nothing in which lurk so many dangers as in self-confidence and self-satisfaction, was followed by the period of the three great kings, Saul, David, and Solomon. In the Word a king always represents a ruling principle: the good kings truth ruling, and the evils kings falsity ruling. We need to be able to work out our problems on the basis of some overall accepted standard. Samuel was angry when the people asked him to give them a king, feeling that they should have been satsified with his direction, since he had never done them anything but good. But the Lord told Samuel to grant the people's request, only making sure that they understood that life under a king would require of them many sacrifices. Samuel's rule represents a state of simple, child-like trust and obedience. We are actually safer and less troubled in such a state, but it does not satisfy our natural desire to think and decide for ourselves, and we have seen that the Lord always permits us to exercise our freedom and rationality even though it is certain that we shall make mistakes and often have to learn the hard way.

The first king—pointed out to Samuel by the Lord Himself and afterward chosen by lot in the sight of all the people—was Saul. He was the only kind of king the people would have accepted at that stage, an active young man of impressive appearance. He represents the truth of the Lord as it first appears to us when we wish to be governed by it, something to obey and follow in an aggressive approach to the problems of life. Saul accepted his appointment with sincere humility and with the intention of being directed by the Lord through the mouth of Samuel. In just the same way, at the start we mean to be humble and to look to the Lord for guidance. Saul immediately won a victory over the Ammonites, who as we remember from the story of Jephthah represent external rather than internal temptations. But his self-confidence was aroused by his victory and in his next conflict he went ahead on his own instead of waiting for Samuel as he had been told to do, and this broke his connection with the Lord and made it impossible for him ever again to be completely victorious.

This shows us the nature of our first idea of the Divine. We mean well, but we feel so sure of our own judgment that we go ahead without waiting to make sure we are right. Our lesson for today contains a very clear example of this in Saul's foolish command to his men not to eat anything until they had completed their pursuit of the enemy. We cannot go all the way to spiritual victory in one burst of speed. As we learned in the lesson on the quail and manna, the Lord gives us nourishment day by day, with natural pleasures also when we need them, and regular sabbaths of rest. The way to heaven is a lifelong road to be followed under the Lord's constant direction.

But our first idea of the rule of truth—which is based on what in the story of Ishmael we learned to call our natural reason—does produce some genuine good. It teaches us by experience something which has before been mere memory-knowledge with us, the fact that the Lord really can give us power to overcome in temptation. This conviction is pictured by Saul's son Jonathan. He also was brave and eager, but he did not depend on himself. His character is summed up in his words to his armorbearer: "It may be that the Lord will work for us: for there is no restraint to the Lord to save by many or by few." And he also left to the Lord the decision as to whether or not the time was ripe for attack.

The result of Jonathan's small victory was the opening of the way for the dispersion of the Philistine army, which was seized with a "trembling" and began to beat down one another. This seems a strange thing in the letter, but there are other stories in the Word in which a similar thing happens. It pictures a very familiar phenomenon. When we are beset by the temptation to do as the world does, the arguments in favor of the world's ways seem very strong; but if we have the courage to defy the world in some instance, the whole structure of worldly argument totters and confusion and conflict arise among its defenders. Try it sometime. When you know you are right about something in which everybody is against you, a simple, well-chosen verse from the Word thrown unexpectedly into the discussion will upset their whole position. This is a very practical reason for reading the Word constantly and memorizing passages from it. Remember how often the Lord answered His opponents by simply quoting the Scriptures. Jonathan represents this confidence in the Lord's power.

Jonathan's eating of the honey is an interesting story in itself. He had not heard his father's order and so he disobeyed innocently; as soon as he tasted the honey "his eyes were enlightened." So when he was told of his father's command, he could see that it had been a foolish one. Honey represents enjoyment or pleasure, usually of a natural kind. It is mentioned often in the Word. The honey that Jonathan tasted represents a sense of satisfaction in his own accomplishment. Such a feeling, since it has self in it, is contrary to some of the commands of the letter of the Word, but a clearer sight shows us that such a literal interpretation cannot be the true one, for the Lord Himself provides us such moments of satisfaction because they are needed by us in our imperfect states. People in their first zeal often make the way of righteousness unnecessarily hard, as Saul did in this case. The people, however, recognized, as most people usually do, that the ones who really do good are not the ones who are hard on other people; so they refused to allow Saul to destroy Jonathan. In a later lesson we shall see the part which Jonathan played in the transfer of the kingship from Saul to David.

## Adult

Important thoughts for the Adults are the nature of Saul's rule and the meaning of Jonathan and his small victory. Another very helpful topic of discussion is the shortsightedness of placing evil in the enjoyment of any of the good things of the world which have been provided for our use and refreshment. The Lord's example and not any assumptions and prejudices of men should be our guide here. The Lord Himself supplies us with a warning and direction in this matter in Matthew 11:17-19.

In I Samuel 7:13 we read: "So the Philistines were subdued, and they came no more into the coast of Israel: and the hand of the Lord was against the Philistines all the days of Samuel." Yet in our chapter for today, with Samuel still Judge and recognized as the Lord's spokesman, we find that the Philistines are again gathered in great strength to attack Israel and that many of the Israelites are in hiding for fear of them, and in chapter 13 we learn that the Philistines have so extensive a control in the land that the Israelites have no smiths and their armies no weapons of war. In the letter this would seem to be contradictory, but it is not so in the internal sense. The "days of Samuel" are our states of childlike trust and obedience, as we saw in our last lesson. But by the time of today's lesson, although the people still in a measure acknowledge Samuel as their head, they have another leader whom they really prefer to Samuel.

You will recall that when Samuel was old and had made his unworthy sons judges, the people had asked for a king to lead them against their enemies. When, as adults, we have suffered the decline of our early religious zeal, as Israel declined in the time of the Judges, and then have come to the realization that we are in real spiritual danger and must return to the guidance and protection of the Lord, our first state is one of sincere humiliation and simple obedience, which Samuel represents. But very few adults can "hold" this state. The world looms very large and we become fearful of losing spiritual ground. We want something more specific than a general assurance to lead us—some system of truth furnished with arguments with which to meet our temptations. We want a warlike king instead of a peaceful prophet, although we still recognize the prophet as our judge.

The three kings represent successively higher concepts of the Lord's truth. Saul, we remember, was accepted by the people because of his appearance. The Lord chose him as the first king because he was the only kind of leader the people would have respected at that time. We know that the Lord always accommodates His revelation of Himself to our states. He permits us to see only so much of His truth as we are capable of applying to life. Saul was a brave and sincere man and in the beginning humble. When we first turn from childlike trust, we do not mean to become self-confident—we have had our bitter experience with trying to lead ourselves. But we have not yet become wise, and our self-will is stronger than we think. Saul won his first victory, a victory over the Ammonites, the same external enemy whom Jephthah had conquered. Then he felt that he was established and sure of victory, and he began to make his own decisions instead of waiting to be directed by Samuel—so the Philistines were in the saddle again. Thus the new attack by the Philistines is really in the days of Saul and not in the days of Samuel.

Our first concept of the truth is, like Saul, superficial and hasty. It is based on our natural reason which judges by appearances and is stubborn and headstrong. But it wins some victories and it also has other good results. It gives us fresh experience of the power of the Lord which confirms what we were taught in our earlier years. This development is represented by Saul's son Jonathan, who was not dismayed by the apparent power of the enemy because he knew that "there is no restraint to the Lord to save by many or by few."

The stories of Jonathan in the Word have great appeal. Among the Bible characters he is a general favorite, and to many Bible readers the question of why Jonathan had to be killed with his father is a real problem. Again the internal sense gives us a clear answer. Saul's line had to perish because a natural understanding of truth, however excellent, must give place to a spiritual understanding if we are to become spiritual men and women.

Yet Jonathan played a very important role in this transition. He was the only one really responsible for such victories as his father won over the Philistines, because it was his fearless trust in the Lord which showed the Israelites the actual weakness of their enemy. In chapter 13 we learn that when Jonathan was in command of a third of his father's small army, he boldly attacked and overcame one of the Philistine garrisons; and in our chapter today he attacks the main body of the Philistines with no one but his armorbearer to help him. The setting of this story reminds us forcibly of the words of Abraham in the parable of the rich man and Lazarus: "Between us and you there is a great gulf fixed." It is the same gulf which Jonathan and his armorbearer crossed when they climbed down one rock and up another—down the rock of self-confidence and up the rock of reliance upon the Lord. The parable, however, treats of the condition in the other life when the gulf has become "fixed" by our refusal to cross it in this world.

The initial slaughter by Jonathan and his armorbearer resulted immediately in a great trembling in the army of the Philistines. They were thrown into confusion and began to fall upon each other. A similar phenomenon occurred in the story of Gideon. It is an accurate picture of what happens to the Philistine attitude in us when we make even a small attack upon it in the Lord's name. The arguments which have supported our pride in our own intelligence are immediately discovered to be really weak and conflicting, and they melt away.

The incident of Jonathan's eating the honey is very interesting. Honey represents enjoyment of a natural kind. Many of the literal commands of the Word would seem, like Saul, to forbid such enjoyment, and many Christian groups through the centuries have based their claim to salvation on the renunciation of all natural pleasures. While Saul, symbolizing the natural understanding of the meaning of the Word, is on the throne, we feel with Jonathan that any indulgence may have been a sin. But Jonathan was given to see that his father's command had been unwise and the people supported Jonathan because his victories had proved to them that the Lord was with him rather than with his father. The ascetic life is not the life the Lord wishes us to live. The good things of this world are created by Him for our enjoyment and are means by which we are enabled to serve Him and our neighbor.

Isaiah 7:14-15 tells us: "Therefore the Lord himself shall give you a sign; Behold a virgin shall conceive, and bear a son, and shall call his name Immanuel. Butter and honey shall he eat, that he may know to refuse the evil, and choose the good." Jonathan's eyes were enlightened when he had tasted the honey.

---

## From the Writings of Swedenborg

*Apocalypse Explained*, n. 619[8]: "There was also much honey in the land of Canaan at that time, because at that time the church of the Lord was there, as can be seen from the first book of Samuel, where it is said that they came into a forest, where there was honey upon the face of the ground, and there was a stream of honey, and Jonathan's eyes were opened by tasting the honey (14:25-27, 29). 'Jonathan's eyes were opened by tasting the honey' because 'honey' corresponds to natural good and its delight, and this good gives intelligence and enlightens, from which Jonathan knew that he had done evil; as we read in Isaiah, 'He shall eat butter and honey, that he may know to reject the evil and to choose the good.' For at that time correspondences exhibited their effects outwardly, since all things of the Israelitish Church consisted of correspondences, which represented and signified things celestial and spiritual."

---

## Suggested Questions on the Lesson

P. Who was the first king? *Saul*
P. Why did the people like him? *tall, strong*
J. What enemy did he first conquer? *Ammonites*
J. What weaknesses did Saul have? *impatient, disobedient, lacked faith*
J. With what enemy did he have trouble? *Philistines*
P. Who was Saul's son? *Jonathan*
P. How was he different from his father? *trusted the Lord*
J. What did Jonathan and his armorbearer decide to do? *attack Philistine camp*
P. Why did Jonathan think two men could win a victory over so many? *faith*

J. In what kind of place did they face the enemy? *rocky*
J. What sign did Jonathan ask of the Lord? *If they say, "Come . . ."*
P. What happened in the Philistine army after Jonathan's victory? *panic*
J. What order did Saul give to his men when they started after the Philistines? *no food*
J. What did Jonathan do? *ate some honey*
J. What did Saul try to do to him? *kill him*
J. Who saved Jonathan? *people*
I. What does a king represent? *ruling principle*
S. What does Saul represent? *superficial idea of truth*
S. What does Jonathan represent? *knowledge from experience*
S. What is pictured by the Philistines' being thrown into confusion? *arguments which support self-pride conflict with themselves*

## SAUL SPARES AGAG

*I Samuel 15*

The teachers should all be familiar with the events of the chapters between 8 and 15, but the events to be reviewed in class are the anointing of Saul, his later choice by lot, the people's satisfaction with him, his first victory, and his first defection as described in chapters 10:8 and 13:8-14.

---

### Doctrinal Points

*The Lord is pure, unselfish love and seeks above all to drive selfishness out of our hearts for the sake of making us happy.*

*Our first understanding of the Word is based on external appearances.*

*Faith in the Lord involves obedience to Him even against our own judgment.*

*We need to recognize clearly how many of our thoughts spring from our hereditary self-love.*

---

### Notes for Parents

We are beginning the period in Israel's history when the nation attained its largest dominion and its greatest importance among nations. We remember that importance in the world was what they were looking for when they asked Samuel to give them a king. Through a series of the three great kings—Saul, David, and Solomon—they did achieve their goal, but they had to learn by bitter experience that security and happiness do not come from worldly power.

Saul was their first king, chosen for them by the Lord because He knew that the only kind of king who would impress them at that time was one like Saul. Saul stood head and shoulders above all the other men, and they respected him for his apparent strength. When we are young, we too judge by the outward appearance of a thing.

Saul had the strength and the weakness of youth. He was brave and eager, but he was also self-confident, hasty, and impatient. He won his first battle, and it turned his head so that he never again was willing to follow exactly the Lord's instructions as they came to him through Samuel, although he and all the people knew that Samuel was the Lord's prophet. Our chapter today tells of his act of disobedience, which finally cost him the kingdom. The Amalekites were a wily foe. When they first attacked Israel in the wilderness at Rephidim, the Israelites conquered them only because Moses went up on the mountain and with the support of Aaron and Hur kept his hands lifted to the Lord until the sun set.

All our ability to resist temptation—brought on by our inward foes—comes from the Lord. When we forget this and trust in our own goodness and wisdom, we often find that our judgment of what is best to do is at variance with the Lord's commands. Like Saul, we do not want to give up things which seem useful and pleasant to us even when the Lord has told us to do so. We do not strike at the root of our trouble, which is self-love and self-satisfaction. In the language of parable, we keep king Agag alive.

---

## Primary

Be sure the children know that Saul was the first of three great kings who ruled over the whole land, and try to make them see why it was that Saul got into trouble even though he really meant in the beginning to be good. He thought he knew better than the Lord what ought to be done, just as children sometimes do not fully obey their parents because their own way seems better. Review the story of Israel's first battle with Amalek (Exodus 17:8-16) and compare the method of the victory there with Saul's victory and his disobedience.

Saul meant to be a good king, and he won his first battle. But this first victory made him feel too sure of himself. Samuel was still the Lord's prophet, and Saul knew that he ought to do just what Samuel told him to do. But Saul was impatient. The next time an enemy threatened, he gathered his army and did not wait for Samuel to come and offer the sacrifices, as he was supposed to do, but went ahead and offered them himself. And then Samuel came and told him that because he had not strictly obeyed the Lord, his kingdom would not be a lasting one.

In our lesson today what enemy is to be attacked?
Where have we heard of them before?
How were they conquered the first time?
What does Samuel tell Saul to do?
How did Saul disobey the Lord this time?
What excuse did he give?
What did Samuel tell him?
What happened to Agag?

You know sometimes when you have been naughty, you go and hug and kiss your mother and think that will make her forget your naughtiness. She likes your hugs and kisses, of course, but she would be happier if you loved her enough to mind her, and your life would be happier too.

---

### Junior

In this lesson again something of the general spiritual meaning can be given to the Juniors through a study of Saul's good and bad points and his excuse for sparing Agag and the cattle. This kind of confidence in our own superior judgment begins sometimes when we are very young, and the story can be a helpful warning.

The Lord had chosen Saul to be Israel's first king because He knew that they would judge by his outward appearance and that they would have to learn by experience that appearance is sometimes deceiving.

Saul's first battle was against the Ammonites in the cross-Jordan country, and he won it. This made the people sure that he was the right one for their king, but unfortunately it also made Saul himself too sure of his own power and ability. He was well-meaning and brave, but not very wise. So when the Philistines rose up and threatened Israel again, Saul was in too much of a hurry to take the proper means of approach to the battle. He knew that although he was king, Samuel was still the Lord's prophet, and Samuel had told him to wait seven days for him to come and offer sacrifices before the battle. But Saul grew impatient and on the seventh day offered the sacrifices himself before Samuel got there. Then Samuel told him that because he trusted in himself instead of obeying the Lord, his kingdom would be short-lived.

Both the Ammonites, over whom Saul had won his first victory, and the Philistines were open enemies of Israel; and both had collected armies and prepared to attack before Saul went out to meet them. But now Samuel tells Saul to hunt out and attack an old enemy which did not seem to be threatening them at the moment.

Who was this enemy?
When have we heard of them before?
How was the victory won that first time?
What was the method of attack of the Amalekites?

Saul did not hesitate to obey the Lord's command to go out against the Amalekites. He was a strong man and liked to fight. And he and his army won a complete victory. But he did not obey the Lord completely. He thought he knew better.

What had Samuel told him to do to the Amalekites?
How did he disobey?

Saul destroyed everything that seemed to him bad and worthless, but he could not resist the temptation to save what looked valuable. Once before—in Joshua's time—someone had disobeyed in this same way, and Israel had suffered for it. You will find the story in Joshua 7.

The wars of Israel picture our battles against our selfish desires and wrong thoughts. We all are willing to fight these things, because we know that they do us harm and make trouble for us. But we are often like Saul. We want to destroy only what we clearly see to be harmful and to keep the things which seem pleasant and which we enjoy—"the best of the sheep and of the oxen"—even though the Lord has told us to get rid of our selfishness completely. In fact, we sometimes rather like our weaknesses. Have you ever heard someone say, "Oh, I have a terrible temper," as if he were rather proud of it? He learns, as a matter of common sense, to control his temper whenever losing it would make him ashamed of himself, but with his family and friends he rather enjoys showing it off. We "save the king" when, while destroying what appears outwardly bad, we leave the root of the trouble untouched in our hearts.

What excuse did Saul give for saving the best of the cattle?
What did Samuel tell him?
How did Saul try to keep Samuel from leaving him?
What happened?
What did Samuel say it meant?
What happened to Agag?

## Intermediate

Identify Saul as the first of the series of three great kings. Stress the immaturity of the understanding of divine truth which he represents and the reason for his failures. Young people are hard to reason with when they are in the heat of an argument with their parents in favor of something they want, but if the realization that their present understanding may be rather limited has been brought home to them in Sunday school, when they are in a quiet and receptive mood, it may come back to them when they need it and prove a help to their parents.

In the Bible, a king represents a ruling principle. All three great kings of the Israelites—Saul, David, and Solomon—were chosen by the Lord and represent the Lord's truth governing in our lives. But our understanding of the Lord's truth develops gradually as we use it. We have to learn many things by experience. At first we have only a natural understanding of the Word and of its application to life. We mean to obey the Lord, but our judgment as to what He would have us do is hasty and shallow. This level of understanding is represented by Saul. The Lord chose Saul as the first king because he was the only kind of leader the people would have accepted and followed at that time. I Samuel 10:23-24 tells us that he was "higher than any of the people from his shoulders and upward," and so they were delighted with him. They judged him by his appearance, as we are all prone to judge things before experience has taught us to look more deeply.

Saul won his first battle, which was with the Ammonites in the cross-Jordan country. The cross-Jordan country represents the outward plane of conduct. The natural understanding of truth represented by Saul can easily see and resist temptations on this plane. But Saul's first victory gave him a confidence in himself which was his undoing. We have already learned how, when his enemy was the Philistines, he was too impatient to wait for Samuel to come and offer the necessary sacrifices, and instead offered them himself. His army overcame the Philistines not through Saul's leadership, but by means of the exploit of his son Jonathan, who trusted in the Lord instead of in himself. And we rememeber that at that time Samuel told Saul that his kingdom would not be of long duration.

Our natural understanding of truth, pictured by Saul as king, is pleasing to us, and is able to overcome some external evils; but it is easily deceived by appearances and is impatient with the Lord's commands when they do not appear to bring immediate results. Our story today illustrates the inadequacy of this degree of understanding.

The enemies that the Israelites were to destroy were the Amalekites, descendants of Esau. Esau, the twin brother of Jacob, represents goodness on the natural plane, while Jacob represents truth. When they were separated and striving against each other, many evils resulted. Esau went to live in the wilderness, as good intentions always do when they are without truth to guide them. One of the bad results of this separate life is liable to be an inner feeling of satisfaction with one's own good intentions. We feel sure that we "mean well" and therefore that our own ideas of right and wrong must be correct. This is a deep-seated kind of self-love, often not recognized as an enemy at all until it suddenly leads one into trouble. Amalek, as a descendant of Esau, represents false ideas which spring from hidden self-satisfaction, often leading to discouragement in the face of the demands of spiritual living. The Amalekites always struck from ambush, as we learned in our lesson about Israel's first battle with them at Rephidim, or they combined with other enemies, as they had in the time of the Judge Gideon (Judges 6:3). And we remember that at Rephidim they were conquered only by Moses going up on the mountain and keeping his hands uplifted to the Lord. We cannot conquer this temptation when we are self-confident.

Apparently, although they were known to be hostile, the Amalekites were not openly attacking in Saul's time. But the Lord through Samuel commanded Saul to hunt them out and utterly destroy them. Saul was willing enough to make the attack and won a victory, but he again set up his own judgment against the Lord's and did not completely obey. He saved the king (who symbolizes the principal falsity) alive, and brought back the best of the sheep and oxen (which represent the outward manifestations of this evil) which to our natural reason seem to be harmless and even useful.

When Samuel pointed out Saul's disobedience, Saul claimed that he had saved these things as sacrifices to the Lord. This pictures a very common excuse for disobeying the commandments. For example, sharp practices in business are winked at when part of the resulting fortune is used for endowing charitable institutions. A common example of this evil was condemned by the Lord in Mark 7:9-13.

Samuel as prophet pictures the Word, and his garments the letter of the Word. Saul's tearing Samuel's mantle pictures his unwillingness to keep the truth whole. This was the reason why the kingdom had to pass from his line.

*Basic Correspondences*

Saul = a natural understanding of divine truth

Agag = self-satisfaction ruling in the life

---

**Senior**

The teacher should study the quotations at the end of the lesson and be prepared with examples of "Amalek temptations" suited to the experience of the class. The effort should be to show the young people how prone we are to accept thoughts and arguments which favor our own natural self-interest as true.

Israel, after conquering the Holy Land under Joshua, became lax under prosperity and, in the period of the Judges, was more and more troubled by its enemies until it came to desire a king who could organize concerted resistance.

Samuel, the last of the Judges, at the Lord's command anointed Saul, and Saul was welcomed by the people because of his height and fine appearance. Saul, the first of the three kings of the united nation, represents a natural understanding of the truth such as we are likely to have when we are young people. It desires to serve the Lord and is eager for action, but it is impatient under delays and, reasoning from appearances, is liable to set itself up as a better judge of what should be done than even the Lord. Saul won his first victory over the Ammonites; but in his struggle against the Philistines refused to wait for Samuel's sanction and won only because his son Jonathan, who did trust wholly in the Lord, opened the way for his army.

At that time Samuel rebuked Saul and told him that the kingdom must pass out of his line, which pictures the fact that as we progress, a natural understanding of the truth is not sufficient to rule our lives.

Our story today shows still more clearly Saul's strength and weakness. The two foes he had so far overcome were open enemies, gathered in force for attack. Now he is told to seek out and destroy the Amalekites, an enemy who never attacked openly, but lay in wait for their foes. Saul is perfectly willing to attack this foe also and wins a victory, but contrary to the Lord's command to destroy the enemy utterly, he saves the king and the best of the sheep and oxen, again setting up his own judgment above the Lord's command, and drawing final condemnation upon himself.

Swedenborg says that Amalek represents "falsity from interior evil." We know from our own experience how readily we see as good those things which serve our self-interest, even when we sincerely believe we are trying to do right. A natural understanding of truth inevitably condemns only the obvious evils, and takes to itself the fair-seeming practices—the best of the sheep and oxen—leaving untouched the deep selfish root idea—represented by king Agag. Saul's claim that he saved the sheep and oxen as a sacrifice to the Lord also has a familiar ring. In business, in society, and in political life today many basically selfish and wrong acts are excused with the argument that "the end justifies the means."

When Samuel told Saul that the kingdom was to be taken from him and started to move away from him, we read that Saul caught hold of the skirt of Samuel's mantle and tore it. Samuel, we remember, represents the Word; so his mantle represents the letter of the Word. Saul's weakness was his unwillingness to keep the letter of the divine command. To symbolize this Samuel's garment was torn by his hand. Our spiritual power is dependent upon our obedience to the divine commands. Our own judgment must not be allowed to interfere with this. The Lord is always and forever wiser than men.

One of the quotations at the end of this lesson describes more exactly the temptation represented by Amalek, and its source. You remember that Amalek was the first enemy the children of Israel actually had to fight after they left Egypt. It was the battle at Rephidim, when Moses went up on the mountain and Aaron and Hur held up his hands to the Lord throughout the battle, because when he let his hands fall, Amalek prevailed. The quotation refers to the last verse of that story (Exodus 17:16) which says that "the Lord will have war with Amalek from generation to generation." Swedenborg calls the evil spirits whom Amalek represents "evil genii" because of their malignancy and subtlety. The thoughts they inspire in us appeal to our natural selfishness, and our first natural understanding of truth, with its tendency to self-confidence, is no match for them. Saul alone could not "root out" the Amalekites. Only the humble acknowledgment of our own weakness and self-love and the persistent lifting of our thoughts above worldly and selfish considerations to the Lord can win a complete victory.

---

## Adult

The best discussion material for this class will probably be based on the general correspondence of Saul and the enemies he could and could not overcome. In a church society we need constantly to help people of all ages to understand each other, to distinguish between good intentions and wisdom, to make allowances for each other, and to work together harmoniously in the Lord's service.

The three great kings who ruled over the whole land—Saul, David, and Solomon—all picture the Lord's divine truth ruling in our life. The enemies they fought are symbolic of evils and falsities within ourselves which oppose the rule of divine truth. Yet Saul, David, and Solomon were not perfect men, nor were they always victorious. Divine truth is received by us individually in different ways and in each of us differently at different stages of our progress through life. In a general sense the period of the kings represents an adult state, a time when we are making our own choices and are responsible for them. And also this period represents a part of the regenerate life. The Holy Land has been entered and has become our home. And we have also passed through the temptation to imagine that no more effort is required of us—the period of the Judges—and are ready to resume the conquest of our inner and outer evils under the rule of divine truth. We accept the Word as our guide—Samuel is still the Lord's prophet. Why are we not always victorious?

It is because our understanding of the truth is imperfect and because our inherited tendency to self-love and self-assertion is ever present and active, whether we recognize it or not. Saul represents divine truth as we first see it at this stage of regeneration. He was acceptable to the people because he stood head and shoulders above them. The Lord had told Samuel to let the people have their king, and He had chosen Saul and commanded Samuel to anoint him. The Lord leads each of us as best He can according to our states, preserving our freedom.

A study of attitudes of "young adult" groups in churches will help us to understand the reign of Saul. Usually they mean well, and they start out with the recognition of their inexperience. When Samuel first told Saul that he was to be king, Saul said: "Am not I a Benjamite, of the smallest of the tribes of Israel? and my family the least of all the families of the tribe of Benjamin?" And later, when at Mizpah the lot fell upon Saul, Saul had "hid himself among the stuff." And Saul, like the young adults in the church, was brave and eager and very willing to go into battle; and he won his first battle. It was against the Ammonites, who were attacking Jabesh-Gilead in the cross-Jordan country. It represents resistance against an obvious external temptation. But this first victory was all that was needed to disclose Saul's inadequacy for the kingship. For it "turned his head." It gave him confidence in himself instead of in the Lord. When we are young, we are much like Saul in this respect. It takes only a very little success and praise to make us self-confident and impatient of advice or control.

In the story of Saul and Jonathan and the battle with the Philistines, you remember, Saul had been told to wait seven days until Samuel should come and offer the proper sacrifices before beginning the battle. But Saul saw the Philistine reinforcements coming in and his own men deserting, and he decided that he himself could offer the sacrifices as well as Samuel. Like Saul, our first understanding of divine truth is based on appearances. We are impatient with delay and in a hurry to "get things done." It was only after Jonathan, who trusted in the Lord instead of in himself, had by his simple exploit thrown the Philistine army into confusion that Saul was able to attack and defeat it. The Philistine temptation to think that knowing the truth will save us without obedience to it can obviously not be overcome by confidence in self.

This lesson gives us Saul's final failure, although he continued to be king in name for some time afterward. The Amalekites were the first enemy who attacked the Israelites after they left Egypt. We have had the story of this first battle at Rephidim, which the Israelites won only because Moses went up into the mountain and, with the help of Aaron and Hur, kept his hands lifted to the Lord until the sun went down. The Amalekites represent "falsity from interior evil." Swedenborg, in speaking of Amalek in AC 8593, says: "Interior evil is that which lies inwardly concealed with man, hidden in his will, and thence in his thought, no trace of which appears in his externals, as in his actions, speech, and face." He says that those in the other world who are in this kind of evil are not called evil spirits but "evil genii," and that in their effort to influence us they "do not attack the truths of faith, but the goods of faith; for they act by means of depraved affections, whereby they pervert good thoughts, and this in a manner almost incomprehensible," and that they "never attack a man openly, nor when he is capable of vigorous resistance; but when it appears that a man is falling so as to yield, they are suddenly at hand, and push him on to a complete fall."

We can see why Saul—picturing the natural understanding of divine truth, based on appearances—was seduced by this enemy into sparing the things which seemed to him good, and so also sparing the king—the ruling principle—of the Amalekites. Swedenborg (in the same number quoted above) refers to the evil genii again in connection with verse 32 of our chapter: " 'To go delicately' signifies the outward blandishments of such spirits in the presence of others." It takes a good deal of experience for one to be able to see through the specious arguments of such spirits, and older people should be wise enough to help young people patiently through their period of "snap judgments."

Read carefully verses 22 and 23 of our lesson. Saul's yielding to this temptation in the face of the Lord's explicit commands finished his actual kingship, for we read in the very next chapter that Samuel was sent to anoint David and that as soon as David was anointed "the Spirit of the Lord departed from Saul." The tearing of Samuel's robe by Saul was the sign of this change. AE 395[5] tells us: "The words of Samuel make clear that 'the rending of the skirt of the cloak' signified the rending of the kingdom from Saul, for he said after it was done, "Jehovah hath rent the kingdom of Israel from thee this day,' 'a king' and 'his kingdom' signifying the Divine truth of the church, and 'the skirt of a cloak' signifying Divine truth in ultimates, that is, all Divine truth in general; for the kings that were over the sons of Israel represented the Lord in relation to Divine truth, and their kingdom signified the church in relation to Divine truth; therefore this historical fact signifies that king Saul was such that he could no longer represent the Lord, and that the representation of the church would perish if the kingdom were not rent from him."

## From the Writings of Swedenborg

*Arcana Coelestia*, n. 8593: "Interior evil is that which lies inwardly concealed with man, hidden in his will, and thence in his thought, no trace of which appears in his externals, as in his actions, speech, and face. They who are in such evil study by every method and art to hide and hoard it under the semblance of what is honorable and just, and under the semblance of love of the neighbor; yet still they devise nothing else within themselves than how they can inflict evil, and so far as they can they do inflict evil by means of others, taking care that it should not appear to be from them; they also color over the evil itself, that it may not seem like evil. The greatest delight of their life is to meditate such things, and to attempt them in concealment. This is called interior evil . . . They who are in this evil do not attack the truths of faith, but the goods of faith; for they act by means of depraved affections, whereby they pervert good thoughts, and this in a manner almost incomprehensible. . . . These infernal genii never attack a man openly, nor when he is capable of vigorous resistance; but when it appears that a man is falling so as to yield, they are then suddenly at hand, and push him on to a complete fall . . . From all this it can be seen what is the quality of those who are represented by Amalek, and why the judgment came upon Amalek from Jehovah that there should be perpetual war against them."

*Apocalypse Explained*, n. 395[3]: "'Prophets' signify those who teach truths from the Word, and in an abstract sense, the truths of doctrine from the Word; and because of this signification of 'prophets' they were clothed with a mantle of hair, 'the mantle of hair' signifying Divine truth in ultimates."

## Suggested Questions on the Lesson

P. Who was the first king? *Saul*

P. How was he chosen? *by lot*
P. Why did the people like him? *tall, strong*
J. In what part of the country did he win his first victory? *across Jordan*
J. What was the second enemy he fought? *Philistines*
P. What mistake did he make? *did not wait for Samuel*
P. By whose help was the victory finally won? *Jonathan*
P. In our lesson for today, what enemy is Saul told to attack? *Amalek*
J. Where have we heard of the Amalekites before? *first enemy in wilderness*
J. How was the first battle against them won? *Moses' hands held up*
J. What did the Lord tell Saul to do to them? *destroy completely*
P. How was Saul disobedient? *saved king, best animals*
J. What did Samuel tell him? *he would lose kingdom*
J. What sign was given of this? *torn robe*
P. What happened to Agag? *Samuel killed him*
S. What do the Amalekites represent? *falsity based on interior evil which leads to discouragement*
I. What does Saul as king represent? *worldly idea of truth*

## THE ANOINTING OF DAVID

*I Samuel 16*

The teachers should reread I Samuel 13 and 15 to recall what was the weakness of Saul. With all but the youngest children, it would be well to review briefly the two incidents in which Saul disobeyed Samuel, and to point out how they indicate Saul's tendency to judge by appearances. This is the most important lesson for the young people in connection with the change from Saul to David.

---

### Doctrinal Points

*We need a spiritual understanding of truth to direct our lives.*

---

### Notes for Parents

The story of Saul's reign over Israel teaches us that we cannot rely upon appearances to guide our judgment of what we should and should not do. Saul meant well and he was a strong and eager leader, but he was not wise. Like many young people—and many older ones who have never really grown up—he was in too much of a hurry to get things done and not willing to believe that the Lord really knew better than he did at all times. He recognized Samuel as the Lord's prophet, but he did not pay strict attention to Samuel's instructions and obey them. How hard it is for all of us to obey the simple command, "Rest in the Lord, and wait patiently for him"! The Lord always knows the right time and the right way. It is for us to learn and do His will.

I Samuel 16:7 gives us the key to the difference between Saul and David, not only in the Bible story but in our own lives: "The Lord seeth not as man seeth; for man looketh on the outward appearance, but the Lord looketh on the heart." Every good thing the Lord gives us and also every unwelcome thing He permits to come to us can bring us to a better state of heart if we will use it in the right way.

But deep changes do not take place all at once. Saul remained on the throne for a long time after David was anointed and although, as our chapter tells us, he loved David greatly at first, he later came to hate him and even tried more than once to kill him. When we are young and inexperienced, we form habits of thought and feeling which are very hard to break even after we have acknowledged that other ways are higher and better. All that is selfish in us rises up to oppose the change. But once we see the higher principle, the Lord's spirit "departs from Saul and enters into David," and if we keep trying, the Lord will give us victory in the end.

David had many faults, but he obeyed the voice of the Lord. Under him all the enemies of Israel were conquered, Jerusalem was taken and the ark of the Lord brought there, and the borders of Israel were extended more widely than ever before. And David was also "the sweet Psalmist of Israel." Many of the Psalms were given through him. And further, when the Lord came into the world, He chose to take on a finite humanity from the line of David and to be born in Bethlehem, the city of David.

---

## Primary

Tell the children that Saul could not keep the kingship because, although he meant well, he was in too much of a hurry and would not do exactly as Samuel told him to do. Little children often have this same failing. Then center the lesson around the difference between Saul and David, David's occupation as a shepherd and his skill in playing the harp, and finally the meaning of anointing. Read aloud I Samuel 16:6-7 to show that even Samuel was tempted to judge by outward appearance. Tell them that David did not actually become king for some time, that Saul later became jealous of him and even tried to kill him, but that David was always Saul's friend, and mourned for him when he died.

When Saul was first told by Samuel that he was to be king, he was very humble and wondered why he should have been chosen. But after all the people had welcomed him as king and after he had, with the Lord's help, been successful in his first battles, he began to think too well of himself. As we say today, "his head was turned" by success. He forgot that Samuel was the one who spoke for the Lord, and he thought he did not have to obey Samuel.

Now the Lord tells Samuel to anoint a new king.
Where does he send him?
What do you know about Bethlehem?
Why did Samuel think Jesse's oldest son must be the new king?
What did the Lord tell Samuel?
How many of Jesse's sons were rejected?
Why was his youngest son David not present?
What did David look like?
What happened to him when Samuel anointed him?
What happened to Saul at the same time?
David is called "the sweet psalmist of Israel."
Most of the Psalms were given through him.

David did not become king immediately after he was anointed. Saul was still on the throne and David had to prove himself to the people before they could accept him. Let us read how this proving started. Read I Samuel 16:14-23.

---

## Junior

Show the class where Bethlehem is on the map and make the connection with the Lord's birth. Read aloud Luke 2:1-4. Review the meaning of anointing. Stress the correspondence of the ass and the sheep in connection with the first appearance of Saul and of David in the story. Compare Saul and David as to their qualifications for the kingship. Connect David with the book of Psalms.

Saul was brave and he meant well, but he was hasty and impatient. He wanted to follow his own judgment instead of doing what Samuel told him to do, although he knew that Samuel was the Lord's prophet. So, although Saul won his first battles, he soon began to lose, and Samuel was sent to tell him that the kingdom would be taken from him.

Now the Lord tells Samuel to anoint a new king. The new king was to be very different from Saul. The Lord said He would choose a man after His own heart (I Samuel 13:14). David was to be a great warrior also, even greater than Saul, but he had other qualities which Saul did not have.

Where was David's home?
Who else long afterward was born in Bethlehem?

Look up Luke 2:1-4 to see why Joseph and Mary went to Bethlehem. They were both descendants of David. And the Lord was to be called, among other things, "the son of David."

What was Saul doing when Samuel first met him?
What was David doing when Samuel found him?

All the animals in the Bible correspond to—or represent—various affections or "likings" that we have. The ass pictures the liking for reasoning from the way things seem on the outside. The sheep pictures innocence, which is the desire to depend on the Lord for guidance, so that we may be sure not to do harm to anyone. Suppose you have a chance to beat someone in a game by cheating a little. What difference would it make whether you were "looking for asses" or "keeping sheep"? Ask your teacher to help you answer this question.

What happened to David when he was anointed?
What happened to Saul at the same time?

The anointing of David by Samuel was a sign that the Lord's power had been transferred from Saul to David, but David was to have many experiences before the death of Saul would open the way for all the people to recognize him as king. Throughout this time David was loyal to Saul and did all he could to help him, although Saul soon became jealous of David because the people liked him. Saul came to hate David and even tried to kill him more than once.

What was the first way in which David helped Saul?

Have you ever seen a harp?* It is one of the stringed instruments. Several musical instruments are mentioned in the Bible, and Swe-

*The small Biblical "harp" or lyre should not be confused with the large, intricate instrument used in a modern symphony orchestra. —*Ed.*

denborg tells us that they picture different ways of expressing our love for the Lord.

What musical instrument was used in the capture of Jericho?
Is that a stringed instrument?

David was to be the great fighting king of Israel. Under him all the enemies within the Holy Land were conquered and the borders of Israel were extended farther than at any other time. Jerusalem was captured and made the capital of the country, and the ark was brought there and placed in a new tabernacle on Mount Zion. But David was always a musician also. He is called "the sweet psalmist of Israel." Many of the Psalms were given through him. They are called "Psalms of David," but he himself, when he was about to die, said: "The Spirit of the Lord spake by me, and his word was in my tongue." (II Samuel 23:2)

## Intermediate

The fallacy of judging from appearances should be stressed. These children are at the age when they form hasty judgments and are very sure they are right. Through the stories of Saul's mistakes and the difference between Saul and David, they can be led to realize that there is a higher kind of judgment into which they will grow later, and this will be a great help to their parents in dealing with them.

As we read the story of Saul and his hasty and unwise actions, we see how our natural reason fails at crucial points. Everything Saul did seemed reasonable to him, and he could not believe that what Samuel told him to do was really wiser. Judging things by their outward appearance and always looking to the immediate external results as the test of what is best, our natural reason cannot deal with inner problems or wholly trust the wisdom of the Lord's commands. It is always saying of spiritual truth: "I can't see how this can be so."

David as king also represents the rule of truth, but it is truth understood in a deeper and more spiritual way. When our natural reason is seen to be faulty, we look for some deeper understanding to guide us. The character of this deeper understanding, which is pictured by David, appears from his occupation. He was a shepherd. That is, the deeper understanding of truth is founded on a desire to cherish and protect innocence, which is essentially the desire and willingness to be led by the Lord, and not merely, like the natural reason pictured by Saul, on a desire to reach a "common-sense" answer to our problems. You remember that Saul, when Samuel met him, was looking for his father's asses. Look up the correspondence of the ass and the lamb.

As soon as David was anointed, the power from the Lord departed from Saul. Just as soon as we have seen that we must think from spiritual principles, we begin to find a great deal wrong with common sense. But Saul is still acting as king. We cannot change our habits of thought in a moment.

At first, Saul was aware of his new position only by his recurring "black moods," and David was able to be his armorbearer and to soothe him with his music. Several musical instruments are mentioned in the Bible, and Swedenborg tells that they picture different ways of expressing our love for the Lord. Wind instruments are symbolic of simple and direct expressions of affection, but stringed instruments stand for expressions of it by means of truths. David was to be called "the sweet psalmist of Israel," and many of the Psalms were written through him. The book of Psalms is usually referred to by Swedenborg as the book of David.

We might say that David's playing before Saul was a form of reasoning from love. Have you ever been cross and irritable with your mother, for example, and suddenly come to yourself through the single thought of how much you really love her? Our love for the Lord, if we take time to express it, will cure many "black moods." This is one of the special uses of the regular reading of the Word and of prayer. They make all our selfish reasonings seem unworthy—as they are. When the Lord came into the world, He came as divine truth to show us how to live. So He was born of the line of David and was called "the son of David." And He was born in David's birthplace, Bethlehem. The word *Bethlehem* means "house of bread," and Swedenborg tells us that Bethlehem corresponds to "truth from good."

The description of David given in verse 18 of our chapter is interesting. The first impression that we get of him at the time of his anointing (verses 11 and 12) is that of a young boy, but here he is called "a mighty valiant man, and a man of war." To worldly people spiritual truths often seem beautiful but childish. It is only when we have come into displeasure with ourselves and recognize our need of help and comfort, as Saul did when the "evil spirit" was upon him, that we can feel the power of spiritual truth. David was to be the fighting king who overcame all the enemies of Israel within the Holy Land. He trusted in the Lord instead of in himself, and so the Lord's power could be with him. If we trust in the Lord and obey Him, He can give us victory over all our inner foes.

*Basic Correspondences*

| | | |
|---|---|---|
| David | = | the rule of divine truth as seen by our spiritual reason |
| Bethlehem | = | truth from good |
| musical instruments | = | expression by truths, as in words |

## Senior

The transition from Saul to David is beyond the actual experience even of the Seniors, but they can understand its meaning, and it will help to prepare them to meet the failure which will inevitably attend many of their early efforts to lead the Christian life as they see it. It may also soften a little the hardness of their early judgments and give them a more sympathetic understanding of the point of view of older people. The correspondence of the harp and its occurrence here will be interesting for discussion. The quotation from the *Apocalypse Explained* at the end of the lesson gives the basis for this discussion.

With every one of us who is developing spiritually the time comes when he sees clearly that he can no longer be satisfied with the rule of his natural reason. He must have a new "king," a deeper and more spiritual understanding of the truth, to direct his life. For we deeply want to "be good." We do not want to do harm, as we are always unintentionally doing when our natural reason is on the throne. This desire to be good, to be led by the Lord instead of by self, is represented by the fact that David, when he was called by Samuel, was tending his father's sheep, just as the character of Saul's kingship was pictured by his search for his father's asses. Our own understanding, based on what we see around us in the world, is not enough to lead us against any of our deeper enemies. Like Saul, it is hasty and impatient, and unwilling to acknowledge as evil anything that "looks good." The story of Saul's failures is told especially in chapters 13 and 15.

David's home was in Bethlehem, the "house of bread," which Swedenborg tells us represents "truth from good." That is, the primary desire to be good and to do good enables us to see truth more deeply and so to detect and dispel those deeper evils which the natural reason overlooks or condones. Living under this new principle we shall not, when we face a decision, say, "What will produce the most immediate external results?" but, "What will be really right in the Lord's sight?"

The anointing of David pictures our first recognition that this deeper rational is our true "king." But there is a long way to go before David becomes king in fact. Habits of thought and feeling are hard to change. Saul is still on the throne. The spirit of the Lord has departed from him, but Saul still directs Israel. In the Bible story there is a long struggle ahead between Saul and David. This is characteristic of our period of transition from very young manhood and womanhood to real maturity. We see the true order of life, but the habits of youth cling to us and let go with great reluctance.

In the first realization of the weakness of our natural reason, pictured by Saul's dark moods, we welcome the comfort which the higher reason brings. So David at first became Saul's armor-bearer and soothed him with his harp. But as soon as we begin to see that our natural reason must actually be dethroned and the higher reason become dominant in our lives, all the hells in us rise up and try to destroy the new king. Saul was to make several attempts to kill David. Yet David always helped Saul, and mourned for him when he was killed. Older people look back upon their lives and wish they could have kept their first energy and self-confidence and at the same time gained the wisdom of maturity. But this cannot be. The two states are distinct. One does not develop out of the other. David was not Saul's son. He was not even his younger brother, as Isaac was the younger half-brother of Ishmael. He came of an entirely different line. Each of the two types of rule has its own time and place in our lives.

---

## Adult

Discussion should center in the difference between Saul and David, in the meaning of the continuance of Saul's reign after David was anointed, and in the meaning of the fact that David was not of Saul's line.

Swedenborg tells us in several places that David represents "The Lord in respect to Divine truth." He has a good deal to say of David in this connection (AE 205 and elsewhere). We know that inmostly the whole of the Old Testament treats of the Lord's life and that all the leading figures in it represent the Lord in one or another aspect. We should, therefore, think of David and others as representative figures whose external lives were ruled over by divine providence in such a way that their record in the Scriptures might, through correspondence, express divine truth for all men in all times. There was a real David, a man like other men, compounded of good and evil, an individual soul just as important to the Lord as any other soul and no more. Of him we know little. But of David, the actor in the great drama of Scripture, we are told much. The many prophecies in which the Lord is connected with David all refer to David in this representative character; so we need not be confused by the statements that the Lord was "of David's line" and "the Son of David." The Lord Himself pointed this out to the Pharisees in Matthew 22:41-46.

In our study, however, we are trying consistently to relate the Scripture story to our own lives as well as to the Lord's life. So we must try to see what David means in us. The three great kings all represent the rule of divine truth, but on successively higher levels. Saul, as we have seen, represents divine truth apprehended in an external and necessarily superficial way. David pictures a more spiritual understanding of truth—"The Lord hath sought him a man after his own heart." "For the Lord seeth not as man seeth; for man looketh on the outward appearance, but the Lord looketh on the heart." Everything about David places his meaning on the spiritual plane of the mind. He is a "mighty valiant man, and a man of war, and prudent in matters [or in speech]"; yet he is called while guarding sheep, signifying the protecting of innocent affections. He is a "cunning player on the harp," the symbol of "spiritual truth" (AC 419). Later we shall find that he overcomes Israel's internal enemies, at last occupies Jerusalem, and brings the ark there.

Divine truth does not change, but our understanding of it changes. We must pass from our first natural and external understanding to a spiritual understanding of it which will enable us to see through appearances, to expose and correct deeper evils, and to set our internal house in order. When the results of our first efforts to apply truth to life are unsatisfactory, we must realize that the truth has not failed, but that our understanding of it is inadequate and that we must seek a deeper understanding. If our desire to do good remains steadfast, we shall be led, in our search for a new "king," to Bethlehem, the "house of bread," which Swedenborg tells us signifies "the spiritual of the celestial" (AC 4594) or "the truth of good." This is the same place to which the Wise Men were led to find the Incarnate Word. That is, by patient effort and with the Lord's guidance, our good desire will lead us to an understanding of truth which will enable our desire to accomplish corresponding good results.

This change in our understanding of truth is not accomplished in a moment. In I Samuel 15:35 we read, "And the Lord repented that he had made Saul king over Israel." We know that this again is the language of appearance. The Lord does not change His mind, but our apprehension of His will with regard to our conduct does change. So in the letter of the story He tells Samuel to cease mourning for Saul, to fill his horn with oil, and go to Bethlehem to anoint the new king. When we realize that our understanding of truth has been too superficial and has led us to make mistakes, we recognize the necessity of a new understanding, and the Lord's love working in us discovers and anoints a new "king." But we cannot at once remove Saul. The habits of judgment which we have formed are still dear to us; in the ordinary affairs of life they still hold sway. Only in critical cases do we seek out and depend upon the new leader. Nor is our new understanding sufficiently developed to take immediate control. It must be tried out over a long period until we come to trust it fully. So Saul continues to reign, and David, although anointed king, becomes recognized only gradually. But the spirit of the Lord has departed from Saul and is with David. We are conscious of the lack in our old understanding and of the fact that we have transferred the real authority to the new.

The first relationship between Saul and David is interesting in its suggestions. Swedenborg says, "Because the 'harp' signifies confession from spiritual truths, and spiritual truths are those by which angels of the Lord's spiritual kingdom are affected, and which disperse the falsities of evil, Saul's evil spirit was driven away by David's playing." (AE 323[12]) Saul at first loved David greatly and made him his armorbearer. It seems at first as if the old understanding and the new can go hand in hand, as if we can keep our familiar judgments as to right and wrong, only employing the new deeper insight to cleanse them of their obvious falsities and to bolster them up in their attacks upon evil. Sometimes, for example, one who has been brought up believing a strictly literal acceptance of the Scriptures and is used to drawing certain obvious lessons from the letter, may be led—through attacks on his faith which he cannot meet—to accept a spiritual interpretation of the Word. He sees that it is true, and uses it to cope with particular perplexities and doubts; yet he clings to his old ideas of the literal sense wherever it has proved satisfactory to him, and for a long time refuses to recognize that the whole must be interpreted according to its spiritual meaning. Or, a young person who has found himself mistaken in some of his judgments sees that a higher principle will help him to revise those particular judgments; yet he hesitates to apply it to other judgments in which he has not been forced to admit himself mistaken.

Habits once formed, whether mental or physical, are hard to break, and Saul lingers on the throne a long time, at first friendly to David and then actively antagonistic to him when he realizes that David must eventually wholly supplant him. Yet once David is anointed, his power gradually increases and Saul's power wanes. Saul's son, however friendly to David he may be, cannot occupy the throne. Even the best and truest offspring of our natural understanding can serve only as a temporary help to the establishment of the higher judgment. We are reminded of the Lord's words concerning John the Baptist: "Verily I say unto you, Among them that are born of women there hath not risen a greater than John the Baptist: notwithstanding he that is least in the kingdom of heaven is greater than he." There is the same discrete degree between the natural and the spiritual understanding of truth that there is between reformation and regeneration.

## From the Writings of Swedenborg

*Apocalypse Explained*, n. 205: "By 'David' in the Word the Lord is meant, because by 'kings' in the Word the Lord in respect to Divine truth is represented, and by 'priests' there the Lord in respect to Divine good. The Lord is represented especially by King David, because David had much care of the matters of the church, and also wrote the Psalms. . . . That David might represent the Lord in respect to Divine truth, the Lord was willing to be born of the house of David, and also to be called 'the Son of David,' 'his Root and Offspring,' also 'the Root of Jesse.' But when the Lord put off the human from the mother, and put on the Human from the Father, which is the Divine Human, He was no longer David's son."

*Arcana Coelestia*, n. 419: "As celestial things are the holy things of love and the derivative goods, so spiritual things are the truths and goods of faith; for it belongs to faith to understand not only what is true, but also what is good. The knowledges of faith involve both. But to *be* such as faith teaches is celestial. As faith involves both of these, they are signified by two instruments, the harp [lyre] and the organ [Panpipe or syrinx]. The harp, as everyone knows, is a stringed instrument, and therefore signifies spiritual truth; but the organ, being intermediate between a stringed instrument and a wind instrument, signifies spiritual good."

*Apocalypse Explained*, n. 323: ". . . the 'harp,' as being confession from spiritual truths. This is signified by 'harps,' because the harp was a stringed instrument, and by such instruments spiritual things, or those that are of truth, are signified, while wind instruments signify celestial things, or those that are of good. Such things are signified by musical instruments because of their sounds, for sound corresponds to the affections; moreover in heaven affections are perceived by sounds; and because there are various affections, and various sounds are produced by musical instruments, therefore these instruments, by correspondence and consequent agreement, signify affections. In general, stringed instruments signify such things as belong to the affections of truth, and wind instruments such as belong to the affections of good; or, what is the same, some instruments belong to the spiritual class, and some to the celestial class . . . Because the 'harp' signifies confession from spiritual truths, and spiritual truths are those by which angels who are in the Lord's spiritual kingdom are affected, and which disperse the falsities of evil, and with these the spirits themselves who are in them; so: 'When the evil spirit was upon Saul, David took a harp and played with his hand; and so rest was given to Saul, and the evil spirit departed from him' (I Samuel 16:23). This was done because kings represented the Lord in respect to the spiritual kingdom, and therefore signified spiritual truths; but Saul then represented the falsities that are opposed to these truths; and these were dispersed by the sound of the harp, because the 'harp' signified the spiritual affection of truth. This then took place because with the sons of Israel all things were representative and thus significative; it is otherwise at this day."

---

## Suggested Questions on the Lesson

J. What did the Lord tell Samuel about Saul and his line? *to lose kingdom*
P. Where did the Lord send Samuel to find a new king? *Bethlehem*
P. Who else was born in Bethlehem? *Jesus, also Benjamin*
P. What did Samuel think when he saw Jesse's eldest son? *here was the one*
P. What did the Lord tell him? *not this one*
J. How many sons of Jesse did the Lord reject? *seven*
P. What was David doing when they sent for him? *tending sheep*

J. What happened to David when he was anointed? *spirit of Lord came on him*

J. What happened to Saul at the same time? *evil spirit troubled him*

P. What did David look like? *ruddy, handsome*

J. What other qualities did he have? *warrior, poet, obedient to God*

P. On what instrument did David play? *lyre (harp)*

J. How did David come to Saul's attention? *soothed with music*

J. What position did Saul give him? *armorbearer*

J. What book in the Bible was written in part through David? *Psalms*

I. To what does David correspond? *truth understood spiritually ruling in life*

S. What is pictured by Saul's continuing on the throne after David was anointed? *old habits hard to change*

## DAVID AND GOLIATH

*I Samuel 17*

The Word gives us many events in the history of the three great kings, but in our course we have only four lessons on each of the three. We need therefore to keep in mind their relative significance rather than the various events of their reigns. They represent three stages in our regeneration as adults, the rule of truth on three different planes. Saul is the truth seen and applied according to external appearances. This is a hasty, superficial, and imperfect judgment. Saul's failure came from his desire to get things done in a hurry and his unwillingness to obey the Lord's commands when his own judgment did not coincide. David represents the same truth but seen in its deeper application to motives and thoughts, with the recognition of our own inherent weakness and need of the Lord's guidance and help. Solomon represents the same truth after it has been obeyed until it has come to be written on our hearts. Keeping this outline in mind will enable the teacher—even with little children—to put the emphasis in each story where it belongs. This is especially necessary in our story for today, in which there are so many interesting details for the children that the point of the story is apt to be lost sight of.

### Doctrinal Points

*True reasoning must be based on spiritual principles.*
*Our self-esteem is a "giant" which stands in our way spiritually.*

### Notes for Parents

Children always love the story of David and Goliath. Boys love to imagine themselves to be David. This is good, if only we can lead them to realize that David overcame Goliath not by his own physical strength or by the use of weapons like Goliath's, but because he trusted in the Lord's help and chose the weapons with which the Lord provided him.

We ourselves are so familiar with this story as one to tell to our children that sometimes we forget that it was not written just for children. Our own souls are the battleground on which the forces of the Lord and the forces of evil are drawn up against each other. The Philistines are in us, the temptation to be satisfied with ourselves and with what we know without trying to learn and do better all the time, the temptation to overestimate our own ability and to underestimate the importance of obedience to the Lord. The giant Goliath is our self-esteem, and his heavy weapons and armor are all the arguments we use to defend what we like to do. But the Lord sees to it that David is in us also, the shepherd boy who gained his wisdom and strength by defending his father's sheep, and who knew that if he obeyed the Lord, the Lord would give him victory. We all have some knowledge of the Lord and of His commandments, which we learned in childhood, and we all have some experience of the strength which comes from doing right.

And we all have David's weapons, the five smooth stones from the brook and the sling with which to use them. The brook is the Word of God and the stones are the simple statements in it which we have learned to believe because we have tested their truth. The sling is the power which the Lord has given each one of us to see how these truths apply to life and how we should direct them against our evils.

We have the Lord's own example to help us in understanding this story. When the Lord was tempted by the devil in the wilderness (Matthew 4:1-11), He did not argue with the devil. He used three quotations from the Word, three "smooth stones from the brook," and with each one He hit the particular temptation squarely "in the forehead." No matter how big and unconquerable our own special faults seem, every one of us can overcome them just as David overcame Goliath, if we have trust in the Lord instead of in self, knowledge of what the Lord teaches us in His Word, and courage to use that knowledge.

## Primary

The story is an easy one to tell. Be sure to tell the children that David was a shepherd and that his home was in Bethlehem, and to connect this with the Christmas story. Point out that Goliath was self-confident because of his size and equipment, but David conquered because he trusted in the Lord.

Who was the first king of Israel?
Why did the people like him?
Who anointed Saul to be king?
What was wrong with Saul?
What did Samuel tell Saul?
The Lord told Samuel to anoint a new king.

This man was David. He lived in Bethlehem. Do you know who else long afterward was born in Bethlehem? It was the Lord Jesus. Do you remember how the angels gave the news of the Lord's birth to the shepherds at Bethlehem? David was a shepherd, too. He was only a young boy when Saul anointed him, and it was to be many years before he actually became king.

The Philistines were still fighting the Israelites. They had with them a great giant named Goliath. He came out every day and offered to fight one of the Israelites, and the Philistines said that if anyone could kill Goliath, they would all serve the Israelites. But for a long time no one dared fight him.

Three of David's older brothers were in the army, and one day his father sent him to see how they were getting along and to take them some food from home. David saw Goliath come out and dare any Israelite to fight him. So David offered to go out against him. He was not afraid like the others because he trusted in the Lord. The Lord had already helped him to kill a lion and a bear which had been stealing some of his father's sheep, and he knew the Lord always helped those who did right.

What did Saul offer David to fight with?
Why could he not use Saul's armor?
What weapons did he have?
Did David or Goliath attack first?
How did David overcome Goliath?
With whose sword did he cut off Goliath's head?

### Junior

The Juniors needed the lesson about Saul's impatience and self-confidence. Point out that Goliath was self-confident, too. They will easily understand the correspondence of Goliath and of the smooth stones from the brook, and will be interested in the origin of the giants. Have them locate the places on a map, and look up all the Bible references. This class especially might easily be absorbed in the fascinating details of the story; so its broad connections and application to their own lives need to be emphasized.

The man to be king after Saul was to be a very different kind of person; Samuel said, "The Lord hath sought him a man after his own heart." The new king was to be David. He was to prove himself a great warrior also, but he had other qualities which Saul did not have.

David's home was at Bethlehem. Long afterward someone else was to be born in Bethlehem.

Who was it?

Joseph and Mary were both descendants of David and that was why they went to Bethlehem to be enrolled for the Roman taxation. The Lord was also called "the son of David." When Samuel went to find David to anoint him, David was keeping his father's sheep. You remember that it was the shepherds keeping watch over their flocks near Bethlehem who first received the news that the Savior had been born. The Lord afterward called Himself "the good shepherd." Sheep are gentle, trustful animals, and whenever a shepherd is mentioned in the Word, we should think of one who protects and cares for the virtues of gentleness, trust, and innocence. This is what the Lord wishes to do for us, and when we are in these good states, we may be sure that He is near us.

The anointing of David by Samuel was a sign that the Lord's support was transferred from Saul to David, but David was to have many experiences before he actually became king. Saul continued on the throne for many more years and David did all he could to help Saul, but Saul soon came to hate David because he saw that the Lord was with David instead of with himself. I Samuel 16:14-23 tells of the first association between Saul and David, when David was able to soothe Saul with his harp. David was called "the sweet psalmist" of Israel. Many of the Psalms were written by David under inspiration from the Lord. A psalm is a song of praise.

In our chapter for today what enemy is still attacking Israel?
Find on a map the valley of Elah where the two armies were drawn up.
How did the Philistines propose to settle the conflict?

We have heard of giants before. Read Genesis 4:4. Some of the descendants of these giants from the Most Ancient Church were still living in the Holy Land when the children of Israel came back to it from Egypt. You remember the report of the spies (Numbers 13:22-23, 33). Read also Joshua 11:21-22. The giants picture the selfishness which is born in each one of us as a result of all the evils in our ancestors from the beginning. We usually think of selfishness as not wanting to share things with others. But this is only one rather obvious kind of selfishness. A much more common and serious kind is thinking of oneself as the most important thing in the world, wanting our own way, and blaming other people if we don't get it.

This selfishness, which Goliath pictures in our story, seems very big and powerful, and it is hard for us to make up our minds to face it. We say, "I can't help it; I was born that way." The Israelites were afraid to go out and fight Goliath. But David was not afraid of Goliath. Why wasn't he?

David could not wear Saul's armor because he had not "proved" it. Do you know that each of us gets for himself a kind of spiritual armor? (See Ephesians 6:11-17.) The truths which we learn and use are our armor. They protect us against evil and help us to resist it when it attacks us. But we hear many truths which we do not yet understand and which we have not tried to practice—they are of no immediate use to us because we have not "proved" them in our own lives. Evil, or selfishness, also uses truths to defend itself. We do this every time we argue in favor of something we want to do which we really know is wrong. Goliath had very powerful armor and weapons, didn't he?

What were David's weapons?

The stones had become smooth by long action of the water of the brook. They picture those truths from the Word which we have tried out and found effective and have stored up in our memories, as David put the stones in his shepherd's bag. Read Matthew 4:1-11 and see if you can pick out the "three smooth stones" which the Lord used against the devil when He was tempted in the wilderness.

Notice that David did not wait for Goliath to come to him. He ran to meet him boldly and attacked first.

What story have we had in which the men who were eager for the battle were the ones chosen?

David's first stone struck Goliath in the forehead, just as the Lord's quotation to the devil in each case hit right at the principle involved in the temptation.

Whose sword did David use to cut off Goliath's head?

This teaches us that after we have used the plain "Thou shalt not" of the Scriptures to stop our temptation short, we can pick up the arguments with which we were defending our selfishness and see how they really work just the other way.

---

## Intermediate

The correspondence is clear and interesting throughout. The lesson may well be centered around the meaning of the weapons of Saul, David, and Goliath.

The change from the Judges to the kings in Israel pictures the time when we realize that we must have the Lord's truth as a general ruling principle in our lives, instead of just going to the Lord for help when we are in serious trouble. Saul pictures our first efforts to use this truth as a ruling principle. Our first idea of it is natural and superficial; so it fails at crucial points. Judging things by their outward appearance and looking in everything to immediate external results seems to us "common sense," but we soon find that common sense cannot solve any of our real problems. This is because common sense deals with material things and the Lord's commands have our spiritual development in view, and our common sense does not trust the Lord's wisdom. This was Saul's failing and so his rule was not a victorious one and had to be terminated.

David as king also represents the rule of the Lord's truth, but it is truth understood in a deeper and more spiritual way. When our natural reason is seen to be faulty, we look for some deeper understanding to guide us. The character of this deeper understanding, which is pictured by David, appears from his occupation. He was a shepherd. That is, a deeper understanding of truth is founded on the desire to be good inside as well as out, for sheep picture the innocent, trustful affections which come to us from the Lord and are necessary if we are to keep close to Him. The Lord called Himself the "good shepherd." We need to remember also that David was born in Bethlehem, and that Joseph and Mary went to Bethlehem on the night of the nativity because they were "of the house and lineage of David." And the Lord was called "the son of David."

As soon as David was anointed, the power from the Lord departed from Saul. Just as soon as we have seen that we must think from spiritual principles, we begin to find a great deal wrong with mere common sense. But Saul is still acting as king. It is not possible to change our habits of thought in a moment. David, however, was able almost immediately to help Saul by playing his harp for him (I Samuel 16:14-23). You may recall from our lesson on the first days in the wilderness, when Moses sang a song of triumph and Miriam used her timbrel, that Swedenborg says of the musical instruments mentioned in the Word that they picture different ways of expressing our love for the Lord. Wind instruments symbolize simple and direct expressions of the affection, but stringed instruments stand for expression of affection by means of truths. David was later to be called "the sweet psalmist of Israel." We might say that David's music was a form of reasoning from love.

When David went out to fight Goliath, he could not fight in Saul's armor because he had not "proved" it. Saul's armor pictures reasonings which up to this time have seemed sensible to us. David relied on the Lord instead of on his own strength. He used only his simple sling and the stones from the brook which he had put in his shepherd's bag. These picture a few truths from the Word which have been proved by experience and stored up in the mind for use.

Goliath, descendant of the giants of the Most Ancient Church (Genesis 6:4), symbolizes the deep-seated tendency to self-love and self-esteem born in each one of us. He was the champion of the Philistines, who picture our tendency to be satisfied with ourselves as we are and with knowing truth without using it to recognize and fight our evils. Goliath's defiance makes us think of the common expression: "You can't change human nature."

David's first shot struck the giant in the forehead, so that he fell on his face to the ground. When the Lord was tempted in the wilderness, He did not argue with Satan. In each temptation He chose the one right verse from the Scriptures which struck straight at the ruling idea of the temptation, and said, "It is written, Thou shalt not . . ." This is the way we are to meet temptation, and if we do we can overcome it, no matter how strong it seems. Afterward we can see how foolish the arguments were with which we had been trying to defend our selfishness. David cut off Goliath's head with Goliath's own sword. After Goliath was out of the way, the Israelites could pursue and conquer the Philistine army. Once we really get rid of our self-satisfaction, the way way is open to spiritual victory. Our pride in self is the "giant" that stands in our way every time.

*Basic Correspondences*

| | | |
|---|---|---|
| David | = | the rule of divine truth as seen by our spiritual reason |
| Goliath | = | our deep inherited tendency to self-esteem |
| sheep | = | innocent, trustful affections |
| smooth stones from the brook | = | truths from the Word proved by experience |
| musical instruments | = | means of expressing our affections |

### Senior

Here the meaning of the Philistines and of Goliath is the central point to emphasize. Young people need to see clearly the subtle temptation to self-esteem which is in all of us, and the difference—in origin and in effect—between trust in self and trust in the Lord.

With every one of us who is developing spiritually, the time comes when we see clearly that we can be satisfied no longer with the rule of our natural reason. We must have a new "king," a deeper and more spiritual understanding of truth to direct our lives. For we deeply want to "be good." We do not want to do harm, as we are always unintentionally doing when our natural reason is on the throne. This desire to be good, not to do harm, is represented by the fact that David, when he was called, was tending his father's sheep—just as the character of Saul's kingship was pictured by the fact that when called he was searching for his father's asses (I Samuel 9). The ass pictures the affection for natural reasoning, but sheep picture the affection of innocence.

David's home was in Bethlehem, the "house of bread," which Swedenborg tells us represents "truth from good." That is, the primary desire to be good enables us to see the truth more deeply and so to detect and dispel those deeper evils which the natural reason overlooks or condones. Living under this new principle we shall not say, when we face a decision, "What will produce the most immediate external results?" but "What will be really right in the Lord's sight?"

The anointing of David pictures our first recognition that this deeper rational is our true king. But there is a long way to go before David becomes king in fact. Habits of thought are hard to change. Saul is still on the throne. The spirit of the Lord had departed from him, but he still directs Israel. There is a long struggle ahead between Saul and David, in which Saul is jealous of David and tries to destroy him whereas David is always kind and helpful to Saul. This is characteristic of our period of transition from very young manhood and womanhood to maturity. The habits of youth cling to us and let go with great reluctance. The familiar story of David and Goliath pictures one of the earlier steps in this transition, our first successful attempt to judge the fallacy of the grosser arguments which exalt self, in the light of our new deeper understanding of the meaning of life.

The giant Goliath, one of the last survivors of the perverted Most Ancient Church, pictures our deep-seated inherited self-esteem, and his armor and weapons the reasonings which favor it. Goliath comes out in avowed defiance of the living God. He is the champion of the Philistines, those ever-present tendencies to imagine that our knowledge of what is right makes us superior to others, without any real effort to apply that knowledge to the correction and improvement of our own motives and thoughts. David, putting his whole reliance on the Lord, uses as his weapon only a smooth stone from the brook, a simple truth from the Word proved by experience and stored in the memory with a view to use. Slung with all his might it strikes the giant in the forehead, the governing principle of selfishness. After Goliath had fallen, David was able to stand upon him and cut off his head, using Goliath's own sword, the very reasonings which had seemed to favor self.

This story is very important for all of us, for it shows us our most persistent enemy (Israel never fully conquered the Philistines), the nature of the giant which acts as "front" for this enemy, and the one effective means of conquering both. If we think the Philistines are not in us, let us keep their meaning in mind and watch our thoughts and words, and especially our unconscious reactions for even one day. We are all prone to the feeling that our weaknesses are minor ones and after all excusable because in general we are "pretty good people," and to carry on arguments not for the sake of finding out the truth but in order to prove that we are right and the other fellow is wrong. We likewise tend to shrug off people who are different from ourselves as not worth much, and to be on the watch for opportunities to display our superior knowledge or ability. So the giant of self-esteem comes out morning and evening and opposes every step of our spiritual progress. But if we have David's courage and trust in the Lord, we shall find plenty of plain statements in the Word with which we may strike him in the forehead. Read Matthew 4:1-11.

---

## Adult

Perhaps the most important thing for this class is to realize the psychological and spiritual depths in this story which is so often thought of only as "one of the Bible stories children love." It is essentially a story of adult experience.

In the history of Israel the Philistines play an important part. They represent "those in faith separate from charity," those who know the truth and are proud of their knowledge, but have no desire to live according to it. But we need always to remember that our concern is not with others whom we may think to be Philistines, but with the Philistines within ourselves, an ever-present enemy. Every time we excuse ourselves from doing what we know is right, every time we twist the truth in such a way as to support our desires, every time we are contemptuous of another who differs from us, the Philistines are upon us.

Saul is unable to wage a successful war against the Philistines. He is afraid of them, and his men are constantly deserting him for fear of the Philistines. This is because a mere external understanding of truth, being superficial, is easily confused by clever arguments. It cannot see the real fallacy behind their plausibility. It relies upon its own strength in argument, as Saul relied upon his army and his armor, and when it meets an adversary more clever in the use of the same weapons, it has no further strength. We recall that the Philistines had prevented the Israelites from practicing the trade of smith, so that they had no means of making weapons themselves or of sharpening those they did have. The Philistine in us tries to keep control of the truth. When we are trying to justify ourselves in self-seeking and self-exaltation, we do our best to use truths for our purpose, sometimes almost convincing ourselves in the process that wrong is right. This is what Swedenborg means by the falsification of truth. When we are in this Philistine state, our own reasoning is very pleasant and convincing to us, and we will go to any length rather than be proved wrong. This "conceit of self-intelligence" is what is meant by Goliath. We have all had the experience of arguing endlessly, twisting the truth this way and that, rather than admitting ourselves mistaken. This is Goliath coming out morning and evening for forty days to deliver his challenge against Israel.

Throughout the Word weapons of various kinds in a good sense represent truths with which we defend ourselves against evil or attack our spiritual enemies. In the hands of the evil, weapons represent these truths falsified by being used in the defense and support of evil. This makes it easy for us to see the correspondence of the armor of the three chief figures in our lesson. Remember that brass represents external goodness. Have we ever, when trying to defend ourselves in a wrong course we have chosen, or when criticizing someone else whose views did not agree with ours, pointed complacently to certain good deeds of ours and to knowledge and abilities which we possess? Have we ever justified a questionable course on the ground that it was the only "practical" method of accomplishing results? Have we ever in argument said or implied, "If you knew as much as I do, you would agree with me"? This is the heavy brass armor and weapons of Goliath. It is terrifying to Saul and his soldiers.

Saul's weapons and armor are literal truths. The mere external understanding of truth, in the face of attack by apparently stronger reasoning, feels helpless because it has relied on a literal acceptance of the truth and has not felt the Lord's love and power within it. We see this in the fact that often young people who have been strictly brought up at home but have not been made to feel the loving purpose behind their parents' rules fall easy victims to the persuasion of schoolmates who pose as more emancipated. It is hard to face ridicule for something which we have been taught is right but which we ourselves do not see to be right. David the young shepherd could not use Saul's armor because he had not "proved" it. But with his own weapons he had already delivered a lamb of his father's flock from a lion and a bear. He used the weapons he had proved.

David's weapons were his shepherd's staff, his sling, and five smooth stones from the brook. The staff was his reliance on the Lord; the smooth stones from the brook, particular truths of the Word readied by experience (five meaning a few but sufficient); and the sling, the understanding—also gained by experience—which enabled him to direct the truth against a particular evil and to communicate to it the force of his zeal. We all may have David's weapons. The Lord promises support to all who obey His commandments. We all have the Word, the clear stream of truth, and we all have the power to find in it truths which we may prove by experience. We make a sling for ourselves by meditating on the truths of the Word and their application to life and conduct. We should be constantly choosing "smooth stones from the brook" and putting them in our "shepherd's bag" ready for use when an enemy attacks any of our innocent affections.

Another point in David's method is suggestive. "And it came to pass, when the Philistine arose, and came and drew nigh to meet David, that David hasted, and ran toward the army to meet the Philistines." We should not sit down and wait until temptation has launched its weapons, but we should see it coming, go out to meet it, and strike the first blow ourselves. This is one of the things a knowledge of the internal sense of the Word prepares us to do by giving us an understanding of all sorts of temptations, their origin, and the truths with which they may be overcome. We should see to it that our children have as much as possible of this advance preparation for life; for the Christian life demands not mere passive resistance, but active attack upon evil. David's aim was true because his eye was clear. He saw his enemy distinctly and was able to strike him in the forehead. This teaches us the lesson that if we are to overcome a temptation, we must be able to recognize and destroy the governing and directing false principle which is its head. When this is done, the enemy falls, and it is easy enough to examine the arguments it used and to turn them against it, as David, standing upon the giant, cut off his head with the giant's own sword. "And

David took the head of the Philistine, and brought it to Jerusalem; but he put his armor in his tent." The evil principle which has falsified truths must be rejected as contrary to the teachings of the church, but the truths it has used, when separated from it, become ours, part of the widom of experience.

It was by a succession of small victories, won through reliance on the Lord, that David gradually won the confidence of the people. At first, even when we are trying to fight the Lord's battles, we rely upon ourselves, form hasty judgments, and often take hasty action, as Saul did. But experience teaches us the folly of self-confidence, and there grows up gradually within us a deeper understanding of the Lord's truth, which is David. The Lord begins to give us power through a higher principle. Yet it is a long time before our self-confidence is altogether replaced by reliance on the Lord. Saul continued to reign as king for many years. Even after Saul's death David was first made king in Hebron, and it was another seven years before he was accepted by all the people and came to reign in Jerusalem. Full confidence in the power of the truth as the Lord gives it to us must become established in our hearts before it can become the ruling principle in our minds.

---

## From the Writings of Swedenborg

*Apocalypse Explained*, n. 781[12]: "Power was given to David to smite the lion and the bear that took away the sheep from the flock, because 'David' represented the Lord in reference to Divine truth in which those who are of His church are instructed; and a 'lion' signifies the power of spiritual Divine truth, and in the contrary sense, as here, the power of infernal falsity against Divine truth; while a 'bear' signifies the power of natural Divine truth, and in the contrary sense the power of falsity against that truth. But 'a sheep from the flock' signifies those who are of the Lord's church. And as this was represented, the power was given to David to smite the bear and the lion, to represent and signify the Lord's power to defend by His Divine truth His own in the church from the falsities of evil that are from hell. . . . But 'Goliath,' who was a Philistine and was therefore called 'uncircumcised,' signifies such as are in truths without good; and truths without good are truths falsified, which in themselves are falsities."

*Apocalypse Explained*, n. 817[6]: "All the wars that the sons of Israel waged against the Philistines represented the combats of the spiritual man with the natural man, and thence also the combats of truth conjoined with good against truth separated from good, which in itself is not truth but falsity. For truth separated from good is falsified in the idea of the thought respecting it, and for the reason that there is nothing spiritual present in the thought to enlighten it. For the same reason those who are in faith separated from charity have no truth, except merely in their speech or in their preaching from the Word, the idea of truth instantly perishing as soon as truth is thought about. Because this religion exists in the churches with all who love to live a natural life, so in the land of Canaan the Philistines were not subjugated, as the other nations of the land were, and consequently there were many battles with them. For all the historical things of the Word are representative of such things as pertain to the church; and all the nations of the land of Canaan represented things heretical confirming either the falsities of faith or the evils of the love; while the sons of Israel represented the truths of faith and the goods of love, and thus the church."

---

## Suggested Questions on the Lesson

P. Where did David live? *Bethlehem*

P. What was his occupation? *shepherd*

J. Where were the armies of Saul and the Philistines facing each other? *Valley of Elah*

P. Whom had the Philistines chosen to be their champion? *Goliath*

J. What can you tell about Goliath? *nine feet tall, heavily armored*

J. What challenge did he shout to Israel? *"Give me a man . . ."*

J. How had David happened to come down to the army? *to bring food to brothers*

P. What offer did he make to Saul? *"I will fight Goliath"*

P. Why did he think he could overcome Goliath? *trusted God*

J. Why could David not use Saul's armor? *had not "proved" it*

P. What were David's weapons? *sling, five smooth stones*

J. How did he kill Goliath? *sling and stone*

J. With what did he cut off Goliath's head? *Goliath's sword*

S. What do the Philistines represent? *thinking we are better than others because of our superior knowledge*

I. What does Goliath stand for? *inherited pride*

I. What are the smooth stones from the brook? *truths from the Word we have tried and found to be effective*

# THE ARK BROUGHT TO JERUSALEM

*II Samuel 6*

The transition from Saul to David should be centered about Jonathan. The loyalty of both David and Jonathan to Saul, in spite of Saul's jealousy and hatred, should be stressed, and the fact that David could win victories because, like Jonathan, he trusted and obeyed the Lord. The sin of Uzzah and its punishment is the most dramatic part of the lesson for today, but it should not be allowed to dwarf the importance of the actual bringing of the ark to Jerusalem.

---

## Doctrinal Points

*Sin is doing what we know to be wrong.*
*To do what seems to us the "natural" thing may not be right.*
*The laws of God are eternal and not to be changed or interpreted to suit the desires of men.*
*We cannot overcome temptation by reasoning about it.*

---

## Notes for Parents

David, the second great king of Israel, was very different from Saul. He had grown up as a shepherd boy in Bethlehem and, although he also became a great warrior, he never lost the attitude of childlike trust and reliance upon the Lord which is pictured by sheep and shepherds, and which is essential to our spiritual development. "Verily, I say unto you, Whosoever shall not receive the kingdom of God as a little child shall in no wise enter therein." David was also a player on the harp or lyre, and it was through him that many of the Psalms were written.

After David had come to the throne and established his capital at Jerusalem, he knew that he should bring the ark there because the ark was meant to be the center of Jewish life. The commandments are to be written on our hearts. For twenty years the ark had been at the city of Kirjathjearim, where it had been taken from Bethshemesh after the Philistines returned it.

The strange story of Uzzah which is part of our lesson for today has often troubled people because to us it might seem quite natural and right that when the oxen shook the cart on which the ark was being carried, Uzzah should have put out his hand to steady it. It was natural but it was not right. The ark was the holiest thing the Jews possessed. Again and again its power had been demonstrated in their history. But Uzzah was thinking of it as just an ordinary chest, as his act showed. All the Levites knew that only the anointed priests were to touch it, but the people needed to be reminded of its holiness and power. The tables of stone on which the commandments had been written by the finger of God at Sinai were in the ark. The Lord's power comes to us only as we keep the commandments. They are not man-made laws, but the laws of God. We cannot tamper with them and we should trust them completely. They stand forever by their own power.

---

## Primary

Stress the reason why the Lord's spirit departed from Saul, the character of David, and Jonathan as the connecting link in the story. In telling about Uzzah, point out that Uzzah should have known better than to try to steady the ark. Tell the children that after the ark was set up in Jerusalem, Jerusalem became the center of the life of the nation.

The second king of Israel was David. David lived in Bethlehem, the same place where the Lord was born long afterward. The Lord sent Samuel to Bethlehem to anoint David, who was then hardly more than a boy. And after David was anointed, the spirit of the Lord was with him instead of with Saul. You have heard the story of how David killed the giant Goliath.

David was a shepherd boy, but he was also a warrior.
The people praised him so much that Saul became jealous and tried to kill him.
But Jonathan and David had become fast friends, and Jonathan saved him.

David had to run away and live in hiding, but he was loyal to Saul as long as Saul lived.
Finally, however, Saul and Jonathan were both killed in battle by the Philistines, and then David became king.
During his reign he conquered all the enemies of Israel.
This was because he always obeyed the Lord.
He captured Jerusalem and made it his capital.
Then he wanted to bring the ark to Jerusalem.
The ark was at Kirjathjearim, also called Baale.
How did they take it from Kirjathjearim?
What did Uzzah do?
What happened to him?
Why was his act so bad?
Into whose house was the ark taken for a time?
What did it do for the household?
What effect did this have on David?

David went before the ark all the way to Jerusalem with singing and dancing, stopping every so often to offer sacrifices to the Lord. This is how the ark finally came back to be the very center of the life of the Israelites.

David built a new tabernacle for the ark on Mount Zion, one of the hills in the city of Jerusalem.

---

## Junior

In speaking of the punishment of Uzzah, point out that sin is doing what we know to be wrong. The ark was the holiest thing the Jews had, and a sin against it was therefore the most serious sin of all. Have the children look up the references in Chronicles, and also Joshua 9:17, where Kirjathjearim is named as one of the cities of the Gibeonites, and I Samuel 6:21 and 7:1-2, where the ark is taken to Kirjathjearim. This will help to tie today's story in with other lessons they have had this year. See how much the children can tell about the ark.

Samuel told Saul that because of his disobedience the Lord had rejected him and would choose as the next king "a man after his own heart." Then the Lord sent Samuel to Bethlehem to anoint David, and the Bible tells us that after David was anointed, "the spirit of the Lord departed from Saul" and was with David instead.

You remember the story of how David killed the giant Goliath with his sling and a smooth stone from the brook. Before that victory Saul had made David his armorbearer, and David and Jonathan had become sworn friends. David won victories for Saul, but when the people began to sing David's praises and to say that David's victories were greater than Saul's, Saul became jealous and tried to kill David. Jonathan saved David's life, but David had to go into hiding. Finally Saul and Jonathan were both killed in a battle with the Philistines and David was made king. At first he was accepted by only part of the people and had his capital in Hebron in the southern part of the land—you remember that Hebron had been Abraham's home—but after seven years, in which he continued to win victories, the people in the northern part of the country accepted him also. Then he took the city of Jerusalem from the Jebusites and made it his capital.

David's next thought was to bring the ark of God to Jerusalem. Baale (= Judah) is another name for Kirjathjearim. Kirjathjearim was one of the cities which had belonged to the Gibeonite League; you remember the Gibeonites who came to make a peace treaty with Joshua.

How was the ark taken from Kirjathjearim?

This was a violation of the law, for the ark should have been carried on the shoulders of the Levites. If it had been, it could not have been shaken as it was by the oxen, and Uzzah would not have been tempted.

What did Uzzah do when the oxen shook the ark?
What happened to him?

Can you see why his fault was so serious? It was because it showed that he did not really believe in the power of the ark to care for itself. This was something like Saul's attitude toward Samuel's advice, wasn't it? The things we do impulsively show what is really deep inside of us.

What was in the ark?

When people today think that the commandments are not really the Lord's laws for all people in all times, and that they need to be changed a little or explained in such a way as to suit conditions in the world, it is like Uzzah's putting forth his hand to steady the ark. The Lord knows what we need better than we do, and His laws do not change. They have just as much power to bring peace and happiness as they ever had.

Where did David have the ark taken after Uzzah's death?
How long was it there?
What induced David to take it to Jerusalem finally?
In I Chronicles 15:11-15 we learn that this time the ark was carried according to the law.
What did David do as the ark was carried toward Jerusalem?
Who despised him for doing this?
What was her punishment?
Where did David put the ark in Jerusalem?

Read I Chronicles 15:1 and II Chronicles 1:3-6. We learn from these that the tabernacle which David pitched for the ark in Jerusalem was not the original tabernacle, which at this time was set up in Gibeon, one of the Levitical cities. It was still there in the early days of Solomon's reign, but no one knows what finally became of it. The real power in the tabernacle came through the ark, just as we can have power from the Lord only as we keep the commandments.

---

## Intermediate

The lesson for this class should be centered around the meaning of this final journey of the ark to Jerusalem, the various incidents being taken up in the order of the journey. More will be done for this class in the next lesson with the meaning of Mount Zion and of the three kings.

After David's victory over Goliath, he was for a time a favorite with Saul, and David and Jonathan swore eternal friendship. Saul, however, soon realized that it was David whom the Lord favored, and he tried to get rid of him in various ways. Jonathan at first would not believe that his father hated David, but when he was convinced he warned David to flee. In exile David gathered a band of fighting men around him and won victories, always considering himself as the faithful servant of Saul and not making any effort to supplant him. But when Saul and Jonathan were both killed in a battle against the Philistines, the people in the southern part of the land–where David had been living–made him king, the people in the northern part setting up as king a son of Saul named Ishbosheth. David reigned in Hebron for seven and a half years. Then Ishbosheth's own captains murdered him and all the people accepted David as king. He took the city of Jerusalem from the Jebusites and made it his capital, reigning there for another thirty-three years, forty years in all.

The second book of Samuel tells the story of the reign of David. Our lesson is concerned with his bringing the ark of the covenant from Kirjathjearim–where it had been ever since the Philistines returned it–to Jerusalem, where he set it up in a new tabernacle or tent on Mount Zion, one of the hills within the city. At the beginning of this lesson we have the story of a punishment which seems out of all proportion to the crime committed. We might think it quite natural and right that Uzzah, seeing the ark shaken, should put forth his hand to steady it. But we must realize that even in the literal story, all the Jews knew about the ark and its power and how it was to be borne and handled. The ark would not have been shaken in the first place if it had been borne on the shoulders of the Levites as the law required, and Uzzah's act showed a lack of belief in the power of the ark and a self-confident sense of superiority to it. It is the same sort of feeling which prompts people today to say that, although the commandments were right and necessary at the time the Lord gave them, today He would give laws more in keeping with modern ideas of what is right and wrong. The real sin involved in this story is the failure to acknowledge that the laws of God are eternal and are not to be changed or interpreted to suit the desires of men. It is putting the opinions of men above the wisdom of God, and this leads to spiritual death. So Uzzah died there by the ark of God.

David's fear to bring the ark further after Uzzah's death is typical of our reluctance to go the whole way in obeying the commandments when we realize fully all that it involves. It took further experience of the blessings produced by the ark to remove David's fear. This time he took care to have the ark properly carried, and he himself accompanied it, singing, dancing, and offering sacrifices along the way (see I Chronicles 15:11 ff.)

We learn from II Chronicles 1:3-6 that the tabernacle which David pitched for the ark in the "city of David," which was the stronghold on Mount Zion in Jerusalem, was not the original tabernacle. The original tabernacle was at this time in Gibeon, and remained there until after the temple was built, after which we hear no more of it. A tent in the Word represents a state of worship from love.

David was a fighting king, who conquered all the enemies of Israel. The enemies of Israel represent our evils and the battles against them our struggles with temptation. When we are fighting our temptations, our central thought must be simple obedience to the commandments, and the tent or tabernacle is the childlike recognition of their importance which is necessary to us until the victory is won. When we are being tempted, we should not stop to reason with the tempter; we should simply obey the commandments because we really want to be good. You remember how the Lord, when He was in the wilderness, answered the devil each time with a simple quotation from the Scriptures.

At the end of our chapter we have the story of how Michal, Saul's daughter, was condemned to be childless because she despised David for dancing and singing before the ark as it was carried into the city. Michal had been given to David as his wife by Saul while David was still in the court of Saul. She pictures the kind of affection for the Lord which comes from our first natural, self-confident efforts to serve Him. This is not a humble and true love and cannot produce genuine "good fruit" in our lives. We shall perhaps understand this better when we study the difference in meaning between Saul, David, and Solomon.

*Basic Correspondences*

| | | |
|---|---|---|
| a tent or tabernacle | = | worship from love |
| the enemies of Israel | = | our evils and our false ideas |

---

## Senior

The lesson for this class might well be developed through a discussion of the attitude toward the ark of Uzzah, David, and Michal, pointing out at the end by way of summary the difference between Saul's son Jonathan and his daughter Michal. The place of the ark in Jerusalem will be considered further in a later lesson.

Our lesson today concerns the reign of David, the second of the three great kings of Israel. We have seen that Saul represents our first concept of divine truth when, as adults, we accept it as our ruling principle. This first concept is based largely on appearances and on confidence in our own judgment. One might think that Jonathan, who had so much more reliance on the Lord than his father had, should have been able to succeed him as king. But Jonathan, as Saul's son, represents a trust in the Lord based on external rather than internal experience. Such trust is not the kind we really need, although it can help us to maintain our faith until we are ready for a deeper and more spiritual reliance. Jonathan loved David from their first meeting, and the relation between David and Jonathan has come down through history as the outstanding example of true friendship. Jonathan saved David from the jealous rage of Saul and helped him to escape into temporary exile. But before David could come into the actual kingship, Saul and Jonathan both had to die. The kind of faith in the Lord which says, "I can see that the Lord has taken good care of me so far and I believe He will continue to do so," must give way to the kind of faith which says, "I know that whatever happens to me in this world, whether it seems good or bad, is permitted by the Lord to come to me for my spiritual welfare." Obedience to the Lord based on this kind of trust is represented by David.

The bringing of the ark to Jerusalem by David pictures the establishment of the commandments in the central place in our adult lives. The ark was never restored to its place in the original tabernacle after its capture by the Philistines. When it was sent back to the Israelites, it stopped first at Bethshemesh, and then it was taken to Kirjathjearim—called in our chapter Baale of Judah (see Joshua 15:9)—and had been kept there ever since. Kirjathjearim was a city a few miles southwest of Jerusalem. The original tabernacle at the time of our lesson had been moved to Gibeon, one of the Levitical cities, and was still there early in Solomon's reign; after that the Word gives us no further information about it.

David's first attempt to move the ark from Kirjathjearim ended disastrously, because he neglected the proper method of transporting it. The ark was supposed always to be carried on the shoulders of the Levites, which pictures the fact that we should always support the commandments with the power of religious devotion. Instead of this, David had it placed upon a cart drawn by oxen, a picture of a system of thought powered by the natural good affections. There are many practical reasons for obedience to the commandments, which may be expressed in such maxims as "Honesty is the best policy"; but they are not adequate as motives. In the story the oxen shook the cart. Our natural affections often prompt us to question the validity of the commandments and to reason about them in a natural and worldly way. We try to find some natural reason—not divine authority—why they should in general not be discarded. This is Uzzah putting forth his hand to steady the ark. Such attempts are often well meant. They are natural; but what is natural is not always right, as we ought to know. Uzzah had every reason to know that the ark did not need steadying by him, but he did not really reverence it or believe in its inherent divine power. He considered his own strength greater than that of the ark. This was the sin for which he died, for reliance on self and the world is what leads to spiritual death.

The second time David moved the ark, he was careful to have it properly borne and to humble himself before it. This humility before the Lord is contrary to the inclinations of the natural man.

Saul's daughter Michal represents these natural inclinations. Saul had given her to David as his wife while David was still in Saul's court. When David fled into exile, Michal was given by Saul to another of his servants, but she came back to David after he became king. This is a picture of the way in which our natural inclinations seek the easy and outwardly successful path. But our natural inclinations are not the affections which produce spiritual fruit because they despise the spiritual virtue of humility, as Michal despised David. "Therefore Michal the daughter of Saul had no child unto the day of her death."

## Adult

The relation between Saul, Jonathan, and David is a good starting point. Then discuss the general meaning of the last journey of the ark and of Uzzah's act and its punishment. Finally, tie the lesson together with the relation between Saul, Jonathan, David, and Michal. Stress the fact that the natural never develops into the spiritual. There is a discrete degree between them.

Jonathan is in a sense the connecting link between Saul and David. His friendship for David has become the classic example in history. We all know the stories of the anointing of David by Samuel at Bethlehem, when the spirit of the Lord rested upon him, having departed from Saul, the story of David's soothing Saul by playing the harp, and of his victory over Goliath. Then follows the account of David's further victories and of Saul's growing jealousy when the people began to hail David instead of Saul as their hero, and the account of Saul's efforts to get rid of David and of Jonathan's success in saving him, of David's flight and long exile, and of his victories while in exile.

David, like Saul, represents the Lord's truth ruling, but it is the truth understood in a new and deeper way, an understanding based on internal instead of on external considerations. We recall that when Samuel first found Saul, Saul was looking for his father's lost asses; but David, when he was called, was tending his father's sheep. The ass represents the affection for natural reasoning, the sheep the affection for innocence.

But David did not immediately supplant Saul, even after he had been anointed and the spirit of the Lord had passed from Saul to him. Long after we recognize the necessity of a deeper understanding of truth, the old natural habits of thought and feeling persist. Even after Saul was dead, his descendants still disputed the kingdom with David, and for a time the kingdom was actually divided. The division was essentially the same as the later division after the death of Solomon, the southern portion of the land accepting David as king—with Hebron as his capital—and the northern portion, together with the cross-Jordan country, adhering to Ishbosheth, a son of Saul. In this division, as later, the southern portion represents the inner affectional life, the northern portion the intellectual or thought realm, and the cross-Jordan country the external life. The meaning of this for us as individuals is not hard to see. David is anointed king when we realize that our first external understanding of the truth is not adequate to protect us against the attacks of evil and falsity, and that a deeper and more spiritual understanding is necessary. Saul dies and David becomes king in Hebron when, by trial and experience, our hearts have confirmed our allegiance to the new principle. But David does not become king over the whole land until we have rid ourselves of the habits of thought and conduct which sprang from our early superficial understanding.

After Jerusalem was taken, David determined to bring the ark there. In AE 700 we are told that the three last stages of the journey of the ark picture "the progress of the church with man from its ultimate to its inmost; and this because such progressions are effected by means of Divine truth, which was signified by the ark; for the man of the church progresses from the natural to the spiritual, and through that to the celestial, and this continually from the Lord by means of His Divine truth; the natural is the good of life, the spiritual is the good of charity towards the neighbor, and the celestial is the good of love to the Lord."

The death of Uzzah is a striking incident. People often feel that Uzzah's deed was a perfectly natural impulse and well-meant, and did not deserve the punishment it received. It can be pointed out, even as to the literal sense of the story, that Uzzah the son of Abinadab, in whose house the ark had been kept for many years, must have been perfectly familiar with the laws concerning the handling of the ark and with the consequences which had in the past overtaken those who broke these laws. No impulse could have been strong enough to induce him to break the law if his reverence for the ark and belief in its power had been deep and sincere. His act was the expression of an inherent confidence in himself and distrust of the Lord's power for which he was really punished. Our impulses spring from habits of thought and feeling, and our habits are formed by our own choice and consent.

But there is a deeper lesson to be learned from the story of Uzzah. The ark represents divine truth. We have this truth in the Word, and we have ample evidence of its power in the history of the church and in the lives of individuals. There is not one of us who does not know that we should reverence the Word, should approach it only with the desire to learn how to live rightly, and should trust its power to accomplish its purpose. Yet how easily, when we are bent upon having our own way in some matter, when our good affections falter, as the oxen stumbled, we fall victims to the temptation to think that we know better than the Lord, to rely upon our own power and intelligence to think that we are doing the Word service by seeking natural explanations for the strange and wonderful occurrences recorded in its letter and trying to discover in the ideas and customs of the Hebrew people something on which they may rest. The attempt to steady the ark of the Lord, to substitute our own power for the Lord's power, our own intelligence for the guidance of the Lord's truth, leads to spiritual death. For spiritual life can be received only as we look to the Lord and trust in Him. When we think of the Word as merely a human book and try to find meaning in it on that basis, rejecting what cannot be naturally explained, we commit the sin of Uzzah. When we think of the Lord's teachings as in any way limited by His "times," we commit the sin of Uzzah. When we give more weight to the judgment of our contemporaries than to the Word of the Lord, we commit the sin of Uzzah. And there we also die "by the ark of God."

Jerusalem represents the Lord's spiritual kingdom, and Mount Zion in Jerusalem represents the inmost of the church. It was upon Mount Zion that David placed the ark in a tabernacle which he had erected for it. David's finally taking the stronghold of Zion from the hands of the Jebusites pictures the final overthrow of the idolatries which hold possession of the inmost heart. This can be accomplished only through a spiritual understanding of truth. The placing of the ark on Mount Zion represents the final uncompromising establishment of the commandments as the only laws to be tolerated in the heart. When this is done, David's kingdom is fully established and he can go out from Jerusalem to the conquest of the Philistines, the Moabites, and the Ammonites.

The incident recorded at the end of our chapter has also its important lesson for us. Saul's daughter Michal had been given to David by Saul at the time when David was living in Saul's court. If we read the story in I Samuel 18, we find that Saul hoped that David would be killed in trying to provide the dowry he demanded for Michal. After David went into exile, Saul gave Michal to another husband. While David was reigning in Hebron, he demanded the return of Michal, and Ishbosheth took her from her husband and sent her back to David (II Samuel 3:13-16). Michal represents the natural affections which develop out of our first self-confident interpretations of the Lord's truth. They like to follow the easy path, attaching themselves to whatever opinion seems popular from time to time. It is significant that although Jonathan, the good element in the development from our first understanding, died with his father, Michal lives on and is still attractive to David. It is harder to overcome natural inclinations than natural reasonings. Michal's true character as the veritable daughter of Saul appears when she despises David and taunts him for his humility before the ark. Jonathan, although he had to die, served a good purpose. But no good ever comes of Michal: "Therefore Michal the daughter of Saul had no child unto the day of her death."

## From the Writings of Swedenborg

*Apocalypse Explained*, n. 700[28]: "Their playing and sounding all kinds of musical instruments, and David's dancing when the ark was brought up, represented the gladness and joy that result from the affection of truth and good from the Lord through the influx of Divine truth, which was signified by the 'ark'; the instruments mentioned, on which they played in the first journey from the house of Abinadab to the house of Obed-edom, represented gladness of mind from a natural and spiritual affection of truth; and the dancing of David, also the shouting and sound of the trumpet represented joy of heart from the affection of spiritual and celestial good. Harmonies of musical sound are from the spiritual world, and signify the affections with their gladnesses and joys."

## Suggested Questions on the Lesson

P. Who was the second king of Israel? *David*
P. Who anointed him? *Samuel*
J. Did he become king as soon as he was anointed? *no*
J. Who became his great friend? *Jonathan*
J. What made Saul jealous of David? *"Saul has killed his thousands, David his ten thousands!"*
P. Who saved David when Saul tried to kill him? *Jonathan*
J. How did Saul and Jonathan die? *in battle with Philistines*
J. What great city did David take and make his capital? *Jerusalem*
P. What did he want to bring there? *ark*
I. Where was the ark at this time? *Kirjathjearim*
P. What happened to Uzzah and why? *struck dead for steadying ark*
J. Who laughed at David for singing and dancing before the ark? *Michal*
J. What was her punishment? *to remain childless*
J. Where did David put the ark in Jerusalem? *Mount Zion*
I. What does the ark represent? *commandments loved and obeyed*
S. What is pictured by bringing the ark to Jerusalem? *putting divine law in center of life*
S. What is pictured by Uzzah's act? *doubting power of God's truth*

## DAVID AND NATHAN THE PROPHET

*II Samuel 12:1-25*

Introduce the lesson by reminding the classes that Saul's disobedience in the case of the Amalekites led to Samuel's saying that the kingdom "was departed" from him. The immediate anointing of David resulted. Then review David's life while Saul continued on the throne, and finally speak of the difference between the two men and of David's achievements as king, before taking up the incident of our lesson.

---

### Doctrinal Points

*The Lord permits sorrow to come to us only for our good.*
*The written Word of God is all parable.*
*Truth is given us in order that we may judge our own states rather than those of others.*
*We never become so good that we are no longer in danger of falling into evil.*

---

### Notes for Parents

The second king of Israel was David. Immediately after the first disobedience of Saul (I Samuel 13), the Lord sent Samuel to Bethlehem to anoint David. At that time David was only a boy keeping his father's sheep, and it was a long time before he became king in the sight of the people. We all know many stories of his early years.

After Saul's death only the people of the southern part of the Holy Land at first accepted David as king. He reigned seven years in Hebron before he was recognized by all the people. Then he captured Jerusalem, made it his capital, and brought the ark there. From that center he carried on a completely successful campaign against all the enemies of Israel and extended its borders farther than they had ever been extended before.

David is sometimes held up to children as a great hero—one to be imitated. The Israelites so considered him. But we should never take this attitude toward the men and women in the Bible story. There is only one example which we ought to place before our children, and that is the Lord Jesus Christ.

Our story for today shows us that David, in spite of all the fine things that he accomplished, was only an imperfect man and liable, as we all are, to yield to temptation. He broke both the commandment against adultery and that against murder, feeling that his high office would save him from punishment. Samuel was now dead, and the Lord spoke to David through another prophet, Nathan. We remember that the Lord speaks to us through the Word. The Word is our prophet. And our chapter shows us just how the Lord through the Word comes to us when we have sinned. Nathan told David a simple parable, and when David—not thinking that what Nathan was telling him had anything to do with what he himself had done—condemned the man in the parable, Nathan said, "Thou art the man." As we read the Word, we can see clearly the faults and the sins of the men and women whose lives are portrayed there. Then, if we have sinned in the same way, there comes to us suddenly the conviction: "Thou art the man."

If we acknowledge our sin and repent, as David did, we can learn by the experience and still produce good, but we do not escape the consequences of our sin. David's first son by Bathsheba died. Evil cannot produce good. We cannot break any one of the commandments without suffering for it. They are just as binding today as when they were given by the Lord from Sinai.

---

### Primary

These children should remember David's birthplace and the story of David and Goliath. They are old enough to understand why Nathan approached David with a parable. Tell them what David's punishment was, and that it teaches us that good never can come from evil.

The second king of the Israelites was David.
His home was in Bethlehem.

What do we think of when Bethlehem is mentioned?

David was only a young boy when he was anointed, and Saul continued to be king in the eyes of the people.

But the spirit of the Lord was with David now instead of with Saul.

But finally Saul was killed in battle, and later David was crowned king. Like Saul, David was a great warrior, but David did not trust in himself as Saul had done. He obeyed the Lord, and so the Lord could be with him and give him victory over all the enemies of Israel. One of the cities he took was Jerusalem. He made it his capital and brought the ark there and had a new tabernacle made for it.

But later in life he committed a great sin.

He had Uriah the Hittite killed so that he could marry Uriah's wife, Bathsheba.

Whom did the Lord send to rebuke him?

What story did Nathan tell David?

How did David judge the man in the story?

Then what did Nathan tell him?

How did David receive this statement?

Why do you think Nathan told him the story first?

What was David's punishment?

---

## Junior

The Juniors should have a more detailed account of David's life and accomplishment. Draw as much as possible of this from their own memories. When the story for today is reached, the teacher will find in the Junior notes several lessons within the grasp of this age group which may be brought out.

The story of David's early life is one we have all read. Let us see how much you remember of it.

Where was David born?

What was he doing when he was anointed?

What talent did he have which brought him to Saul's attention?

What enemy did he overcome single-handed?

What weapon did he use?

Who was his special friend in Saul's court?

Why did he finally have to flee from Saul?

David's first capital was Hebron, where he reigned for seven years over the people of the southern part of the land. Hebron had been Abraham's home and at the time of the division of the land it was given to Caleb. After Ishbosheth's death, the people of the northern part of the land came under David's rule also. He conquered Jerusalem—which the Jews had never before been able to take from the Jebusites who possessed it—and made it his capital. You remember how he brought the ark there and put it in a new tabernacle because the Lord had told him that he was not the one who should build the temple. Because David obeyed the Lord, the Lord could give him victory over all the enemies of Israel, and he extended the borders of the land farther than they had ever extended before.

People sometimes think that the men in the Bible story whom God prospered must have been altogether good. They think of them as heroes to be imitated. Those who think this have a hard time explaining our story for today, for David had done a very wrong thing. He had seen a beautiful woman named Bathsheba and wanted to marry her, and when he found she was already married, he had her husband placed in the front line of a battle so that he would be killed. Then he married Bathsheba. He knew he was a great king and perhaps he really imagined he could do no wrong. But no one ever reaches that point.

Nathan the prophet was sent to David by the Lord. Nathan did not immediately charge David with his sin. When someone finds fault with us, our first impulse and effort is to defend ourselves, isn't it? Instead Nathan told David a simple little story apparently about other people. David could see clearly the wrong which the rich man in Nathan's story had done, and he judged him very severely. Then Nathan said, "Thou art the man." And David could see that he really had done the very same thing, and he could not help acknowledging his sin.

What was David's punishment?
How did David take the sickness of his child?
How did he surprise his household when the child died?
What reason did he give?

Who was the second son of David and Bathsheba?

There are many lessons in this story. One important one is that we should look at our own conduct squarely and be willing to judge it honestly. We must be willing to let the Lord through his Word say to us, "Thou art the man." Another lesson is that there is no escaping the consequences of wrongdoing. We may think we have "got away with it," but every wrong we do actually destroys something good in us which might have grown up, like David's child, to give us greater happiness. The Lord has to permit such losses, or we should never try to improve.

And there is another lesson. What is done cannot be undone, but if we acknowledge our sin, as David did, and accept the justice of the consequences, we can use the experience to help us to become stronger and more useful. This is why David and Bathsheba were allowed to become the parents of Solomon, the greatest of the three kings.

The people in the Bible story were men and women just like us, with many faults as well as virtues. The Lord wants us to learn from them both what to do and what not to do. The whole of the Word is a parable which the Lord has told us through His prophets, just as surely as he sent Nathan with his parable to David. We are meant to read the Word and think about it and judge ourselves by it, so that we can see and acknowledge our faults and try to do better from day to day.

---

## Intermediate

The lesson of the story for today is an important one, and as it can be drawn directly from the letter, we have done nothing this time with particular correspondences except for the general difference between Saul and David.

David was humble and obedient and trusted the Lord. He pictures the rule of divine truth as it is understood from a spiritual perception instead of in a natural way. We have had the stories of David's playing his harp or lyre to sooth Saul, of his early fight with Goliath, and of his friendship with Saul's son Jonathan, who saved him from his father's jealous rage and helped him to escape. For Saul continued to be king as long as he lived. As soon as David was anointed, however, "the Spirit of the Lord departed from Saul and an evil spirit from the Lord troubled him." This was why David, even in exile, increased in favor with the people. When Saul and Jonathan were finally killed in a defeat at the hands of the Philistines, another son of Saul, Ishbosheth, was crowned king by Abner, the captain of Saul's army, but David was made king in Hebron by all the people of the southern part of the land. This is the first time the division of the land into north and south appears in the Bible story. David reigned seven years in Hebron and then Ishbosheth was assassinated by two of his own captains, and the northern part of the country also accepted David as king.

David, like Saul, was a fighting king, and because he obeyed the Lord he was not defeated as Saul had been. He extended the boundaries of the land, subdued all its enemies, and took Jerusalem, which was one of the cities that had stood out against the Israelites up to that time. David made Jerusalem his capital and brought the ark there, putting up a new tabernacle for it, because the Lord told him that he was not to be the one to build the temple.

David always obeyed the commands of the Lord when they came to him personally through a prophet. But as time went on and successes continued to come to him, he forgot that the fundamental laws of God are the ten commandments. The background of our story for today is found in chapter 11. David saw a beautiful woman named Bathsheba and wanted her for his wife, although he already had several wives. With the Israelites of that day it was not considered unlawful for a man to have more than one wife. But Bathsheba was the wife of Uriah the Hittite. David first broke the commandment against adultery and then attempted to conceal his sin by having Uriah sent into the front line of the battle, where he was killed.

The story of David's sin and its punishment should show us plainly that the persons in the Bible story are not meant to be examples to us in the sense that their conduct is always to be copied. They were weak and often evil men, and the Lord uses their lives to show us what not to do as well as what to do. When the Word describes David as a man after the Lord's own heart, it is not the man that is meant but the faculty which he represents in the spiritual sense; and this faculty—even after it has gained dominion in our lives—must constantly be kept subject to the judgment of the commandments or it will go astray, as David did when he considered himself great enough to be above the commandments.

If Nathan had gone to David and charged him directly with his sin, David's first thought would have been to defend and excuse his conduct. We know that this is always our natural reaction to a direct rebuke. But when the case was presented to him as a story about other people, his mind was free to pronounce righteous judgment.

This is just the way in which the Lord calls our attention to our sins—through his prophets in parable. We read the stories and teachings of the Word first in an impersonal way. We form our judgments of them unhampered by thoughts of self. Then, when our judgment is formed, the Lord says to us through our conscience, "Thou art the man." The deep lessons of the Word lie concealed in the simple and seemingly commonplace stories of the letter. These stories lie in our minds until the moment comes when we need the lesson. Then they are suddenly quickened to life and present application.

David had become so great that he thought himself above the commandments. We are all subject to this same weakness. Most of us lead outwardly correct lives, gain the respect of our neighbors, and come to consider ourselves established as good Christians. Then some strong desire of ours meets an obstacle. In order to satisfy it we must do something which is technically forbidden by the commandments. Unconsciously we argue, "I am a good person. I would not have a desire which was really wrong. This thing I want would further the good work which I can do in the world. Therefore it cannot be wrong for me to remove the obstacle. The end justifies the means."

But Nathan's simple parable brought David down to the valley of humiliation. Read the fifty-first Psalm as an expression of this state. The heading of the Psalm reads, "To the chief musician, a Psalm of David, when Nathan the prophet came unto him, after he had gone in to Bathsheba." It is a Psalm which we all need to repeat frequently as a reminder of our weakness and need of direction.

*Basic Correspondences*

David = the rule of divine truth as seen by our spiritual reason

---

## Senior

Several lessons should be drawn from this chapter for the Seniors: the nature of the Word and why it is written in parable form, the necessity of obedience to the commandments however sure we may feel of ourselves, the general meaning of marriage and of its perversions, the fact that sin always brings punishment, and the good use we may make of such experiences, provided we repent. It is the repentance which brings the good.

We are all well acquainted with the general story of David, the second great king of Israel. He represents a deeper and more spiritual understanding of divine truth than Saul. Such an understanding does not develop overnight. David was anointed by Samuel immediately after Saul's act of disobedience, and at that time the spirit of the Lord departed from Saul and was with David instead. But Saul continued to be king in the eyes of the people, and after Saul's death his son Ishbosheth was crowned and ruled for seven years over the people of the northern part of the land. David had also been crowned and was ruling in Hebron. This pictures a time in our lives when we have realized that our first natural understanding of the Lord's Word and what it requires of us is not adequate—that we need to look into divine truth more deeply and in a humbler spirit; but still our immediate impulse is to judge by appearances. We get rid of any habit only gradually.

When David finally came into full control, he subdued all the enemies of Israel, captured Jerusalem and brought the ark there, and extended the borders of Israel farther than they had ever been extended before. The spiritual understanding of divine truth, once firmly established in our minds, removes many temptations which have formerly troubled us and gives us a firmness of purpose and a breadth of view of which we have not dreamed before.

Then comes our story of David's sin. We are tempted to forget that even our established character is not a guarantee of salvation, that the commandments can never be broken with impunity no matter how important we are or how far our regeneration has progressed. David saw and desired Bathsheba, the wife of Uriah the Hittite, and not only committed adultery with her but afterward tried to conceal his sin by using his royal power to send Uriah to a battle station where he would certainly be killed.

It would be hard to find a story in the Word which illustrates the general principles of the New Church doctrine of the Sacred Scriptures more clearly than this of David's sin and its results. David here is obviously a sinner; yet he is the Lord's anointed, to whom it was promised that his line should never fail. We see then that it is not the man that is laudable but the thing he is chosen to represent. We see that men, just as they were, could be chosen by the Lord as his instruments in the giving of the Word. And in Nathan's parable and its effect we have a clear example in the letter of the manner in which the Word speaks to us and the reason why it is given in parables.

David, as we have seen, represents in our individual lives the rule of the principle of divine truth; but our understanding of this truth, even when it has risen above mere appearances and become spiritual, is still imperfect, just as David was, and prone to be obscured by our own selfishness and prejedices. It is easily led astray by a desire for anything which appears beautiful but is not rightfully yours, and we all tend to justify ourselves in taking the means necessary to get what we feel we should have. The marriage relation represents inmostly the union of divine love and divine wisdom in the Lord, and all perversions of this relation represent attempts to join evil to truth, or good to falsity. When we try to justify ourselves in doing wrong to satisfy some selfish desire, we commit spiritual adultery.

The Word, pictured by Nathan the prophet, by presenting our problems to us in an objective form, clears our vision and enables us to distinguish impartially between right and wrong. It is easy to judge the conduct of the people in the Bible story, and then all we need is to turn the same judgment upon ourselves—to hear the voice of Nathan saying, "Thou art the man."

David repented and was forgiven, but he did not escape the consequences of his sin. The death of Bathsheba's first son pictures the fact that nothing spiritually living can be produced as a direct result of wrongdoing. But her second son, Solomon, conceived after David's repentance, became the greatest of Israel's kings. This pictures the fact that genuine repentance and humility may lead to greatness.

This is a distinction we need to keep constantly in mind. We often hear it argued that good comes out of evil, that certain necessary virtues are developed by war, that a young man is better for having "sowed his wild oats." This is not true. Evil always results in a loss, no matter what course may be followed afterward. But our freedom provides that after this loss, if we choose to accept it as a lesson, repent, and change our ways, we may still go on to great things. We cannot go back and undo the wrongs we have committed—although we can sometimes reduce their consequences to others—but we can start afresh with the bitter experience as a warning. We cannot be what we might have been, but we can be something else which is good.

---

## Adult

Again and again, as in this story of Nathan's parable, the lesson is brought home to us that as long as we are in this world we are liable to temptation and liable to yield to it. There are plenty of discussion topics here, but try to make this general lesson the outstanding one. It may be pointed up by reading to the class Ezekiel 18:20-24.

David, the second king of Israel, represents the rule of divine truth spiritually understood. This understanding of the truth is first recognized by us as a result of our realization of the inadequacy of our natural understanding of it—represented by Saul—but it is a long time before it comes into full control in our life. We all know the stories of David's early life—his being called from tending his father's sheep at Bethlehem to be anointed by Samuel, his being called to Saul's court because of his skill in playing the lyre, his victory over Goliath, and his friendship with Saul's son Jonathan, who helped him to escape when Saul's jealousy would have killed him. We can see these incidents as picturing the first relations between the spiritual and the natural understanding of divine truth in our minds. We have a similar picture in the story of the relations of Joseph with Potiphar and Potiphar's wife (Genesis 39), and the period when David was in exile may be compared with the time when Joseph was in prison, the David stories of course representing the cycle at a later period in our life than the Joseph stories.

Even after Saul's death, David did not immediately come to the throne, for Abner, the captain of Saul's host, crowned Saul's son Ishbosheth. David was at the same time crowned in Hebron by the people of the southern part of the land, and reigned there for seven years. At the end of this time Ishbosheth was assassinated by two of his own captains and the northern tribes also accepted David. This temporary division of the land foreshadowed the final division which took place after Solomon's death. The southern part of the land represents the heart or will and the northern part the mind or understanding. Hebron had been Abraham's home. David's ruling there first pictures the fact that the heart—and especially the innocent states stored up in us as remains from our earliest infancy—accepts the rule of spiritual truth before the mind fully yields to its control. It was not until David had been anointed king by the northern tribes that he captured Jerusalem, which up to that time had been firmly held by the Jebusites. He made it his capital and brought the ark there, and from that center went on to full conquest of the enemies of Israel, extending the borders of the

Holy Land farther than they had ever extended before.

As we read the long story of David, we cannot help being struck by the sudden change which takes place in his fortunes beginning with II Samuel 11, when he first sees Bathsheba, covets and takes her, and arranges to have her husband Uriah killed in battle. From that time on, although David continues as king and actually retains all the territory he has conquered, he is plagued by internal troubles, beginning with the conspiracy of his son Absalom and ending with that of his son Adonijah. In our chapter for today, Nathan the prophet foretells this: "Thus saith the Lord, Behold, I will raise up evil against thee out of thine own house."

The turning point in David's life and career came at the moment when he, too, at last became confident in his own might and careless of the commandments. David knew the commandments and knew that his rise to power had been won for him by the Lord and not by his own strength or wisdom. Yet when he wanted Bathsheba, he did not hesitate to break the commandments to get her and even used his authority as king to establish his possession. The crimes of adultery and murder are in themselves deadly to spiritual life. Pure marriage love is the love from which all heavenly loves flow, and its opposite closes heaven; and we have seen in an earlier lesson that innocence is essential to heavenly states. Adultery and murder are characteristic of the hells (Matthew 5:21-28). David's yielding to the temptation to commit these two crimes shows us how even the spiritual understanding of the Lord's truth may be misused and led to justify our evil desires, if we allow ourselves to think that we have reached a state in which the commandments may be transgressed with impunity. It is possible for us at any time, no matter how far we have progressed in regeneration, to fall into hell if we cease to test our lives by the commandments. Indeed, the further we have progressed the deeper the hell into which we may fall, if we use the Lord's gifts for selfish purposes and turn the power which he has put in our hands to the injury of others (Ezekiel 18:24). One of the trends of modern thought is in the direction of the relegation of the commandments to the realm of outworn statutes. This is particularly evident in connection with the problem of marriage. Children should be taught from the very beginning by example as well as by precept that the marriage relation is beautiful and sacred and that anything which lessens our regard for it or makes us less fit to receive and enjoy its blessings should be avoided as a deadly plague. To know the beautiful teachings concerning marriage revealed through Swedenborg and then to yield to the temptation to treat the marriage vows lightly or to enter into other relations is like the sin of David.

If Nathan had come to David and charged him outright with his sin, David's immediate impulse would have been to justify himself in one way or another and perhaps to get rid of Nathan. But Nathan put the matter before David's own judgment in an impersonal way which left David's judgment free to see the simple right and wrong involved. There was nothing in the parable to touch David's self-love and so blind his judgment. And his judgment was immediate and clear. Then, when Nathan said, "Thou art the man," David realized that he had freely judged himself, and that whatever punishment came to him was just. This is exactly the way in which the Lord points out to us our evils by means of the Word. The Word presents to us in parable form every possible spiritual situation into which we may come, leaving us free to judge the right and wrong involved and to see the inevitable results of evil. Then, if we are listening to the prophet's voice, it says to us in each of our weaknesses and sins, "Thou art the man." If we store our memories with the letter of the Word and try to see its application to our lives, we are prepared to face our problems objectively and to judge justly.

The child of David's unlawful union with Bathsheba died. No living spiritual principle can come from the attempt to evade our obligation to obey the letter of the commandments, even in the interest of something which appeals to us as beautiful and which, if properly acquired, is innocent and good. Good does not come out of evil. But David repented. His fasting before the child died pictures our natural hope that the consequences of our sin may be avoided. But once they have fallen and been accepted, we are shown that, like David, we must rise and begin anew, and that if we do, we may still use the bitter experience rightly and develop new strength.

---

## From the Writings of Swedenborg

*Arcana Coelestia*, nn. 10801-10803: "The royalty itself is not in the person, but is adjoined to the person . . . The royalty consists in administering according to the laws of the kingdom, and in judging from justice according to these laws. The king who regards the laws as above him, consequently himself as below the laws, is wise; but he who regards himself as above the laws, consequently the laws as beneath him, is not wise. . . . he who regards the laws as beneath him, and thus himself as above them, makes the royalty to consist in himself, and either believes himself to be the law, or the law which is justice to be from himself; consequently he arrogates to himself that which is Divine, and under which he must be."

---

## Suggested Questions on the Lesson

P. Who was the second king of Israel? *David*
P. Where was his home? *Bethlehem*
P. What was his first occupation? *shepherd*
P. Who anointed him? *Samuel*
J. How did he come to Saul's attention? *played lyre*
J. How did he conquer Goliath? *sling and stone*
J. Where did David first reign? *Hebron*
J. How long did he reign there? *seven years*
P. After he became king over all the land, what city did he take as his capital? *Jerusalem*
P. What precious thing did he bring there? *ark*
J. What did he accomplish for Israel? *conquered all enemies*
J. What sin did he commit? *took Bathsheba*
P. Who was sent by the Lord to rebuke him? *Nathan*
P. What parable did Nathan tell David? *rich man, poor man, one ewe lamb*
P. How did David judge the man in the parable? *should die*
P. Then what did Nathan tell him? *"Thou art the man"*
J. How did David take Nathan's condemnation? *repented (see Psalm 51)*
I. Why did Nathan tell him the parable first? *to get unbiased judgment (also fear of his own life)*

S. What is the difference in correspondence between (1) Saul, and (2) David?
*(1) worldly idea of truth*
*(2) spiritual idea of truth*

## THE WISDOM OF SOLOMON

*I Kings 3*

The things that should especially be remembered about David are that before Samuel anointed him he was a shepherd of Bethlehem, that he was a musician and also a great warrior, and that the book of Psalms was in part written through him.

---

### Doctrinal Points

*We have peace only when we love to do right.*

---

### Notes for Parents

When anyone says that someone is "a regular Solomon," we know that he means that the person is unusually wise. Our story today tells us how Solomon came to be so wise. He was a son of David, but not one of his older sons. In fact he was a young man—perhaps not more than twenty—when he came to the throne, and in our chapter he himself says to the Lord, "I am but a little child: I know not how to go out or come in." But we are also told that "Solomon loved the Lord." And when the Lord appeared to him in a dream and said, "Ask what I shall give thee," Solomon did not ask for riches or power or long life, but for an understanding heart, that he might "discern between good and bad" and judge his people wisely. In other words, Solomon's wisdom was grounded in humility, love to the Lord, and the desire to do right in the Lord's sight. We read in Psalm 111:10, "The fear of the Lord is the beginning of wisdom: a good understanding have all they that do his commandments." No one can be wise who imagines that he knows enough to do right without constantly looking to the Lord for guidance and strength.

And trusting in the Lord and obeying His commandments is the only road to peace. The name *Solomon* [*Shalom*] means "peaceful." All our conflicts and distresses come from trust in self or in others instead of in the Lord. The forty years of Solomon's reign were years of peace. The fame of his wisdom spread, and kings and queens came to him for instruction and advice. In accordance with the Lord's promise he also acquired great riches. Chapter 10 especially tells of the glory of his kingdom.

But the crowning work of Solomon's reign was the building of the temple at Jerusalem. David had wanted to build it, but had been told that he must not because he was "a man of war." The temple of the Lord is a picture of a character built according to the Lord's commandments. It is the crowning work of every good life. It is really the work of the Lord in us as we put away our selfish thoughts and desires and make way in our souls for His unselfish love to flow in. Battles with temptation must first be fought—this is pictured by the reign of David—but as the battles are won, peace and happiness follow.

Why did not the glory of Solomon's kingdom continue? The answer to this question forms the background for a later lesson.

---

## Primary

The story of Solomon's dream is a simple one. The children should learn what he asked for and what the Lord promised him. Tell them that to have a wise and understanding heart means to be able to know what the Lord wants us to do and to love to do it, and point out that when we really love someone, we will try to behave in such a way as to make that person happy. This is also an opportunity to review the names of the great leaders of Israel and see what the children remember about each.

What special talents did David have?
What book in the Bible is called "the book of David"?

David was a great warrior and conquered all the enemies of Israel. When the time came for him to die, the Lord sent Nathan the prophet to him and told him that his son Solomon—one of his younger sons—was to be king after him. So David, even before he died, had the priests anoint Solomon to be king. One of Solomon's older brothers tried to set himself up as king, but the people accepted Solomon.

The name *Solomon* means "peaceful."
What did Solomon ask of the Lord?
What did the Lord promise him?

The Lord kept his promise to Solomon, as He always keeps His promises. Solomon became so wise that kings and queens came to ask his advice. And he also became very rich and owned all sorts of beautiful things.

Solomon had peace throughout his reign.
Several chapters in I Kings tell about his wisdom and glory and possessions.
His greatest work was the building of the temple at Jerusalem.
Solomon and David each reigned forty years.

---

## Junior

The Juniors need the lesson of Solomon's request very much, for they are nearing the age when judgment is likely to be hard rather than wise and loving. Suggest that they learn and use the lines from the last verse of the League Hymn: "Give us to think as angels think, and feel as angels feel." Go over with them the story in verses 16 to 28 of our chapter, and help them to see that it took an understanding heart to find the truth in the case of the two women. Also have them read the suggested passage in II Chronicles. This is a good opportunity to show them the usefulness of the books of Chronicles and to tell them also that, like the book of Ruth, they do not have an inner sense.

What book of the Bible is sometimes called "the book of David"?

David did not have a peaceful reign, but he was successful against his enemies and brought the kingdom of Israel to its greatest extent and power. He captured Jerusalem and set up his capital there on Mount Zion, one of the two principal hills in the city, and he brought the ark there and put it in a new tabernacle.

The Lord had told David through Nathan the prophet that Solomon, one of his younger sons, was to be his successor. So David, near the end of his life, had Solomon anointed as the next king, and the people accepted him willingly.

The name *Solomon* means "peaceful." Solomon had peace

throughout his reign, which like David's lasted forty years.

Where did Solomon go early in his reign to make offerings to the Lord?

The old tabernacle which was built at Sinai and which, when we heard of it last, was set up at Shiloh, was now at Gibeon, with all its furnishings except the ark. Read II Chronicles 1:1-6, which gives us some interesting facts. The two books of Chronicles, like the book of Ruth, do not have an inner sense. But since they are part of the ancient Hebrew records, they contain some of the same stories in slightly different form, and we learn from them additional details which the Lord did not choose to make part of the Word.

What did Solomon in his dream ask of the Lord?
What did the Lord promise him?

This request and its fulfillment were the cause of Solomon's greatness. The story of the two mothers in the last part of our chapter gives us an example of the kind of wisdom which comes of an "understanding heart." We are not really wise until we have come to love to do right, and also to understand and sympathize with the good desires of other people.

The Lord had promised David that Solomon should build the temple. David himself had wanted to build it, but the Lord told him he could not because he was a man of war. The building of the temple is a picture of the building of our characters by the Lord as we come into the love of obeying Him. David's battles, like all the battles in the Word, picture our times of temptation, and it is only after we have won the victory over temptation that we really love to obey the Lord.

The temple that Solomon built was not the one of which we read in the Gospels, but it was built on the same site, Mount Moriah, the second hill in Jerusalem. Mount Moriah is thought to be the place where Abraham went intending to sacrifice Isaac. Mount Zion, where David's tabernacle was set up, was a fortified citadel.

The Lord fulfilled His promise to Solomon. Several chapters of I Kings tell of Solomon's riches and beautiful belongings, and of his glory. Kings and queens came from afar to see him and ask him questions.

### Intermediate

Review the three kings and their meaning. Point out that the David state supplants the Saul state altogether, while the state represented by Solomon grows naturally out of that represented by David—Solomon was David's son. Touch on the fact that it was Solomon and not David who built the temple.

David was a warrior king. Under him all the enemies of Israel were overcome. And he was allowed to conquer Jerusalem and to establish the ark there in a new tabernacle which he set up on Mount Zion. He wanted to build a temple for the ark, but he was forbidden to do so because he was "a man of war." The temple is a picture of heavenly character. We have to fight against temptations, but the state of struggle is not the ideal state and is only a preparation for the building of character. The temple of character is built in us by the Lord as we clear the way for His entrance into our hearts.

When Solomon, the son of David, succeeded his father on the throne of Israel, one of his first acts was to offer sacrifices to the Lord at Gibeon. Here the old tabernacle with its furnishings had finally been set up (see II Chronicles 1:1-6). Although the ark was no longer in it, the people still regarded the old tabernacle as their principal place of worship and all the regular ceremonies were maintained there, as they had been at Shiloh in the time of Samuel. In going there Solomon was dedicating himself as best he could to the service of the Lord, and it was there that he had his well-known dream in which the Lord said to him, "Ask what I shall give thee." Solomon made the wise choice of "an understanding heart" as the most desirable of all gifts which the Lord might grant him. The Hebrew word here translated "understanding" actually means "hearing." The ear and hearing correspond to obedience.

An understanding heart—or an obedient heart—is the symbol of true wisdom, the ability to distinguish between right and wrong, which comes from a genuine desire to do right in the Lord's sight. Swedenborg tells us many times that we can be enlightened by the Lord only when we study the Word from a desire to learn what is true and *do* it. Solomon's wisdom became famous and kings and queens, like the queen of Sheba, sought his counsel.

Solomon did build the temple. His name means "peaceful." We have peace only when we love to do right, and the Lord builds a heavenly character in us in proportion as we come into this love. Read I Kings 6:7. The temple is the dwelling place of the Lord in our hearts. This is built silently by the Lord from the materials which we have prepared. Every time we make ourselves remember one of the Lord's commandments and obey it, we are fashioning a "stone" or a "timber" which the Lord can use in our temple. The temple was seven years in building. We remember the six days of creation and then the sabbath of rest. The whole of our life is needed to complete our temple.

Saul pictures our attempts to do right in our own strength and from our own ideas of what must be right. The kingdom of heaven can never be established in us on this basis. David pictures our attempts to do right according to the truth we find in the Word, trusting in the Lord for guidance and strength. In this way we can recognize and conquer our inner evils and establish the Lord's rule in our minds as well as in our outward lives. But Solomon pictures the final state of regeneration when we do the Lord's will from the love of doing it. Then there is peace. All the riches and beautiful possessions of Solomon, which are described in several chapters of I Kings, represent the beautiful things which we have in our souls when Solomon is on the throne.

The wisdom which comes of an understanding heart is illustrated in the story of Solomon's dealing with the two mothers in the last part of our chapter. Even in the letter we can see that Solomon was given to understand the feeling that would be in the heart of the true mother, who would sacrifice her own claim to the child rather than have it destroyed. But there is a deeper meaning in the story. A son always pictures truth. The pretended mother pictures those who do not really care for the truth, but want to seem to possess it. The true mother represents those who really love the truth and are willing to acknowledge that it is not their own in order to keep it alive. An understanding heart in its inner meaning is the acknowledgment that all truth and goodness are the Lord's and not our own.

*Basic Correspondences*

| | | |
|---|---|---|
| the ear and hearing | = | obedience |
| the temple | = | true character in which the Lord dwells |
| Solomon | = | the rule of divine truth as seen when we have come to love to obey it |

## Senior

The Solomon state can be illustrated for the Seniors from their own experience. Let them think of temptations which they had in early childhood and felt very strongly—such as eating things on the sly—and which they have entirely overcome. In respect to such things they already have come to love to do right instead of wrong, and so are at peace. The implications of "an understanding heart" will furnish ample material for discussion.

The three kings, Saul, David, and Solomon, represent stages in our regeneration. Under Saul we keep the commandments from a sense of duty, thinking principally that they will prosper us in the world and get us to heaven. Under David we keep them from an understanding of the Lord's purpose in giving them to us and a desire to correct our inner as well as our outer life. Under Solomon we keep them because we have learned to love to keep them. Then they are written in our hearts and we are no longer in a constant state of struggle against our own selfish desires. The name *Solomon* means "peaceful." To love to do the Lord's will is peace. And what Solomon asked of the Lord was "an understanding heart."

There is a difference between knowledge, intelligence, and wisdom. One may have a great deal of knowledge, but if he cannot organize it and apply it to his life, he is not intelligent. And he is not wise until he has proved his knowledge and his intelligence by life experience.

The temple was built by Solomon. The materials, stone and wood, basic symbols of truth and goodness, were brought from outside the Holy Land, and each piece was fashioned before it was brought. Our temple is built of the truth and goodness we have made our own by applying it in our daily life. We fashion its stones and timbers by our victories in temptation, but we do not actually build the temple in this way. The stones and timbers must be brought to the Lord. Our temple is a heavenly character, and it is built in us by the Lord. It rises up silently within us–read I Kings 6:7–and at the end of seven years (that is, when the Lord sees that we have reached the full measure of the goodness we are willing to achieve), it stands forth in its final form as we pass into the spiritual world.

The oracle or Holy of Holies of the temple was entirely covered with gold leaf, a symbol of the love which should be in our hearts. When all was complete, the ark was brought into it, and then "the glory of the Lord filled the temple" and Solomon had a solemn dedication service. This is a beautiful picture of a life dedicated to the Lord's service, with the commandments at the center kept willingly from love to the Lord. Such a life is full of the glory of the Lord.

The Lord's promise to Solomon to add to him the riches and glory for which he had not asked was fully kept. The chapters telling of his marvelous possessions picture in the internal sense the spiritual riches of a truly good life. Every detail has its meaning.

We do not reach the Solomon state in its fullest sense until our life in this world is over, but we do have repeated limited experiences of it as we overcome one temptation after another. When we recognize any given evil in ourselves, fight against it with the Lord's help, conquer it, and come to love its opposite, we know something of the peace and beauty and spiritual riches which are in store for the faithful, and which are pictured by the glory of Solomon's kingdom.

The story of the two mothers in the latter part of our chapter is a vivid picture of what is meant by wisdom. We are not wise until we acknowledge from the heart that all truth is from the Lord and not the product of our own intelligence. A son always pictures truth. The two women are different kinds of affection for truth, the one genuine, the other pretended. The true mother would rather give up her own claim to the truth than have it perverted. The pretended mother would rather destroy the truth than acknowledge it to be anything but her own. At the bottom of all the false teaching in the world today concerning the Lord and the Word can be found the unwillingness to acknowledge that there is any higher authority than man's own intelligence. If you will keep this firmly in mind and analyze the reasons given you in the business and professional world and in college for disbelief in the Lord and the Word, you will be able to stand on your own feet spiritually and be saved from swallowing a great many falsities.

---

### Adult

The meaning of the three kings should be reviewed and the process of the development of wisdom clearly explained. Then discussion should center on the fact that the Lord's request of Solomon in verse 5 is addressed to each one of us also, and on the importance of our choice.

Solomon's accession to the throne of Israel pictures the coming of a new state. There are a number of important general points to note in connection with it. (1) The new king is a son of the preceding one, whereas David was of a different line from Saul. (2) Solomon is anointed by the express command of David, and almost immediately assumes full power. (3) He does not have to conquer any of his kingdom nor to defend it, but instead is freely consulted and assisted by other kings. (4) He is free to build, to adorn his land, and to amass riches.

In AE 654[29] Swedenborg says that Solomon represents "the Lord in relation to His celestial kingdom and His spiritual kingdom." That is, Solomon, whose name means "peaceful," enters into the fruits of David's reign. He does not have to undo any of David's work. We have seen that this was not true of David's accession, which was marked by difficulty and delay through conflict with Saul. The change from a natural understanding of truth to a spiritual understanding is slow and difficult. But when the spiritual understanding is established and has been exercised and strengthened by years of successful conflict with the evils which oppose our regeneration, there comes a time when we pass from conflict to peace, the celestial state in which we do right because we love to do it. David dies, in the sense that we no longer have to obey truth against our will, for we no longer will anything which is contrary to the truth. This peaceful or "celestial" state is represented by Solomon. Love to the Lord and love to the neighbor are so firmly established in our hearts that the Lord can give us a perception of the truth. This is the highest goal of the Christian life, but it is a state to which few of us attain. "To him that overcometh will I give to eat of the tree of life, which is in the midst of the paradise of God."

We may wonder why, if Solomon represents this highest state, he was permitted to marry so many wives and to worship other gods as well as Jehovah. We shall see that these very things led to the breaking up of Solomon's kingdom, and that they represent temptations which assail us even in this highest state and which must be resisted. But the stream of truth which ultimates itself in the letter of the Word, spoken and acted out so often by evil men, has always inmostly a pure meaning relating to the life of the Lord. When we think of Solomon as a representative of the Lord after His coming into the world, his many marriages and his tolerance of the worship of other gods picture the Lord's love reaching out and seeking to draw to Him the good of all religions and offering salvation to all who seek to live rightly from a religious principle whether they know His true name and character or not.

Solomon asked in his dream, "Give therefore thy servant an understanding heart to judge thy people, that I may discern between good and bad." This desire involves the very state which Solomon represents, a heart so established in what is good that it has a perception of truth. We should make a distinction between *knowledge*, *intelligence*, and *wisdom*. Knowledge is the accumulation of facts in the memory, facts about spiritual as well as about natural things. Knowledge is the necessary basis for all our thought.

For example, we must know the commandments before we can use them in our lives. Intelligence belongs to the rational faculty and is the power of arranging our knowledges and applying them to the various situations in which Providence places us. Without intelligence we cannot judge our conduct in relation to the commandments. But wisdom is of the heart as well as the mind. When we have learned the commandments and consistently applied them to our conduct, we come to *know* them by experience as the laws of life. In connection with this development, verse 1 of our chapter is particularly interesting when we remember that Pharaoh's daughter would represent the affection for memory knowledges. Read also I Kings 7:8 and 9:24. Millo was one of the ramparts of Jerusalem (cf. II Samuel 5:9).

We are wise when, through experience, the commandments are written on our hearts. For what we truly *are* proceeds out of the heart (Matthew 12:34-35). No matter how much we know or how cleverly we can reason, if we do not love goodness we are not wise, and we cannot attain this wisdom without long practice in keeping the commandments. "Whosoever heareth these sayings of mind, and doeth them, I will liken him unto a wise man . . . And everyone that heareth these sayings of mine, and doeth them not, shall be likened unto a foolish man . . ." (Matthew 7:24-26) The same lesson is strikingly taught in Psalm 14:1: "The fool hath said *in his heart*, There is no God." If we have acquired an "understanding heart," we can indeed judge the "Israelites" within ourselves and discern between good and bad. The Lord's reply to Solomon makes us think of His words in Luke 12:31: "But rather seek ye the kingdom of God; and all these things shall be added unto you."

In all languages there are fairy stories based upon the granting of wishes. All children are familiar with this idea. Usually these stories are worked out on the basis of an unwise choice and its disastrous results. There is a general truth underlying all such stories—one wonders if all could perhaps be traced to something in the Ancient Word—and as a rule they lead children to think, however superficially, of what would be a really wise wish. Actually the Lord says to each one of us in our early youth, when we are looking forward to life, "Ask what I shall give thee." And He also says to us, "Ask, and it shall be given thee; seek, and ye shall find: knock, and it shall be opened unto you." We are free to choose our own goal and to work for it, free to mold our lives to the attainment of one objective or another. But the Lord does better for us than the fairies in the story: He tells us beforehand what the wise wish is, and warns us of the disastrous results of foolish wishes. He tells us that life in this world is very brief and that we have eternity before us, and also that we must make our choice here. He tells us that if we choose to wish and struggle for the things of this world, we may indeed attain them, but when our short life here is over, we shall face eternal poverty. But if we choose to wish and to work for eternal goods, we shall have them without fail, whatever our external lot in this world may be.

And the Lord also tells us that the eternal goods may be ours now as well as in the other life. To the man who planned to build ever-larger barns and to take his ease, eat, drink, and be merry, the Lord said: "Thou fool, this night thy soul shall be required of thee: then whose shall these things be, which thou hast provided? So is he that layeth up treasure for himself, and is not rich toward God." But to His disciples He said: "There is no man that hath left house, or parents, or brethren, or wife, or children, for the kingdom of God's sake, who shall not receive manifold more in this present time, and in the world to come life everlasting." The Lord's promises do not fail. If we make Solomon's choice when the Lord first puts the question to us, and are faithful to that choice ("if thou wilt walk in my ways, to keep my statutes and my commandments"), Solomon's peaceful and glorious kingdom will surely be ours.

---

## From the Writings of Swedenborg

*Arcana Coelestia*, n. 1555: "Few, if any, know how man is brought to true wisdom. Intelligence is not wisdom, but leads to wisdom; for to understand what is true and good is not to be true and good, but to be wise is to be so.

Wisdom is predicated only of the life—that man is such. A man is introduced to wisdom or to life by means of knowing, that is, by means of knowledges. In every man there are two parts, the will and the understanding; the will is the primary part, the understanding is the secondary one. Man's life after death is according to his will part, not according to his intellectual part. The will is being formed in man by the Lord from infancy to childhood, which is effected by means of the innocence that is insinuated, and by means of charity toward parents, nurses, and little children of a like age; and by means of many other things that man knows nothing of, and which are celestial. Unless these celestial things were first insinuated into a man while an infant and a child, he could by no means become a man. *Thus is formed the first plane.* But as a man is not a man unless he is endowed also with understanding, will alone does not make the man, but understanding together with will; and understanding cannot be acquired except by means of knowledges; and therefore he must, from his childhood, be gradually imbued with these. *Thus is formed the second plane.* When the intellectual part has been instructed in knowledges, especially in the knowledges of truth and good, then first can the man be regenerated; and, when he is being regenerated, truths and goods are implanted by the Lord by means of knowledges in the celestial things with which he has been endowed by the Lord from infancy, so that his intellectual things make a one with his celestial things; and when the Lord has thus conjoined these, the man is endowed with charity, from which he begins to act, this charity being of conscience. In this way he for the first time receives new life, and this by degrees. The light of this life is called wisdom, which then takes the first place, and is set over the intelligence. *Thus is formed the third plane.* When a man has become like this during his bodily life, he is then in the other life being continually perfected. These considerations show what is the light of intelligence, and what is the light of wisdom."

---

## Suggested Questions on the Lesson

P. How was David different from Saul? *obeyed direct orders of the Lord*
P. What special talents did David have? *musician, poet*
J. What book in the Bible was given in part through David? *Psalms*
J. What was accomplished in David's reign? *peace*
J. Where did David set up the ark? *Jerusalem*
P. Who was the third king of Irael? *Solomon*
P. Whose son was he? *David and Bathsheba*
J. What does his name mean? *peaceful*
J. Where did Solomon go to worship the Lord? *Gibeon*

J. What was at Gibeon? *tabernacle*
P. Who spoke to Solomon at Gibeon in a dream? *the Lord*
P. What did the Lord ask Solomon to do? *"Ask what I shall give you"*
P. What did Solomon ask the Lord to give him? *an understanding heart*
J. What did the Lord tell him? *he would have it, plus riches and honor*
J. What did Solomon build at Jerusalem? *temple*
P. How long did Solomon reign? *forty years*
I. What is represented by Solomon? *loving to live the Lord's will*
S. Why did Solomon and not David built the temple? *heavenly character comes only when one is at peace with God*

## BUILDING THE TEMPLE

*I Kings 6*

The connection is easily made through David's desire to build the temple and the Lord's answer. The reason for this answer, as given in I Kings 5:3, should be stressed because of its spiritual meaning. The succession of Solomon and the difference between his reign and David's should be mentioned again. Very little can be done in one lesson with the details of the temple. The fullest statement of these will be found in the Junior notes. Its general characteristics and materials and type of decoration may be covered, and mention should be made of Solomon's dealings with Hiram king of Tyre, as given in I Kings 5.

---

### Doctrinal Points

*Our character is built out of the materials we furnish by our choices day by day.*

*An understanding heart is true wisdom, i.e., the ability to distinguish right from wrong and to choose freely to do right.*

*When we determine to serve the Lord, all our natural knowledges can be employed in His service.*

---

### Notes for Parents

Saul had been told that because of his unwillingness to obey the Lord in all things, his line would not continue on the throne of Israel; and we have seen that the second great king was not Saul's son, but David. David did obey the Lord, and the Lord promised him that there should always be a descendant of his on the throne. Even before he died David had his favorite son Solomon anointed to be the next king. The name *Solomon* means "peace," and Solomon's reign was one of peace and great glory; for David had conquered all of Israel's enemies, and the Lord, in addition to making Solomon very wise, gave him great riches.

Solomon was allowed to build the first temple in Jerusalem. We remember that the tabernacle, although its walls were of boards, was really a tent, because the children of Israel were constantly moving from place to place through the wilderness, and even after they entered the Holy Land, they were in constant conflict and did not have a fixed center for their national life. This is a picture of our own individual state during the greater part of our lives in this world. Spiritually we are constantly changing from one place to another and constantly at war with the weaknesses and evils in our own natures. Our worship of the Lord, our thought about Him and our obedience to His commandments, must go with us from state to state and must keep the quality of childlike dependence upon our Heavenly Father. This is symbolized by the tabernacle.

But when David took Jerusalem, the nation then had a strong, permanent national center and David brought the ark there. Then in the peace which followed David's conquests, Solomon could build the temple, which pictures a lasting spiritual character. Paul says, "Know ye not that ye are a temple of the Lord?"

All the materials for the temple were prepared outside of the city of Jerusalem, so that "there was neither hammer nor ax nor any tool of iron heard in the house, while it was in building." By our free choice of right thought and action as we struggle against our temptations from day to day we fashion the materials out of which the Lord is silently building the temple within us—the spiritual character which at the end of our time in this world will stand forth complete as we enter the beautiful world where we shall find our eternal homes.

---

## Primary

Review the names of the three kings and something of the difference between David's reign and Solomon's, which made it possible for Solomon to build the temple. Tell them the difference between a temple and a tabernacle, and take up the temple by comparison. The characteristics of Solomon's reign are important, and his league with Hiram should be described.

David asked the Lord if he might build a temple in Jerusalem to take the place of the tabernacle he had made for the ark, but the Lord told him through the prophet Nathan that he was not the one who should build the temple. He was to have a son who would build it. This son was Solomon, the third great king of Israel. See if you can learn the names of the three kings—Saul, David, and Solomon—so well that you will always remember them.

Solomon was a very great king. He did not have to fight battles because David had conquered all the enemies. So all through his reign there was peace instead of fighting. Solomon's name means "peace." Early in his reign the Lord offered to grant him a wish, and Solomon wished for a wise and understanding heart so that he could rule his people well. The Lord was pleased with this wish and in addition to a wise and understanding heart gave him great riches. People came from far away just to see his treasures and to ask him questions.

Solomon built several beautiful buildings.

What did he build for the Lord?
What were the outside walls made of?
Where was the stone cut?
What were the inside walls?
The cedar came from the Lebanon mountains.
Hiram, king of Tyre, helped Solomon to get it.

The Holy of Holies, where the ark was kept, was called the oracle or inner sanctuary. Here Solomon set up two giant figures of cherubim, made of olive wood overlaid with gold. Their outspread wings touched in the center over the ark, and they were so big that the other tips of their wings touched the outer walls.

The Lord told Solomon that if the people would truly worship and obey Him, He would always be with them and bless them.

It took seven years to build the temple. When it was finished, Solomon had a great dedication service with sacrifices and a feast, and brought the ark from David's tabernacle and put it in the oracle in the temple.

### Junior

It is in this class that the plan and details of the temple should be found most interesting, especially in comparison with those of the tabernacle. This will take most of the lesson time, but be sure the children also understand why Solomon instead of David built the temple.

David was a fighting king. He was successful against his enemies and brought the kingdom of Israel to its greatest extent and power. The Lord had told David through Nathan the prophet that his son Solomon was to be his successor. So David, near the end of his life, had Solomon anointed as the next king, and the people accepted Solomon.

The name *Solomon* means "peace." Solomon had peace throughout his reign, and he reigned, as David did, forty years. Early in his reign he went to Gibeon to make offerings to the Lord. The tabernacle which had been made at Sinai was at this time set up at Gibeon with all its furnishings except the ark. At Gibeon the Lord appeared to Solomon in a dream and offered to give him anything he asked for. Solomon asked for wisdom. This request and its fulfillment were the cause of Solomon's greatness. He was so wise that not only his own people but other kings and queens came to listen to him. The Lord also gave him great riches, for which he had not asked. The chapters which tell of his reign are full of descriptions of his possessions.

David had wanted to build a temple in Jerusalem, but the Lord told him that his son should be the one to build it. Our lesson today tells about the building of the temple. This temple which Solomon built was not the one of which we read in the Gospels, but it was in the same place. There are two hills in the city of Jerusalem, Mount Zion and Mount Moriah, separated by a valley. Mount Zion, the western hill, was the fortified citadel, and when David brought the ark to Jerusalem, he placed his tabernacle for it there. But Solomon built the temple on the eastern hill, Mount Moriah (II Chronicles 3:1), and the two later temples, the temple of Zerubbabel and the temple of Herod (the temple of the Gospel story) were built on the same site. Perhaps you remember that it was on Mount Moriah that Abraham tried to sacrifice Isaac.

What were the dimensions of Solomon's temple?
What materials were used to build it?
What is said about the way in which it was built (verse 7)?
What were the inside walls made of?

The cedar for the walls of the temple, as well as the fir [probably cypress] for the floor and doors, came from the mountains of Lebanon. Hiram, king of Tyre, who was a firm friend of both David and Solomon, furnished the skilled workmen who cut it, and Solomon's men worked with them. Read I Kings 5:8-11 to see what Hiram agreed to do and how Solomon paid for the work.

The details of the structure of the temple are not easy for us to work out from the brief account given in our chapter. There is another account of it as the prophet Ezekiel was permitted to see it in vision many years later. This description is found in chapters 40 to 48 of the book of Ezekiel. A New Church minister, the Rev. T. O. Paine, about a hundred years ago made a very thorough study of the two accounts and has given us in his book what is probably the most accurate picture we can form of the building and its surroundings.* You can see from reading our chapter for today that the proportions of the temple were the same as those of the tabernacle, that it was divided into two parts, as the tabernacle proper was, and that the oracle, which was the Holy of Holies where the ark was placed, was a cube just as it had been in the tabernacle.

The temple, however, being a permanent building, could have additional features. It had a broad porch in front, the roof of which was supported by two great brass columns. These and all the other brass furnishings were cast by another Hiram—not the king—and are described in I Kings 7:15-22. The "chambers" described in verses 5 and 6 of our chapter were built against the side walls of the temple on the outside, but they opened into the temple. These

*T. O. Paine, *Solomon's Temple*, Boston: George Phinney, 1861. (There were also several later editions.) —*Ed.*

were used as treasure chambers to hold all the gold and silver articles and the trophies of victory. The furnishings of the temple were similar to those of the tabernacle, except that there were ten lampstands instead of one in the Holy Place.

From Ezekiel we get an idea of the great outer court, in which were not only the great altar and laver but also ten smaller lavers, as well as chambers for the priests who were on duty, and places for roasting and boiling the parts of the sacrifices which were the portion of the priests for their own eating. And the outer gate was a whole building in itself.

Our chapter tells us also of two figures which Solomon had made for the oracle.

What were they?
Of what were they made?
How tall were they?
How long were their wings?
What were they overlaid with?

Chapter 8 tells of the great feast of dedication when the temple was completed, and of Solomon's prayer that the Lord might always dwell in it to receive the worship of his people and hear their prayers and forgive their sins.

---

### Intermediate

The general meaning of the three kings can be brought out clearly in this lesson. Stress the reason why the temple was built by Solomon and not by David, and the meaning of verse 7. The thought that the Lord builds our character out of the materials we furnish by our choices from day to day is helpful for young people of this age.

We remember that David was a fighting king. Under him all the enemies of Israel were overcome. And he was allowed to conquer Jerusalem and establish the ark of the covenant there in a tabernacle set up on Mount Zion. But because his work was the work of struggle and conquest, he was not allowed to build the temple. We have to fight against temptations, but the state of struggle is not the ideal state and is only a preparation for the building of heavenly character.

When Solomon, the son of David, succeeded his father on the throne of Israel, one of his first acts was to offer sacrifices to the Lord at Gibeon. Here the old tabernacle and its furnishings had finally been set up, and although the ark had been removed from the Holy of Holies, the regular ceremonies of worship were maintained and it was regarded as the principal place of worship. In going there Solomon was dedicating himself as best he could to the service of the Lord, and it was here that the well-known dream was granted him in which he made the wise choice of an "understanding heart" as the most desirable of all gifts which the Lord could give him. An understanding heart is a synonym for true wisdom, the ability to distinguish between right and wrong and to choose freely to do right. Solomon's wisdom thenceforward became famous, and kings and queens, like the queen of Sheba, sought his counsel.

Solomon did build the temple. The temple pictures the dwelling place of the Lord in our hearts, and this is built silently by the Lord out of good states which we produce by doing right in our daily life. Every time we make ourselves remember one of the Lord's commandments and obey it, we are fashioning a "stone" which can be used in our "temple." Read verse 7. It took seven years to build the temple, just as the building of a true human being, described in the Creation story, took seven days. *Seven* represents what is holy.

You remember that Saul pictures our natural understanding of truth and David our spiritual understanding of it, after we have grown up and learned by experience that we must be ruled by the truth. Solomon pictures the love of truth ruling. When we make ourselves do right because we know we shall get along better if we do, Saul is our king; when we do right because we want to please the Lord, David rules; but when doing right has become our habit and we love to do it, Solomon is on our "throne."

The difference between the temple and the tabernacle is brought out in two ways. The tabernacle, as we have seen, represents worship from the heart in a childlike state. The temple, a permanent building made of stone, represents a more mature acceptance of the Lord based on an understanding of the truth, and therefore more permanent. Not only stones went into its construction but also cedar and cypress brought from the mountains of Lebanon with the cooperation of Hiram, king of Tyre. Hiram is the symbol of a right principle governing worldly knowledges. He had been David's friend and had furnished materials for David's house. Now the same Hiram furnishes materials for the temple. When we are bent on serving the Lord, all our natural knowledges can be made useful.

The other representative of the change from the tabernacle to the temple state is found in the change of location from Mount Zion to Mount Moriah. These two hills were both within the city of Jerusalem. Mount Zion, which was the stronghold of the city, represents the "celestial" principle of the church, that is, the love of goodness. Mount Moriah represents the "spiritual" principle of the church, that is, the love of truth.

The plan and proportions of the temple were the same as those of the tabernacle, but some of its furnishings were multiplied, as we learn from chapter 7. Our appreciation of the truths of the Word, like the lampstands in the Holy Place, is multiplied when we have advanced in understanding, and so is our ability to make our outer lives serviceable to the Lord.

*Basic Correspondences*

| | | |
|---|---|---|
| Saul | = | a natural understanding of truth |
| David | = | a spiritual understanding of truth |
| Solomon | = | truth obeyed from love |
| Mount Zion | = | the celestial church |
| Mount Moriah | = | the spiritual church |
| seven | = | what is holy |

## Senior

The meaning of the three kings should be made clear in this class. Young people should know that although they will not arrive at the Solomon stage for many years, the state he represents is the ideal toward which they are working. They are preparing materials from day to day from which the Lord can build their characters. They should have clearly in mind from the first what is their part and what is the Lord's, as a check to the universal tendency to self-praise.

The three kings, Saul, David, and Solomon, represent stages in our regeneration. Under Saul we keep the commandments and study the Word from a sense of duty and with the feeling that being Christians will prosper us in the world and get us to heaven. Under David we do the same from an understanding of them and of the Lord's purpose in giving them to us. Under Solomon we study and keep the law because we have learned to love it. Then it is written in our hearts and we no longer are in a constant struggle against our own selfish desires. We are at peace. *Solomon* means "peace." What Solomon asked of the Lord was an "understanding heart."

There is a difference between knowledge, intelligence, and wisdom. One may have a great deal of knowledge, but if he cannot organize it and apply it to his life, he is not intelligent. And he is not wise until he has proved his knowledge and intelligence by experience.

The temple was built under Solomon. David had wanted to build a temple, but the Lord, speaking through Nathan the prophet, told him that his son should be the one to build it, and we learn in I Kings 5:3 that this was because David's work was the work of conquest. While we are fighting our evils and weaknesses we must remain in the childlike state of worship and trust represented by the tabernacle. In overcoming our temptations we are preparing the way for the building of the temple of spiritual character, but it is really the Lord's spirit inflowing in the peaceful times which follow our victories which does the actual building. The same lesson is taught by the fact that "there was neither hammer nor axe nor any tool of iron heard in the house while it was in building." The materials for the temple, stone and wood—truth and goodness—were brought from outside the Holy Land and each piece was fashioned before it was brought. Our "temple" is built of the truth and goodness we have made our own by shaping our outward lives according to what is true. It rises up silently within us and at the end of seven years—when the Lord sees that we have reached the full measure of holiness we are willing to achieve—it stands forth in its final form as we pass into the spiritual world.

The "oracle" of the temple, or Holy of Holies, was entirely covered within with gold leaf, a symbol of the love which should be within our hearts. When all was complete, the ark was brought into it. Then the "glory of the Lord" filled the temple and Solomon held a solemn dedication service. It is a beautiful picture of a life dedicated to the Lord's service, with the commandments at the center kept from love to the Lord.

The Lord's promise to Solomon to add to him riches and glory for which he had not asked was fully kept. The chapters telling of his marvelous possessions picture in the internal sense the spiritual riches of a truly good life. Every detail has its meaning. In its fullest sense we do not reach the Solomon state until our life in this world is over, but we do have repeated experiences of it as we overcome one temptation after another. As we recognize any given evil in ourselves, fight against it with the Lord's help, conquer it, and come to love its opposite, we experience something of the peace and beauty and spiritual riches which are in store for the faithful, and which are pictured in the story of Solomon's kingdom.

---

## Adult

In this class, after a brief survey of the lesson, consult the members to see which phase of the subject will make the most profitable discussion. The teacher will need to study not only the chapter for the day but also I Kings 5-9, and should look through Ezekiel 40-48 for additional background.

The three kings all represent the Lord's truth—or the Word—

accepted as our ruling principle in our adult lives, but with varying degrees of understanding. Natural understanding, pictured by Saul, cannot of itself produce any higher degree. Saul's line had to perish. But spiritual understanding does produce lasting spiritual results. David was promised that there should never be lacking one of his line to sit on his throne, and we remember that the Lord chose to be born into the house and lineage of David. So David's son followed him as king, and Solomon's gift from the Lord was an "understanding heart."

As Jonathan played an important role in the transition from Saul to David, so there was another man—a king—who played an important role in the transition from David to Solomon. Even after a spiritual understanding of truth has wholly succeeded natural understanding as ruler in the life, the natural plane of thought and activity continues as a necessary and serviceable basis of the character. In I Kings 5 this fact is brought out in the agreement between Solomon and Hiram king of Tyre. We are told in the writings that Tyre and Sidon represent knowledges of good and truth (AC 2967) and that Hiram represents the nations that are outside of the church but with whom there are knowledges of good and truth (AE 514[7]). Hiram was a friend of both David and Solomon, helping David in the building of his own house and Solomon in the building of the temple, as well as of his other structures. In the individual life Hiram pictures our good "Gentile" states, states in which we are absorbed in learning scientific and rational truths and training our minds in intelligent thinking, not seeing clearly perhaps the relation to the Lord and the church of what we are doing, but intending to make unselfish use of whatever we acquire of knowledge and ability. All that we gain in this way can be made serviceable to our regeneration, first in developing orderly spiritual thinking—David's house—and later in building true heavenly character, the church in us, for which the temple stands. When the knowledge and ability we have gained is thus used to build up the church in us, this very outer region of our minds is fed with truth and good from the Lord and lives from Him: "And Solomon gave Hiram twenty thousand measures of wheat for food to his household, and twenty measures of pure oil: thus gave Solomon to Hiram year by year." An example of this process might perhaps be found in our acquisition of the knowledge of ancient history and the habit of trying to trace historical causes. We find such study interesting and desire to make it useful in some way. Then, once we catch a glimpse of the correstpondence of the ancient people and lands and begin to see their history as spiritual drama and, in the Word, relate it to the Lord's life and to our own spiritual states, our knowledge of ancient history "comes alive," and every detail that we have stored in our memory becomes useful in our spiritual development and is filled with higher and deeper meaning.

David wished to build the temple of the Lord but was told through Nathan the prophet that this privilege must be left for his son. Solomon gives us the reason for this in his reply to Hiram: "Thou knowest how that David my father could not build an house unto the name of the Lord his God for the wars which were about him on every side, until the Lord had put them under the soles of his feet." Heavenly character, the house of the Lord in us, is not built by our own knowledge or rationality, even when that is spiritually enlightened; nor is it built while we are passing through temptation. It is built in the states of peace which follow victories, built by the Lord's spirit flowing in silently where the enemy has been cast out.

Swedenborg tells us many times to guard against the thought that what goodness we have is our own, and tells us that it is always the Lord's goodness in us. We merely open the door by turning away from evils and toward the Lord. So the temple was built silently, every piece having been prepared elsewhere, as the various truths and goods which go to make up a heavenly character come to us as a result of experiences in every field of our activity, and our character grows silently through our full period of opportunity, which is our life in this world. "So was he seven years in building it." Swedenborg gives us a further suggestion as to the reason why Solomon and not David was permitted to build the temple. In

DP 245, in discussing the relative meaning of David and Solomon, he says that the temple signifies both the Divine Human and the church: David could not build it because he represents the Lord before His coming into the world, whereas Solomon represents the Lord after His coming. Another interesting thought is suggested in AE 654[33]: "As every man of the church has a spiritual, a rational, and a natural, therefore Solomon built three houses, the house of God or the temple to stand for the spiritual, the house of the forest of Lebanon for the rational (for 'cedar' and thence 'Lebanon' signifies the rational), and the house of the daughter of Pharaoh for the natural." That is, when the soul has really found rest in the Lord, it takes on an appropriate and beautiful form not only with reference to things of the church, but with reference to intellectual and even to external worldly things.

In studying the correspondence of the various details of the temple, we should recall our knowledge of the tabernacle and consider the similarities and the differences between the two. The tabernacle represents the celestial church and the temple the spiritual church (AR 585), the tabernacle being the Lord's dwelling place in a more childlike, less intellectual stage of development. In HH 223 we are told that the houses of worship in the celestial heavens are of wood, while those in the spiritual heavens are of stone, because wood corresponds to good and stone to truth. Thus the walls of the tabernacle were of wood, but those of the temple were of stone. The cedar with which they were covered pictures the good coming from the rational understanding of truth. This could be carved into beautiful forms of cherubim, palm trees, and open flowers, which suggest thoughts about the Lord's providence, His saving power, and the great variety of blessings which come to us from Him. The gold which overlaid it is the love which makes the truth beautiful. In II Chronicles 3:1 we learn that Solomon's temple was built on Mount Moriah in Jerusalem instead of on Mount Zion, where David's tabernacle had been. Swedenborg tells us in many places that Zion represents the celestial church. Therefore it was fitting that a tabernacle should have been erected there but that the temple, which represents the spiritual church, should in the letter have been built on Mount Moriah. Wherever Zion and Jerusalem are mentioned together in the Word, Zion refers to the celestial church and Jerusalem to the spiritual church.

The brief account of the structure of the temple which is given in our chapter is filled in and amplified in the description of it as it was showed to Ezekiel in vision some years after its destruction (Ezekiel 40-48). From a long study of the two accounts the Rev. T. O. Paine, a New Church minister, in the middle of the last century demonstrated the identity of the two by drawing a careful plan of the temple as given in our chapter and an equally careful one of the temple of Ezekiel's vision and finding that when the two plans were superimposed, they not only coincided, but each supplied details which the other lacked, indicating that they were intended to be complementary.

## From the Writings of Swedenborg

*Arcana Coelestia*, n. 7847[4]: ". . . in the supreme sense by 'temple' is meant the Lord as to the Divine Human, as He Himself teaches in John 2:19-22. Therefore in the representative sense by a 'temple' is meant His church. . . . Because the 'posts' and 'lintels' signified the truths and goods in the natural which serve for introduction . . . therefore in the temple of Solomon the posts were made of olive wood . . . 'Olive wood' signified the good of truth, or the good which is of the spiritual church."

## Suggested Questions on the Lesson

J. What was David's principal work? *conquering enemies*
J. Why could he not build the temple? *needs time of peace*
P. Who did build it? *Solomon*
P. What does the name *Solomon* mean? *peace*
J. Who furnished some of the materials for the temple? *Hiram*
J. How did Solomon pay him? *grain, oil, cities*
P. What were the principal materials? *stone, cedar, gold*
J. How was the temple like the tabernacle? *same general plan*
J. How was it different? *more elaborate, permanent*
J. Where in Jerusalem was it built? *Mount Moriah*

J. Why was it built more quietly than most buildings? *stone cut and shaped at quarry*

P. How long did it take to build it? *seven years*

I. What are pictured by (1) Saul, (2) David, and (3) Solomon? *obeying truth from (1) duty, (2) reverence, and (3) love*

S. What is meant in our lives by David's not being permitted to build the temple? *character takes final form only after temptation battles*

S. What is meant in our lives by the temple materials' being prepared before they were brought to Jerusalem? *forming character by right actions in outer, everyday life*

## THE GLORY OF SOLOMON

*I Kings 9; 10*

The important lesson for all classes is that the glory of Solomon could not have been achieved without David's victories and that it could not have been enjoyed except in a state of peace. The teacher should be familiar with the main points in David's reign.

---

### Doctrinal Points

*We cannot become good without passing through temptations, and temptations are conquered by means of truth.*

---

### Notes for Parents

The lesson today is about Solomon, the last king to reign over the whole nation, the third and greatest of her kings. The children need to hear often the names Saul, David, and Solomon, so that they will know them well. Like the names Abraham, Isaac, and Jacob, they are landmarks in the Bible story. Not only are they mentioned again and again in the Bible—in the New as well as in the Old Testament—but the two periods of the patriarchs and the kings are the high points of the Old Testament story, as childhood and the fullness of maturity are the two high points in our lives. Jewish history began with Abraham and led up to Solomon. The life of each one of us begins with the beautiful, innocent, trustful state of infancy and, if we choose wisely, culminates in the peaceful and glorious state which is pictured by Solomon.

For Solomon's reign is the picture of a heavenly or regenerate character, and the name *Solomon* means "peace." Most of us know some fine, upright, wise old person whom everyone in the community admires and praises, to whom everyone may go for advice, sure of a sympathetic hearing and wise judgment. The character of such a person has not been developed overnight. It is the result of a lifetime of effort to learn and do the Lord's will. Our first impulse is to say, "I wish I could hope to be like that when I am old." We can if we are willing to follow the same course. Saul and David were fighting kings. They overcame the enemies and made the glorious reign of Solomon possible.

In Solomon's reign the fruits of victory were enjoyed. All sorts of treasures were brought to him. The few enemies that remained in the land paid the "tribute of bondservice," and all his own people served him, each in his proper station. Kings and queens, like the queen of Sheba in our lesson, came to hear his wisdom. And in his time the temple was built at Jerusalem, the house of God in the heart and mind. This is the picture of the heavenly character which is the true goal of every human life.

---

## Primary

Mention Solomon's wish and show the children simply what an understanding heart is. Also mention the building of the temple by Solomon. Then tell some of the wonderful things Solomon had, as background for the story of the visit of the queen of Sheba. Develop the idea that Solomon's riches and honors were the result of Solomon's wise choice.

After Saul died, David became king. David was a great warrior and conquered all the enemies of Israel. Just before he died, he had his son Solomon anointed to be king after him. The name *Solomon* means "peace." That is easy to remember because Solomon's reign was a peaceful one. He did not have to fight any enemies.

He built a beautiful temple at Jerusalem in which to place the ark.
He also built many other buildings and cities.
He married the daughter of the Pharaoh of Egypt.
His friend Hiram king of Tyre furnished him cedar wood from the forests of Lebanon.

Solomon had a dream in which the Lord told him to ask for whatever he most wanted, and Solomon had asked for "a wise and understanding heart." The Lord was pleased with this wish and granted it, and He also gave Solomon riches and glory and a long life.

Solomon had a throne made of ivory overlaid with gold, with a figure of a lion on either side of it, and it had six steps leading up to it with a lion on either side of each step. And Solomon had a fleet of ships, which brought him gold and silver from other countries, and ivory and apes and peacocks.

The wisdom and glory of Solomon became so well known that kings and queens came from other countries to see his treasures and to ask him questions.

About what particular queen do we read in our lesson?
Why did she come to Solomon?
What presents did she bring him?
What did she say after she had talked with him?

---

## Junior

The Juniors will be interested in a brief review of David's relations with Saul and the accomplishments of his reign. Make this an introduction to the greater glory of the peaceful reign of Solomon. Have the children do map study and look up the Bible references.

David was a fighting king. Even while Saul was still living, the people came to trust David rather than Saul. This made Saul so jealous that he tried to kill David. But Saul's son Jonathan loved David and helped him to escape. David had to live in exile for many years, but he never worked against Saul. He gathered a band of fighting men around him and won victories for Israel. Finally Saul and Jonathan were killed in battle and David became king. He was crowned first in Hebron and reigned there seven years over the southern part of the land. One of Saul's sons was made king over the northern tribes, but his reign did not prosper and after he was killed the whole country accepted David, crowning him again at Jerusalem. In all he reigned forty years. He brought the ark to Jerusalem and wanted to build a temple for it, but the Lord told him the temple was to be built by his son; so he placed the ark in a new tabernacle. Under David the Israelites conquered all their enemies and became a leading nation.

Who was the third king of Israel?

David had several sons older than Solomon, but he had chosen Solomon to succeed him on the throne; so before he died, he had Solomon anointed. The name *Solomon* means "peace." The story of David's reign is full of wars and fighting, but when Solomon came to the throne, the few enemies within the land who had not been destroyed were paying tribute to the king of Israel, and the kings and queens in all the surrounding nations looked to Israel as the leading nation of the district.

Solomon himself was sought out by all for his glory and wisdom. For in the beginning of his reign he had taken advantage of an opportunity to make a very wise choice. Read I Kings 3:5-15. Chapters 5 and 6 of I Kings tell of the building of the temple at Jerusalem, and chapter 7 tells of other structures which Solomon built. In all his building he received help from a friend of his father David, who is mentioned again in our lesson today.

Who was this friend?
What did he furnish king Solomon?
What did Solomon give Hiram?
Whose daughter was Solomon's first wife?
What did Solomon do with the enemies who were left in the Holy Land?

Read verses 26-28 of chapter 9. This is the first time we have heard of the Israelites' having ships.

What queen came to see Solomon?

Sheba was a kingdom in the southwestern corner of the Arabian peninsula along the Red Sea, the district now known as Yemen. In those days it was a long journey away from the land of Canaan.

Why did the queen of Sheba come to Solomon?
What did she bring him?
What did she say after she had seen and talked with him?

Read carefully the description of Solomon's throne in verses 18 to 20 of chapter 10.

What metal is most prominent in the description of Solomon's treasures?
What is said about silver?

If you think of all the enemies in the Holy Land as picturing the selfish and wrong things in us which the Lord wants us to fight, you can see that Solomon's reign is a picture of the peaceful, happy, beautiful state of a person who has overcome his temptations. Such a person has a heart full of love for the Lord and the neighbor and is very wise. Everyone goes to him for advice because he has what Solomon asked for: "a wise and understanding heart." The reason gold is so prominent in the description of Solomon's treasures is because gold is the symbol of love.

---

## Intermediate

The general correspondence of the three kings and the meaning and effect of the possession of a wise and understanding heart are the important subjects for this class.

David reigned forty years in all, and his reign was one of constant fighting. You remember that forty pictures a state of temptation. We have to pass through many temptations and to overcome many selfish feelings and false ideas before we reach a state of peace. The name *Solomon* means "peace." Solomon had no enemies to fight because David had conquered them. Solomon was greater than David, but his greatness was founded on David's victories. We cannot jump from ignorance to wisdom without passing through a long period of study, and we cannot pass from selfishness to unselfishness without overcoming many temptations.

Solomon was David's favorite son and was anointed, by David's command, just before David died. Early in his reign the Lord appeared to Solomon in a dream and offered to grant him whatever he most wished. Solomon asked for "an understanding heart." The Lord was pleased with the wish and said that because Solomon had asked for this instead of for riches and power for himself, he should have a wise and understanding heart and also riches and honor and long life.

Think what a wise and understanding heart means. It means a heart full of love for other people with wisdom to understand and help them. If a person has such a heart, he is not always thinking about himself, envying other people, and unhappy because he cannot have everything he wants. And because his dearest wish is to be helpful to the Lord and the neighbor and there are always thousands of ways of doing that—no matter what one's own circumstances are—he can always have more and more of what he most wants. And also he is loved and honored by other people, and people come to him with their problems and troubles.

Do you see how our two chapters for today picture just such a life? Solomon did a great deal of building. First he had built the temple of the Lord in Jerusalem and then he built houses for himself and for his wife, who was the daughter of the Pharaoh of Egypt. And he rebuilt cities which had been destroyed by earlier enemies. A person who is genuinely desirous to help others builds first the temple of the Lord in his own character and then is constantly helping to build happy lives for other people. In this he is able to to make use of all the natural knowledges and powers available, just as Solomon used the beautiful cedar wood and the skilled workmen sent him by Hiram king of Tyre. He has all the rational knowledge and principles he needs, as Solomon had horses and chariots. Every faculty of mind and body is able and willing to serve his purpose, as Solomon had his ministers and his attendants and his cupbearers. His judgment is established on a high and firm throne and he has power to maintain it; this is pictured by the lions on either side of Solomon's throne and on either side of the six steps which led up to it. Solomon's navy—the first and the only successful navy of Israel—pictures his ability to procure ideas and services from many other people. And throughout the description notice how often gold is mentioned and remember that gold corresponds to love.

The familiar story of the visit of the queen of Sheba to Solomon sums up the honor in which he was held. She came from a distant country and brought him very valuable presents, just as the magi did who came to worship the Lord when He was born. She had heard even in her far-off land of the glory and wisdom of Solomon, and when she had seen and talked with him, she said that the half had not been told her. This story teaches us that even those of great attainments have yet something to learn. The riches and knowledges of the world and the human mind seem very wonderful to us at first, but if we "follow on to know the Lord," as the prophet Hosea puts it (Hosea 6:3), we finally come to know and to possess the true riches.

*Basic Correspondences*

| | | |
|---|---|---|
| Solomon | = | an understanding of truth based on humility and trust in the Lord |
| forty | = | temptation |
| ivory | = | rational truth |
| ships | = | knowledges which can convey wisdom to the mind |

---

### Senior

Stress the unique power possessed by the person who has attained a heavenly character. It is especially important for young people of this age to see clearly the beauty and value of such an ideal. Even to see it as an ideal will often help them to recognize evil for what it is and to reject it.

The reign of Solomon was the high point in ancient Hebrew history. In Solomon's time all the alien peoples living in the Holy Land paid tribute to Solomon, and the kings and queens of other nations came to Jerusalem to see his glory and to hear his wisdom.

We have seen that the history of the Jews throughout is a divinely directed and recorded picture of the course of our individual lives as well as of the life of the human race as a whole and inmostly of the Lord's life on earth. Each of us starts, as this nation started in Abraham, from a small ignorant beginning, with a nature full of self-love and conceit, but with a call to follow the Lord and a promise that, if we obey Him faithfully, He will care for us and bring us eventually to all happiness. We go on as they did with many backslidings, many mistakes and failures, many battles, and some victories. But if we keep trying, looking always to the Lord for help, we shall gradually come into an orderly state of life, overcome our spiritual enemies—first the external and then the deep inner temptations—and eventually attain a heavenly character, which means that our hearts will finally be full of the Lord's unselfish love, our minds will delight in His truth, and our outer lives will be rich in service to the Lord and the neighbor.

When we are young, we are able to recognize the beauty of such a character, but the things of the world make such a strong appeal to us that sometimes we are not sure the attainment of goodness is worth the sacrifices involved. The picture of Solomon's glory is given us in the Word as an answer to this doubt. It took a long time to reach the Solomon stage. It takes any one of us a long time to reach the inner peace and beauty of a heavenly character, but it is the only thing really worth the effort of a lifetime. All the worldly successes we may gain will pass away, but heavenly character may be ours to eternity.

Solomon's reign was a reign of peace—the name *Solomon* means "peace." When we have learned to love to do the Lord's will, we no longer have to struggle against evil in our hearts. We are at peace. We still have weaknesses and limitations, but we have control of them (9:20-21); all our faculties give willing and orderly service to our spiritual life (9:22-23). All the things we have learned about the natural world become serviceable to us and find their proper place in our spiritual thinking (9:11). Our minds range over the whole field of learning and bring back treasures (9:26-28). Solomon's navy was the first and the only successful navy the nation ever possessed. Some sixty or more years later their navy was lost under King Jehoshaphat (I Kings 22:48). Belief in the Lord and in His providence is the only principle which enables us to see things in their true proportions and relationships. When this belief is weakened, our "navy" is lost.

And Solomon's glory and wisdom made an impression on all the world around him. In I Kings 4:34 it is said, "And there came of all people to hear the wisdom of Solomon, from all the kings of the earth, which had heard of his wisdom." The example we know of these visits is that of the queen of Sheba, described in our chapters for today. Swedenborg says that Sheba represents "the celestial things of love and faith," and that the gifts which the queen of Sheba brought, "the camels that bare spices, and very much gold, and precious stones" (10:2), represent "the things of wisdom and intelligence in the natural man" (AC 3048). And Solomon's throne is a picture of the loftiness and power of the judgment which is possible to those in true heavenly states. Such people make a deep impression on others by their wisdom and understanding.

The person who has passed through the states of reformation and regeneration to the point of character represented by Solomon inevitably stands out above his fellows and is aptly described in verses 23 and 24 of chapter 10: "So king Solomon exceeded all the kings of the earth for riches and for wisdom. And all the earth sought to Solomon, to hear his wisdom, which God had put in his heart."

---

## Adult

The story is familiar to most adults. The class will probably be interested in the development of some of the details of the correspondence, as one is apt to read such chapters as these with little thought beyond the impressiveness of the story in the letter.

For the purpose of our present lesson only two review points need be especially mentioned. One is that David's reign was one of almost continuous fighting, resulting in the virtual conquest of all the enemies which had been troubling Israel. The other is that, although David brought the ark to Jerusalem, he was forbidden to build the temple there. We learn from I Kings 5:3 that the reason was that he was in the midst of wars, and I Chronicles 22:8 and 28:3 say that it was because he had been a man of war and had shed blood. The reign of David represents the period when we are engaged in temptation conflicts–forty signifies temptation–and, although these conflicts are the necessary preparation which we ourselves with the help of the Lord make for regeneration, they are not regeneration. Regeneration is the inflow of the Lord's unselfish love into the heart from which self-love has been cast out. The building of the temple is the building of regenerate or heavenly character, the house of the Lord in the individual, and this is the work of the inflowing divine love. We recall that when the temple was built, the stones were prepared before they were brought to the site "so that there was neither hammer nor ax nor any tool of iron heard in the house, while it was in building." (I Kings 6:7) The temple rose silently, just as a regenerate character is built in us by the Lord quietly after we make the necessary preparation. David's conquests prepared the way, but David could not build the temple. "The kingdom of heaven cometh not with observation" (Luke 17:20).

The name *Solomon* means "peace." Solomon's reign was one of peace, and it pictures the fully regenerate state, the state of glorification in the Lord and its analogue, regeneration in man. It is the state in which self has been so brought under control that the commandments of the Lord are written on the heart, and the life is one of willing and joyous service to the Lord and the neighbor. Solomon, in his dream at Gibeon (I Kings 3:5-15), had asked for "an understanding heart," and the Lord had granted his petition and promised him also riches and honor and long life.

Our two chapters for today in their inner meaning describe the spiritual riches and honors which a regenerate person enjoys. They begin, we should note, with a solemn charge to be faithful, and a warning against falling away from the high state attained. Then comes the curious incident of Solomon's gift of twenty cities in Galilee to Hiram king king of Tyre and Hiram's displeasure with the cities; in spite of which he sends Solomon "six score talents of gold." Hiram represents the external man. In all Solomon's building Hiram had furnished him with beautiful cedar from Lebanon and skilled workmen. This pictures the fact that our character is built only by making use of everything that is good and suitable and capable in our natural knowledges and faculties. We recall that the tabernacle was constructed of materials "borrowed" from the Egyptians. In return, the internal man, or rather the Lord through the internal man, gives the external "twenty cities in the land of Galilee," all the heavenly doctrines needed for use in external living. Hiram's distaste for these cities pictures the inherent inability of the external man to understand and appreciate heavenly things. Yet the external man, in the regenerate state, attributes all its goodness to the Lord: this is Hiram's giving of the six score talents of gold.

Solomon is a builder. The regenerate man is not a destroyer; he restores the cities others have destroyed. And some of the cities he builds are "cities of store" where truths and goods are stored up for use in time of need. Solomon also erected other buildings, his own house, and a house for his wife, the daughter of Pharaoh. But we note that the house he built for her was not in Jerusalem. Pharaoh's daughter represents the affection for natural knowledges, an essential "helpmeet" but dwelling outside the Holy City.

Chapter 9 ends with the account of Solomon's navy, the first navy and the only successful one ancient Israel ever possessed. The regenerate man is able to communicate with those outside his own religious borders and to bring back treasures from these contacts.

Chapter 10 begins with the well-known visit of the queen of Sheba to Solomon. Swedenborg says (AC 3048) that Sheba signifies "knowledges of things celestial and spiritual." The fact that this kingdom was outside the Holy Land indicates that it represents knowledges possessed by the Gentiles. And it is interesting to find that the Sheba who was the father of this nation is identified as the grandson of Eber, who is mentioned in Genesis 10:28. Eber, according to Swedenborg, is the first real person mentioned in the Scriptures, the ancestor from whom the Hebrews took their name, and the founder of the second Ancient Church. It is therefore quite natural that there should have been in that country remains of the knowledges of celestial and spiritual things. The queen of Sheba had treasures to bring to Solomon. What is said of the spices she brought is especially interesting, because spices correspond to "interior truths in the natural which are from the good there" (AC 4748). Swedenborg often speaks of the Gentiles as being in good more than those of the church. But the queen of Sheba also had questions which only Solomon could answer.

Thinking of Solomon as the fully regenerate man, we understand why there is so much mention of gold in these chapters, since love in the heart is the impelling motive of such a man. We can also understand why silver "was nothing accounted of in the days of Solomon." It was not because truth was despised but because it was so plentiful and so easy of attainment. Verse 27 expresses this by saying that the king "made silver to be in Jerusalem as stones." "And cedars made he to be as the sycamore trees that are in the vale, for abundance," expresses the wealth of rational thought which is possible to the regenerate man. This is also clearly pictured in Solomon's throne. A throne always denotes judgment. It was made of ivory overlaid with pure gold, the rational truth of the natural man used as a foundation for the expression of celestial good—the wise and understanding heart. It was reached by an ascent of six steps, the successive victories which lead to such a state, and each step and the throne itself were guarded on either side by a lion, the power of mind and heart which the Lord alone can give. Have we not all recognized the power of clear-sighted judgment possessed by a truly good man? His judgment sits enthroned above the confused tangle of worldly ideas and reasonings. "So king Solomon exceeded all the kings of the earth for riches and for wisdom. And all the earth sought to Solomon, to hear his wisdom, which God had put in his heart."

---

## From the Writings of Swedenborg

*Apocalypse Explained*, n. 514[7]: "Although these are historical facts [concerning Solomon's navy and the loss of the navy under Jehoshaphat] they contain a spiritual sense as well as the prophecies (Isaiah 23:1, 2, 14 and 60:9); "the ships made in Ezion-geber, at the shore of the Red Sea, in the land of Edom,' signified knowledges of the natural man, for these contain in themselves, and as it were carry, spiritual wealth, as ships carry worldly wealth; for the 'Red Sea' and 'the land of Edom,' where Ezion-geber was, were the outmost border of the land of Canaan, and the 'outmost borders of the land of Canaan' signify the outmosts of the church, which are knowledges including knowledges of truth and good. 'Gold and silver' (I Kings 10:22) signify the goods and truths of the internal church; 'ivory, apes, and peacocks,' signify the truths and goods of the external church; knowledges here meaning such knowledges as the ancients had namely, knowledges of correspondences, of representations, and of influxes, and respecting heaven and hell, which especially included and were serviceable to the knowledges of truth and good of the church. 'Hiram' signifies the nations that are out of the church with whom also there are knowledges of good and truth; and that the 'ships' under king Jehoshaphat 'were broken' signifies the devastation of the church in respect to its truths and goods."

## Suggested Questions on the Lesson

J. How long was David's reign? *forty years*
P. What was the name of the king after David? *Solomon*
P. What does the name *Solomon* mean? *peace*
J. What did Solomon ask of the Lord? *wisdom*
J. What did the Lord promise him in addition? *riches and honor*
J. What did Solomon build which David had been forbidden to build? *temple*
J. What else did Solomon build? *houses for self, wife*
J. Who furnished him cedar wood and skilled workmen? *Hiram*
J. What did Solomon give Hiram? *twenty cities*
J. Who was Solomon's first wife? *Pharaoh's daughter*
J. What did Solomon have which the Israelites had never had before? *navy*
P. What queen came to visit Solomon and why did she come? *Sheba, to prove him with hard questions*
P. What did she say about him after she had talked with him? *wiser than reported*
J. Can you describe Solomon's throne? *six steps, twelve lions, gold-plated ivory*
I. Why is gold mentioned so many times in these two chapters? *gold = love of wisdom*
S. What does Solomon as king represent? *fully regenerate person*

# SOLOMON'S LAST YEARS

*I Kings 11:1-13, 26-43*

Solomon was the second son of David and Bathsheba and the third king of Israel. The meaning of his name should be told in all classes, as well as the difference between his reign and David's. His wisdom and glory and his building of the temple should be noted. In the lesson for today stress the fact that his wives led him into the worship of idols, rather than the fact that he had a great number of wives. Connect the rending of Jeroboam's garment with the rending of Samuel's robe by Saul (I Samuel 15:27-28).

---

## Doctrinal Points

*The Lord is constantly trying to reach those in evil and falsity.*

*The Word is written in such a way that it may reach those in evil.*

*People who are in falsities may be saved if there is charity in their hearts.*

*True charity reaches out to everyone but does not treat the good and the evil just alike.*

---

## Notes for Parents

Our chapter for today again teaches that no one in this world becomes so good and so wise that he is beyond temptation and the possibility of falling into sin. This life is given us that we may of our own free will choose the heavenly life and progress in it as far as we are willing to progress, and we do this by recognizing the selfish tendencies which are ours by nature and overcoming them one by one with the Lord's help. If we are regenerating, the older we grow the deeper the evils we are likely to see in ourselves. This sometimes troubles and discourages us, but actually it is a sign of progress.

Solomon succumbed to his temptation instead of resisting it. He had been richly blessed. He was the second son of David and

Bathsheba and was chosen by his father—under inspiration from the Lord—and crowned at his father's command even before David died. He did not have to fight for his throne,* and his enemies had all been conquered for him, so that his reign was one of peace and increasing glory. The very name *Solomon* means "peace." When he first came to the throne, he was young and felt very humble and weak, and he asked the Lord to give him wisdom to rule his people well. In this humble state he could and did receive wisdom—wisdom never comes from ourselves. And the Lord also gave him great riches, and the right to build the temple in Jerusalem.

But Solomon, like David, eventually came to feel that he was above the law instead of subject to it. This is the great temptation which inevitably comes with success and prosperity. In our own day and age we do not have to look far to find examples of it, but we are likely to think of examples of the more obvious kind. Our real concern is with the more subtle form of it to which we may all be subject no matter how poor our outward circumstances are. Theoretically we recognize that the highest goal we may strive for is a heavenly character. This has nothing to do with material wealth or poverty: anyone may attain it if he will. And the mark of this character is love to the Lord and the neighbor, the Lord's own spirit, in the heart. If we have this, we have the wisdom and the glory of Solomon. How can we be tempted then? Just as Solomon was—by forgetting that everything in the world is not fit to be loved, that we must still study and obey the letter of the Word, and that we must not let our love blind us to evil and falsity. If we yield, as Solomon did, to this temptation, the "kingdom" can still be taken from us.

---

## Primary

Teach the children about Solomon's reign and the meaning of his name, and drill them in the names of the three great kings. They will be interested in the rending of Jeroboam's garment. The lesson proper should be taught as a prep-

---

*Except against his brothers. —*Ed.*

aration for the story of the division of the kingdom.

After David died, his son Solomon became king. The Old Testament was not first written in our English language. It was written in Hebrew. In that language all names have meanings. See if you can remember that the name *Solomon* means "peace." We have learned that both Saul and David were fighting kings, and that David, because he obeyed the Lord, was given victory over all the enemies of Israel. So when Solomon became king, the country was at peace, and Solomon had no enemies to fight.

One night, not long after Solomon became king, the Lord appeared to him and told him to make a wish for whatever he most wanted. Solomon did not ask for riches or power, but for wisdom to rule his nation well. The Lord was pleased with Solomon's wish, and told him that he should have great wisdom and also the riches and power he had not asked for. And so his wish came true.

Solomon was so great and had so many beautiful treasures and was so wise that other kings and queens came to see his glory and to ask him the answers to the questions that were bothering them. He married the daughter of Pharaoh, king of Egypt, and built her a house, and he built himself another house. And the Lord also allowed him to build a beautiful temple in Jerusalem for the ark, to take the place of the tabernacle.

But it is not always good for a person to have everything he wants.
What did Solomon do that was wrong?
Why should he have known better?
What did the Lord tell him?
Was all the kingdom to be taken from Solomon's son?
Who was to have part of it?
How was Jeroboam told what was to happen?

## Junior

A good lesson for the Juniors is in the contrast between Solomon's wisdom and glory and the sins of his later years. We had the same general lesson with David. We must never rely on a period of good behavior to excuse later sins.

The name *Solomon* means "peace." Because David had conquered all the enemies of Israel, Solomon's reign was a peaceful one. Not long after David died and Solomon came to the throne, Solomon had a dream one night in which the Lord said to him, "Ask what I shall give thee." Solomon did not ask for riches or glory but for wisdom to rule his people well. And the Lord was pleased and promised Solomon the wisdom he had asked for and also the riches and glory he had not asked for. Solomon became so wise that kings and queens came from other countries to ask him questions, and he did have great riches and many beautiful possessions. In I Kings 10:22-23 we even read that "the king had at sea a navy of Tarshish with the navy of Hiram: once in three years came the navy of Tarshish, bringing gold, and silver, ivory, and apes, and peacocks. So king Solomon exceeded all the kings of the earth for riches and for wisdom." Solomon was also allowed, you remember, to build a beautiful temple in Jerusalem to house the ark.

You know that sometimes you have a "good" day. You are happy, you are feeling helpful, and you do what your parents and teacher want you to do without having to be nagged or even reminded. Then along toward the end of the day you have a chance to do something that you know you ought not to do, but it looks like it would be a lot of fun and you think, "I've been so good all day, I ought to be allowed to have *some* fun." But when your mother finds out, what she says is, "You've been so good all day; why did you have to spoil it?" Solomon was just a man after all.

Who was Solomon's wife?
What bad thing did he now do?
Why was it bad?
When he was old, what did his wives lead him to do?
What did the Lord tell him would happen?
When was this to happen?

At that time people did not consider it wrong to have more than one wife, but the Lord had commanded them strictly not to take any wives from among the idolatrous nations who were their enemies in the Holy Land. Solomon disobeyed this command, and the very thing happened which the Lord knew would happen. Solomon was led away by his wives into the worship of their idols. Then enemies began to rise up again and threaten the peace of his kingdom, and finally one of his own servants turned against him.

Who was this servant?
What position had Solomon given him?
What prophet did Jeroboam meet?
What did Ahijah do?
When was the same kind of sign given before?
What did Ahijah tell Jeroboam?
What did Solomon try to do?
Where did Jeroboam take refuge?
How long was Solomon's reign?

---

## Intermediate

In the doctrinal points for this lesson attention is given to the celestial sense rather than to the spiritual, and none of this sense is given in the Intermediate notes this time. Stress the point that true charity does not treat the good and the evil alike. It is suggested that the teacher bring it out in connection with the illustration of the spoiled child. The important lesson for the Intermediates is in the inevitable results of disobedience.

We have learned that the three kings of Israel represent the rule of divine truth in our lives, and that they differ in character and accomplishment because our understanding of divine truth develops and deepens as we try to live according to it. Saul represents our first natural understanding of it, based on judgments formed from appearances. David represents a spiritual understanding, based on the recognition that appearances are deceiving and that there are spiritual principles which transcend natural ones. Both Saul and David spent most of their time fighting. The Lord says to us in Isaiah 1:16, "Wash you, make you clean; put away the evil of your doings from before mine eyes; cease to do evil." This is a summary of the work of Saul and David—the overcoming of the enemies of our souls—which must be accomplished first. Then Isaiah 1:17

continues, "Learn to do well." This is the work of Solomon.

Swedenborg tells us that Solomon represents "the Lord in relation to His celestial kingdom and His spiritual kingdom." The celestial principle is love; the spiritual principle is truth. So under Solomon we are obeying divine truth understood in a still deeper way because we have come to love the Lord and the neighbor. Perhaps we can understand this better is we think of a simple example. We know that divine truth is summed up in the ten commandments. Suppose then we take the commandment "Thou shalt not steal." We all at first have a natural desire to possess the good things which other people have. Even very little children are tempted to take things which do not belong to them. We begin to control this desire because we find that stealing gets us into trouble. Obedience from this motive is symbolized by Saul. Then we are taught the principle of love to the neighbor, which is a spiritual principle, and we see that it is right and control our impulse to steal not from fear of punishment but because we really see that stealing is wrong in the Lord's sight; this is symbolized by David. But if we continue in the process of regeneration, we come to the point where we no longer covet what belongs to our neighbor; we enjoy his pleasure in it and would give him more if we could. All temptation to steal is gone and we are at peace; this is symbolized by Solomon. The name *Solomon* means "peace."

In other lessons we have had the stories of Solomon's dream in which he asked the Lord for widom and was granted riches and glory also, of the visit of the queen of Sheba and the details of Solomon's glory, and of the building of the temple at Jerusalem. But now we come to the dark shadow which falls over the latter part of Solomon's reign, brought on by his own sin. For all his glory and wisdom, Solomon—like David—was a mere man with the same selfish inclinations that we all have, and with our common tendency to rely upon our general good character to excuse our sins.

In our chapter Solomon is not rebuked because he had seven hundred wives, for we remember that at that time polygamy was considered allowable. It was rather because he took wives from among the idolatrous nations in the Holy Land, against the Lord's express command. In the Bible women before they are married represent affections for truth (or falsity), and women after they are married represent affections for the good (or evil) which their husbands picture. Solomon early in his career married the daughter of Pharaoh king of Egypt, which pictures taking to himself the affection for the memory-knowledge of truth. This is right and necessary, for we must learn truth from the letter of the Word and from doctrine as a basis for a good life. And Solomon might without blame have taken other wives from nations which had not been forbidden—nations which have in general a good correspondence. But the nations in the Holy Land were enemies of Israel, and their women represent affections for falsity and evil.

Did you ever know a person who was so unwilling to criticize anyone that he excused all sorts of wrong things? Mothers sometimes do this with their children, and then we say the children are "spoiled." This is like Solomon's loving women from evil nations. When we let our love for someone blind us so that we do not recognize and try to correct wrong things, we are committing the sin of Solomon. The Lord had told the people plainly (Exodus 34:16; Deuteronomy 7:3-4) why they must not marry wives from these nations: it was because such wives would turn their hearts to the worship of their idols. And this happened even to Solomon, who had been greatly blessed by the Lord and should certainly have remained faithful to Him. Whenever we admit into our minds the thought that any commandment of the Lord may be broken without resulting harm, we are opening our minds to the entrance of all sorts of falsity and are led further and further away from the heavenly life. The "kingdom" is taken from us.

We shall study the actual division of the kingdom later, but we should note here that the seeds of this division were sown by Solomon's sin. As we have said before, no great change really takes place suddenly. We may seem to be getting along all right in spite of our sins—Solomon was allowed to keep his throne until he died—but the consequences begin piling up. Solomon was told that his son would be able to hold only a part of the territory over which he had reigned, and he saw his enemies beginning to gain power. He also learned that Jeroboam, one of his own favored servants, had been promised by the Lord that he should rule over ten* of the tribes. There was nothing Solomon could do to prevent these consequences.

*Basic Correspondences*

| | | |
|---|---|---|
| Solomon | = | divine truth understood from love |
| women before marriage | = | affections for truth or falsity |
| women after marriage | = | affections for good or evil |

## Senior

The Seniors are old enough to see how this story can relate to the Lord's mercy and at the same time have an application to temptation in our own lives. We cannot too constantly stress with the young people the need of perpetual watchfulness and the fact that we never reach a state in which we can safely trust in self. This story is particularly apt for this purpose.

If you ask the "man on the street" what he knows about Solomon in the Bible, the chances are that his first and perhaps his only answer will be, "Well, he had a lot of wives, didn't he?" Shakespeare wrote, "The evil that men do lives after them; the good is oft interred with their bones." Solomon was the greatest of the kings of Israel. We are told in I Kings 10:23 that "he exceeded all the kings of the earth for riches and for wisdom." He built the temple at Jerusalem. Yet what the average person remembers is the thing which caused the downfall of his kingdom.

*See Bruce, *The First Three Kings of Israel*, pp. 549 ff. See also *The Sower*, Vol. 2, p. 331. *Note:* There is a good bit of inconsistency in the letter of the Word in regard to the total number of tribes: there are either twelve, or thirteen, if you count Ephraim, Manasseh *and* Levi. It is true, however, that whenever the tribes are listed by name, they will invariably add up to twelve; but some of the names will vary from list to list. In the dividing of the kingdom there is some obscurity about where to place both Benjamin and Simeon. Thus in I Kings 11:31-32 one *might* conclude there were only eleven tribes. —*Ed.*

We have had the story of David's sin and also the story of Saul's disobedience. The pattern is the same: a period of success led each of the three to set himself up in his own mind as superior to the commandment of the Lord. The lesson in the letter is obvious: Breaking the commandments never leads to good, and no finite human being ever becomes so perfect or so wise that he can safely cease to "search the scriptures."

But there are deeper aspects of our story for today which the New Churchman may study. The quotation at the end of this lesson is chosen to give you an idea of the inmost or celestial sense of this part of Solomon's life, the sense which relates to the Lord. "The Lord is good to all: and his tender mercies are over all his works." The writings tell us many times that not only does the Lord save all those Gentiles who preserve charity in their hearts in spite of the falsities in which they are brought up, but that His love is constantly reaching out to those in evil, trying by every possible means to lead them to see and acknowledge their evils and to turn from them. This is why so much of the Word is written in terms of vengeance and punishment, as well as why so many improper practices, like polygamy, were permitted to continue. They not only were representative of the states of the people of that time, but they kept them from falling into still deeper evils, and thus are actually expressions of the Lord's love for all mankind.

But in our Sunday school lessons our particular concern is with the spiritual sense of the Word, that sense which relates to the spiritual states of the individual man and woman. What does the story of Solomon mean for our personal lives? We have learned that a king represents truth (or falsity) ruling, and that the three great kings of Israel–Saul, David, and Solomon–represent divine truth ruling, understood in deeper and deeper ways as we advance in regeneration. Saul symbolizes a natural understanding of it and David a spiritual understanding. The task of both these kings was to seek out and overcome the enemies of Israel. Our first need after the outer life has been set in order–the period of reformation, pictured by the wilderness journey–is to wage war against evils and falsities in our own hearts and minds and overcome them with the Lord's help. This is not accomplished all at once. The books of Joshua and Judges describe our first efforts, with their successes and failures, and the two books of Samuel our later, better-organized attack which results in victory. Throughout this long struggle, although we have moments of victory with its satisfactions, we are never really at peace.

Finally, however, the enemies are conquered and Solomon comes to the throne. The name *Solomon* means "peace." We have come into a state in which we accept the rule of divine truth not from fear of the consequences of disobedience nor even because we see that the truth is from the Lord and therefore is to be obeyed, but from love, love to the Lord and the neighbor in the heart. We no longer want to do wrong things. Therefore we have no battles to fight: we are at peace. It is in the period of Solomon that the temple is built silently, "of stone made ready before it was brought thither: so that there was neither hammer nor ax nor any tool of iron heard in the house, while it was in building." Perhaps you know some old person who has apparently reached this Solomon state. Everyone loves and admires him. All kinds of people go to him for advice, as the queen of Sheba and others went to Solomon. We say he has a beautiful character. There is no evidence of weakness, temptation, or struggle in his life. Granted that not many reach such a state in this life, we know that a few do. Is it true that such a man has passed beyond the possibility of temptation?

Our chapter for today answers this question. It begins with the word *But* [KJV]. There is a temptation, and a very deep one, which accompanies this state. Solomon succumbed to it. It is the temptation to see nothing but good in everyone, to close one's eyes to evil and falsity and forget that it is never safe to ignore them. This leads the person gradually to condone evil and to accept false ideas without correcting them even in his own mind. Solomon's wives "turned away his heart after other gods." The acceptance of a false idea by a person known to be unusually good gives that falsity tremendous support and leads many astray.

And there is a way in which each one of us is subject to this temptation, even though in general we may be far from the Solomon stage of regeneration. When we love and admire someone very much, we may be tempted to excuse and justify his shortcomings, and to copy his faults as well as his virtues. At such times we need to remind ourselves of Solomon's sin and its conseqences, and to say to ourselves: "There is none good but one, that is, God. . . . if thou wilt enter into life, keep the commandments."

---

## Adult

Probably the best discussion material for this class will be found in the difference between the celestial and the spiritual sense of this chapter and in the danger of refusing to recognize and condemn evil and falsity on the ground that we are taught to look for the good in everyone. Some useful examples may be found in the Intermediate and Senior notes.

We may think of the series of the three great kings—Saul, David, and Solomon—as picturing the increasingly full and satisfying rule of divine truth in our lives as we progress in regeneration and understand it more and more deeply. Consider this divine truth as it is summed up in the two great commandments, love to the Lord and love to the neighbor. From the beginning of our regeneration we recognize these as the essential foundation of a heavenly life.

When we are in the "Saul stage" of understanding, they mean that we should attend and support the church, obey the commandments in their literal sense, assist those about us when they are in trouble, and give to various charitable causes—perhaps take an active part in such work. This understanding enables us to overcome some of our more obvious selfish tendencies, but it inclines us toward self-satisfaction rather than toward humility, and we make mistakes and must eventually see that it is inadequate.

When we study the two great commandments more deeply, especially in the light of their internal meaning, we come into the David stage. We do not discard the good practices which we have developed, but we examine them with a view to finding out what has been genuinely good in the Lord's sight and what we have been doing merely to be seen of men. In our worship we try sincerely to humble ourselves, and in our good works we learn to discriminate between the good and the evil, seeing that it is the good in everyone which is the neighbor to be helped, and that thoughtless and indiscriminate giving may actually promote evil. In this David stage we find within ourselves many "enemies" hitherto unnoticed. The reign of David is a long series of wars and conquests. And here, too, there is the temptation which comes with victory. But if we are willing to accept the Lord's rebuke and repent of our evils, eventually Solomon is born.

In AE 654[29] we read that Solomon represents "the Lord in relation to His celestial kingdom and His spiritual kingdom." Under Solomon the celestial principle, which is pure unselfish love, is in control of our understanding of divine truth. We now go to church and do good to the neighbor not to be seen of men and not from a sense of our duty to humble self and serve the Lord, but because we love the Lord and the neighbor. We are deeply thankful to the Lord and happy in the happiness of others. The long struggle against the enemies without and within is over and we are at peace. The name *Solomon* means "peace." The great wisdom and glory of Solomon are representative of the state of the soul at this time, and it is in this stage that the temple of heavenly character is built silently within us out of materials prepared beforehand.

Yet here again victory brings the inevitable temptation. Our chapter for today begins with the word *But* [KJV]. There is always a "but." The writings tell us that even in the heavens the angels sometimes have to be reminded that their own selfish nature is still with them and that it is only by the Lord's mercy that it is kept quiescent there. We all probably know some old people who apparently have reached the Solomon stage. They live beautiful lives. Their advice is sought on many problems and they stand out as examples in the community. But sometimes we see in them also evidence of Solomon's sin. They are so kindly that they "love" everyone, bad and good alike. They see only good and close their eyes to evil. So they condone false ideas and by so doing lead others astray.

AE 654[46] points out to us the law which Solomon broke. It is given in Deuteronomy 17:15-17 and includes these words: "Thou shalt in any wise set him king over thee whom the Lord thy God shall choose . . . but he shall not multiply horses to himself . . . Neither shall he multiply wives to himself, that his heart turn not away: neither shall he greatly multiply to himself silver and gold." And section 47 of the same number explains that horses in this case signify "false knowledges which are fanciful" and that "As wives signify affections of truth and good, which become the affections of evil and falsity when one man has several wives, it is said 'neither shall he multiply to himself wives that his heart turn not away.' And as 'silver and gold' signify the truths and goods of the church, but here falsities and evils, when they are regarded only from the natural man, it is said 'neither shall he multiply exceedingly to himself silver and gold.'" The section ends with these words: "Because Solomon not only procured for himself horses from Egypt, but also multiplied wives, and heaped up silver and gold, he became an idolater, and after his death the kingdom was divided."

Solomon's original and chief wife was the daughter of Pharaoh king of Egypt. The number of the *Apocalypse Explained* from which we have been quoting concerns Egypt and contains several references to Solomon. In section 3 of that number we read, "'Egypt' signifies in the Word the natural man in both senses, good and bad," and in section 33: "Because Solomon represented the Lord in relation to both the celestial and the spiritual kingdoms, and as all who are of both these kingdoms are in intelligence and wisdom through the knowledges of truth and good and knowledges that confirm these, therefore 'Solomon took the daughter of Pharaoh to wife, and brought her into the city of David' (I Kings 3:1); "And afterwards he built for the daughter of Pharaoh a house beside the porch' (I Kings 7:8). By this also was represented that knowledge, upon which all intelligence and wisdom is based, is signified by 'Egypt' in a good sense. And as every man of the church has a spiritual, a rational, and a natural, therefore Solomon built three houses, the house of God or the temple to stand for the spiritual, the house of the forest of Lebanon for the rational (for a 'cedar' and thence 'Lebanon' signifies the rational), and the house of the daughter of Pharaoh for the natural."

This leads us to the consideration of the celestial sense of our chapter, and it is important that we understand something of this, for the question is often asked, "How could Solomon represent the Lord when he had seven hundred wives and three hundred concubines?" The writings give us a very clear explanation of this. In DP 245 we read: "Solomon was permitted to establish idolatrous worship. This was done that he might represent the Lord's kingdom or the church, with all the varieties of religion in the whole world . . . And because the Lord after the glorification of His Human had power over heaven and earth . . . so Solomon His representative appeared in glory and magnificence, and possessed wisdom above all the kings of the earth, and also built the temple." The Lord's love reaches out to people of all religions and to the evil as well as to the good, and the laws of permission are His way of leading us without interfering with our freedom.

But we must not take these laws of permission into our own hands and use them as justification for indulging our own selfish inclinations. Solomon—both as an individual and as king of Israel—broke a law which he knew, and he and his people suffered accordingly. Read here also AC 3246[3-4] which tells us that concubinage, while permitted to the earlier church, is not allowable for Christians. We are all responsible for doing our best to live up to the highest truths which have been revealed to us.

---

## From the Writings of Swedenborg

*Divine Providence*, n. 245: "Solomon was permitted to establish idolatrous worship. This was done that he might represent the Lord's kingdom or the church, with all the varieties of religion in the whole world; for the church instituted with the nation of Israel and Judah was a representative church; therefore all the judgments and statutes of that church represented the spiritual things of the church, which are its internals; that people itself representing the church, the king representing the Lord, David representing the Lord who was to come into the world, and Solomon the Lord after His coming. And because the Lord after the glorification of His Human had power over heaven and earth . . . so Solomon His representative appeared in glory and magnificence, and possessed wisdom above all the kings of the earth, and also built the temple. Furthermore, Solomon permitted and set up the worship of many nations, by which the various religions in the world were represented. His wives, seven hundred in number, and his concubines, who numbered three hundred . . . had a like signification, for a 'wife' in the Word signifies the church, and a 'concubine' a religion."

---

## Suggested Questions on the Lesson

P. Who was the second son of David and Bathsheba? *Solomon*
P. Who was the third king of Israel? *Solomon*
J. What did he ask of the Lord? *wisdom*
J. What did the Lord give him? *that, plus wealth, fame*
P. What did he build in Jerusalem? *temple*
J. What sin did he commit? *married many foreign women*
J. To what further sin did it lead him? *idolatry*
P. What did the Lord tell him? *kingdom would be lost*
J. Would this happen before he died? *no*
J. How much of Solomon's kingdom would his son have? *one (two?) tribes [cf. I Kings 11:32]*
J. Who was to be king of the rest? *Jeroboam*
J. Who was Jeroboam? *servant of Solomon*
J. Who told him he would be king? *Ahijah*
J. What sign was given him? *torn robe*
J. What did Solomon try to do? *kill him*
J. Where did Jeroboam take refuge? *Egypt*
I. What does Solomon represent? *peace of soul*
S. What does Solomon's sin picture? *excusing or ignoring evil*

## ELIJAH AND AHAB

*I Kings 17; 18*

All the notes this time begin with the division of Solomon's kingdom, and this background material is very important to the understanding of the lesson. The teacher should read at least I Kings 12 to have the facts concerning the division clearly in mind. The reasons for the breaking up of the kingdom should be discussed with all the classes above the Primary.

---

### Doctrinal Points

*When we have come into a regenerate state, our minds are more immediately subject to temptation than our hearts.*

*Unselfish love—the Lord's love—in our hearts is the only thing that can give us happiness.*

---

### Notes for Parents

Sometimes when everything goes well with us for a while, we become overconfident and forget that we must still "watch and pray" that we "enter not into temptation." Long-continued success is not always good.

We remember that kings and queens came to Solomon to consult with him and ask his advice. As time went on, he made alliances with women from the idolatrous nations whom his people had been told to destroy. He "loved many strange [foreign] women," brought them into his household, set up places of worship for their idols, and finally began to worship those idols himself. This is a picture of the way in which we, when all is going well with us, often fall in love with the pleasures and possessions of the world and forget the first commandment.

In order to support all his wives and to keep up the splendor of his court Solomon had to levy heavy taxes, and the people became restless under their burdens. After Solomon's death they petitioned his son Rehoboam to lighten this burden. His wise older counsellors advised him to grant their petition, but instead he listened to the young men and tried to show his power by making the burdens heavier. So the ten northern tribes rebelled and set up an independent kingdom, which was called Israel. The southern kingdom, called Judah, remained faithful to Solomon's line, kept its capital at Jerusalem, and continued the worship in the temple. But Jeroboam, the first king of Israel, in order to keep his people from going to Jerusalem to worship, set up two golden calves, one in Bethel and one in Dan in the far north. The kings of Israel were uniformly evil and idolatrous. Their reigns, for the most part, were short and stormy, and the royal line changed often. This is a picture of what goes on in our minds when we forget the worship of the Lord and allow ourselves to reason from selfish and worldly considerations.

One of the most powerful and successful of the kings of Israel was the Ahab of our story for today. History rates him as a great king, but the Bible says of him that he "did evil in the sight of the Lord above all that were before him." Remember what the Lord had said to Samuel: "The Lord seeth not as man seeth; for man looketh on the outward appearance, but the Lord looketh on the heart." This is something we all need to think of often. So in the days of Ahab the Lord sent the great prophet Elijah to declare that the land was to suffer a prolonged drought. The worldly mind is unable to receive truth from the Lord—the rain of heaven. When we are absorbed in selfish pursuits, the Lord still speaks to us in His Word, warning us of our danger. And He still preserves in us, hidden in our memories, the verses from the Bible which we have learned or heard in our childhood, just as He preserved Elijah until Ahab had reached a point at which he had to recognize his need of help and so became willing to listen.

Elijah's test is one which we all need to think about very seriously. The prophets of Baal worked hard all day and even "cut themselves after their manner with knives and lancets," but no fire from heaven descended upon their altar. Similarly, we may work very hard—even injure our health—in the pursuit of worldly possessions and power, but it does not make us happy. Happiness comes only from unselfish love in the heart, and the Lord alone can give us this as we worship Him and obey His commandments. We cannot serve self and the Lord at the same time. Jesus told his disciples: "Ye cannot serve God and mammon." As Elijah said to the people, "How long halt ye between two opinions? if the Lord be God, follow him."

---

## Primary

Tell the children simply that after Solomon's death his kingdom was divided, and that the people in the northern part stopped going to the temple to worship and finally became so bad that the Lord sent the prophet Elijah to warn them. Teach the children the name *Elijah*. Then tell them about the drought and its results and go over the story of the two chapters as simply as possible. Read as much as possible from the Word, since there is little in the letter of this story which the children cannot understand, and no paraphrase of it can possibly be more dramatic and powerful.

Do you remember what Solomon asked of the Lord? It was a "wise and understanding heart." And you remember the Lord granted his wish and also gave him power and riches and all sorts of beautiful possessions. Wouldn't you think that Solomon would have been so grateful to the Lord that he would always have loved and obeyed Him?

But you know your parents do a great many lovely things for you, and yet you do not always obey them, do you? When you want very much to do some selfish or naughty thing, you are likely to forget all about obeying. That was the way it was with Solomon. He got to thinking he could do anything he pleased, and so his people began to be dissatisfied with him.

After Solomon's death his son could not hold the kingdom together.

It was divided into two kingdoms, the southern one called Judah and the northern one Israel.

The people of Israel forgot the Lord and set up two golden calves to worship, one in Bethel in the southern part of their kingdom and one in Dan in the north.

Finally one of their kings, Ahab, set up also the worship of the god Baal, the god worshiped by his wife, Jezebel.

What great prophet did the Lord send to rebuke Ahab?
What did Elijah tell Ahab?
When Ahab and Jezebel tried to kill Elijah, how did the Lord take care of him?
When Ahab was finally ready to listen to the Lord, what did Elijah tell him to do?
Where did the people gather?
What was the test to be?
How did the prophets of Baal try to persuade their god to hear them?
How did Elijah build his altar?
How did the Lord show which was the true God?
What did the people all say when the fire fell?
What did Elijah tell them to do?
What did Elijah do to the prophets of Baal?
What happened afterward?

---

## Junior

After your introduction, follow with the story of Elijah, using a map to locate the brook Cherith, Zarephath, Carmel, and Jezreel. (Note, however, that the location of the brook Cherith has never been exactly fixed.) Have the class look up and read Luke 4:24-26 (*Sarepta* [KJV] is the Greek form of *Zarephath*). The correspondence of the worship of Baal, of the drought and consequent famine, and of the fire from heaven can easily be understood by children of this age, and the meaning of the choice offered and of the test and its result is an important lesson.

Who was the third great king of all Israel?
What does his name mean?
What did he ask of the Lord?
What did the Lord also give him?
What did he build?

Even Solomon's great wisdom did not insure him against temptation. In his later years he did something which led to the breaking up of his kingdom. He was so great that he could have anything he wanted, and so he married a great many wives, women of different nations and religions. Then he built them temples for the worship of their gods, and naturally this led other people away from the worship of Jehovah and so divided and weakened the nation. And finally even Solomon himself began to worship these other gods.

It took a great deal of money and manpower to do all this and to keep up the grandeur of Solomon's court, and this meant that the people were heavily taxed and began to be dissatisfied.

When Solomon died and his son Rehoboam came to the throne, the people asked him to lighten their burden. The old men advised him to do as the people asked, but the young men urged him to show his power by increasing the burdens instead. He listened to the young men, and the people rebelled and the kingdom was divided, only the southern part, called Judah, remaining faithful to the line of Solomon. Judah kept its capital at Jerusalem and continued the worship in the temple. But the ten tribes in the northern part of the land set up a kingdom which they called Israel, making Shechem their capital and taking Jeroboam, a former general under Solomon, as their king. In order to keep them away from Jerusalem, Jeroboam set up two golden calves for them to worship, one in Bethel and the other in Dan.

When Jeroboam set up the golden calves, it was prophesied that his line should not continue on the throne of Israel. This prophecy was fulfilled, but the later kings continued the worship of the golden calves and brought in the worship of other idols as well. Many of them were killed by violence, and the royal line changed many times. Our lesson today is about the most wicked king of them all.

What was his name?
What was the name of his wife?
What god did they worship?
What great prophet was sent to warn Ahab?

Ahab and Jezebel blamed Elijah for the drought which followed, but the Lord took care of him.

Where did he hide first?
Who brought him food?
When the brook dried up, where did the Lord send Elijah?
What did Elijah ask the widow to do?
What did he promise her?
What other wonderful thing did he do for her?

Look up Luke 4:25-26 to see how long the drought lasted. (*Elias* is the Greek form of *Elijah* and *Sarepta* the Greek form of *Zarephath.*) Look up Zarephath on a map and also see how the country was divided after Solomon's death.

The Lord saw that suffering had made the people—even Ahab—willing to listen to Him. Read from the Word the story of Elijah's return and meeting with Obadiah (I Kings 18:1-16). Even evil men may have good servants. When we are in selfish states, our "good servants" are the memories we have of what we have been taught about right and wrong, especially from the Word. It was through the good Obadiah that Elijah could reach the ear of Ahab.

Look up Carmel on the map. It is a long ridge. One end of it juts out into the sea and the other end overlooks the plain of Esdraelon or Jezreel, through which the brook Kishon runs. It was at this brook long before that Deborah and Barak overcame the army of Sisera.

Read carefully from the Word I Kings 18:21-24, which tells of the test Elijah proposed to the people. The worship of Baal represents putting ourselves first in everything we do. Sometimes people are willing to work very hard and even to suffer in order to gain selfish ends. This is like the prophets of Baal, jumping about all day and calling on Baal and even cutting themselves with knives. The prophets of Baal are all the thoughts and arguments that try to make us believe that it is right to be selfish. See if you can think of some of these arguments.

What did Elijah build?

Read carefully I Kings 18:31-35 about his preparations. He wanted to prove to the people that nothing they could do would interfere with the Lord's answer.

What happened when he called upon the Lord?

The fire from heaven is a picture of the Lord's love—unselfish love—which always comes down into our hearts when we offer what we have to Him instead of thinking of ourselves in everything we do. Unselfish love is the only thing which really brings happiness.

Selfish people sometimes have fun for a short time, but they soon begin to want something else and are never truly satisfied or happy. If we stop to think, we can all see that this is so, just as the people acknowledged the lord when they saw the fire come down.

When the people were ready to worship the Lord again, the rain came. You remember that water pictures truth. Rain from heaven is the Lord's truth coming down to us. When we turn away from our selfish thoughts and begin to worship the Lord, His truth can be revealed to us.

---

## Intermediate

Something can be done with the meaning of Solomon's temptation and its results, stressing especially the weaning away of Israel from worship at Jerusalem. The protection of Elijah by the Lord, the meaning of the drought and famine, the return of Elijah when Ahab had been brought to a humble state of mind, and the meaning of the suggested test are all powerful lessons and easy to present.

The reign of Solomon presents an ideal of heavenly life. Under him the ancient Hebrews enjoyed their greatest prosperity and prominence. But this state could not last. The Word gives us teaching for life. Our lives are not a continual upward progress. We know that no sooner have we gained the victory over one temptation than we find ourselves faced with another. Every victory has its inherent temptation, the temptation to be self-satisfied and to imagine that we are now strong enough to do as we please.

During the latter part of Solomon's reign his very prosperity and grandeur led him to take wives of many nations, to build temples to their gods, and to burden his people with heavy taxes in order to keep up all his glories. So the seeds of division were sown. And at last even Solomon himself fell into idolatry. Only when we reach heaven can a state of lasting peace be attained. Here in this world, if our characters are to grow, we must always be discovering new and deeper evils in ourselves to be fought and overcome.

After Solomon's death the kingdom split in two. Judah, the southern kingdom, remained under the kingship of Solomon's line and kept its capital at Jerusalem. Israel, the northern kingdom, took Jeroboam as its king, setting up its capital first at Shechem and later at Samaria. Israel and Judah represent the two parts of our natures, the understanding and the will. When these are in agreement, we are at peace; but unfortunately we often find them at war. We never wholly desire what our minds see to be right, and often we desire to do right but fail because of wrong ideas in our minds. So most of the rest of the Old Testament story, until the coming of the Savior, is a story of two warring kingdoms, each having a succession of kings and both eventually falling captive to their enemies. Judah had some good kings but the kings of Israel were uniformly evil. This pictures the fact that we sometimes mean well even after our ideas have become false. The particular evil which caused havoc was the setting up of false gods, as in our lives it is the tendency to serve self and to fall in line with the ideas of those in the world around us. The people of Israel and Judah were weak because they forsook Jehovah, in whom alone was their strength. We are weak whenever we turn away from the Lord.

Jeroboam, in order to keep his people from going up to Jerusalem to worship, set up two golden calves, one in Bethel and one in Dan, and established this worship for Israel. This pictures the setting up of "natural" goodness and learning and worldly success above the things of the spirit. We recall that Shechem and Bethel were the sites of Abraham's first two altars. Now they are wholly perverted. The history of Israel is the history of violence and of frequent changes in the royal line. The evil is constantly traced to the setting up of the golden calves. It is said repeatedly of the successive kings of Israel, "He walked in all the ways of Jeroboam the son of Nebat, and in his sin wherewith he made Israel to sin."

Elijah appeared in the reign of Ahab, one of the most powerful and most idolatrous of the kings of Israel. Ahab had a long and outwardly prosperous reign. Secular historians consider him one of the greatest of the kings, but the letter of Scripture gives him no praise. He married Jezebel, daughter of the king of the Zidonians, who has come to be regarded as one of the most wicked of all the women of history. She led Ahab and the people of Israel into the worship of Baal, which pictures self-love ruling.

Israel under Ahab and Jezebel pictures our minds when they are governed by false and selfish principles. We have come to set up ourselves above everything else. When our minds are in such a state, we want to forget the teachings of the Word of God. Elijah, the prophet of the Lord, represents the Word. Ahab and Jezebel tried to destroy Elijah, but the Lord preserved him, first at the brook Cherith near the Jordan as long as there was any water in the brook, and then at Zarephath, far to the north on the Mediterranean Sea, which pictures what we might call the "back of our minds." Perhaps we imagine that we are never in the extreme state pictured by Israel in this story; but we really are in it every time we are bent on having our own way, arguing in favor of ourselves and closing our eyes to the truth we know which forbids what we want to do.

Elijah's first appearance in the Bible story is with the prophecy of drought and famine. When self becomes the center of our thought and life, no "rain of truth" from the Lord can fall into our minds and no "fruit of goodness" can grow in our acts. But after a while we begin to realize that having our own way is not making us happy after all. Nothing seems to be prospering with us. Our "land" is dry and barren. Then of our own accord we begin to try to find out what is really wrong with us. Ahab set out to find water. And that is just where the Lord can begin to help us again. Ahab had a servant named Obadiah who "feared the Lord greatly." In each one of us, however far we may stray from the right, there is a memory-knowledge of right on which we depend to keep our conduct in some external order, as Obadiah was "over the house" of Ahab. It is by means of this memory that the Lord speaks to us. It is easy to see why, in their search for water, Ahab and Obadiah went in different directions and why it was Obadiah who found Elijah.

Elijah told Ahab to gather all the prophets of Baal at Carmel for a test. Carmel is a high promontory overlooking the Miditerranean at one end and the valley of Jezreel or Esdraelon at the other. This valley was the site of many crucial battles—including that between the armies of Barak and Sisera. The ascent to Carmel is a picture of raising our thoughts to a plane where we can view all our accumulated knowledge and all our past experience in temptation and victory, and so freely reason out the problem of allegiance to self or to the Lord.

The prophets of Baal, the arguments in favor of self, worked hard, but they could draw no fire from heaven. Fire from heaven is unselfish love, which alone can give us happiness. Only obedience to the commandments, Elijah's altar of twelve stones, brought this fire from heaven—in spite of all the arguments against it, pictured by the barrels of water. When we see this and determine to turn from selfishness and serve the Lord, our land is once more watered by the rain and again becomes fruitful.

*Basic Correspondences*

| | | |
|---:|---|---|
| Israel in the divided kingdom | = | the understanding |
| Judah in the divided kingdom | = | the will |
| Elijah | = | the prophetic Word |
| Baal | = | self as a god |

## Senior

There is so much in this lesson for the Seniors that the teacher will do well to go through the whole lesson as rapidly as possible and then let the questions and comments of the class suggest its further development.

Our study of the Old Testament from the time of Abraham has seemed to indicate a gradual progression, reaching its climax in Solomon. But the story of Solomon teaches us a deep and much-needed lesson. Success has its temptations. We never in this world reach the point when we do not need to be on our guard against our own weaknesses and evils.

Solomon's wisdom and grandeur attracted to him the great of

many nations. He began to take wives from these nations, although the Hebrew people had been commanded not to do so. In the life of the soul this is a picture of our tendency to adopt the likes and tastes of those among whom we live without examining them to see if they agree with our religious principles. This is one of the faults into which we are particularly likely to slip just when we think we are established in the good life. Solomon built temples and altars to the idols which his wives worshiped and ended by worshiping these idols himself.

So his kingdom came to an end with his death, and his son was able to hold only the southern part—two tribes. In general, in the divided kingdom, Judah represents the will and Israel the understanding. United under Solomon these two parts of the land picture the times in our lives when we both know what is right and want to do it. But such states are brief. Doubts arise in our minds. Is it worthwhile to give up our own way always and serve the Lord? Is not the sacrifice too great? The Israelites rebelled against the price they seemed to be paying for the grandeur of the united kingdom. Rehoboam, Solomon's son, instead of listening to the advice of his more experienced counselors, tried to keep his people in line by adding to their burdens. So the northern kingdom broke away and accepted another king, Jeroboam.

Jeroboam, to keep the people from drifting back into their old allegiance, set up the worship of golden calves at Bethel and Dan. The golden calves picture "natural" goodness, the setting up of external good works as the real good, independent of recognition and service of the Lord. How easy it is for us to fall into the popular idea that material benefits are the real good works, and that it does not matter whether or not one thinks about God and worships Him so long as he is kind and charitable in external ways! But no deed is really good which is not inspired by the intention of serving the Lord and directed by His truth. Without this we attribute our good works to ourselves, and this is the beginning of spiritual decline, as the setting up of the calves was the beginning of the Israelites' downfall.

The line of David continued on the throne of Judah to the end, and several of its kings were good men who maintained true worship and carried out reforms. But it was not so in Israel. Chapter 16 tells of a series of short, stormy reigns, which picture our state of mind when the will and the understanding are divided. No principle can long rule in the mind which looks to self as supreme. The whole history of Israel is the record of a series of evil, idolatrous kings and of frequent, violent changes in the royal line.

Then Ahab, the most wicked of them all, came to the throne. He took to wife Jezebel, who has come down in history as the synonym for evil in women. They both worshiped Baal, which pictures the love of self ruling in the life. It is not hard to see why drought and famine were the result. Spiritual drought and famine are always the result of putting self first.

Against this dark background we have the wonderful history of Elijah. Elijah, like all the prophets, represents the Word. What Elijah said to Ahab the Lord through His Word says to us when we fall into self-centered and evil ways. Somewhere in our minds, no matter how hard we try to silence it, is a voice from the Word, which the Lord preserves and feeds as He did Elijah. And eventually we are driven by spiritual drought and famine to seek out Elijah and listen to him.

Chapter 18 presents one of the most striking and powerful pictures in the Bible. Every detail is interesting in the letter and still more so in its spiritual meaning. The three and a half years which the drought lasted represent the fullness of time in a selfish state and the preparation for a new beginning. At the last of this period even Ahab was looking for water. He had with him his servant Obadiah, a God-fearing man. Obadiah pictures that memory of a better kind of life which persists even with the evil and through which alone the mind of an evil man can be reached. Notice that in the search for water Ahab went one way and Obadiah another, and it was Obadiah who met and recognized Elijah.

Elijah called all the people together to Mount Carmel to witness a test between Baal and Jehovah. To make the test between self-worship and worship of the Lord we have to raise our minds to higher levels of thinking than our everyday ones. The prophets of Baal, who are many, picture all the reasonings which favor self-love. Some examples of these reasonings are: "You have to look out for yourself; no one else will"; "God helps those who help themselves"; "You have to be practical and realistic in this world." These reasonings are constantly active in our minds—they cry all day to Baal. But there is one thing which self-love cannot do for its devotees: it cannot bring them happiness, the fire of unselfish love, the Lord's own fire.

Elijah's altar of twelve stones pictures the setting up of the Lord's laws to govern our lives. The bullock sacrificed is the recognition that all the good we may do comes from the Lord. The water poured over the sacrifice is all the worldly reasonings which we have held to be true and which we imagine make the worship of the Lord useless. But upon the altar erected to the Lord, divine fire fell and the people were convinced. Baal's prophets were destroyed. Then abundant rain followed, meaning that we are enabled to see and understand divine truth once more, and our life again can become happy and fruitful.

## Adult

This is a very important lesson for the Adults because it describes and analyzes a temptation which we are all subject to right up to the end of our lives, and perhaps more especially we of the New Church. We can make no compromise between belief in the Lord and the Word and acceptance of worldly reasonings, and we should teach ourselves to examine the ideas of modern churchmen and Bible students to see which of them are really valid and which are based on rejection of the Lord and the Word. Elijah's words in I Kings 18:21 are addressed to us.

We are coming to the closing chapters of the history of the ancient Hebrew church. Let us pause to review briefly the outline of this history: the beginning in the call of Abraham to leave his own country and his father's house and go to the land of Canaan; the gradual development and growth through Abraham, Isaac, and

Jacob; the settlement in Egypt under Joseph; the bondage, the call of Moses, the deliverance, and the wilderness journey, during which the commandments were given, the tabernacle built, and the twelve tribes molded into a nation; the initial conquest of the Holy Land under Joshua; the confused period of the Judges, when "every man did that which was right in his own eyes" and they fell into one difficulty after another; the transition under Samuel when they were brought back to the worship of the Lord; and finally the period of the kings, when under Saul, David, and Solomon they were brought into order, conquered all their enemies, captured Jerusalem, built the temple, and became for a short time a powerful, peaceful nation to whom other nations paid tribute.

It is not hard to see in this outline the story of the spiritual development of a man or woman from the first childish consciousness of the necessity of doing right instead of merely having one's own way, through the experiences of early education and development, the temporary bondage to natural knowledges and pleasures, the long and often painful and protesting struggle to bring the external life into order according to the commandments, the long-sought establishment in the land of spiritual living, the temptation to be satisfied with half-conquest and to compromise with one's deeper evils instead of rooting them out, the graudal unifying of the life by means of the adoption of ruling principles of a more and more interior character, until one tastes the power and peace which come only to a life inmostly devoted to the service of the Lord.

But this is not the end. Such states do come to regenerating men and women even in this life, but they pass. They are only foretastes of heavenly happiness. We need these states, but we cannot remain in them because we are always finite and imperfect. Our ideal, the Divine Humanity, is eternally ahead of us; our test is in Him–not in ourselves. So with every victory are associated new temptations, exposing deeper evils in us and opening the way–if we are faithful–for new conquests. We are told (I Kings 11:1) that King Solomon loved many foreign women and in verse 4 that "it came to pass, when Solomon was old, that his wives turned away his heart after other gods: and his heart was not perfect with the Lord his God." The realization and enjoyment of victory and peace have performed their use, and the Lord permits evil once more to appeal to our affections, exposing some weakness of which we have not been conscious and starting us on a new spiritual task.

Swedenborg tells us that Israel represents the spiritual or "thinking" side of the church and Judah the celestial or "loving" side of the church in general or in the individual (AC 4292), the relation to the Lord of the understanding and of the will. Many interesting things are said of the reason for the division of the kingdom with reference to the Israelitish Church as a representative church (see especially AC 8770), but we are trying rather to relate the stories of the Word to the individual life. The history of the divided kingdom is the history of adult life. We all know from experience that desire and understanding do not always go together. We have good desires which we do not have the knowledge to carry out in act, and we have bad desires which we know better than to carry out. We ourselves are often in a "divided" state, desire pulling one way and judgment another. When desire and reason go hand in hand there is satisfaction and accomplishment, but if we remain too long in that state we slip into self-satisfaction and self-indulgence. These lead to division again, for it is in the divided state that we acquire new truths which point out our selfish feelings. The Lord has provided for this sort of division in order to make it possible for us to change. Our natural desires are selfish. If our thoughts were always in complete subjection to them, we should always think only the things which suited our selfish purposes, and the Lord could not reach us. However, the separation of thought and affection should be temporary, always looking toward reunion on a higher plane. When we have good desires, we should seek the wisdom to carry them out. When we learn new truth, we should cultivate the desire to put it in practice. A good desire which does not seek its appropriate knowledge not only fails to accomplish anything good but also rapidly degenerates into self-love, while truth which we are satisfied merely to know still more quickly becomes lost in the realm of fruitless reasonings. It was because Israel and Judah remained stubbornly separate that both were eventually taken captive.

Ahab was the seventh ruler of the separate kingdom of Israel. He was not a descendent of its first king, Jeroboam. In fact, the reigning house in Israel had already been changed by violence three times. When our thought life is separated from its true purpose of serving for the growth of spiritual character, it is easily upset by every new and revolutionary idea. The kings of Israel had been uniformly evil, but it is written of Ahab that he "did evil in the sight of the Lord above all that were before him." He not only continued the worship of the golden calves, which Jeroboam had set up, but he married Jezebel, daughter of the king of the Zidonians, who worshiped Baal, and set up a temple and altar to Baal in Samaria itself, which his father had made capital of Israel. The worship of Baal pictures the perversion of worship of the Lord into worship of self. The writings tell us (AE 159) that Jezebel represents the delight of the loves of self and the world or "the church completely perverted," and (AE 324[21]) that the worship of Baal represents worship from the loves of self and the world. So under Ahab—in our correspondence—the thought life has degenerated further than the setting up of "external good works"—the golden calves—as the highest good, and has come to consider self-gratification the object of life. Then drought and famine came. When once we make up our minds that the object of life is to serve self, our minds are shut against truth from the Lord and everything in us which can nourish spiritual life dies. "No Divine truth flowing in out of heaven could be received because of the falsities of evil, which were signified by 'other gods' and by 'Baal,' whom they worshiped." (AE 644[8]) The falsities of evil are the perverted reasonings which always spring up in our minds when we want to defend our selfish desires. We all know how we close our minds against good advice when we are bent upon having our own way. Under these conditions there could be neither dew nor rain in the land.

In this crisis the Lord sent Elijah. The mission of a prophet was always to denounce evil and prophesy its punishment and to encourage the good by promising reward. Consequently the prophets were always hated by the evil and cherished by the good. We know that there were many other prophets besides those whose sayings are recorded in the Word; in chapter 18 we read of a hundred prophets whom Obadiah saved from Jezebel. The Israelites doubtless received much direct instruction as to their external conduct from such prophets throughout their history. But those whose sayings found place in the Word transmitted a message of permanent and universal import. Of these Elijah is one of the most important, so important that he is used throughout the Word as a symbol of the prophetical parts of the Word. We recall that Moses and Elijah, symbolizing the Law and the Prophets, were seen talking with the Lord at His Transfiguration. Swedenborg tells us that in the Word as it is in the heavens, in place of the name Elijah appears "the prophetical Word" (SS 71). In our lives Elijah stands for the Word prophesying, denouncing evil, showing us what the results of our evils will be if we persist in them, and showing us also the rewards of a good life. In the New Testament John the Baptist performs the same office and is called "Elias [Elijah] which was for to come" (Matthew 11:14). Today we do not need prophets in the flesh because we have the Word. The Word tells us all we need to know. If we do not reach the heavenly life, it is not because the Lord has failed to warn us just as He did not fail to warn Ahab through Elijah.

Elijah was preserved by the Lord at first in the land itself beside the little stream Cherith. The ravens which fed him represent the most natural thoughts about right and wrong which, though not true, can be used by the Lord to maintain some spiritual life. We recall that a raven was first sent out by Noah after the ark came to rest on Mount Ararat. When the stream dried up, Elijah was sent outside the land until the time was ripe for his return. In the same way, the Lord always preserves in us something of the Word, keeping it alive as long as possible in our active consciousness and then in the external region—"the back of our minds"—whence it can be recalled when we become desperate over our condition. A widow represents one who wants to be good but lacks truth. In the state of our life pictured by Israel under Ahab, a widow outside the Holy Land represents perhaps some little remainder of kindly feeling of an external type, something which can be appealed to, and with which there is, like the widow's son, some seed which may grow into spiritual life. Elijah found the widow almost dead, gathering two sticks with which to prepare her last meal and oil. This represents a time when there is almost no nourishment left even for the the promptings of external kindliness. Elijah gave her a strange command: "Make me thereof a little cake first," meaning: "Do something, however small, in recognition of the Lord, and the little remains of goodness will be tided over and maintained until the way is again opened for truth to enter the life." Many people who have no real knowledge of the Lord and who in general lead self-satisfied and self-centered lives still hold in their memories a verse here and there from the Word which may from time to time influence their actions. The Golden Rule is perhaps the commonest of these. Do we not see in such instances Elijah preserved by the widow of Zarephath and in turn preserving her? Not uncommonly we are allowed to see the working out of the rest of the story. The widow's son died, picturing a time when life suddenly becomes empty and useless, when a person sees no possible happiness in the future. Then the Word which has remained with him shows its power and renews his spiritual life by lifting up what he had thought dead and restoring it. He recognizes the power and its Source and turns to the Lord. However worldly and selfish we become, however persistently we shut out the voice of the Lord speaking to us through His Word, divine providence preserves Elijah somewhere on the outskirts of our minds so that to the very end of our life in this world there may be some little opportunity left for us to hear and repent.

The time came when even Ahab was forced to look for water. He took with him his servant, the God-fearing Obadiah, and it is significant that in their search Ahab went one way and Obadiah another, and it was Obadiah who found Elijah and brought Ahab to him. Ahab's greeting was, "Art thou he that troubleth Israel?" Self-interest always finds the voice of the Word troubling. Then follows the test. The people were summoned to Mount Carmel—picturing the fact that the whole mind must be lifted up where it can see and judge clearly in spiritual light. Elijah stated the issue clearly: "How long halt ye between two opinions? if the Lord be God, follow him: but if Baal, then follow him." This is the fundamental issue which the Word places before every one of us. Love to the Lord and love of self are diametrically opposed to each other. If we choose to serve the Lord, we must put self-interest out of our considerations; if we choose to serve self, we must not expect any of the blessings promised to those who serve the Lord. We cannot serve the Lord on Sunday and self the other six days. We cannot serve self until we have made a fortune and then make up for it by building a church or endowing a hospital. If we say we believe in the sole Deity of Jesus Christ, we must study His life and follow Him, instead of thinking we or other men know better than He what the wise life is. If we say we believe the Sacred Scriptures to be the veritable Word of God, we must accept them as providentially given and preserved and not try to change them to suit men's ideas of what the Lord ought to have said. In our story, when Elijah declared the alternative, the people did not know what to answer. If we listen for any length of time to the promptings and demands of worldly and selfish reasoning, we become confused and hesitate to make the choice boldly.

There were many prophets of Baal but only one prophet of the Lord—many false ways but only one true one. The voices of worldly reasoning are many and loud. The prophets called upon Baal all day. They jumped about and even cut themselves with knives and lancets. Of a prophet we suspect to be false we may at times hear someone say, "He must be right. Think how hard he has worked, how he has given his whole life to the study of this thing!" But the fire from heaven does not fall upon the sacrifices of those who do not worship the Lord. The fire from heaven is the Lord's unselfish love coming into the heart, which alone can give happiness. Those who look to self and to human intelligence for direction are never satisfied.

Elijah repaired the altar of the Lord which was broken down. He built his altar of twelve stones. We must return to the worship of the Lord and accept all the truths of the Word as necessary to genuine goodness. We must prepare our sacrifice according to the Lord's order, doing whatever good we do in His name and not in our own. Then we may let men argue about it all they like, as Elijah allowed them to drench the sacrifice with water until the water ran all around the altar: it will make no difference. For when we call upon the Lord, He will hear and crown our efforts with happiness and peace, which are the evidence of His presence. The people who are happy are those who do not think of themselves but who look upon life as an opportunity to serve the Lord. We are happy when we have forgotten ourselves in love for the Lord's work. If we will go up to Carmel and observe the test, we shall have no doubt of the truth.

Then the people were ordered to take all the prophets of Baal and let not one of them escape, "and Elijah brought them down to the brook Kishon, and slew them there." When we have really seen that the Lord is the only one worthy of our service, we must search out all the false reasonings which have defended our self-love and destroy them in the light of truth from the Word. Then Elijah told Ahab to eat and drink. Our "individuality," which has led us so far astray, is allowed to recover strength so that when the rain begins—when truth again flows into the mind from the Word—we may go forward to a new spiritual state.

---

## From the Writings of Swedenborg

*Arcana Coelestia*, n. 4844[12]: "What is related of Elijah, that when there was a famine for want of rain in the land he was sent to Zarephath to a widow, and that he asked of her a little cake, which she was first to make and give to him, and was afterwards to make for herself and her son, and that the barrel of meal with her was not consumed, and the cruse of oil did not fail, was representative, like all the other things related of Elijah, and in general all that are in the Word. The famine that was in the land because there was no rain, represented the vastation of truth in the church; the widow in Zarephath represented those outside of the church who desire truth; the cake which she was to make for him first, represented the good of love to the Lord, whom, out of the little she had, she was to love above herself and her son; the barrel of meal signifies truth from good, and the cruse of oil charity and love; Elijah represents the Word, by means of which such things are done."

## Suggested Questions on the Lesson

P. What did Solomon build? *temple*

J. What did Solomon later do which was wrong? *worshiped idols*

J. What was the result? *kingdom divided*

P. What were the names of the two parts of the divided kingdom? *Israel, Judah*

P. In which one was Jerusalem? *Judah*

J. What did the first king of the northern kingdom do to keep his people from going to Jerusalem to worship? *set up two gold calves*

J. Whom do historians consider the greatest king of the northern division? *Ahab*

J. What was his wife's name? *Jezebel*

J. What disaster happened during his reign? *drought*

P. What great prophet was sent to warn Ahab? *Elijah*

P. What did Ahab try to do to Elijah? *kill him*

P. How did the Lord take care of Elijah? *ravens fed him*

J. When Elijah came back, what test did he suggest to Ahab? *"The God that answers by fire . . ."*

J. Where was this test carried out? *Mount Carmel*

J. How long did the prophets of Baal call upon their god? *all day*

P. How did Elijah prepare his altar? *twelve stones, twelve barrels of water*

P. What happened when Elijah called upon the Lord? *fire came*

J. What did the people say? *"The Lord is God"*

J. What happened to the prophets of Baal? *Elijah killed them*

J. What came as a result of this test? *rain*

I. What do (1) Israel, and (2) Judah, represent?
*(1) the mind or understanding*
*(2) the heart or will*

S. What does Elijah represent? *the prophetic Word*

## ELIJAH AT HOREB

*I Kings 19*

This lesson follows immediately after the last one, so there is no transition problem. However, for all but the two youngest classes an understanding of the reasons for the division of Solomon's kingdom and of the nature of the kingdom of Israel is as important as the specific story for today. Thus the teacher might begin by reviewing these points.

---

### Doctrinal Points

*The Lord is always trying to reach us, no matter how bad we become.*

---

### Notes for Parents

Against the background of the glorious reign of Solomon this lesson again presents a dark picture. Our states of high attainment do not last. New temptations appear. Success brings its own dangers. To the very end of our lives we need to be on our guard against the subtle attacks of our natural selfishness. Even the best people, especially those who have become very gentle and loving, have the temptation to excuse and then to condone selfish and false things in the people about them. The very first verse in chapter 11—immediately following the description of Solomon's treasures—begins, "*But* [only in KJV] king Solomon loved many strange women." The strange or foreign women represent the desires which do not belong in a life devoted to the service of the Lord and the neighbor. We admit these to our minds in a spirit of charity and presently find that we have taken them to our hearts as our own and are acting from them.

So the northern tribes in the land, which picture the intellectual part of our nature, revolted against Solomon's son and set up a separate kingdom. They established the worship of idols, and their history, that of the kingdom called Israel, is one of constant revolt and fighting. Their kings became progressively worse. Under Ahab, their most powerful king, the Lord sent the prophet Elijah to rebuke and warn the people. After three years of drought and famine and the wonderful test at Mount Carmel described in chapter 18, Ahab and the people were convinced of the power of the Lord; but Jezebel, Ahab's evil wife, was enraged and sought to kill Elijah.

In the Bible a prophet always represents the Word of God. When we are forced to admit that the Word of God is telling us the truth about ourselves, everything that is selfish in us rises up, like Jezebel, to try to silence it. Elijah's flight to Horeb, which is Mount Sinai where the commandments were given, is a picture of our discouragement with ourselves at such a time and of how the Lord gently and wisely sustains us and revives our courage so that we may go on. The Lord was not in the wind, the earthquake, and the fire, but in the still small voice which followed them. The Lord does not send our troubles upon us. Our own evils and the evils of others cause them, and the Lord saves us from the consequences as far as it is good for us. But sometimes He has to let us feel these consequences so that we may be impressed enough to listen to the still voice which tells us to take heart and go on trying.

---

## Primary

Remind the children that when Solomon died the country was divided into two kingdoms, Israel and Judah, and that in Israel the kings were wicked and worshiped idols. Have them tell who Jezebel was and why she hated Elijah. Be sure they know that a prophet is one who speaks for the Lord. Remind them of what had happened at Horeb and point out that this was why Elijah wanted to go there. If you have time, read them Genesis 21:22-34 in connection with Elijah's stop at Beersheba, which means "well of the oath."

After Solomon's death his kingdom was divided.
His son, Rehoboam, reigned in Jerusalem over the southern kingdom, which was called Judah.

Ten tribes formed the northern kingdom, which was called Israel.
Their king was a man named Jeroboam, and their capital was Shechem.
All the kings of Israel were wicked and idolatrous.
The worst one was Ahab, whose wife was a woman named Jezebel.
Jezebel was a worshiper of the idol Baal.
The Lord sent His prophet Elijah to Ahab.
Elijah proved to the people that the Lord was the true God, and they allowed him to destroy the prophets of Baal.
What did Jezebel say when she heard it?
Where did Elijah go to escape her?
How did the Lord help him in the wilderness?
Horeb is another name for Mount Sinai.
What do you remember about Mount Sinai?
What three great signs did the Lord give Elijah on the mount?
What came after them?
Do we have a still, small voice in us?
What did the Lord tell Elijah?
Who was to be prophet after him?
What did Elijah find Elisha doing?
How did he show Elisha that he was to follow him?
What did Elisha ask?
What offering did he make?
What position did he take while Elijah lived?

## Junior

Have the class study a map as you talk of the division of the kingdom, and be sure they know the names of the two divisions, the capital of each, and the location of the golden calves. They can easily understand why Israel rebelled against Solomon's line. They will want to study the map again for Elijah's flight, and to find Elisha's home, as well as Syria and Damascus.

You would think, wouldn't you, that Solomon's descendants could have maintained his glorious kingdom for many generations. But when people have everything they want and everyone looks up to them, they sometimes grow careless and imagine that everything they think must be true and that everything they want must be right. They forget that they must go on trying to learn and do the Lord's will if they want to remain great. Read the first nine verses of chapter 9 again to see the warning the Lord had given to

Solomon. But Solomon forgot. In his old age he married wives from among the many nations which sought his favor. He built places of worship for the various gods his wives served, and finally he even began to worship with them. In order to support his grandeur he levied heavier and heavier taxes, and the people began to grow dissatisfied.

So after Solomon died, the ten northern tribes revolted against his son Rehoboam. They set up a separate kingdom called Israel, with its capital at Shechem, and made their leader in the revolt, Jeroboam, king. Rehoboam's kingdom was called Judah and continued faithful to the line of Solomon; its capital was Jerusalem.

Jeroboam was afraid that if his people went up to the temple at Jerusalem for the great feasts, they would gradually drift back into allegiance to their true king. So he established a new worship. He set up two golden calves, one in Bethel and one in Dan, and decreed elaborate feasts in connection with their worship. So he turned the people of Israel away from the Lord, and all his successors followed in his footsteps. There were a number of good kings in Judah after Solomon, but every king of Israel was evil. The worst was Ahab, whose wife was Jezebel, a worshiper of the idol Baal. The Lord sent Elijah the prophet to Ahab with a warning, and Elijah proved to the people that the Lord was the true God, and slew the prophets of Baal. Jezebel was the patroness of the prophets of Baal. Naturally she was enraged by their death.

Where did Elijah go to escape her?

Find Beersheba on your map. We associate it with Abraham and Isaac. Most people have times when they are discouraged, especially when they have tried very hard to do right and apparently accomplished nothing.

What happened to Elijah in the wilderness beyond Beersheba?

The Lord is always at hand to encourage us and to revive our spirits with enough of His goodness and truth—the cake and the water—to sustain us for whatever we must do. Angels actually minister to us just as they did to Elijah, only we cannot see them.

Do you remember another name for Horeb?
What happened there?

Elijah knew that the Lord had spoken to Moses at Sinai; so he went there hoping to receive a message from the Lord. And the Lord did speak to him there. When we try to find out what the Lord wants us to do, we sometimes have to go through experiences which will really prepare us to listen and obey. The wind and the earthquake and the fire are pictures of the upsetting things which come to us and make us look to the Lord for help. The Lord was not in them. That is, the Lord does not bring them upon us. He merely permits them to come to us to make us stop and think. The still small voice is His. He speaks to our minds through His Word when we are thinking and meditating quietly about what He would like us to do. Conscience is often spoken of as a still small voice, but we should remember that our conscience can tell us only as much of what is right as we have learned from the Word. That is, the Lord can speak to us from every passage of the Word which we have stored in our minds.

First the Lord gave Elijah something new to do. Then He encouraged him by telling him that he was not alone as he had thought himself to be. There were still seven thousand in Israel who had not bowed the knee to Baal.

Who was to be the next king of Israel?
Who was to be the prophet after Elijah?
What was Elisha doing when Elijah found him?
What did Elijah do to Elisha?
What did Elisha ask to do first?
What offering did he make?

Sometimes today, when some leading person is succeeded by another who promises to follow in his footsteps worthily, you read in the papers that the person's "mantle" has fallen on his successor, and you will know that the expression goes back to this story. In the Word garments picture the thoughts with which our desires and affections clothe themselves. They are true or false thoughts depending on whether our desires are good or bad. Since

Elijah was the Lord's prophet, his mantle pictures the "clothing" of the Lord's truth, which is the letter of the Word of God. The literal story of the Bible is the mantle of the prophet which brings the Lord's truth to us.

---

## Intermediate

The general correspondence of the division of the kingdom, of Ahab and Jezebel, of Elijah, and of Jezebel's hatred of Elijah should be discussed.

Solomon's glory is a picture of a beautiful state which every one of us may attain in some degree if he will. But the history of the Old Testament did not end with Solomon. His reign was also a turning point, and a long decline followed it. The seeds of this downfall were sown by Solomon himself. He had been warned (I Kings 9:1-9) that he and his people must remain faithful to the Lord if they wanted their prosperity to continue. The first eight verses of chapter 11 tell us how Solomon turned away from the Lord and led his people into the worship of other gods. After his death the northern tribes revolted and formed a separate kingdom, which was called Israel. The southern kingdom, which remained faithful to the line of Solomon, was called Judah. Perhaps you remember that David reigned seven years over the southern tribes before he became king over the whole land, and perhaps you remember what that meant.

The division was a natural one. It pictures a division which exists in every one of us. Judah represents our heart or will, and Israel our mind or understanding. You can remember this easily because the south is warmer than the north and we are familiar with the expressions "a warm heart" and "cold reason." Our hearts and our minds do not always work together as one. Sometimes we want very much to do something good but we lack the wisdom to carry out our good desire, and sometimes we know just what we ought to do but don't want to do it. In such situations, our "Judah" and "Israel" are divided and working against each other. Judah kept its capital at Jerusalem where the temple was, and several of its kings were good kings who tried to bring the people back to the worship of the Lord. Our hearts have more good impulses than our minds have true thoughts. We shall have a lesson about one of these good kings of Judah soon.

But Jeroboam, the first king of Israel, who had led the revolt against Solomon's son, was determined to keep his people from going to Jerusalem to worship, because he thought that if they did, they might be drawn back to their true kings. He established his capital at Shechem, and he set up two golden calves for the people to worship, one in Bethel and one in Dan. A king represents a ruling principle. Jeroboam represents the principle that human reason determines what is right and not revelation from the Lord. All the kings who succeeded Jeroboam in Israel followed his example. So Israel represents our minds ruled by the false principle that we do not need the Lord to tell us what is right.

The most powerful and successful, but the worst of these kings was Ahab. He married Jezebel, daughter of the king of the Zidonians, who was a worshiper of Baal, and they set up the worship of Baal in Israel itself. Some of the enemies in the land had worshiped Baal before this. You remember that Gideon's first work for the Lord was to throw down an altar which had been built to Baal. The worship of Baal is the worship of self–pure selfishness–and Jezebel pictures the enjoyment we get from being selfish. She was the patroness of the prophets of Baal.

It was in the time of Ahab that Elijah, the greatest of the Old Testament prophets, appeared. We think of him as the greatest because he came to be recognized as a symbol of all the prophets. The prophet Malachi (Malachi 4:5) said that Elijah would come again, and the Lord Himself (Matthew 17:10-13) said that this prophecy was fulfilled in John the Baptist, not meaning that John the Baptist was a reincarnation of Elijah, but that he brought the same message from the Lord. At the time of the Transfiguration Moses and Elias (Elijah) were seen talking with the Lord, to represent that the Law and the Prophets taught of Him. The appearance of this great prophet in the time of Ahab shows that no matter how far our minds go astray, there is always in them some knowledge of the Word of God which the Lord can raise up to rebuke and warn us.

Chapter 18 tells the wonderful story of how Elijah proved to Ahab and the people that Baal was powerless to bring them happiness and that the Lord was the true God, and of how he slew the four hundred and fifty prophets of Baal by the brook Kishon. The people promised to obey the Lord, but Jezebel was so enraged by the death of her prophets that she swore to kill Elijah. Our natural selfishness tries to silence the Lord's voice in our minds. Elijah had to flee. He imagined that he was the only one in Israel who really desired to serve the Lord, and he begged that he might die. Sometimes we try our best and apparently make no impression. We say, "What's the use?"

Elijah's journey to Horeb and return picture the Lord's dealing with us in our states of discouragement. We are not forced. We are allowed to rest. The angels, who are always with us, speak to us in our quiet states and point out to us a little goodness, a little truth—the cake baked on the coals and the cruse of water—which we have learned by experience. This is enough to give us strength to go to Horeb, to return to the commandments as the laws given us by God, which cannot fail. We are shown how our troubles lead us to the Lord. The wind, the earthquake, and the fire are not the Lord speaking to us, as some people think, but are the effects of His presence on the worldly and selfish things in us. When they have passed and we can be quiet, we hear the still small voice.

Then Elijah was sent back to prepare others to carry on his work. He was encouraged by the knowledge that he was not alone in his worship of the Lord. He was to train another who could carry his message more powerfully. He was to cast his mantle upon Elisha. The mantle of the prophet pictures the letter of the Word. Elisha also was to speak for the Lord. Notice that Elisha was plowing with twelve yoke of oxen when he was called. Oxen picture the affection for leading useful lives, and the number twelve signifies completeness. So the ground of Elisha's ability to become a prophet was the wholehearted desire to be useful, and he was glad to begin his preparation as Elijah's servant.

*Basic Correspondences*

| | | |
|---|---|---|
| Judah | = | the heart or will |
| Israel | = | the mind or understanding |
| Ahab | = | a false principle ruling in the mind |
| Jezebel | = | the delight of the love of self and the world |
| Elijah | = | the prophetic Word |
| Elijah's mantle | = | the letter of the Word |

## Senior

In addition to the points discussed with the Intermediates, call attention to the meaning of the fact that the Lord was not in the wind, earthquake, and fire. Point out that the upheavals in our lives are not sent by the Lord, but are permitted to come to us when we need them as preparation for listening to the still small voice.

Elijah is perhaps the best known of the prophets, partly because of the power of the familiar stories concerning him in the Word, and partly because the ancient Hebrews recognized him as typifying the prophetical part of the Word just as they recognized Moses as standing for the Law. We remember that the three disciples who saw the Lord transfigured saw Moses and Elias (Elijah) talking with Him. Elijah was prophet in Israel in the time of the divided kingdom.

Judah represents the heart or will and Israel the mind or understanding. When a person has grown up with good habits and established himself in a good civil and religious life, he sometimes forgets, as Solomon did, that he must continue to watch his motives and thoughts, as well as his acts, and keep them faithful to the Lord's truth. Just as Solomon did, he unites himself to many ideas and aims belonging to the world around him and foreign to his religious principles. Then he finds himself in a divided state. He continues to have good intentions—Judah remained more or less faithful for a long time—but his mind is full of worldly ideas and governed by principles opposed to the acceptance of the Word.

Elijah, like all the prophets, represents the Word of God. He was raised up by the Lord to rebuke and warn Ahab, the most powerful and most evil of the kings of Israel. Ahab had brought into Israel the worship of Baal—self-worship—because he had married Jezebel, daughter of Ethbaal ("Baal's man") king of the Zidonians. Jezebel represents the delights of the love of self and the world. She is sometimes considered the worst woman in history, and the expression "a regular Jezebel" is an epithet applied to women who do great harm to those around them. She maintained four hundred and fifty prophets of Baal. The powerful story of the test carried out by Elijah at Carmel and of his slaying of the prophets of Baal is told in the chapter preceding our chapter for today.

Ahab and the people were convinced by the proof Elijah offered of the power of the Lord. But Jezebel was merely enraged. When the truth is presented to us in convincing form, everything that is selfish in us rises up to fight it.

Elijah's discouragement and flight picture the feeling we sometimes have that our deep selfishness is too strong for us and that it is of no use for us to struggle against it. The Lord's dealing with us in this state is beautifully pictured in the incidents of Elijah's journey. First he went to Beersheba, "the well of the oath," Abraham's home, which pictures going back to our childhood state of simple trust in the Lord's promises. This must be our first step when we are discouraged. There Elijah left his servant, the reasonings proper to the natural man, and went a day's journey into the wilderness—one more step in admission of his helplessness. There he sat down under a juniper tree. (This is not the juniper with which we are familiar, but a species of broom which is common in the wilderness of the Sinai peninsula. It was useful for shade. John Worcester in *Plants of the Bible* suggests that it pictures a belief in the working of the Lord's providence upon earth.) Elijah "requested for himself that he might die." In the letter this means complete discouragement, but inwardly it suggests rather the desire to be emptied of self. And this is borne out by the fact that he then lay down and slept, for in sleep our self-consciousness is dormant and the Lord can draw nearer to us. The coming of the angel twice with bread and water is the refreshment and enlightenment which the Lord grants as soon as self-will is wholly put aside, renewing both the mind and the heart. In the strength of that food Elijah went to Horeb, or Sinai, always the symbol of the commandments, and there braved the wind, the earthquake, and the fire—symbols of temptation in thought, act, and will—and was given to recognize that the voice of the Lord was not in these, but in the quiet meditation which follows when they are past. Then he was comforted with the assurance that there were still seven thousand in Israel who had not bowed the knee to Baal. There are always people who are ready to stand with us for what is right if we look for them.

Elijah was sent back to complete his own work by preparing another to carry it further. Elijah and Elisha both represent the letter of the Word, but Elisha, as we shall see later, represents the letter used with a deeper understanding of its source and meaning. The fact that when Elijah found him, Elisha was ploughing with twelve yoke of oxen pictures the truth that the effort to do good as fully and thoroughly as possible is the best ground for an ability to understand the Word and to use it for spiritual help.

---

### Adult

The last point mentioned for the Seniors should be stressed in this class also. Perhaps the best discussion topics are Solomon's sin, the golden calves, the meaning of Jezebel, and the general significance of Elijah's return to Beersheba and to Horeb.

Solomon's death marks the passing of the state of joy in doing the Lord's will. The sense of duty remains—his son Rehoboam—in our hearts for a long time. The southern part of the land—Judah—remained faithful to Solomon's line and kept its capital at Jerusalem and its chief worship at the temple. A number of its kings were good. But there is a state of resistance to the rule of the Lord in our minds. The ten northern tribes refused to accept Rehoboam and set up a separate kingdom called Israel, with its capital at Shechem. Jeroboam, the leader of the revolt, was its first king.

Jeroboam naturally was not anxious that the two kingdoms should be reunited, and he recognized that his people would be likely to go back to their old allegiance if they were allowed to continue in their familiar manner and place of worship. So he set up new objects of worship in new places—the golden calves at Bethel and Dan—and inaugurated a new feast to hold the people's interest within the limits of his own territory. "By a calf is signified the good of the external or natural man." (AC 9391[2]) We are familiar with the thought that the oxen and calves in the Old Testament sacrificial law picture our affections for useful work of an external kind, which should be made sacred to the Lord, that is, done from love to Him and with the recognition that all power to do good is from Him. When the calf is made an object of worship instead of a sacrifice, it means the setting up of external good works as the all of religion, enabling us to give ourselves credit for goodness.

Ahab was the seventh ruler of the separate kingdom of Israel. The reigning house in Israel had already been changed by violence three times. When our thought life is separated from its true purpose of furthering the growth of the heavenly kingdom, it is easily upset by every new and revolutionary idea. The kings of Israel had been uniformly evil, but it is written of Ahab that he "did evil in the sight of the Lord above all that were before him." He not only continued the worship of the golden calves, but he married Jezebel, the daughter of the king of the Zidonians, who worshiped Baal and set up a temple and altar to Baal in Samaria itself, which Ahab's father had made capital of Israel. The worship of Baal pictures the perversion of worship of the Lord into worship of self. The writings tell us (AE 159) that Jezebel represents the "delight of the loves of self and the world," or "the church completely perverted," the worship of Baal representing "worship from the loves of self and the world" (AE 324[21]).

Jezebel was the cause of Elijah's flight to Horeb. Ahab and the people had been convinced by the great demonstration at Mount Carmel of the impotence of Baal and the power of Jehovah, had promised to serve Jehovah, and had willingly seized the four hundred and fifty prophets of Baal and brought them down to Elijah at the brook Kishon to be slain. The voice of Baal speaking to the mind had been silenced. But the delight of self-love was still very much alive and in the person of Jezebel rose up to slay Elijah.

Jezebel's threat completely discouraged Elijah and caused him to flee. In this flight he left Israel altogether and went far to the south, first to Beersheba, the southernmost city of the Holy Land, prominent in the story of Abraham, and then on to Horeb. When one lacks sufficient understanding of the Word to enable him to defend it against the attacks of the loves of self and the world, his only salvation is in a return to childhood states of trust and obedience. Elijah took another step in the right direction when from Beersheba he went a day's journey into the wilderness and sat down under a juniper (broom) tree and "requested for himself that he might die." This seems to be a picture of complete discouragement, but as is frequently the case the internal meaning is very different. It expresses the recognition of one's own helplessness and ignorance, willingness to rely on the protection of divine providence, and the desire to be completely emptied of self. This is carried further by his lying down to sleep, sleep being the state in which consciousness of self and the world is relinquished and the Lord can come in closer contact with us. The immediate influx of the Divine into this state is pictured by the appearance of the angel with food and drink. The cruse of water is the truth needed, and the cake baked on the coals suggests goodness which has been developed by experience.

This is enough to give us strength to endure temptations until we reach Horeb or Sinai, i.e., the assurance that the commandments are the eternal laws of God. On the mount sheltered in a cave—a state of relative obscurity—Elijah was given the experience of witnessing the wind, the earthquake, and the fire—a demonstration of the upheaval which takes place in the mind, heart, and conduct of the natural man when he tries to conform to the will of God. But he was told that these effects were not the voice of God. They are the necessary reformation which must take place before a person can really hear the still small voice. Then Elijah was ready to leave the cave, wrapping his face in his mantle—making use of the veiling protection of the letter of the Word. He was given the encouragement of knowing that he was not alone in his efforts to serve the Lord, since there were still seven thousand in Israel who had not bowed the knee to Baal. And he was given instructions for the reorganization of Israel: a new king in Syria, a new ruling principle in the external life; a new king in Israel, a new ruling principle in the mind; and a new prophet, a new and stronger voice of the Lord in the land. The occupation of Elisha when Elijah found him pictures the life of devotion to useful service and the desire for the truth needed for such service which are the necessary ground for the commission of messenger of the Lord.

## From the Writings of Swedenborg

*Apocalypse Explained*, n. 159: "As all perversion of the church springs from those two loves, namely, from the love of self and the love of the world, 'Jezebel' signifies the delight of these loves. . . . Every man is such as his love is, and every delight of his life is from his love; for whatever favors his love he perceives as delightful, and whatever is adverse to his love he perceives as undelightful. . . . Those, therefore, who are loves of self and of the world, that is, they, with whom these loves reign, have no other life's delight, or no other life than infernal life. For these loves, or the life's delights from them that are permanent, turn all their thoughts and intentions to self and the world. . . . It is otherwise when man loves God above all things, and his neighbor as himself; then the Lord turns the interiors which are of man's mind, or of his thought and intention, to Himself, thus turning them away from man's proprium [what is his own], and elevating them, and this without man's knowing anything about it. From this it is that man's spirit, which is the man himself, after its release from the body is actually turned to its own love, because that constitutes his life's delight, that is, his life."

## Suggested Questions on the Lesson

J. What three buildings did Solomon erect? *temple, two palaces*

J. What happened to the kingdom after Solomon died? *divided*

J. What had Solomon done which brought this about? *idolatry, heavy taxes*

J. What were the two divisions of the land called? *Israel, Judah*

I. What do these divisions picture? *division of one's heart and mind*

J. What worship was set up in Israel, and where? *gold calves at Dan and Bethel*

P. In our lesson for today, who is king of Israel? *Ahab*

P. What was his wife's name? *Jezebel*

P. Who was the Lord's prophet? *Elijah*

P. Why did Jezebel want to kill Elijah? *he had killed prophets of Baal*

J. When Elijah fled, where did he go first? *Beersheba*

J. How did the Lord encourage him in the wilderness? *an angel fed him*

J. Then where did Elijah go? *Horeb*

P. What else was Horeb called, and for what do we remember it? *Sinai, ten commandments*

J. What happened when Elijah was in the cave on the mountain? *Lord spoke, gave signs*

P. Was the Lord in the wind, the earthquake, and the fire? *no*

P. What came after them? *still small voice*

J. What did the Lord tell Elijah which encouraged him? *seven thousand still true to the Lord*

J. What did the Lord tell Elijah to do? *anoint new kings, choose his successor*

J. What was Elisha doing when Elijah found him? *plowing*

S. What is pictured by the Lord's speaking in the still small voice? *times of quiet meditation after temptations, when we hear the Lord speaking to us through our conscience*

## ELIJAH'S MANTLE

*II Kings 2*

The lesson should begin with a brief review of the story of the division of Solomon's kingdom and the reasons for it. The substitution in Israel of the worship of the golden calves at Bethel and Dan in place of worship in the temple at Jerusalem makes an excellent connection between the general lesson of the divided kingdom and the mission of Elijah and Elisha.

---

### Doctrinal Points

*The power of the Word is exercised through its literal sense.*

*It is of divine providence that one becomes aware of the teachings of the Second Coming.*

*We never reach a point where we no longer need to study the Word.*

*If we see the spiritual meaning and God's love speaking through it, the letter of the Word will have new and much greater power in and through us.*

---

### Notes for Parents

I wonder if we haven't all at some time been just a little bit irritated by some dear old lady who was so good she just couldn't believe anything bad of anyone? We knew she was good and that it is right to look for the good in everyone, but when we were perhaps trying to correct some fault in one of our children and she insisted on shielding him and saying the child was such a little dear that we didn't need to worry about him, we couldn't help feeling that something wasn't quite right. The story of the division of Solomon's kingdom after his death shows us that there really is something wrong in refusing to recognize and condemn evil either in ourselves or in others. It is a very deep temptation which comes to everyone who reaches the beautiful state pictured by Solomon's reign, the state when one has come to love to do right. We are tempted then to feel that we can't do wrong, and no one ever reaches that state in this world.

After Solomon's death the whole northern part of the land and the cross-Jordan country rebelled against Solomon's son and set up an independent kingdom. Worse than this, they set up two golden calves, one in Bethel and one in Dan, as their centers of worship, so that they would no longer have to go to the temple at Jerusalem. When we have struggled with the temptations of our earlier lives and established what we believe to be a good character, it is all too easy to fall into the thought that we no longer need to study the Bible or go to church and that if we are kind and helpful and honest in our dealings with our neighbors, the Lord cannot expect any more of us. Then our attention becomes centered on the things of this world only. This was what happened to the people of the northern kingdom when they separated themselves from the worship at Jerusalem.

It was to these northern tribes that the Lord sent the two great prophets Elijah and Elisha. All the prophets spoke from the Lord. Our "prophet" is the written Word of God. If we hear and obey it, the Lord can lead us and take care of us. Our story for today tells how, when Elijah's work was over, he asked his servant and disciple Elisha what last wish he could grant him, and Elisha asked for a double portion of Elijah's spirit. Elijah told him that if he saw him when he was taken away, his wish would be granted. Then Elisha did see the horses and chariot of fire which carried Elijah to heaven in a whirlwind, and Elijah's mantle fell back to earth for Elisha to wear. This is a beautiful picture of how the Bible in the literal form which we know comes to us with double power once we really see that it is not just a book written by men but that it comes to us from God and connects us with heaven.

## Primary

The story is easy to tell and one in which the children will be interested. Emphasize the distinction between Elijah and Elisha and the relation between them. Elisha acted for a time as Elijah's disciple and servant and then became his successor. Before telling the conclusion of the story read to the children verses 9 and 10. The granting of a wish always catches a child's imagination. We remember how many fairy tales are based on this theme, but do not mention this fact to the children unless they bring it up themselves. If they do, be sure to impress upon them that the Word is not a fairy story. In fact, the idea as it appears in the fairy stories doubtless goes back to the instances recorded in our Word and in the Ancient Word, as so many universal modes of thought and speech do.

Do you remember what the Lord promised Solomon after he built the temple? He promised that if the people would obey his laws, He would always be with them in the temple and take care of them.

But the people didn't remember. After Solomon died and his son Rehoboam became king, a man named Jeroboam persuaded half the people to rebel against Rehoboam and set up a new kingdom. They accepted Jeroboam for their king. The other half of the people remained faithful to Rehoboam.

Jeroboam was afraid that if his people continued to go up to the temple at Jerusalem to worship, they might change their minds. So he set up two golden calves for them to worship.

Jeroboam was a wicked king, and all the kings that followed him were wicked too. Jeroboam's part of the land was called Israel and Rehoboam's part was called Judah. One of the very worst of the kings after Jeroboam was Ahab, and he had a wife called Jezebel who was even worse than he was. While Ahab was king, the Lord tried to save the people of Israel by sending a great prophet to warn them. His name was Elijah. Elijah showed Ahab in many ways just how foolish he and his people were to turn away from the Lord and worship idols. Ahab was almost persuaded, but Jezebel hated Elijah and tried to kill him.

But the Lord always protected him.
When Elijah was old, he was told by the Lord that a man named Elisha was to succeed him.
How did they cross the Jordan?
What wish did Elisha make?
What did Elijah tell him?
How was Elijah taken to heaven?

Did Elisha see it?
How did Elisha get Elijah's mantle?
What did he do with it?
Near what city did this happen?
What did some of the prophets learn from the miracle?

---

## Junior

Try to do more in this class with the division of the kingdom, using a map. This is an excellent opportunity for a map review lesson, comparing the Holy Land as divided among the tribes with this division into two parts and with the later division into three in the time of the Gospel story.

Solomon reigned forty years in peace and honor, but during the last part of his life he was led away from perfect allegiance to the Lord. He married a great many wives from other lands and set up in the Holy Land altars to their various gods. Also in order to keep up his splendor and the palaces for his wives he taxed the people very heavily. So after he died ten of the tribes rebelled against his son Rehoboam and set up a new kingdom in the northern part of the land with its capital at Samaria. This new kingdom was called Israel and the southern part of the land, which remained faithful to Solomon's son, was called Judah and kept its capital at Jerusalem.

The kings of Israel were uniformly wicked kings, not worshiping or obeying the Lord. The Lord sent many prophets to warn them. One of the greatest of these was Elijah. Perhaps you remember some stories of the miracles he performed through the Lord's power. King Ahab and his evil wife Jezebel made many attempts to destroy him. Our lesson today is concerned with the end of Elijah's life. The Lord had told him that Elisha was to be his successor, and he had called Elisha to go with him as his disciple and servant.

How did Elijah and Elisha cross the Jordan?
What power had parted it once before?
What wish did Elisha express?
What did Elijah tell him?
What did Elisha see?

If you should see such a thing as that, you could never forget it, could you? You would know that Elijah had been a real prophet or speaker for the Lord. No matter what anyone said or did, you would be sure you were right and would tell him so. That is like Elisha's double power. When we learn the commandments and try to obey them because our parents and teachers tell us we should, they have power to make our lives orderly; but when we are older and see that the commandments are really the Lord's laws, given to lead us to happiness and heaven, they have double power in our lives.

What fell from Elijah as he was caught up to heaven?
His mantle was well known by the people, especially by the "sons of the prophets."
So when they saw Elisha with Elijah's mantle, they knew he was Elijah's successor.
What did Elisha do with the mantle which proved this?
What miracle did Elisha perform for the sons of the prophets in Jericho?
As Elisha was going to Bethel, what did some children call him?
What happened to them?

This does not seem to us a very serious offense, does it? But in those days it was considered a disgrace to be bald, and "bald head" was a very bad name to call anyone. Elisha was the Lord's prophet and had to be respected by the people. When you are older, you will learn more of what this part of the story means.

---

## Intermediate

The correspondence of the time of the divided kingdom as it applies to us individually is important for this class, and also the meaning of Elijah and Elisha and of the double power given to Elisha and why it could be given.

The divided kingdom is a picture of a state in which we often are. At heart we want to be good, but our minds find all sorts of excuses for our being selfish instead. Judah represents the heart and Israel the mind when they are divided in this way. All the kings of Israel were bad. In fact, they grew worse and worse in spite of the many prophets the Lord sent to warn them, the greatest of whom were Elijah and Elisha. In his old age, when Jezebel had vowed to take his life, Elijah fled to Horeb and asked the Lord to take him out of his troubles, and the Lord sent him back to do some last things, one of which was to anoint Elisha to be his successor. In our lesson for today Elijah has done all the things he was commanded to do and his work is ended. Elisha has been with him for some time as his disciple and servant, and now his worthiness to succeed his master is to be proved.

First Elisha refused to turn back from following Elijah in his last journey. The Gilgal from which they started is not the Gilgal near Jericho, but another Gilgal just north of Bethel. The journey of the two prophets from Gilgal first to Bethel, then to Jericho, then to and across the Jordan pictures the way in which the letter of Scripture reaches down from the heights to the very outmost plane of our lives. It is in this outmost plane that we are in danger of losing our connection with the Lord by thinking of the letter of the Word as a mere dead relic of the past.

But Elisha, because he wished to obey the Lord, was given a new assurance. Horses are symbols of intelligence and a chariot the symbol of doctrine, the kind of organized teaching which enables our intelligence to work effectively and to carry us on from state to state, in this case even to heaven. Fire, of course, pictures divine love. Elijah, as the Lord's prophet, stands for the Word; Elisha also stands for the Word, but for the Word as seen from a higher understanding. When Elisha saw Elijah taken up to heaven by the horses and chariot of fire, he knew beyond question that Elijah's power had been a heavenly power coming from divine love, and this knowledge gave Elisha himself a double power. If we read the Word because we know we ought to and try to obey it for the same reason, it will indeed work miracles in our lives. But if we see within it its spiritual meaning and how the Lord's love is speaking to us through it, it has a new and much greater power in and through us.

Elijah's mantle pictures the letter of the Word. We should note that when he used it to part the water, he "wrapped it together," and later Elisha did the same. This pictures the fact that we need to see the teaching of the letter of the Word as a whole if we are to use it effectively in our lives. We cannot pick and choose what we like to believe and forget the rest. We must have an organized knowledge of its teaching. And no matter how much we know of the inner meaning of the Word, the power is still in the letter. We should all learn as much as possible of the letter of the Word and cultivate the ability to "quote Scripture" in times of need for ourselves and for others.

The rest of our chapter gives us two incidents in the beginning of Elisha's career as a prophet. First he showed the power to make the bitter waters of Jericho sweet. Jericho was in the plain near the head of the Dead Sea, the lowest spot on the face of the earth. The sons of the prophets there picture our efforts to correct the lowest plane of our lives, the cravings of our senses. The truth is bitter to us on this level, but the new understanding of it which Elisha pictures furnishes a new cruse—a new container—full of salt to make it sweet. Salt is the symbol of "the desire of truth for good." This means the urge to apply truth to our lives as soon as we learn it. When we have this desire, truth is sweet to us and makes our lives fruitful. Then Elisha started up toward Bethel and the little children came out and called him "baldhead." This is almost the only place in the Bible where little children are used in a bad sense, except in the passages where the Israelites are told to destroy their enemies including the little children.* Usually we think of the innocence and trust of little children, but little children are also ignorant and incapable of judgment. They represent beginnings. When they do good things, they picture beginnings of goodness, but when, as here, they do bad things, they picture the beginnings of evil. The hair, which is the outmost thing of the body in which there is life, represents our most external thoughts and deeds. The hair of the prophet represents obedience to the commandments in the outmost form. To call Elisha "baldhead" is to ridicule the necessity of learning and obeying the command-

*See, for example, Psalm 137:9. —*Ed.*

ments and in general to ridicule the letter of the Word. This leads people into gross external evils, pictured by the bears from the woods, and to spiritual death.

*Basic Correspondences*

| | | |
|---|---|---|
| the prophet's mantle | = | the letter of the Word |
| salt | = | the desire of truth for good |

## Senior

There are important lessons for the Seniors in this story. They will soon face the temptation to yield to the ideas in the world about them concerning the Word, and to think that if they measure up to the world's standards of goodness, they need no longer go to the Word for guidance. They need also to be shown that since, under divine providence, they have been introduced to the teachings of the Second Coming, a responsibility has been laid upon them to live the more spiritual life demanded by these teachings.

Elijah and Elisha, as prophets of the Lord, both represent the Word. The Word comes to us, as the prophets came to Israel, to show us our evils, to warn us, and also to show us the way of true happiness, to heal our griefs and troubles.

We recall that after the death of Solomon ten of the tribes, the whole northern half of the Holy Land and the cross-Jordan people, rebelled against Solomon's son Rehoboam and set up an independent kingdom called Israel with its capital at Samaria and its worship centered in the images of two golden calves, one at Bethel and one at Dan on the northernmost border. When we allow worldly reasoning to lead us away from worship of the Lord and come to think that if we do the outward kindly acts which the world praises, we are good people, we have, like Israel, separated ourselves from Jerusalem and set up golden calves in place of the ark and the temple. At the bottom of our hearts we may still acknowledge the Lord and admit that we ought to be led by Him—Judah, the southern kingdom, remained faithful to the line of David and nominally to the worship of Jehovah. The two books of kings are principally concerned with the history of the divided kingdom, the story swinging back and forth from Israel to Judah to Israel again, just as our attention alternates between our good intentions and our false reasonings when our minds and hearts are not in harmony. For when the mind turns from the guidance of the Lord, it goes further and further astray. The kings of Israel were increasingly evil.

The Lord through the Word does all He can to bring us back to the true way of life, as He sent Elijah and Elisha to Israel. In our lesson for today Elijah's mantle represents the letter of the Word. Folded together—that is, accepted and understood as a consistent whole—it is able to part the waters of Jordan, just as the ark had done long before. Swedenborg tells us that the power of the Word is in its fullness in the letter. We can see how this is. Take, for example, the twenty-third Psalm. We can study it verse by verse, learn more and more of its spiritual meaning, and understand it and its application to life better the more we learn; but all this is contained in the actual words of the Psalm, and we never reach the point where we do not need and love to repeat the Psalm in its letter. The more deeply we understand it, the more it affects us as we say it. So Elisha received a double portion of Elijah's spirit because he was permitted to see Elijah taken up to heaven by the horses and chariot of fire.

The two familiar stories told in the rest of the chapter are closely connected with the same thought. The prophet's hair as the outmost expression of his life, as well as his mantle, pictures the letter of the Word. So to call Elisha "baldhead" was equivalent to denying the holiness of the letter of the Word. The children who did this were torn by she-bears from the wood. Bears are hairy animals and picture an affection for the outmosts of things. So today those who deny the divine inspiration of the Word are often absorbed in the study of its letter as a mere human production; studying it in this way, they get further and further from the Lord. Their very study gradually destroys their spiritual life.

The story of the "healing" of the spring by putting salt in it is easily understood if we remember that salt represents the element which unites truth to goodness. Truth produces nothing unless it is lived. When we learn new truth, we should not go on doing just as we did before. Each new truth we learn should make a change in our life. This is especially true of the new truths the Lord made known in His Second Coming. We cannot be truly New Churchmen and continue to live the same old worldly, stumbling lives. If our "spring" is barren, it is because we need the "salt" of active application of newly learned truths to our own thought and conduct.

---

## Adult

The meaning of Solomon's sin and of the division of the kingdom and the setting up of the golden calves makes a good discussion topic to begin with. This should be followed by a discussion of the meaning of the wrapping together of the mantle, Elisha's vision, its result, and Elisha's first acts as prophet.

The transition from the peaceful, triumphant reign of Solomon to the divided kingdom is a sudden and striking one. Why did Solomon's kingdom not endure? The external reasons, as stated in the letter, seem inadequate. One would have expected the whole people to be too proud of their obvious glory and prosperity and of their great capital and beautiful temple to be tempted to rebel. The answer is to be found in the spiritual meaning of Solomon's own later acts. We recall that in the latter part of his reign he married many wives from other nations and set up altars so that they might worship their own gods, and finally began himself to worship those gods in addition to his own. There is a grave warning for us in this story. Solomon's reign at its best represents the highest state we can reach, when we have come to obey the truth from love. But this highest state carries with it a deep temptation, the temptation to imagine that now we can do no wrong and to be proud of our own all-embracing love. This leads to an unwillingness to see anything but good in ourselves and others, and to a state in which we excuse and finally embrace many attractive forms of evil. At heart we still intend to be good—as Judah remained faithful to Solomon's line and continued the temple worship—but our minds, having accepted the idea that everyone who does the outward kindly acts which the world recognizes as good is a good person, are led further and further astray. After Jeroboam set up the golden calves in Bethel and Dan to keep his people from going to Jerusalem to worship, the kings of Israel, who represent the governing principles in the mind, became more and more wicked.

The Word is full of warnings against this state. No matter how good our intentions may be, it is the mind (i.e., our thought life) to which the Word must address itself. So it was to Israel, the rebellious northern kingdom, that the great prophets Elijah and Elisha were sent. In AC 5321[5] we learn that "by both Elijah and Elisha was represented the Lord as to the Word." In the writings they are frequently mentioned together and no clear distinction is drawn between the two. Yet we know there must be a distinction. The power of Elijah passes over to Elisha in double measure, indicating that Elisha must represent a more potent presence of the Lord through His Word than Elijah. The Word in our minds increases in power as we progress in understanding and experience. We are familiar with the thought that garments picture external truths, like the language with which we clothe our thoughts. The prophet's mantle pictures the letter of the Word, "the Word in ultimates" (AE 395[4]), in which, we are told, the power of the Word is in its fullness. The same number gives us a detailed explanation of the parting of the Jordan by Elijah's mantle. As the Jordan represents the first truths which initiate us into the church, the mantle wrapped together—that is, the sense of the letter of the Word taken as a whole—has power to part the waters for us. We must have a knowledge of the general teaching of the Scriptures before we can rightly understand the particular passages of the Word which are presented to us. Failing such general knowledge, we are often baffled by the waters of Jordan: particular passages do not yield their true meaning and are turned into falsity. So in AC 4255[4] we are told that the dividing of the Jordan pictures the "removal of evils and falsities." The same miracle was accomplished by the ark in Joshua's time, because the ark represents the commandments and the commandments are a summary of the whole teaching of the Word.

When Elijah first called Elisha (I Kings 19:19), he cast his mantle upon him, and now Elisha assumes the mantle which Elijah drops, both these incidents representing the transfer of the representation of the Word from Elijah to Elisha.

Elisha asked for a double portion of Elijah's spirit. Those who grow up in the New Church and are introduced gradually to a knowledge of the spiritual sense of the Word are not conscious of the transition from Elijah to Elisha; but for one who has tried to understand the Word from a knowledge of the letter only and then finds the New Church teaching concerning correspondences, the experience of Elisha is a very real one. Elisha was told that if he saw Elijah when he was taken into heaven, his request would be granted. Elisha saw first a chariot of fire and horses of fire which parted Elijah from him. That is, Elisha's eyes were opened to see a representation of the Word in the heavens; the chariot of fire pictures "the doctrine of love and charity from the Word" and the horses of fire "the doctrine of faith therefrom" (AC 2762). And then he saw Elijah lifted up by a whirlwind into heaven. When we are permitted to see that within the letter of the Word there is a heavenly meaning which teaches a consistent doctrine of love to the Lord and the neighbor, the Word is lifted up as by a whirlwind in our minds. The letter, Elijah's mantle, remains but now has a double power. This is a very real experience. When we study the Word in the light of correspondences, passages which have been obscure and even meaningless to us are lighted up and become effective helps for life; and not only that, but we find ourselves acquiring an ability to remember and to quote the Word in our conversation with others and to pass on something of our new understanding and especially something of the recognition of the power of the Word.

The meaning of the healing of the waters of Jericho is explained in detail in AC 9325[9-10]. Jericho, as a city near the Jordan, pictures an external or natural teaching concerning the letter of the Word. If there is not the desire to apply these teachings to life, the waters are bitter and produce no fruit. The new cruse pictures new knowledge of good and truth and the salt "the longing of truth for good." The spring of the waters, into which Elisha cast the salt, is "the natural of man which receives the knowledges of truth and good, and which is amended by the longing of truth for good." When we see the Word only in its external meaning, many passages have no effect upon our lives because we cannot see their application. We often seem to read the Word without effect—our land is barren. This state can be healed by the added power which comes with our new understanding. If we have the desire to apply what we learn, every passage which we read with our new understanding can be made effective in our lives.

An example of this is found in the last verses of our chapter, where we are shown the office of the prophet in pointing out and condemning evil. As in the story of Uzzah, the punishment seems to us at first too severe for the offense, and here again a literal understanding of the passage has sometimes turned people away from the Word. But when we realize that Elisha represents the Word and his hair the letter of the Word, we see that to call Elisha "thou baldhead" is to ridicule the letter of the Word. Children always picture beginnings. Thus our story teaches us the danger of beginning to take the letter of the Word lightly, even through mere thoughtlessness, to make jokes about it or to laugh at such jokes, to make light of any of its stories. The punishment of the children was that they were torn by bears from the wood. Bears picture "those who read the Word and do not understand it." If we allow ourselves to break down our reverence for the letter of the Word, we become a prey to all those arguments and influences which emanate from the study of the Word as a mere natural history product. This is spiritual destruction. "For all the power and sanctity of the Word are gathered up and have their seat in the sense of the letter; for without this sense the Word could not exist, since without it the Word would be like a house without a foundation, which would be shaken by the wind, and thus be overthrown and fall to pieces." (AE 781[11]) See also AC 3301[9], AR 573, and SS 39.

## From the Writings of Swedenborg

*Apocalypse Explained*, n. 395[4]: "Because Elijah represented the Lord in relation to the Word, which is the doctrine of truth itself, and Elisha continued the representation, and because 'mantle' signified Divine truth in general, which is the Word in ultimates, so the mantle divided the waters of Jordan. . . . 'Elijah's casting his mantle upon Elisha' signified the transference to Elisha of the representation of the Lord in relation to the Word; and that 'the mantle fell from Elijah when he was taken away, and was taken up by Elisha,' signified that this representation was then transferred to Elisha, for Elijah and Elisha represented the Lord in relation to the Word and they were clothed according to what they represented, "the mantle' signifying the Word in which is Divine truth in general, or Divine truth in the whole complex. 'The dividing of the waters of Jordan by Elijah's mantle,' first by Elijah and afterwards by Elisha, signified the power of Divine truth in ultimates; 'the waters of Jordan' signifying, moreover, the first truths through which there is introduction into the church, and these first truths are such as are in the ultimates of the Word."

## Suggested Questions on the Lesson

J. What happened to Solomon's kingdom after he died? *divided*
P. What were the two divisions of the kingdom called? *Israel, Judah*
P. Which remained faithful to the line of David? *Judah*
P. What two great prophets were sent to Israel? *Elijah, Elisha*
P. When Elijah's work was ended, what did Elisha ask? *double portion of power*
P. What did Elijah tell him? *granted, if you see me go*
P. What vision was granted to Elisha? *fiery chariots and horses*
P. What fell from Elijah as he was taken up to heaven? *his mantle*
J. How did the sons of the prophets know that Elisha had become the successor of Elijah? *saw him part waters of Jordan with mantle*
J. What miracle did Elisha perform for them? *"healed" water*
J. What name did some children call Elisha? *baldhead*
J. Why was this so bad? *a sign of disgrace*
J. What happened to the children? *mauled by bears*
I. What do the two parts of the divided kingdom represent? *mind, heart*
I. What does the prophet's mantle represent? *letter of Word*
S. What is the difference in correspondence between (1) Elijah, and (2) Elisha?
*(1) Word studied from obedience*
*(2) Word studied with awareness of inner sense*

## ELISHA AND NAAMAN

*II Kings 5*

The teachers should review I Kings 12, in which the story of the division of the kingdom is told and also the setting up of the two golden calves which led Israel into idolatry and consequent steady decline. Mention Elijah and Elisha and their mission, and then introduce the story for today by speaking of Syria as one of the enemies harassing Israel.

---

### Doctrinal Points

*The Lord alone can heal.*
*Truth comes only from the Lord by means of the Word.*
*Natural knowledge cannot cure our inner evils.*
*Genuine love does not look for reward.*

---

### Notes for Parents

We all know from our own experience what it is to have a divided mind. Sometimes we mean well but find that we do harm rather than good because we have in our minds wrong ideas of what ought to be done. And still more often perhaps we know in our minds what is right but do not want to do it. When heart and mind, i.e., will and understanding, are at variance in this way, our strength and peace both diminish. This is what is pictured by the division of Solomon's kingdom after he died—the division of the Holy Land of a heavenly character. The warmer southern kingdom represents the heart or will, and the northern kingdom the understanding. The southern kingdom, which was called Judah, remained faithful to the line of Solomon and kept its capital at Jerusalem, with the temple as its center of worship. But in the northern kingdom, which was called Israel, the very first king, Jeroboam, set up two golden calves for the people to worship, and all the succeeding kings continued in this idolatry. Our hearts are likely to cling for a long time to the worship of the Lord in which we have been brought up, but our minds tend to be led astray by worldly and selfish reasoning.

The Lord sent two great prophets to rebuke and warn the kings of Israel—first Elijah and after him Elisha. Our "prophet" is the Word of the Lord, and sometimes unfortunately we pay as little attention to it as the kings of Israel did to Elijah and Elisha. Often people outside of the Christian altogether are more willing to hear the Word than we are. It is these good Gentiles who are pictured by Naaman the Syrian. He wanted very much to be healed of his leprosy, as the good Gentiles long to be spiritually clean. At first he could not believe that a simple thing like washing in the Jordan could cure him, and felt that the rivers of his own land must be just as good. This is a natural first reaction when one is told that faithful keeping of the commandments is the essential, and is better than all worldly reasoning. But once he was healed, he accepted Elisha's God wholeheartedly.

---

## Primary

After reading the story for today dwell on the figure of the little maid who, even in captivity, was sorry for her master and wanted to help him. Tell the children what leprosy is. Drill them on the names *Elijah* and *Elisha*. The rest of the story will carry itself.

The two greatest prophets sent to warn Israel were Elijah and Elisha. They did many wonderful things, helping the good people and punishing the bad ones. Because they obeyed the Lord, He could give them great power.

In our story today, what enemy has been troubling Israel?
Who was the leader of the Syrian army?
What disease did he have?
Who suggested a way to cure him?

Naaman himself must have been a kind man or the little maid of Israel would not have been so eager to help him.

What did the king of Syria do for Naaman?
What did Elisha tell him to do?
How did he at first take Elisha's advice?
What happened when he had washed in Jordan seven times?
Elisha would not take any reward from Naaman.
But his cure convinced Naaman that the God of Israel was the true God, and he vowed that he would never worship any other.
What did he ask Elisha to give him?
What happened to Elisha's servant Gehazi, and why?

---

## Junior

Use a map of the divided kingdom as the basis of discussing the introductory material. If your class has at hand a map of the Holy Land as divided among the tribes, the two maps may be compared. Point out Syria and Damascus. In the story of Naaman the Juniors can be given something of the spiritual meaning, as suggested in the last part of their notes. Water as truth is one of the easiest correspondences to make clear, and the difference between the Jordan and the rivers of Damascus follows. Explain also what leprosy is and what it represents.

At the very beginning of his reign Jeroboam made a disastrous mistake. He was afraid that if his people went to the temple at Jerusalem to worship and to take part in the great feasts every year, they might be persuaded to return to the rule of Rehoboam. So he set up two golden calves, one at Bethel in the southern part of his kingdom and the other at Dan in the far north; and he established regular worship of these idols with sacrifices and feasts to satisfy the people. As a result the people of Israel were turned away from the Lord, and all sorts of wickedness prevailed. The kingship in Israel did not stay long in one family. Several of the kings were murdered by their own servants, and many of the reigns were very short. Again and again we read of the new king: "And he did evil in the sight of the Lord, and walked in the way of Jeroboam, and in his sin wherewith he made Israel to sin." There was not a single king of Israel who was called good. And the enemies of Israel soon began to take advantage of this condition.

We have had three lessons about the great prophet Elijah, whom the Lord sent to rebuke and warn the people of Israel, including the story of how Elijah was finally taken up into heaven by a chariot and horses of fire, and how his mantle fell from him upon Elisha, who had been his follower and had been promised a double portion of his spirit. Elisha continued Elijah's work.

Our lesson for today is part of the story of Elisha. At this time Syria, a strong nation to the northeast of Israel, was getting the upper hand, making raids and carrying off the treasures of the kingdom and even some of the people. The capital of Syria was the great city of Damascus. Study a map to see how the Holy Land was divided, where the two capitals were, where the two golden calves were set up, and where this new enemy was located.

Who was the captain of the army of the king of Syria?
What disease did he have?
Who told him how he might be cured?
What did the king of Syria do for him?
What did the king of Israel do when he read the letter?

You see, the king never thought of Elisha. People today, when they find themselves in trouble, often forget that the Lord has given us his Word to heal our ills. They try everything and even despair before it occurs to them to ask the Lord's help.

What did Elisha tell Naaman to do?

The Jordan, which people had to cross to enter the Holy Land, pictures the truths which the Lord tells us are necessary if we are to enter the heavenly life. Look up Matthew 19:17. The Jordan as the entrance to the Holy Land pictures the ten commandments. So Elisha's advice to Naaman means that if we want our souls to be healthy, we must first of all keep the commandments. And it is not enough to keep them once: we must form the habit of keeping them. This is what is meant by Naaman's washing in Jordan seven times.

The nations which were Israel's enemies did not recognize the Lord. They represent the people who think only of succeeding in the world. The Abana and Pharpar, rivers of Damascus, picture maxims developed by worldly thought, such as, "You have to look after yourself first," and "You can't mix business and religion." These sound sensible, and many people like them much better than the ten commandments. Naaman thought the Abana and Pharpar were better rivers than the Jordan.

Who persuaded him to try Elisha's remedy?
What happened?
Of what did this convince Naaman?
Did Elisha accept the reward Naaman offered him?
What did Naaman ask him for?
What did Elisha's servant try to do?
What was his punishment?

Gehazi's sin of taking pay for Naaman's healing teaches us that we must never take credit to ourselves for any good we do. It is always the Lord, working through us, who does the good. Gehazi became a leper because the disease of leprosy pictures trying to appear good when we are really selfish, that is, doing right for what we can get out of it.

---

### Intermediate

The lesson for this class is the correspondence of Israel and Judah and their separation, and the correspondence of the Jordan and the rivers of Damascus. Explain that profanation is knowing the truth and turning it to selfish purposes instead of obeying it.

The kings of Israel were all wicked kings. Most of their reigns were short, and some of them were murdered by their own followers. No one family could keep the kingship long. And enemies from without were constantly threatening. This is a picture of the restlessness and dissatisfaction which prevail in the worldly mind.

The Lord sent great prophets to Israel to rebuke and warn both the kings and the people. You recall the wonderful stories about Elijah which we have recently had; and you remember how, when Elijah was taken up into heaven by a chariot and horses of fire, his mantle and power fell to his follower, Elisha. The story of Elisha runs from chapter 2 through chapter 13 of II Kings. Our chapter for today is just one incident in this story.

The Syrians at this time were a wealthy and powerful people bent on conquering the world. Their capital was the great city of Damascus. Syria pictures the knowledge of truth and good, but when it is an enemy of Israel it means that this knowledge has been turned to selfish purposes. The rivers of Damascus are the ideas which are current in such a state of mind, ideas of how best to get along in the world. Naaman was a principal servant of the king of Syria, captain of his army. He is pictured as a good man, but a leper. Our natural powers are the good servants who work for us, whatever our character may be. Leprosy was a terrible disease, characterized by lifelessness of the skin. The skin at first appeared extremely white, but as the disease progressed, decay set in so that sometimes the hands and feet and even the features of the face would rot and drop off. Leprosy pictures a state in which there is no spiritual life—no real goodness—in what we do. We may put on an appearance of doing good, but it is only superficial and does not last. Sometimes, however, people in this state, like Naaman, realize their condition and long to change, to become really good all through. Naaman, coming from outside the Holy Land, pictures the good Gentiles who have never had an opportunity to learn about the Lord.

The Lord always helps those who sincerely want to know what is right. They are led to the Word—often, it seems, as if by chance. The little maid brought captive out of the land of Israel was such a seeming chance. She had been in contact in her early childhood with the knowledge of the prophet in Israel and cared enough for her master to tell him where he might find a cure for his leprosy. You remember that the prophets always represent the Word. Naaman went first to the king of Israel, as people turn to the teachings of some church which seems to be the leading one, expecting to find guidance there. But if the church has become worldly and has lost its touch with the Word and its dependence upon the Word, as the king of Israel had forgotten the very existence of Elisha, it is powerless to help. Elisha had to remind the king. Then Naaman went to Elisha.

Elisha told Naaman to go and wash in Jordan seven times. We remember that the Jordan, the boundary of the Holy Land, pictures the truths we must know and obey if we are to enter into heavenly states of living–particularly the ten commandments. Naaman at first thought that the Abana and the Pharpar, rivers of Damascus, were better than the Jordan; that is, that the worldly ideas he had had before were more important than keeping the commandments. But, when his servants urged him to try the simple advice, he decided to make the experiment, and he was healed. Elisha's taking no reward for the healing is a picture of our recognition of the fact that it is the Lord always who does the good, not ourselves.

The result of wishing to be praised and rewarded for the good we do is pictured in the story of Gehazi. He became a leper because the desire for reward and praise takes all spiritual life out of our good works.

*Basic Correspondences*

| | | |
|---|---|---|
| Israel | = | the mind or understanding |
| Judah | = | the heart or will |
| Syria | = | knowledges of good and truth |
| leprosy | = | profanation of truth |
| rivers of Damascus | = | worldly ideas of good |

## Senior

Stress the insidious nature of worldly reasoning and the deterioration of the character when once we admit into our minds doubt of the binding nature of the commandments. Steady obedience to the Word is the essence of the lesson, and young people preparing to go out into the world especially need this lesson.

In the fourth chapter of Luke, when the people of Nazareth asked the Lord to prove His power by performing miracles there in the town where He had grown up, He cited to them two Old Testament stories to show that in the Lord's sight the good Gentiles might be more capable of being healed than the "chosen" people.

One was the miracle which Elijah performed for the widow of Zarephath and the other was our story for today—the story of the healing of Naaman the Syrian by Elisha. Elijah and Elisha, as prophets of the Lord, both represent the Word.

In the Word Syria pictures knowledges of good and truth, but in our story Syria has become the enemy of Israel. When such knowledge as we have is turned to selfish and worldly purposes, it can do us harm rather than good. This is indicated by Naaman's leprosy. Leprosy pictures the state in which good is done for the sake of getting along better in the world. There is no spiritual life in such good.

But many people grow up in environments where this idea prevails and, like the Gentiles who know nothing of the Word, accept it from ignorance of anything better. Naaman was in good repute with his master, and he was evidently kind to his servants, or the little maid would not have felt free to offer advice. He was prepared to pay generously for his cure. And, once convinced, he was willing to change his allegiance from his former gods to the Lord. In other words, he was a good Gentile and so could be healed.

In contrast to him was the king of Israel, who did not even remember the existence of the Lord's prophet at a time when he most needed him. He represents the worldly principle prevailing in the mind of a person brought up in the church, whereas the little maid who had been taken captive to Syria represents the remains of childhood affection for the Word preserved by the Lord for this same time of need.

Elisha's command to wash in Jordan seven times is the command to cleanse our lives by obeying the commandments persistently until they become our habitual rule of life. The hard part for us, as for Naaman, is to admit that the commandments are greater than the precepts of the world, and to humble ourselves to obey them. But only by so doing can we make our lives really clean and sound.

There are more interesting details in this story than can possibly be taken up in one lesson. The little maid carried off from Israel into Syria and surviving there to save her master is a beautiful picture of our innocent childhood states stored up within us to lead us later in the way of repentance and regeneration. Elisha's permission to Naaman to go with his master when he went into the temple of the God Rimmon pictures the Lord's mercy in recognizing our human frailty. It reminds us of the parable of the unjust steward. Gehazi's sins and its punishment remind us that we must never take credit to ourselves for the good the Lord is able to do through us, for just to the extent that we do accept credit we ourselves are spiritual lepers.

---

## Adult

Naaman's leprosy and its cure are the best discussion topic. They picture a common state and need in our modern life. Elisha's first treatment of Naaman points up the fact that the Word remains closed until we choose to obey its simplest precepts.

The story of Naaman the Syrian is a striking one. It is explained in some detail in AE 475[18] (see the quotation below). In Luke 4:27 the Lord Himself refers to this story, suggesting that it was easier for Naaman the Gentile to be healed than for the many lepers that were in Israel; this is a part of His condemnation of the people of Nazareth for not receiving Him. We know that the good Gentiles in the Word represent those who wish to be good but do not know how, from no fault of their own. When Syria is an enemy of Israel it pictures falsification of the knowledges of truth and good through dependence upon human instead of upon divine wisdom.

Naaman was a leper. In AC 6963 we read that leprosy pictures "the profanation of truth" and that "to believe in truths and to live contrary to them is to profane them." According to that definition, we are all lepers, for not one of us lives up to all the truth he knows and believes in. Yet we may all be like Naaman, desiring to be clean and willing to go to the Word for the means. The "lepers of Israel" picture those who do not wish to amend their lives. Chapters 13 and 14 of Leviticus enumerate many forms of leprosy, some curable and some incurable, and give the laws relating to them in detail. So there are many kinds and degrees of profanation, forms which may be corrected, and deeper forms, even to the "unforgivable sin" (Luke 12:10). DP 231 gives us a very interesting account of seven types of profanation.

Naaman's leprosy was presumably one of the milder forms, since it apparently did not interfere with his office as captain of the king's army or with his family life. The means of his being led to go to Elisha is interesting—the little maid who had been carried captive out of Israel. When, like the Syrians, we are confident of our own knowledge of what is right and of our ability to direct our own lives, we often attack Israel—that is, we argue against the authority of the teachings of the church—and we feel that we are victorious. Sometimes in the process we acquire some little affection for some of the things of the church which we can make serve our own purposes. And we all have some remains of innocent affection left from our early childhood. The Lord uses these, when we wake to our spiritual need, to direct us to the Word.

Naaman went first to the king of Israel, offering to purchase healing from him. In the same way, people in need are likely to go first to the most obvious representative of religion in their community, with the idea of "getting into church work" without searching out "the prophet"—that is, without trying to find out what the Word really teaches. They are not only disappointed themselves, but they often make trouble for the organization to which they have turned, as Naaman frightened the king by demands which the king could not satisfy.

The Jordan pictures the simple precepts which introduce people into the Holy Land of spiritual living—especially the commandments. We cannot enter this land without obeying the commandments. Naaman expected Elisha to come out and show him some special manifestation of power, but Elisha merely sent him a message. The Word is no respecter of persons. It does not have one method for the rich and another for the poor. It offers no one instantaneous regeneration. It says to every person alike, "Go and wash in Jordan seven times"—that is, "Go, learn the commandments and keep them faithfully until they shall have had time to do their work in your life—until your life is clean in the sight of God." But Naaman was angry and said, "Are not Abana and Pharpar, rivers of Damascus, better than all the waters of Israel? may I not wash in them and be clean?" We do not like to submit simply to the commandments. We like to think that our own ideas of right and wrong are better. Men think the world has outgrown the commandments, that new conditions demand new standards. Abana and Pharpar picture man-made ideas of right and wrong. But Naaman's servants persuaded him to try the prophet's prescription. So, when we reach the point where we realize that we must have some new knowledge, some new way of life, that we need the help of the Lord, our common sense should tell us at least to try the simple method which has cured men and women for ages. "My father, if the prophet had bid thee do some great thing, wouldest thou not have done it?" How prone we are to demand some new, startling, heroic mode of life! But steady, persistent obedience to the Lord's laws is the only road to a clean life, the only road to any real life. We simply do not know better than the Lord. "O Lord, I know that the way of man is not in himself: it is not in man that walketh to direct his steps."

When Naaman had been healed, he went back to thank the prophet and offered to reward him, but Elisha would accept nothing. This is one of the many passages in the Word which teach that we can never pay our debt to the Lord. Whatever righteousness we may attain is not ours, but the Lord's in us. The Lord gives us His gifts freely and our part is merely to keep ourselves in a state in which we are capable of receiving them and transmitting them to our neighbor. So Naaman went away promising to serve the Lord. But presently Elisha's servant, Gehazi, caught up with him and accepted a reward from him on the pretext that it was needed by someone else. Sometimes we go through a spiritual experience which leaves us in a state of humility and gratitude to the Lord, but when we have gone "a little way," our natural selfishness catches up with us, demanding that we give ourselves some credit for our good behavior and supporting its claim with various pretenses. Naaman "lighted down from the chariot" to meet Gehazi, as we too often are ready to abandon the teaching which is carrying us forward in a new resolution because of the prompting of a selfish thought. But Elisha was not deceived by Gehazi's lies. The Word penetrates the excuses with which we seek to cover our selfishness. "The Lord looketh upon the heart." And then Gehazi was punished with Naaman's leprosy. In the light of the Word self-interest is seen for what it really is, a disease which, if not rooted out, will spread throughout the system until it deprives us of spiritual life.

## From the Writings of Swedenborg

*Apocalypse Explained*, n. 475[18]: "'Naaman a leper of Syria' represented and signified those who falsity the knowledges of truth and good from the Word, for 'leprosy' signifies falsifications, and 'Syria' the knowledges of truth and good. 'The waters of Jordan' signified the truths that introduce into the church, which are the knowledges of truth and good from the Word, for the river Jordan was the first boundary across which the land of Canaan was entered, and 'the land of Canaan' signified the church; this is why 'the waters of Jordan' signified introductory truths, which are the first knowledges of truth and good from the Word. Because of this signification of 'the waters of Jordan,' Naaman was commanded to wash himself in them seven times, which signified purification from falsified truths; 'seven times' signifies fully, and is predicated of things holy, such as truths Divine are. Because 'seven times' has this signification, it is said that 'his flesh came again like unto the flesh of a little lad,' the flesh coming again signifying spiritual life, such as those have who are regenerated through Divine truths."

## Suggested Questions on the Lesson

J. What evil did Jeroboam commit? *set up two gold calves*
J. Why did he set up the golden calves? *afraid people would return to Rehoboam*
J. Where were they set up? *Bethel and Dan*
P. What two great prophets did the Lord send to Israel? *Elijah and Elisha*
P. In our lesson for today what nation is troubling Israel? *Syria*

P. Who was the captain of the army of the king of Syria? *Naaman*
P. What disease did he have? *leprosy*
P. Who told him how he might be cured? *captive Hebrew girl*
P. What did Elisha tell Naaman to do? *wash in Jordan seven times*
J. What did Naaman at first say? *rivers of Damascus were better*
P. What happened when he obeyed Elisha? *he was cured*
J. What did he ask Elisha to give him? *two loads of dirt*
J. What did Elisha's servant do? *took a reward*
J. What was his punishment? *leprosy*
I. What do Israel and Judah represent? *mind and body separated*
S. What does washing in Jordan seven times represent? *consistently obeying the commandments*

## THE REIGN OF ASA

*I Kings 15:9-24*

At the beginning of the lesson emphasis should be on the fact of the divided kingdom and the difference between Israel and Judah. Review briefly the story of Elijah and Elisha. Be sure the children know that Judah was the part of the country which remained faithful to the descendants of David and Solomon and continued to worship in the temple at Jerusalem.

### Doctrinal Points

*The thing against which we must guard most constantly is putting anything above service to the Lord as our prime object in life.*

### Notes for Parents

We may wonder why in our assignment this week we go back from II Kings to I Kings, chapter 15. It is only because the two books of Kings, in following the history of the divided kingdom, necessarily shift back and forth between the story of Israel and that of Judah. The four lessons preceding this have been on the northern kingdom, Israel; now we shall have four lessons on the southern kingdom, Judah. The history of Judah comes out most clearly by taking up the stories of some of its good kings, and the first of these, Asa, appears in I Kings 15.

When Solomon's kingdom was divided, the southern part, Judah, remained faithful to Solomon's line and continued the worship in the temple at Jerusalem, while the northern part, Israel, rejected Solomon's son, chose another king, and set up two golden calves, one in Bethel and one in Dan, as the object of national worship. The result was that while the kings of Israel were uniformly idolatrous and became worse and worse, Judah from time to time had good kings who instituted reforms and tried to strengthen worship of the Lord. In both kingdoms the people as a whole were easily led away into idolatry by the pagan nations who lived side by side with them.

We all know from experience what it is to have a "divided mind"—to want to do right and not be sure what is right, or to know what is right and not want to do it. It is this state which is pictured in the Bible by the divided kingdom, Judah in the south representing the heart and Israel in the north representing the mind. The kingdom united and at peace under Solomon is a picture of those times when we are at peace and happy because we both know what the Lord would have us do and want to do it.

After such a state it is our mind which rebels first. We ask ourselves in some new situation, "Is it really worthwhile to follow the Lord wholly?" Selfish considerations appeal strongly to our minds, although our "better nature" clings to the principles which we have been taught from the Word. The good kings in Judah represent such principles. In our story today Asa removes the idols which the people have set up. Once we have become established in the Christian life, we are frequently led to judge ourselves in this way, to see that some of the things which have appealed to us as more important than strict goodness are really unworthy of our effort, and to try to put them out of our calculations.

But often, like Asa, we do not do a thorough job. Verse 14 of our chapter says, "But the high places were not removed." The high places were the elevations which had been built up to hold idols. We may make ourselves see that certain particular things we have been "worshiping" are worthless, but we are not quite willing to give up the self-satisfaction and pride in our own judgment which has supported these pursuits. It is this pride which is represented by high places. It was because Asa stopped short of complete reform that he was moved later to seek the help of the king of Syria instead of trusting in the Lord, and that he gave up the treasures of the temple to gain this help. And finally we read that "in the time of his old age he was diseased in his feet." When we cling to our pride in our own wisdom, we eventually slip back into the ways of the world instead of walking firmly in the paths of the Lord.

---

### Primary

Remind the children of the wicked Ahab in an earlier lesson. Then tell them that Asa was a good king. Tell them about the worship of idols and repeat the commandment against worshiping idols (Exodus 20:2-6). Then tell them how Asa destroyed the idols and brought the people back to the worship of the Lord. The good side of Asa's story is the important one for the little children, but mention the fact that Asa made mistakes, too, as all of us do, and also mention the disease in his feet in his old age. This may seem a very small point, but it will interest the children and will help to fix Asa in their minds. Later its correspondence will be important.

Do you remember how the people in the northern part of the land rebelled against Solomon's son and set up a kingdom of their own? Their first king was afraid that if his people continued to go down to the temple at Jerusalem to worship, as they had been brought up to do, they would in time be drawn back into the other kingdom. So he set up two calves made of gold, one in Bethel just across the border from Jerusalem, and the other in Dan, the city farthest north in his own kingdom. And he appointed ceremonies and great feast days for the worship of these calves, so that the people would enjoy themselves in it. So the people of the northern kingdom never did return to the worship of the Lord. In spite of the warnings of the prophets Elijah and Elisha, whom the Lord sent to them, they became worse and worse until finally the Lord could not help them anymore and their enemies conquered them and carried them all away.

But the people of the southern kingdom had the temple and its worship to keep them reminded of the Lord. They were not very good either, and were often tempted to worship the idols which the other peoples of the land worshiped, and sometimes they even set up idols of their own. Many of their kings were bad, too, but every once in a while there would come a king who was good, who would try to bring his people back to the worship of their true God.

Our story today is about the third king of Judah.
What was his name?
Was he a good or a bad king?
What good things did he do?
What did he not do that he should have done?
How did the king of Israel try to injure him?
To whom did Asa send for help?
What did he use for presents to persuade Benhadad?
How did Benhadad help him?
What physical trouble did Asa have in his old age?

## Junior

This class will be interested in a study of the situation with the help of a map and in discussing how Asa's leaving the high places untouched and turning to Syria for aid would be likely to invite trouble later. The lesson of the result of not doing a thorough job of "cleaning up" is good for this age group.

All the kings of Israel were evil. In spite of the Lord's warnings through the prophets Elijah and Elisha, Israel became worse and worse and finally was taken captive by Assyria and all its people carried away into captivity, never to return.

But the history of Judah was different. In the first place the kings of Judah were all descendants of David. Read verse 4 of our chapter to see why. They were not all good, and the people of Judah were often led away into the worship of the idols of the nations among whom they dwelt. But you remember that the capital of Judah was Jerusalem, where the temple was; so they always had that to remind them of the Lord. Sometimes they neglected the temple and let it fall into disrepair, and one bad king even set up idols in the temple itself. But every once in a while a good king would come to the throne, who would restore the worship of the Lord and bring about reforms. So Judah was able to stand longer than Israel and, although it, too, was eventually conquered and many of its people carried away to the conquering Babylonia, some of the people were left in the land and others were, after a time, allowed to return and rebuild the temple. So it was the descendants of the people of Judah who were the Jews of the Lord's time.

The first of the good kings of Judah was the great-grandson of Solomon.

What was his name?

It is said in verse 14 that "Asa's heart was perfect with the Lord all his days." This means that he always wanted to do right. We shall see that he made mistakes, but his intention was good.

What was the first good thing he did?

Perhaps you remember that in Abraham's time the great cities of Sodom and Gomorrah were destroyed by a rain of "fire and brimstone" from heaven because all the people in them had become so wicked. Afterward those who practiced similar evils were sometimes called sodomites.

What other good thing did Asa do?
What did he not do that he should have done?

This same thing is said of several of the other good kings. It means that though they destroyed the idols themselves, they did not break down the places where the idols had been set up, and so afterward it was easy to put new idols there. The idols were images of various kinds. Some people today still worship such images. We do not worship images, but really anything that we think of as more important to us than obeying the Lord is our idol. People may make an idol of money or social position or political power or sports and pleasures. Sometimes even you, for instance, come to see that you have been caring too much about fun or sports or even eating, and you make up your mind to put that particular enjoyment down in your life to the level where it belongs and not to let it come first in all your thinking and planning. This is like Asa destroying the idols. Grown people do this, too, with their idols. But if they do not go further and recognize that there is something which supports all these idols and leads us into the worship of them—the thought that we ourselves are of first concern in everything—then they are not destroying the high places, and other idols will soon take the place of those they have removed. The "high places" are the feeling of our own importance and wisdom.

Who was king of Israel during most of Asa's life?

He was not a descendant of Jeroboam. Nadab, Jeroboam's son, reigned only two years and then the people, led by Baasha of the tribe of Issachar, rebelled against him. Baasha killed Nadab and became king himself. The royal line in Israel changed several times in this way.

What did Baasha do to trouble Asa?
To whom did Asa send for help?
What did Asa give the king of Syria in return for his help?

In II Chronicles three chapters, 14, 15, and 16, are devoted to Asa's reign. The books of Chronicles are the temple records and do not have an inner sense. But we sometimes learn interesting details from them. So in regard to Asa we learn that he was rebuked through a prophet for trusting the king of Syria instead of the Lord, and that the last part of his reign was less happy than the first.

How long did Asa reign?
What physical ailment did he have in his old age?

---

## Intermediate

The children of this age are able to understand the general meaning of the divided kingdom in us and how hard it is for us to stay good when we let ourselves begin to think in a worldly way about our everyday life. Stress our need of the courage to stand by our religious principles in the face of temptation from companions.

Our lesson today is chosen partly because it is typical of the history of the divided kingdom and partly because Asa has come down in history as a well-known figure in spite of the fact that his story is told in only a few verses.

The Lord kept His promise to David that he should always have a son to sit on the throne of Judah. Evil as many of the kings of Judah were, they were all of David's line. This means that once the heart has accepted the rule of the Lord's truth, it never can quite forget that sovereignty. However bad some of its states are, it is bound to stop now and then and examine itself and try to reform. So the kings of Judah were not all bad. Every little while there was a very good one. The sign of a bad king was the setting up of idols; the sign of a good king was the destruction of them. Idolatry is the setting up of anything as our supreme-goal in life except service of the Lord. We should guard against this more than against anything else.

Spiritual idolatry may creep into our lives without our recognizing it. Up to the time of Asa's reign there is no mention of neglect of the temple worship. The idols were set up in the "high places" outside of Jerusalem. So at first we may continue to go to church and worship the Lord on Sunday but may forget Him during the week in our pursuit of knowledge or money or pleasure. It is recorded that Asa destroyed the idols, but "the high places were not removed." We come to our senses from time to time and dethrone certain false goals which we find to be in control of our thinking in regard to our daily life, but often we do not go quite far enough. We do not destroy the high places, the tendency to trust our own judgment, to assume that what we think is right just because we think it.

If we remember that "high places" used in a bad sense are the opposite of true humility before the Lord, we shall understand the result of this neglect of Asa's. Other good kings had this same weakness. Literally, when the high places were left untouched, people still continued to go to them for worship and it was easy to put new idols in them when the good king was gone. So it is with us: if we do not recognize and break down our tendency to self-esteem and pride in our own intelligence, we merely replace one worldly goal with another, and worship of the Lord gradually dies out of our lives. Later in the story of Judah we find that the temple fell into disrepair and finally that idols were set up in the very temple court.

In this chapter, too, we have the first appearance of the king of

Syria, who was to play an important role in the subsequent history of both Judah and Israel. Syria and Assyria picture the rational faculty—Syria especially that faculty in the natural plane of the mind. We all know that we may use our reason to support either truth or falsity—that we may argue in favor of either. It is not the possession of good reasoning power which makes a person good, but the desire of his heart to serve the Lord and the neighbor. In our story today Syria is brought in as an ally of the good king Asa, but Asa buys this help by giving up the gold and silver of the temple. Syria, which later would become an enemy, thus gained a type of control in Judah. Asa saved his country for the time being but at the cost of later disaster. Read here II Chronicles 16:7-10, which tells how the Lord sent a prophet to Asa to rebuke him for trusting in the king of Syria instead of in the Lord. The two books of Chronicles do not have an inner sense. We do not study them in Sunday school for this reason. But we may often find interesting historical details in them which are not mentioned in the Word itself. Chapters 14, 15, and 16 of II Chronicles are concerned with the reign of Asa. Asa's looking to Syria for help is a picture of trying to support our belief in the Lord and the Word by means of natural things, as people try to find traces of the flood in order to support the story of Noah. In doing this they are really giving up their inner certainty with regard to the Lord and the Word, the gold and silver of the temple.

Asa's weakness in this respect had an interesting result. Verse 23 tells us that "in the time of his old age he was diseased in his feet." The feet represent our outward conduct. When we begin to look to men and to nature for support of our faith instead of trusting wholeheartedly in the Lord, sooner or later we begin to do as other people do instead of governing our conduct by the Lord's laws. We become diseased in our spiritual feet.

*Basic Correspondences*

| | | |
|---|---|---|
| Syria | = | the rational faculty exercised on the natural plane |
| the feet | = | the outward conduct |

## Senior

The best lesson for the Seniors is that of the subtle way in which the will to do right can be undermined by listening to worldly reasoning. They will be facing this temptation constantly from now on and need to be armed against it. Remind them of Elijah's words: "if the Lord be God, follow him: but if Baal, then follow him." The story of Asa is a good illustration of the importance of this choice. The Lord says: "Ye cannot serve God and mammon."

We have seen that the divided kingdom pictures the state of our lives when our desires (Judah) and our thinking (Israel) do not work in harmony. When we have once known the peace and happiness of the state represented by Solomon's kingdom, our hearts cling to the religion which has meant so much to us. We have our selfish and rebellious times—there were evil kings in Judah as well as in Israel. But frequently we examine our lives and try to correct them because we really mean to be good.

The reign of Asa, the third king of Judah, represents one of these times of self-examination. Asa was the great-grandson of Solomon. All the kings of Judah were of David's line. At heart we recognize the Lord's truth as our ruler. Our capital is at Jerusalem and we continue to worship in the temple on Sunday—or at least at Easter and Christmas. The people of Judah continued to go up to Jerusalem for the great feasts. But outside of Jerusalem—that is, in our everyday life in the world—we fall into the habit of doing as "everybody else" does. We set up idols in our high places. The high places represent our self-esteem and self-confidence. The idols are the objectives which worldly people accept as the desirable things of life: money, power, position, pleasure, skills of various kinds. Asa destroyed these idols. It is not hard from time to time to recognize that we have been putting too much time and energy into our sports and recreations, or worrying too much about money, or injuring our health by unnecessary overwork. "But the high places were not removed." We do not give up our self-esteem. In fact, we are rather apt to be proud of ourselves for showing such good sense. And when the high places are left, it is easy to put new idols there. Asa's son was a good king, but his grandson was evil and the land slipped back into idolatry.

During Asa's reign it is recorded that Israel threatened Judah by building a city near Jerusalem to keep people from going out or coming in. So the worldly part of our mind tries to build up arguments to "shut up" our good intentions. In this crisis Asa sought help of the king of Syria and paid him with treasures from the temple and from his own house. People do this when, feeling their beliefs threatened, they try to support them by finding "natural" explanations for the miracles, for example, and "common-sense" reasons for supporting the church and living the Christian life. The treasures they give up are the silver of belief in the Word because it is the Word of God coming to us from the Lord Himself, and the gold of serving the Lord and the neighbor from love. Syria represents the reasoning faculty as applied to external knowledges of good and truth. This faculty may be a friend or an enemy, depending on how it is used. At this point in the story Syria appears as a friend, but since the motive of the service is gain and not true friendship, Asa is really weakened by the alliance and Syria is strengthened and put in a position to become a more dangerous enemy. We all know how easily our own arguments can sometimes be turned against us.

In his old age Asa was "diseased in his feet." When we begin to compromise with worldly reasoning and to look to it for support, and give up our full trust in the Lord and the Word, our daily conduct eventually shows the effect of our weakness. We no longer walk easily and confidently in the Lord's way. We wobble. We yield here and there to worldly ways, not only in our thinking but in our acts. Throughout the Bible walking is a symbol of daily conduct, and we remember that the Lord tells us that the way to destruction is broad but the way to life is narrow and straight. We should remember this when people who are trying to get us to go back on our principles urge us to be "broad-minded."

---

### Adult

The correspondence of the high places and the meaning of Asa's mistake in looking to Syria for help instead of to the Lord are probably the most fruitful discussion topics for this class. Read aloud in class II Chronicles 16:7-10, and point out how the books of Chronicles round out the narrative of the books of Kings in spite of the fact that they do not have an inner sense. Suggest that the class study at home chapters 15, 16, and 17 of II Chronicles and compare them with our assignment from I Kings.

Judah pictures our will—our desires, affections, motives—in their relation to the Lord. When once we have experienced the state pictured by Solomon, the peaceful victorious state in which our wills and our reason unite in serving the Lord, it is not easy for our will to change and become evil. The mind goes astray more readily than the will, if once the will has become regenerate. This is pictured by the contrast between the history of Israel and the history of Judah. Israel degenerated rapidly after the separation, as we have seen; its sovereignty was not passed down in unbroken succession, and its kings were evil. Judah, on the other hand, remained loyal to the line of David throughout its history, and several of its kings were good, although some weakness and compromise was found in most of them. The people of the land were idolatrous and wicked, but the kings endeavored to serve Jehovah. This is a picture of the state of our affectional life when we still wish to be good but have allowed our minds to turn from reliance upon the Word to reliance upon worldly considerations and knowledges. Our ruling principle, the king, for a long time remains prevailingly faithful to the Lord, but our lesser desires and affections, the people of the land, are led to follow our wandering thoughts, and become more and more corrupt until the king can no longer bring them back to order.

A glance at a map of the divided kingdom will help us to see the situation. See how close Jerusalem actually was to the northern border of Judah. When Israel, which should have been a great protecting bulwark, had instead become an enemy, Jerusalem was very vulnerable. The Ramah which is mentioned in our chapter for today is not the Ramah of Samuel. Ramah merely means "a hill," and there were several Ramahs. This Ramah was very close to Jerusalem on the border of Israel. Geba, which Asa built with the materials from Ramah, was just to the east of it, also on the border.

The little incident in regard to Baasha and Asa, considered in the light of this glance at the map, can readily be seen to picture the way in which our mind, once perverted, seeks control of the will by building up a stronghold of reasoning just on the border where our affections must express themselves in ideas. In the early stages of degeneration—Asa was only the third king of Judah—the good will in us is able to tear down this stronghold and to use the same materials, the same facts and arguments, to build another stronghold a little to the east of the former, a little closer to the Lord, which may serve as a defense to our religion instead of a threat. Geba also means "a hill." Every detail in the story of the relations between Israel and Judah throughout this period teaches us something about the interplay of thought and desire in us.

Asa, the great-grandson of Solomon, was a good king. Verse 11 tells us that he "did that which was right in the eyes of the Lord, as did David his father," and verse 14 says that in spite of certain shortcomings "Asa's heart was perfect with the Lord all his days." He "took away the sodomites out of the land, and removed all the idols that his fathers had made." He even removed Maachah, his mother—actually his grandmother—from being queen because she made an idol, and he destroyed her idol. Before Asa came to the throne Judah had had two bad kings, Rehoboam and Abijam. When the intellect abandons its allegiance to the Lord, when the mind ceases to accept the Word of the Lord as revelation, the immediate effect on the heart is bad. But there soon comes a time when the well-meaning heart recognizes at least the obvious evil results and seeks reform. This is Asa. The sodomites, according to Swedenborg, represent an extreme degree of the "love of exercising command for the sake of self and not for use" (SD 5939[e], 6096[29]).

"But the high places were not removed." AC 2722 tells us: "In the Ancient Church holy worship was performed on mountains and in groves; on mountains, because mountains signified the celestial things of worship; and in groves, because groves signified its spiritual things." Later, as with many other representative forms, the significance was lost sight of and the mountains and groves worshiped as holy in themselves. The Israelites even built themselves high places and made images of their groves, turning what was originally holy into idolatry. Read John 4:20-23. High places in a good sense represent exaltation of the Lord, but in a bad sense exaltation of self. Just as the high places in the time of the divided kingdom were set up throughout the land, so the sense of our own importance and intelligence may come to pervade our daily living. There is scarcely a field of our activity where we shall not find it if we examine ourselves honestly. These are our "high places," and as long as we allow them to remain, we shall soon find new "idols" to replace those we may recognize and reject.

In the spiritual sense this failure to remove the high places leads directly to the rest of Asa's story. For even though apparently he kept his good intentions to the end, Asa was led into the serious mistake of looking to men for aid instead of to the Lord. When Baasha, king of Israel, threatened to hem him in, he turned to Syria for help. In II Chronicles 16:7 ff. we learn that the prophet Hanani rebuked Asa for trusting in the Syrians instead of in the Lord and that Asa was angry at the rebuke. Asa had not purged himself of self-esteem. In a good sense Syria represents the right kind of reasoning from the knowledges of truth and good on the natural plane. That there were remains of the Ancient Church in Syria we learned in the story of Balaam and in the story of the Magi. But the character of Asa's reliance on Syria pictures reliance on these knowledges as belonging to the human intelligence, not as coming from the Lord. In return for the aid of the king of Syria, Asa gave him "all the silver and gold that were left in the treasures of the house of the Lord, and the treasures of the king's house." This is a picture of sacrificing interior good and truth for the sake of external immunity and advancement. Without the bulwark of spiritual intelligence, which Israel should have been to Judah, our wills are prone to give up one treasure after another through fear of the strength of our enemies. Once our minds have become convinced that the only valid truth is what men discover for themselves, we begin to give up one by one the treasures which have come to us by revelation.

When Asa was old it is recorded that "he was diseased in his feet." Here again the story as given in II Chronicles adds interesting details. When we have allowed ourselves to turn from reliance on the Lord to trust in the fickle support of human intelligence, even our moral character declines. The feet, as we know, picture our daily conduct, the way in which we walk. We recall how many times the Lord was called upon to heal the halt and the lame. When we undertake to set up human intelligence as the test of truth, we soon become like those who "reel to and fro, and stagger like a drunken man." The Lord knows better than we do what is right. It is the Lord who can say to us, "This is the way, walk ye in it," and "I am the way, the truth, and the life." The quotation from Isaiah just above is from chapter 40, which ends: "But they that wait on the Lord shall renew their strength; they shall mount up with wings as eagles; they shall run, and not be weary; and they shall walk, and not faint."

## From the Writings of Swedenborg

*Apocalypse Explained*, n. 411[12]: " 'In that day they shall reject every man the idols of his silver and the idols of his gold which your hands make for you . . .' This treats of judgment upon those who from self-intelligence believe themselves to be wise in Divine things. Such are those who are in the love of self and the world, and who seek after a reputation for learning for the sake of self; these, because they are unable to see truths, seize on falsities and proclaim them as truths. The falsities that favor their principles and their loves are signified by 'the idols of silver and the idols of gold'; that these are from self-intelligence is signified by 'which your hands have made for you.' "

*Arcana Coelestia*, n. 6435[11]: "In very many passages of the prophetic Word mention is made of 'mountains and hills,' and by them in the internal sense are signified the goods of love . . . Because 'mountains' and 'hills' signified such things, in the Ancient Church their Divine worship also was upon mountains and upon hills; and afterward the Hebrew nation set altars upon mountains and hills, and there sacrificed and burnt incense; and where there were no hills, they constructed high places. But because this worship became idolatrous, through holding the mountains and hills themselves holy, and thinking nothing at all about the holy things which they signified, this worship was therefore forbidden the Israelitish and Jewish people . . . In order however that this representative which had been in ancient times might be retained, the mountain of Zion was chosen, and by it in the supreme sense was represented the Divine good of the Lord's Divine love, and in the relative sense the Divine celestial and the Divine spiritual in His kingdom."

## Suggested Questions on the Lesson

P. What king of Judah is our lesson about today? *Asa*
P. Was he a good or a bad king? *good*
P. What did he do that was good? *destroyed idols*
J. What did he not do that he should have done? *remove high places*
J. How did the king of Israel try to overcome Asa? *built Ramah*
J. To whom did Asa send for help? *Ben-hadad, king of Syria*
P. What did Asa use for presents for the king of Syria? *gold and silver of temple*
P. What physical trouble did Asa have in his old age? *diseased feet*
I. What does idolatry mean for us? *"worshiping" such things as money, power, etc.*
S. What do the "high places" mean? *pride in one's own intelligence*

## HEZEKIAH AND ISAIAH

*II Kings 20*

This is a chapter characteristic of the history of Judah. Start by reminding the children of Elijah and Elisha, and telling them of the captivity of Israel to Assyria. Remind them that all the kings of Israel were wicked kings, and point out that Judah survived longer because several of its kings were good kings like Hezekiah. This is clearly pictured in the story of the prolonging of Hezekiah's life.

---

### Doctrinal Points

*The Samaritans in the New Testament were descendants of the "strangers" (foreigners) brought in to take the place of the captured people of Israel. This means that when we give up right thinking, wrong thinking takes its place, and this has long-lasting consequences.*

*Our good intentions cannot long survive when our minds are captivated by worldly reasoning.*

*External good works are not in themselves "charity."*

---

### Notes for Parents

Our lesson today is about Hezekiah, one of the good kings in Judah, the southern part of the divided kingdom. Hezekiah had tried hard to bring his people back to the worship of the Lord. He had gone further in his reforms than any king before him, but he had a greater handicap than they had had.

We know that Israel, the northern part of the land, had rebelled against the line of Solomon. After that, Judah and Israel were never on good terms with each other, but at least they were people of the same ancestry and tradition. In the early years of Hezekiah's reign in Judah, Israel was conquered by the king of Assyria, and all its people were carried away to lands in the east. They never came back. The king of Assyria sent in people from the east to take their places. Their descendants were the Samaritans of the Gospel story, still despised as foreigners by the Jews even after five hundred years. So with Assyria in possession of Israel, Hezekiah had no protection on the north.

Assyria did try to conquer Judah also, but the Lord saved Judah by a miracle. This story is told in chapter 18.* Then Hezekiah fell sick and was about to die. The story of his prayer to the Lord and of the Lord's answer through the great prophet Isaiah is a simple one. Hezekiah was permitted fifteen more years of life. The life of each of the good kings in Judah prolonged the life of the kingdom of Judah. Every time we acknowledge our evils and try to reform, our spiritual days are lengthened: that is, we have new opportunities for spiritual progress. The sign of the shadow going back on the dial of Ahaz is a picture of this, too. We must not imagine that the Lord turned back the course of the earth with relation to the sun. A spiritual light was given which for a time did away with the shadow. Many of the shadows that seem to hover over our earthly lives disappear when we turn to the Lord for light and help.

## Primary

Hezekiah's sickness, Isaiah's first prophecy to him, his prayer, and his healing, make a simple story to tell. If you have time, take up the sign given to Hezekiah. Call the children's attention to the way in which shadows move as the sun crosses the sky. If it is a sunny day, this will be easy to demonstrate by setting something up on a piece of paper in a window at the beginning of the lesson period and marking the shadow it casts, and then showing the children where the shadow is at the end of the period. They can then understand how surprising it would be if the shadow moved back. This will help to fix the story in their minds. Describe the dial (or degrees) of Ahaz and point out why Hezekiah asked that the shadow go back.

What great prophet was sent to Israel?
What prophet succeeded him?

---

*This story is also told, almost verbatim, in Isaiah 36 ff., and also in substance in II Chronicles 32. —*Ed.*

In spite of all Elisha could do, Israel went from bad to worse.
Finally the Lord permitted the Assyrians to conquer it.
All the people were carried away captive, and they never came back.
The Assyrians brought in people from the eastern countries to take their place.
The Samaritans of the New Testament were the descendants of these foreigners.
When Israel was taken captive, Hezekiah was king of Judah.

Hezekiah was one of the good kings of Judah. He tried very hard to bring his people back to the worship of the Lord. He destroyed the idols the people had set up, and he did something which no king before him had done: he "removed the high places." These were mounds on which the people had set their idols. Without the mounds it would be much harder for the people to go back to idol worship.

But Hezekiah became sick. He had a boil, and he was so sick that he was about to die. He wanted to live longer. So he prayed to the Lord.

What did Hezekiah do?
What was Isaiah's second message?
What sign did Hezekiah ask?
How was Hezekiah cured?

Did you ever eat figs? The ones we usually have are dried, and so they are quite different from the fruit as it grows on the tree. There are a great many fig trees in the Holy Land, and we often read about them in the Bible. The fig has a great many seeds in it, but we can eat the seeds.

What sign did Hezekiah ask for?

The dial of Ahaz was a sundial, but not like the ones people sometimes have out in their gardens today. It was probably a series of steps with a pole set up near them. As the sun moved, the shadow of the pole moved over the steps, darkening one step after another. This was the king's way of telling the time, for in those days they had no clocks or watches. The shadow always moved in the same direction, of course; so if it were to move backwards, Hezekiah would be sure the Lord was performing a miracle for him. This miracle was a sign that Hezekiah was to have more time to live than he had expected.

Who came to him later pretending to be friends?
What foolish thing did Hezekiah do?
What did Isaiah tell him?

## Junior

Use a map to show how, with Israel gone, Judah was open to attack by Assyria and later by Babylon. Stress the meaning of the sign given to Hezekiah. In taking up the last incident in the lesson, point out to them how important it is that we recognize our spiritual enemies and shut them out of our hearts, and that Babylon pictures self-love, particularly the desire to have our own way, a very powerful enemy which we all sometimes fail to recognize as such.

Even Elisha could not reform Israel. Conditions there grew steadily worse, and finally the Assyrians were permitted to conquer it. They carried away all the people into the countries to the east, and these people never came back. Many theories have been formed as to what became of their descendants, but nothing is really known. They were probably absorbed gradually into the populations of the lands where they were settled. You may sometimes see them referred to as the "lost tribes." The Assyrians brought people from the eastern lands in their place to settle the Holy Land. Read the account in II Kings 17:24-33, 41. The descendants of these strangers were the Samaritans of the New Testament.

The rest of the Old Testament story is about Judah. Several of the kings of Judah were good kings who tried to restore the worship of the Lord. Hezekiah was one of the best of them. We want to notice particularly two of the things he did which are mentioned in chapter 18. Of all the previous good kings it is said, "Nevertheless the high places were not taken away." From earliest times people had been in the habit of worshiping on mountains and hills, or of building up mounds or other high structures for this purpose. The idols were set up on such "high places." But in Deuteronomy 12:10-14 we read the command to the Jews not to set up such places of worship of their own choosing after they should be settled in the Holy Land. This command had been disobeyed. Hezekiah destroyed even these high places. Now read Numbers 21:4-9. This serpent of brass had been carefully preserved for hundreds of years, and the people had come to use it as an idol. Hezekiah destroyed this also. It takes great courage to destroy something which people worship. You remember the story of how the people were ready to kill Gideon when he destroyed their altar to Baal (Judges 6:25-32).

With Israel gone, the kingdom of Judah was unprotected on the north. Assyria, which had captured Israel, threatened Judah also. Hezekiah tried to buy them off with presents, even giving them the silver and gold from the temple, but they were not satisfied. Chapter 19 tells how the Lord sent the prophet Isaiah—the same prophet who gave his name to the book of Isaiah—to tell Hezekiah what he should do, and because Hezekiah obeyed Isaiah, the Lord saved Judah by destroying the army of the Assyrians overnight.

Then Hezekiah fell sick, and Isaiah came to him again.

What did he tell Hezekiah?
What did Hezekiah do about it?
What new message did the Lord give Isaiah for him?
What remedy did he order for Hezekiah?
What sign did Hezekiah ask for?

The dial—more accurately translated "degrees"—of Ahaz is thought to have been a column set up beside a flight of steps so that, as the sun moved, the shadow darkened one step after another. There were no clocks or watches in those days, and people told the time by various types of sundial. Of course the Lord did not make the sun turn back in its course. That would have upset the world completely. But He did make it seem that the shadow had gone back, and this was a sign that Hezekiah's goodness had put off the time when Judah would fall. The Lord does not change. But when we turn from evil to good—which is like our part of the earth turning back toward the sun—the Lord can do things for us which He could not have done otherwise. It seems to us as if the Lord had changed toward us, but it is really we who have changed toward Him.

How many more years of life were granted to Hezekiah?

Hezekiah's prayer opened Hezekiah's mind so that the Lord could help him.

What new country appears in our lesson today?
What did Hezekiah do for the messengers from Babylon?
What did Isaiah tell him?

Judah was finally taken captive by Babylon. Many of its people were carried away as the people of Israel had been, but some were allowed to remain in the Holy Land, and after seventy years all of the captives who wished to return were allowed to do so. They rebuilt the temple at Jerusalem, which had been destroyed by the Babylonians, and their descendants were the Jews of the New Testament and are the Jews of today. But we must note one important thing: the ark had disappeared. It was never brought back.

## Intermediate

Although the class should be given the correspondence of the specific story concerning Hezekiah, the meaning of Assyria and Babylon and the separate captivities is of more general importance for their understanding of the Bible story as a whole. This can be pointed up by reference to chapter 18 and to Hezekiah's mistake in admitting into his confidence the emissaries from Babylon.

Even Elisha was not able to stem the tide of evil in Israel. There were twelve kings after Ahab—all evil kings. When we remember that a king represents a ruling principle, we see that this pictures the fact that Israel—the intellectual part of the man—came to be governed by principles more and more false. Finally Israel was completely overcome by Assyria. In the Bible we read much about three countries: the lands of Israel, Assyria, and Egypt. The Holy Land represents the heavenly character, the religious life of a man; Judah, this life in the heart; and Israel, this life in the mind. We have learned that Egypt represents external memory-knowledges. Assyria represents the rational plane of the mind, the plane where memory-knowledges are thought about and made to serve either the Lord or self. These three "countries" in us should work together in the service of the Lord and the neighbor. They are meant to help each other. In Isaiah 19:23 we read concerning the ideal state of man: "In that day shall there be a highway out of Egypt to Assyria, and the Assyrian shall come into Egypt, and the Egyptian into Assyria, and the Egyptians shall serve with the Assyrians." And the next verses say: "In that day shall Israel be a third with Egypt and with Assyria, even a blessing in the midst of the land: Whom the Lord of hosts shall bless, saying, Blessed be Egypt my people, and Assyria the work of my hands, and Israel mine inheritance." But during most of the Israelites' history Assyria was one of their two most threatening enemies. It tried to conquer them, just as people today who reason entirely from the things they know of the natural world argue against the Bible and religion. When the mind turns away from worship of the Lord and comes more and more to accept principles developed by men as its rulers, it is false reasoning which finally carries it away completely, as Assyria did Israel.

With Israel gone, Judah was unprotected on the north. That is, when the mind becomes subject to worldly ideas, the good intentions of the heart cannot long stand. But Judah had several good kings who tried to restore worship of the Lord. Hezekiah was one of the best of these. He even destroyed the "high places," which represent self-satisfaction and self-praise, and the brazen serpent made by Moses in the wilderness (Numbers 21:4-9) which, when it had come to be worshiped as an idol, pictures the belief that the sensual (natural affections) can be separated from the spiritual life and allowed to dominate.

Hezekiah also smote the Philistines. We remember that they picture the temptation to be satisfied with knowing what is right without doing it. It is some time since the Philistines have been mentioned in the Bible story, but we now see that they had never been fully conquered. This is an ever-present temptation.

Hezekiah also tried to rebel against the control of Assyria. In other words, the good intent of the heart tries not to be reasoned out of its attachment to the Lord. But it is soon forced to compromise. Chapter 18 tells us how Hezekiah tried to buy off the king of Assyria by giving him the gold and silver of the temple, even to the gold which covered its doors and pillars.

Sometimes a good man, who at heart loves the religion in which he was brought up, is forced little by little to compromise with the principles of the world in which he moves. At least it seems to him that he is forced to do so in order to save anything of goodness in himself. Actually the compromise accomplishes nothing. The attacks of the enemy increase until the issue becomes clear-cut and the man is forced to make a choice between serving God and serving the world. The account of how the prophet Isaiah was sent to advise Hezekiah and of how, because Hezekiah obeyed his advice, the Lord miraculously saved Judah from the Assyrians is told in chapter 19. The Lord can save us from false reasonings if we obey the commandments of His Word.

But Hezekiah fell sick. Everyone, no matter how good, has deep inherited tendencies to evil. Hezekiah's "boil" pictures the breaking out of such a deep-seated evil. The prophet told him, as the Word says, that the disease was mortal. Then Hezekiah turned his face to the wall—the protection given him by the Lord—and his humility enabled the Lord to prolong his life. Figs picture the doing of useful works of an external kind which helps us to counteract the poison of internal evils. The turning back of the shadow on the dial pictures the prolonging of our daytimes, our good states, when we are humble (Exodus 20:12).

Then a new country, Babylon, appeared in the story and Hezekiah did not recognize it as an enemy because it came with messages which seemed to be friendly. Babylon represents "the love of dominion from the love of self," that is, the feeling that everyone should do as we tell them to do because we think we are better and wiser than anyone else. When our minds have lost their confidence in the truth which the Lord has revealed, this feeling creeps into our hearts, and we do not see clearly the distinction between good and evil. Then we are likely to accept as "friends" many things which are deeply dangerous.

The beginning of the end had come for Judah. The new enemy

gained more and more power and eventually conquered Judah and carried into captivity all of its important people. Only "the poor of the land" were left. The poor always represent the humble in heart who do not set themselves up. Do you know the first of the Blessings (Matthew 5:3)?

*Basic Correspondences*

| | | |
|---|---|---|
| figs | = | good works of an external kind |
| Assyria | = | the rational plane |
| Babylon | = | the love of dominion from the love of self |

## Senior

The same holds true for the Seniors as for the Intermediates with special emphasis on the last incident named. Young people need to be warned against the subtle beginnings of the love of rule which comes from self-love in the heart.

Israel had gone too far astray to be reclaimed. Its kings were all concerned only with their own glory and none of them attempted reforms. Some hundred and fifty years after the time of Elijah, Israel was conquered by Assyria and all its people were carried away captive, never to return. This is a picture of the mind wholly captivated by worldly and naturalistic reasoning. The land was settled by foreigners from the eastern countries whom the Assyrians brought in. Their descendants were the Samaritans of the New Testament story.

With Israel gone, Judah was unprotected. With the mind wholly given over to belief in the supremacy of natural reasoning and no longer accepting revealed truth, the heart becomes a prey to every evil, although "good intentions" persist. Indeed, at the very time when Israel was taken captive, Judah was under the rule of Hezekiah, the best king since Solomon. Even when the mind has ceased to defend revealed truth, there persists stubbornly in the heart a belief in God and a longing for His blessing and protection.

Hezekiah is the first king who is recorded as having removed the "high places," which represent thoughts of self-praise. He also destroyed the brazen serpent, which Moses at the command of the Lord had set up in the wilderness (Numbers 21:4-9) and which had been preserved and come to be worshiped as an idol. The brazen serpent, when it was first set up, pictured the divine sensual of the Lord, through which power can be given us to overcome our sense temptations. When, however, we misunderstand and abuse the sensual by making it an object of worship, we have allowed sense pleasures to dominate our lives. This is pictured by burning incense to the serpent. Hezekiah's breaking it in pieces signifies the decision no longer to allow the sensual to have such a controlling influence.

Because Hezekiah wished to obey the Lord, his people could be saved from the attack of Assyria. Chapter 19 tells this story. The Lord's power is as great today as it ever was. No matter how overwhelming the odds seem, if we will trust in the Lord and look to His Word for direction, the enemy, like the Assyrians, will melt away in the night.

Our chapter for today is a very wonderful chapter picturing the steps by which the good heart, unprotected by an understanding of the truth, must waver between good and evil and gradually degenerate. Humility and simple obedience like Hezekiah's can prolong spiritual health, but with "Israel" gone, "Judah" is open not only to direct attack, which one is able to recognize and resist in the Lord's strength, but to what has been called "infiltration." Without truth in the mind one cannot recognize evil for what it is. This is pictured in the latter part of the chapter.

Babylon represents "the love of dominion from the love of self." This creeps up on us, often in friendly guise. For example, our friends may praise us. We do not really mean to take credit for our good deeds and various abilities, but the praise is pleasant to our natural self and we open our hearts to it, just as Hezekiah showed the messengers from Babylon all his treasures. The hells know our times of weakness, as the king of Babylon "heard that Hezekiah was sick." The object of the "messengers" is to spy out our treasures with a view to robbing us of them, and often we let them into our hearts without inquiring into their source and intent. We are told in II Chronicles 32:25 that after Hezekiah was cured of his illness, "Hezekiah rendered not again according to the benefit done unto him: for his heart was lifted up." This statement is not included in the story as given in the Word, but it gives us another instance of the imperviousness of the people of Bible times which made it possible for the Lord to work miracles among them without affecting their freedom of choice. We need always to remember that without the Lord we are subject to temptation by every sort of evil and cannot always see the temptation involved. We do not fully know our own motives. Only the Lord sees us through and through. We may think we are humble and unselfish, but that very thought is one of self-praise. Babylon, once admitted into Judah, gained in power until it carried Judah away captive.

## Adult

The general line which seems indicated for development with the adults is the gradual encroachment of worldly reasoning and of self-satisfaction possible even after a regenerate state has been reached. The history of the divided kingdom is the picture of this most subtle and dangerous temptation of the adult life of the churchman.

Hezekiah came to the throne in Judah in the third year of Hoshea, the last king of Israel. It was in the sixth year of Hezekiah's reign that Israel was carried away captive by Assyria, and the strangers from the eastern countries, whose descendants were to be the Samaritans of the New Testament, were brought in to resettle the land. This we recognize as a picture of the mind wholly given over to worldly ideas and reasonings. But when we have once experienced the state pictured by Solomon—the peaceful, victorious state in which our wills and our reason unite in serving the Lord—it is not so easy for our wills to change and become evil. The understanding changes more readily than the will, for better or worse, and this is pictured by the contrast between the history of Israel and that of Judah. Israel degenerated rapidly after the separation; its sovereignty was not passed down in unbroken succession; and its kings were consistently evil. Judah, on the other hand, remained loyal to a single line throughout its history, and many of its kings were good, although some weakness and compromise were found in most of them. The people of the land were idolatrous, but the kings endeavored to serve Jehovah. This is the state of our affectional life when we still wish to be good but have allowed our minds to turn from reliance upon the Word to reliance upon human reasonings. The ruling principle in our heart, the king, for a long time remains prevailingly faithful to the Lord, but our lesser desires and affections, the people of the land, are led to follow our wandering thoughts and become more and more corrupt until the king can no longer bring them back into order.

Hezekiah was one of the most thoroughgoing reformers of all the kings of Judah. There may come a time in our lives when we have fallen so far from our best state that we shock ourselves, and we decide upon a complete about-face. Hezekiah "removed the high places, and broke the images, and cut down the groves." He also "brake in pieces the brasen serpent that Moses had made," "rebelled against the king of Assyria," and "smote the Philistines." This is a picture of a thoroughgoing self-examination. AC 2722 tells us, "In the Ancient Church holy worship was performed on mountains and in groves; on mountains, because mountains signified the celestial things of worship; and in groves, because groves signified its spiritual things." Later, as with many other representative forms, the significance was lost sight of and the thing worshiped for itself. So they even built themselves high places and made images of their groves, turning what was originally holy into idolatry. We do this when we cling blindly to forms and phrases of worship which no longer have any meaning for us, when we make the traditional externals of worship the all of religion. The Lord said of the scribes and Pharisees, "Ye pay tithe of mint and anise and cummin, and have omitted the weightier matters of the law, judgment, mercy, and faith" (Matthew 23:23). To understand the meaning of Hezekiah's destruction of the high places read also John 4:20-23. Read the story of the origin of the brazen serpent in Numbers 21:4-9 and the reference to it in John 3:14-15. The brazen serpent properly pictures the glorified sensual of the Lord through which we can receive power from Him to overcome our sense temptations. But the people had come to worship the brazen serpent as an idol, with no desire to correct their evils but only to keep out of trouble. In much the same way, the Christian church came to look upon the Lord's physical suffering as efficacious in itself and to believe that He would save men from the eternal consequences of their evils without any amendment of life on their part. Hezekiah also rebelled against Assyria, but he was not able to maintain his independence. Judah was saved from Assyria by a miracle performed by the Lord for Hezekiah because Hezekiah obeyed His commandment given through the prophet Isaiah. As long as we obey the Lord and trust in Him, no mere argument of the worldly reason can rob us of goodness.

But Hezekiah had previously tried to pacify the king of Assyria by giving him the gold and silver of the temple, even stripping the gold from the gates and pillars. His compromises—which picture our compromises with worldly reasoning—had weakened him greatly. So "in these days was Hezekiah sick unto death." The sickness of the good king means that the desire to be good had almost perished. Isaiah the prophet tells Hezekiah that he is about to die. But our story shows that even at this point, if we turn to the Lord and pray humbly that our good desires may be strengthened and renewed, we have the promise of the Word—Isaiah's second message—that we can be restored. Read Isaiah 1:18, Jeremiah 18:8, and Ezekiel 18:21. The Lord does not change His mind; the change is in us. So long as we are in this world it is never too late for us to turn to the Lord and try to change our ways; and if we do, we are sure of His help.

Boils and ulcers are pictures of some evil which has been hidden in the character and now breaks out into open misconduct. At Isaiah's command a lump of figs was placed on Hezekiah's boil and it was healed. The fig tree is the symbol of the natural man, and its fruit is natural goodness (AE 403[17]). When we have sunk so far that we are living in open evil, the first thing necessary is to correct the outward conduct, to do good deeds instead of bad. When we get into such a state, for example, that we find ourselves constantly saying and doing disagreeable things to others on the slightest provocation, the first remedy to apply is to force ourselves to say something pleasant instead, and to find good that we can do instead of evil. But this is only the first step, the outward reform, and it will not last. Isaiah told Hezekiah that his life should be prolonged fifteen years, and fifteen is one of the symbols for "a little." In II Chronicles 32:25 we are told that Hezekiah did not profit by his lesson, for he "rendered not again according to the benefit done unto him; for his heart was lifted up." If we merely reform our outward conduct and continue to cherish pride and selfishness within, we receive no permanent benefit.

The sign given Hezekiah has always interested Bible readers. Swedenborg tells us that the "steps of Ahaz" (translated "dial of Ahaz") picture the gradual decline of the Jewish Church. As Hezekiah was a good king, its time was prolonged. We may compare this miracle with that found in Joshua 10:12-13. In AE 401[18] we are assured that the sun did not actually stand still—for that would have inverted the whole order of nature—but that the people were given a light from the Lord. Even in nature we know that the sun does not actually go down: it is the earth that turns away from the sun. So it is with the Lord, who is our Sun. The Lord never turns from us, but we turn from Him. When we turn to Him again, our daytime is renewed.

The rest of the chapter shows us the beginning of the end for Judah. Babylon pictures the worst form of self-love which makes one wish to dominate everyone and everything. The desire to impose our will upon others is the direct opposite of the Lord's love; yet this desire often comes into our hearts so gradually and in so pleasing a form that we do not recognize its evil nature until it has gained possession of us. Hezekiah's heart was "lifted up."

When we have done well and are enjoying the satisfactions of a good life, we are easily led to "show our treasures" to the enemy, and the love of dominion creeps in.

## From the Writings of Swedenborg

*Apocalypse Explained*, n. 706[16]: "This sign was given to king Hezekiah as an attestation that the Lord would defend him and Jerusalem from the king of Assyria . . . that king signifying the perverted rational destroying all things of the church; therefore this sign represented also a new church that must be established by the Lord, but here that the time would be extended beyond that indicated to Ahaz just above; 'bringing back the shadow that had gone down on the steps of Ahaz before the sun' signifies a holding back of the time when this should be done, 'the steps of Ahaz' signifying a time, 'here until the coming of the Lord, and the 'shadow' signifying the progress of time from the rising to the setting; that the shadow 'should be brought backwards ten degrees' signifies the extension of the time for many years still, 'ten' signifying many, and the 'sun' which should go back signifying the Lord's coming. But this shall be further illustrated. The Lord's coming took place when the Jewish church was at an end, that is, when there was no good or truth left in it. . . . The entire period of the duration of the Jewish church was represented by 'the steps of Ahaz,' its beginning by the first step, which is when the sun is in its rising, and its end by the last when it is at its setting. This makes evident that by 'the bringing back of the shadow' from the setting towards the rising means the extension of the time. This would take place 'in the steps of Ahaz,' because Ahaz was a wicked king, and profaned the holy things of the church, consequently if his successors had done the same, the end of that church would have quickly come: but as Hezekiah was an upright king the time was extended, for on that account the iniquity of that nation was not so soon to reach its consummation, that is, its end."

## Suggested Questions on the Lesson

P. What king of Judah is our lesson about today? *Hezekiah*
J. What happened to Israel early in his reign? *captured by Assyria*
J. How was Judah saved from Assyria? *angel of the Lord*
P. Who was the prophet in Judah in Hezekiah's time? *Isaiah*
P. When Hezekiah fell sick, what did Isaiah tell him? *you will die*
P. What did Hezekiah do? *prayed*

P. What new message from the Lord did Isaiah bring him? *he would live fifteen more years*
P. What was the matter with Hezekiah? *boil (ulcer)*
P. How did Isaiah cure him? *figs*
J. What sign did Hezekiah ask? *shadow go back ten degrees*
J. What king sent messengers to Hezekiah? *Babylon*
J. What did Hezekiah show them? *all his treasures*
J. What did Isaiah tell him? *that was foolish*
I. How did the captivity of Israel affect Judah? *left it unprotected on north*
S. What do (1) Assyria, and (2) Babylon, represent?
*(1) worldly, naturalistic thinking*
*(2) love of dominion from love of self*

# KING JOSIAH

*II Kings 22*

Israel did not heed the warnings of Elijah and Elisha and was finally taken captive by the Assyrians. All her people were carried away captive and never came back. But in Judah, although there had been a number of wicked kings, and worship of the Lord had declined and idolatry flourished, there had also been several good kings who instituted reforms and tried to restore true worship: Assyria was not allowed to overcome Judah. This brings us to our lesson. All teachers should read chapter 23 as well as 22.

---

## Doctrinal Points

*There must be truth in the mind if the good intentions of the heart are to survive.*

*Whenever we let our minds accept worldly ideas, selfishness begins to creep back into our hearts.*

*As long as we are really trying to do right, the Lord can protect us.*

*If we are sincerely trying to uncover and correct our faults, we do not count the cost.*

---

## Notes for Parents

The Lord once said, "The kingdom of God is within you." In our outward surroundings many things happen over which we have no control, but each one of us is responsible for the state of the kingdom of God in his own soul, in his heart and mind. If the Lord really rules there, if we are trying always to learn and do the Lord's will, then all is well with us, no matter what our outward condition may be.

But sometimes our "kingdom" is divided, as Solomon's was after his death. Sometimes, although in our hearts we mean to be good people. we let all sorts of false ideas creep into our minds. Our minds come to be ruled by what other people think and say instead of by the truth as the Lord gives it to us in His Word. Like Judah, our hearts remain true to the line of David and continue to worship in the temple, but our minds set up the worship of the golden calf in place of the Lord. So the two kingdoms of our Bible story—Judah on the south and Israel on the north—are a picture of the heart and the mind when they are trying to act independently of each other.

The nation was near its end. Israel, in spite of the warnings of Elijah and Elisha, turned more and more away from the Lord. Its enemies grew stronger, and it was finally overcome by Assyria. All its people were carried away captive and never came back. You may see them referred to sometimes as the "lost tribes." This is a picture of the mind when it finally has given in altogether to worldly reasoning.

The heart holds out a little longer. Our good intentions are harder to destroy. Jerusalem and the temple were in Judah, and many of its kings were good. These good kings, like King Josiah in our story today, are pictures of our recurring states of repentance and attempted reform. Every so often we realize what a bad state we have fallen into and resolve to change our ways. We try, as Josiah did, to repair the temple of God within us, which we have been abusing, and then always the book of the law appears. All our knowledge of what is right and wrong goes back to the Bible, and what we know of the Bible comes back when we need it. The kingdom of Judah was spared as long as Josiah lived. As long as we are sincerely trying to correct our faults, the Lord can preserve our souls. But bad habits are hard to break, and after Josiah died, the country slipped back into idolatry and was soon conquered by Babylon. Everything we do or think from day to day has its inevitable effect on that kingdom of God which is within us.

## Primary

The story of the repair of the temple and the finding of the book is simple and interesting. Many of the details of Josiah's reign can be covered in this class. Tell them also about Josiah's death (II Kings 23:29-30) and that his sons were evil kings, so that the Lord very soon permitted Nebuchadnezzar, king of Babylon, to conquer Judah.

Our story today is about one of the good kings of the line of David and Solomon. He reigned in Jerusalem over the part of the country which had remained faithful to Solomon's son. This part was called Judah. Many things had happened since the kingdom was divided. The kings of Israel—the other division of the country—had not been willing to listen to the warnings of Elijah and Elisha. Things in their part of the land had gone from bad to worse until finally—not long before Josiah's time—the Assyrians conquered Israel. They carried all the people away captive and sent foreigners in to take their place.

The descendants of these foreigners were the Samaritans of the Gospel story.
In Judah also there were many evil kings, and idolatry sprang up.
But in Judah there were some good kings too.
Who is the king in our story today?
How old was he when he came to the throne?
What was the first good thing he undertook to do?
What was found when they were repairing the temple?

As soon as the book of the law was read to him, Josiah realized how many wrong things the people had been doing. He had the law read to the people and then he destroyed all the idols, even the altar to the golden calf which Jeroboam had set up in Bethel. Then, when the land was in order again, he had the people celebrate the Passover, the greatest Passover that had been celebrated for many years.

Do you remember when and why the first Passover was celebrated?
The Lord spared Judah as long as Josiah lived.
But when he died, the people went right back to their evil ways.
Judah was later conquered by Babylon.

## Junior

This is the age at which the historical sequence of events is important. As the remaining Old Testament lessons are concerned with the Psalms and the

Prophets, it has been thought best to touch on the completion of the story of the divided kingdom in this lesson, although it goes a little beyond the actual assignment.

Israel did not listen to the warnings of Elijah and Elisha. Its kings and its people turned more and more from the Lord until He could no longer reach and save them. So, in the time when Hezekiah was on the throne of Judah, Israel was taken captive by the Assyrians. All the people were carried away into the lands of the east, and they never came back. You may sometimes hear them referred to as the "lost tribes." There is no record of their later history. They were absorbed by the nations among whom they were settled. They had given up their worship of the Lord, for which their nation had been set apart, and so they had nothing left to keep them from forgetting their nationality. The Assyrians brought foreigners into the land of Israel to settle in their places. There is an interesting story about these people in II Kings 17:24-29, 41. Their descendants were the Samaritans of the Gospel story, who even after hundreds of years were still despised as foreigners by the Jews.

The kings of Judah were not all evil like those of Israel. Idolatry flourished in Judah, too, but they still had the temple at Jerusalem to remind them of their true worship, and every now and then a good king would appear, who would restore the temple worship, destroy the idols, and for a time bring the people back into order. Hezekiah was one of these good kings, and so the Lord was able to save Judah when Israel was conquered. But Manasseh, Hezekiah's son, was the opposite of his father. After Hezekiah's death he immediately swung the country back into idol worship, including the worship of Baal. Hezekiah had destroyed the "high places" which were mounds built for pagan religious rites. The first thing that is said about Manasseh is that "he built up again the high places." He was the worst king Judah had had. He even set up idols in the temple itself. His son Amon followed in his footsteps, but Amon's son was Josiah, the best king Judah ever had.

How old was Josiah when he began to reign?
What was the first good work he undertook?

What did the high priest find when the temple was being repaired?

Read Deuteronomy 31:24-26. This tells us what the book of the law was. The books of Moses are full of warnings of what would happen to the people if they failed to keep the law. You can imagine how a good, conscientious king would feel on hearing these read when his land was in the condition in which Manasseh and Amon left it.

To whom did Josiah send to inquire of the Lord?
What did Huldah say about the punishment of the people?
What did she say about Josiah?

Hezekiah had also been promised peace in his own time. Each of us who does right really helps the world, no matter what other people do.

Josiah remained faithful to the Lord to the end of his life. He destroyed all the idols, including the altar to the golden calf which Jeroboam had set up in Bethel. Even Hezekiah had not done this. Each one of us has special good things that he can do. This is something we need to remember when we are working or playing with others. Everyone is not able to do just the same things, but if each does what he can and notices and acknowledges the good that others do, the whole group will be happy and useful.

For Josiah's sake the destruction of Judah was delayed. Josiah himself was finally killed in battle with the king of Egypt. His sons were not like their father, and it was only a few years before Judah was taken captive by Nebuchadnezzar, king of Babylon. All but the poorest of the people were carried away into Babylon. But there were good people among them who did not forget the Lord. And they had the prophets Ezekiel and Daniel to remind them. So after seventy years of captivity all who wished were allowed to return. They rebuilt Jerusalem and the temple, and it was their descendants who were the Jews of the Lord's time.

## Intermediate

These young people should be brought to understand the need of truth in the mind, if the good intentions of the heart are to survive. Most of them have good intentions, but at this age they are particularly susceptible to persuasion from their companions. The more clearly they can see their lives as a spiritual drama and see the value of standing firmly on the side of right, the more easily they will recognize and overcome such temptations.

While the kings of Israel—the Israel of the divided kingdom—were all bad, a number of the kings of Judah were good. Remember that Judah represents the will and Israel the understanding. Once we have reached the state of love pictured by Solomon's reign, we cannot becaome bad all at once. Worldly reasoning may creep into our minds, but our good intentions are still very real. From the twelfth chapter of I Kings through II Kings the story of the two kingdoms and their decline is told. The story in the Bible goes back and forth from one to the other. This is just what we should expect, for although our will and our understanding may be pulling in opposite directions, they cannot really be separated.

So the idolatries practiced in Israel crept into Judah. When we let our minds accept worldly ideas, selfishness creeps back little by little into our hearts. Suppose, for instance, that there is some pleasure which in our hearts we know is wrong, but when our friends invite us to join in it, instead of saying "no" immediately, we listen to their excuses for doing it. The next step is to say, "That sounds reasonable." Then we begin to think, "After all, I'm good most of the time; I ought to be allowed some fun." And finally we find ourselves doing just as everybody else does. But from time to time we wake up and realize that we are not good—that we have fallen very far from the standards we had decided to live by—and we try to reform. This is the history of Judah: two or three bad kings and then a good one.

We have had the story of king Hezekiah, who not only destroyed the idols throughout the land of Judah, but also broke down the "high places" which his predecessors had left standing. Yet while Hezekiah was on the throne in Judah, Israel was taken captive by Assyria. All her people were carried away captive and never came back, and foreigners were brought in to take their place. This is a picture of a time when our minds give in completely to the ideas in the world around us. We haven't become wholly selfish–Judah still held out–but there are no thoughts left in our minds which can defend our good intentions. Hezekiah's son Manasseh was the worst king Judah had ever had. He rebuilt the high places and restored all the idols, and even set up idols in the temple itself. And his son Amon, who reigned only two years and was slain by his servants in his own house, was also evil.

Then there came a king who made one last great stand against the increasing corruption of Judah. This was Amon's son Josiah. Josiah had come to the throne as a child of eight. Young children of the royal family were, as a rule, under the special care of the high priest. Read the story of an earlier king, Jehoash, as told in chapters 11 and 12. Read also Matthew 18:1-3.

Josiah's first work was to cleanse and repair the temple. We may recall that the temple is the symbol of spiritual character. When we see that we have fallen into such evil states, we begin to examine ourselves with a view to purifying our own hearts. Such an honest and humble attempt is described in verses 4 to 7 of our chapter. And its first result is the rediscovery of the "book of the law," the books of Moses containing the commandments and other laws, and the realization that our lives have departed very far from the right way.

Josiah inquired of the Lord concerning the state into which the nation had fallen and its outcome, and was told through Huldah the prophetess–as Hezekiah had been told through the prophet Isaiah–that the great evils of the people would bring their inevitable punishment, but that the doom would not fall in his time because he had humbled himself before the Lord. As long as we are really trying to do right, the Lord can protect us.

Chapter 23 tells how Josiah destroyed all the idols and the high places, cleansed the temple, and even destroyed the golden calf which Jeroboam had set up at Bethel.* Then he celebrated the

*Although one might infer that the gold calf was destroyed when Jeroboam's altar was torn down, the text does not so state specifically. –*Ed.*

Passover, the greatest Passover that had been held for many years.

But even Josiah's efforts could not stem the tide of evil which had been sweeping over the land. It is recorded (II Kings 23:29) that when Josiah had reigned thirty-one years, the king of Egypt came up against the king of Assyria to the river Euphrates. Josiah went out to meet him, apparently to prevent his crossing the land, and was killed in battle. We remember that the king of Egypt always pictures the principle of reliance on natural knowledges. When our minds have given in to worldliness, we cannot stand in the face of this principle. The king of Egypt put the land of Judah to tribute. He carried away to Egypt Jehoahaz, the son of Josiah who followed him as king, and set up another of Josiah's sons, Eliakim, afterward called Jehoiakim, who was willing to pay tribute. During his reign the king of Babylon became stronger than the king of Egypt and took over the tribute; and when Jehoiakim died, his son Jehoiachin was carried away to Babylon. A little later Jerusalem and the temple were destroyed, all but the poorest of the people were carried off, and the kingdom of Judah was at an end. Babylon represents "the love of dominion from the love of self." This means the feeling that everyone should look up to us and do what we want. It is a very deep evil and one against which we should be especially watchful. We are all in the world to be useful to others—not to be served. In the destruction of character Assyria—which in a bad sense represents false reasoning—first captures the mind, and then, robbed of the bulwark of truth in the mind, the heart soon becomes a prey to this selfish love of dominion.

After seventy years of captivity the people of Judah were allowed to come back and rebuild Jerusalem and the temple. This was because some four hundred years later the Lord was to fulfill the prophecies and be born in Bethlehem, and the Lord had to come where the Word was, and the Jews had the Word. Those who were in the Holy Land when the Lord came were the descendants of those who returned from captivity from Babylon. The descendants of the foreigners brought in by Assyria to take the place of the people of Israel were the Samaritans of the Gospel story.

*Basic Correspondences*

Assyria (in a bad sense) = false reasoning

## Senior

This is a good lesson in which to put into the young people's minds a warning against the danger of allowing worldly reasoning to influence their thinking. The example of the fall of Judah so soon after the fall of Israel teaches this lesson clearly.

In reading the story of the kingdom of Judah we are always particularly struck by the brave efforts of certain kings–Asa, Jehoshaphat, Jehoash, Amaziah, Azariah, Jotham, Hezekiah, and finally Josiah–to stem the tide of evil which was slowly destroying Judah.

We recall that the division of Solomon's kingdom is a picture of the time in the life of a person who has reached a state of regeneration, but then because he relaxes his vigilance against evil begins to admit false ideas from the world around him into his mind. Israel–representing the mind–went steadily from bad to worse from the time when Jeroboam rebelled and set up the golden calves in Bethel and Dan until, while Hezekiah was on the throne of Judah, Israel was taken captive by Assyria. This pictures the time when the mind has given up the fight against worldly reasoning and has accepted the naturalistic arguments which are so popular, with all their false conclusions. All the people of Israel were carried away captive to Assyria, and foreigners were sent in to take their places. It is interesting to read in II Kings 17:24-41 a story of the coming of these foreigners. At the start they were troubled by lions because "they feared not the Lord." So the king of Assyria sent one of the priests back from captivity to "teach them the manner of the God of the land." Then they added this worship to their own idolatries. It is said of them (II Kings 17:41): "So these nations feared the Lord, and served their graven images, both their children, and their children's children: as did their fathers, so do they unto this day." Their descendants were the Samaritans of the Gospel story, and we learn from the Lord's conversation with the woman of Samaria at Jacob's well (John 4:6-26) that they still were in the same confusion in regard to their worship. We know, too, that the Jews of New Testament days—after more than four hundred years—regarded them as foreigners and despised them. The mind of a person who knows he ought to worship the Lord and yet accepts the pronouncements of those who reason from nature alone is in just such a state of confusion.

Our good intentions are likely to hold out longer than our true thinking. Judah could not be taken by the Assyrians. But without the protection of Israel on the north, they could not long maintain their independence. In the same way, when the mind is full of falsity, the heart gives in little by little to the claims of selfishness. It has its times of repentance and reform, but they do not last. Even the good kings of Judah often had to give up the silver and gold stored in the temple in order to save themselves or buy protection from one enemy against another. You will remember how Hezekiah in his old age received the ambassadors of the king of Babylon as friends and showed them all his treasures, and how Isaiah told him that the time would come when Judah would be carried away captive to Babylon. When our minds are full of falsity, we cannot recognize our spiritual enemies until they have control of us. We cannot distinguish clearly and promptly between right and wrong.

Manasseh and Amon, the son and grandson of Hezekiah, were wicked kings, restoring all the idols and high places which Hezekiah had destroyed, and even setting up idols in the temple itself. Then a last attempt to save Judah was made by Amon's son Josiah.

The fact that Josiah came to the throne as a child reminds us of the Lord's teaching that we must become as little children if we are to enter the kingdom of God. Josiah turned his attention first to repairing the temple. When we remember that the temple pictures a regenerate character, we can understand why under the evil kings the temple had been allowed to fall into disrepair. The work of repair was paid for by the offerings of the people, and no accounting was required of the workmen "because they dealt faithfully."

When we are sincerely trying to find out our faults and correct them, we do not count the cost.

Then the high priest found the book of the law. The fact that in the clutter which had accumulated in the misused temple the book of the law had been lost shows how far we can get from the standards we have once accepted when we allow worldliness to creep into our hearts. Think perhaps of a man who, after starting out in life with high ideals, has let himself be led by business competition into more and more questionable business practices. Then suddenly the words "Thou shalt not steal" are repeated in his hearing. If he is a sincere man, he will realize immediately, as Josiah did when the book of the law was read to him, how many things of many kinds he has been doing which were fundamentally wrong. The excuses he has made for himself fall to pieces—Josiah tore his clothes.

When Josiah inquired of the Lord what the outcome would be, the prophetess Huldah told him that the results of the wrongdoing of the people could not be averted, but that because he had humbled himself before the Lord the doom would not fall in his day. And Josiah's reforms were the most sweeping of all that had been attempted. He cleansed and repaired the temple, destroyed the idols and broke down the high places, put away the wizards and sorcerers, and even destroyed the altar and grove which Jeroboam had set up at Bethel.

But evil had too great a hold on the people. Josiah could postpone, but not prevent, the fall of Judah. This should make us think very seriously. It is natural for young people—indeed for all of us—to put off serious thinking about our spiritual responsibility. We think we have plenty of time. We like to assume that we can do what pleases us today and perhaps make up for it tomorrow. But what we do today becomes a part of us and has its effect on our future. Our concern should always be with making today right. Bad habits are formed little by little, and they are hard to break.

Josiah's death teaches this same lesson. It is described in verse 29 of chapter 23: "In his days Pharaohnechoh king of Egypt went up against the king of Assyria to the river Euphrates: and king Josiah went against him; and he slew him at Megiddo, when he had seen him." We have not heard of Egypt for some time, but we remember that it pictures the natural plane of the mind. It is in that plane that the results of our bad habits become fixed. So when Egypt rose up and Josiah tried to prevent their passage across his country, he was killed. Megiddo is a city in the plain of Esdraelon, where many great battles were fought. Swedenborg tells us that Megiddo–like Armageddon in Revelation 16:16, whose name comes from the same root–pictures a love of domineering others, which is a great destroyer of character. It was only a few years after Josiah's death that Judah was overcome by Babylon, and Babylon represents "the love of dominion from the love of self." We need to keep always in mind that humility is the only ground in which spiritual life can grow.

---

## Adult

The effect on Judah of the fall of Israel and its meaning may be the most fruitful discussion topic. Follow this with the lesson to be drawn from the inability of Josiah to avert the consequences of the sins of his people. The teacher will find additional suggestions on this point in the Senior notes.

We have had the story of Hezekiah, of his good reign in Judah, his illness and recovery, his conversations with the prophet Isaiah, and his final weakness in showing all his treasures to the ambassadors of the king of Babylon. Manasseh and Amon, son and grandson of Hezekiah, were evil kings, reestablishing the worship of idols and of Baal, and even setting up idolatrous worship in the temple itself. Amon reigned only two years and was slain by his servants in his own house, and his son Josiah was made king.

Josiah was only eight years old when he came to the throne. We learn from II Chronicles 34:3 that "in the eighth year of his reign, while he was yet young, he began to seek after the God of David, his father: and in the twelfth year he began to purge Judah and Jerusalem from the high places, and the groves, and the carved images, and the molten images." Our lesson tells us that in the eighteenth year of his reign he had the temple repaired. Others before him had cleansed and repaired the temple, but each time when idolatry arose again, the temple soon became polluted and fell into disrepair. The temple is a picture of what our lives should be, of a true heavenly character in which the Lord is worshiped in heart and mind and His laws carried out in every act of outward conduct. When "idols" are set up—that is, when other motives are allowed to rule our lives in place of service to the Lord—heavenly character begins to degenerate. The truths which have formed it—the walls of our "temple"—are broken down, and all sorts of unworthy ideas and practices creep in. When we awaken to the condition into which our character has fallen and begin to repair it, we find that we must use every bit of truth we have which can lead us into connection with the Lord again, like the silver which the keepers of the door of the temple gathered from the people who came to worship. But we note that there was no accounting made of this money. What we do for the Lord should be done willingly and faithfully with no desire for praise or reward.

While the temple was being cleaned out, a book of the law was found. This was undoubtedly the scroll containing one or more of the five books of Moses which had been laid up beside the ark from the time of its completion (Deuteronomy 31:24-26), but had been mislaid and forgotten and perhaps buried under rubbish during the misuse of the temple (AC 9396). When we seek to cleanse and repair our characters, we inevitably "find this book of the law"—we come to realize that only the teachings of the Word can direct us in living a good life. And when, like Josiah, we read the book with humble minds, we realize how far we have fallen from the standards of truly heavenly living. Josiah tore his clothes, which we learn is a symbol of "grief on account of truth being lost" (AC 4763), and we know that truth which has not been applied to life is lost. Then Josiah set out to make sweeping reforms, going even further than Hezekiah; for he not only destroyed the idols, the groves, and the high places in Judah, but went up into what had been Israel and destroyed the altar to the golden calf which Jeroboam had set up at Bethel, fulfilling the prophecy made concerning it in Jeroboam's time (I Kings 13:1-2). We may recall the meaning of Jeroboam's altars. A study of the Word in genuine humility will break down the idea that merely natural goodness is enough.

Josiah was terrified by the curses pronounced against the nation in the book of the law in the event of their forsaking the Lord and pursuing the very course which they had actually been pursuing (Deuteronomy 28:15-68). He sent to Huldah the prophetess to inquire of the Lord whether these things would surely come to pass, and Huldah told him that the prophecies would be fulfilled but that, because of his own humility and righteousness, the doom would not fall in his day.

In the same way, we often wish to feel that the consequences of evil may after all be averted; but the Word assures us that they cannot be escaped, although whatever of humility and genuine goodness we have will also have its reward. This is a lesson which we all need to have clearly in mind; it is taught in the stories of both Hezekiah and Josiah. The effects of evil are inevitable. It is true that so long as we are in the world it is never too late to recognize our evils, repent, and begin to do well and lay the foundation at least of a heavenly character; but we are not the same persons we might have been if we had not done evil. Some opportunities have been lost forever, some of our original possibilities cut off. We can never actually make up for our present wrong acts. Even a brave and conscientious king like Josiah could not save the people from the consequences of their evils. And we must remember that the effect of evil is cumulative. Every time we deliberately choose to do what we know is wrong we make it harder for ourselves to do right the next time. And our lives are to be judged by the very book of the law which Josiah read (see Revelation 20:12). We too should read that book humbly and be shocked to find how far we have departed from its commands, and set about cleansing our lives and repairing the breaches in our characters.

As the crowning act of all his work, Josiah celebrated the Passover. The Passover, we remember, symbolizes deliverance from bondage to evil and falsity through the Lord's victory over the hells. The people were ordered to observe the Passover annually at a certain time. We, if we lived orderly lives, would regularly experience this acknowledgment of the Lord's saving power and the peace and joy which follow it. But as the people had forsaken the Lord, the feast had been neglected and only occasionally, after some great reform like that of Josiah, is its celebration mentioned. So we experience this state all too seldom, for it never comes from self-satisfaction, but from the realization of our debt to the Lord. In the Christian Church the proper preparation for receiving the Holy Supper—the feast which takes the place of the Passover for us—is self-examination and repentance, the same work which Josiah's reforms symbolize.

Our lesson today brings us to the end of the ancient Hebrew nation as a representative of the true Church in the world and in us. In the letter we find that Josiah was killed when he tried to oppose the passage of the king of Egypt through his land (II Kings 23:29). The evils fixed in the natural plane of the mind by long habit are our undoing. He was succeeded by his son Jehoahaz, who after a reign of only three months was removed from the throne by the king of Egypt and carried off to Egypt. The Pharaoh raised another son of Josiah, Eliakim or Jehoiakim, to the throne and exacted tribute. It was in Jehoiakim's reign that the invasion of Judah by Babylon began, but Jehoiakim died and was succeeded by his son, Jehoiachin, before the actual captivity took place. Jehoiachin surrendered and was carried away to Babylon, together with his mother, his wives, and all the princes, warriors, and wealthy men, and the best of the craftsmen. For a time the country was allowed to continue under the puppet rule of a third son of Josiah, whose original name was changed to Zedekiah. Finally Zedekiah rebelled and the army of Babylon destroyed Jerusalem and the temple and carried away all the rest of the people except some of the poorest, who were left to till the ground so that it might be useful to Babylon. After seventy years, however, when Cyrus, king of Persia, had absorbed Babylon, "the Lord put it in the heart of Cyrus" to allow all who would to return. Jerusalem and the temple were rebuilt, and so the Holy Land was tided over until the coming of the Lord.

## From the Writings of Swedenborg

*Apocalypse Explained*, n. 707: "By 'Armageddon' is signified in heaven the love of honor, of dominion, and of supereminence; for from that is the combat, and from that and on account of it is lamentation. . . . The like is also signified by 'Megiddo.'"

## Suggested Questions on the Lesson

J. What part of the divided kingdom remained loyal to the line of David? *Judah*

P. Were all the kings of Judah bad like those of Israel? *no*

P. What king is our lesson about today? *Josiah*

P. How old was he when he became king? *eight*

J. What was the first of his good works? *repaired temple*

J. How were the repairs of the temple paid for? *contributions*

P. What was found when the temple was being repaired? *book of law*

J. What did Josiah do when the book was read to him? *tore clothes*

J. To whom did he send men to inquire of the Lord? *the prophetess Huldah*

J. What did Huldah tell him? *punishment would come, but not in his time*

J. What reforms did Josiah carry out? *destroyed idols, high places, groves, altars*

J. What did he destroy which no king before him had been able to touch? *altar at Bethel*

P. What great feast was celebrated when the country had been set in order? *Passover*

J. How did Josiah die? *killed by king of Egypt*

J. What happened to Judah afterward? *conquered by Babylon*

I. What do (1) Israel, and (2) Judah, represent? *(1) mind or thoughts, (2) heart or feelings*

I. What does the temple represent in us? *our character*

S. What is pictured by the fact that some of the kings of Judah were good? *heart still has times of repentance and reform*

S. Why could Judah not long survive the fall of Israel? *when thoughts are captivated by worldliness, good intentions cannot long survive*

## ZEDEKIAH AND JEREMIAH

*II Kings 24; 25:1-12; Jeremiah 21*

In all the classes try to impress the names of the two nations which conquered Israel and Judah and the fact that the people of Israel were replaced and never returned, whereas the people of Judah were not all carried away, and some returned. Call attention to the destruction of the temple and Jerusalem and mention their rebuilding later.

---

### Doctrinal Points

*The Lord cannot save a person against his will.*

*The books of the prophets often help us to understand the historical books of the Word.*

*We cannot turn to the Lord and expect Him to save us if we are not willing to obey Him.*

*When the mind turns from truth to falsity, goodness in the heart cannot long survive.*

---

### Notes for Parents

The kingdom of Israel was conquered by Assyria and all its people were carried away captive, never to return. Foreigners were brought in to take their places, and the descendants of these people were the Samaritans of Gospel days. We shall hear more about them later when we study the Gospel.

The king of Assyria tried to conquer the kingdom of Judah also and besieged Jerusalem, but the good king Hezekiah asked the Lord's help, and the Lord by a miracle destroyed a large part of the besieging army and caused the rest to go back to their own land. But Hezekiah afterward made a serious mistake. He received some emissaries of the king of Babylon and showed them all his treasures. The prophet Isaiah was then sent to tell him that the king of Babylon would eventually carry off all these treasures and that Hezekiah's own descendants would some day be servants in the court of Babylon.

Our lesson for today tells us about the fulfillment over a hundred years later of this prophecy. Babylon had increased in power and had absorbed Assyria and extended its control even to Egypt. Only one of the kings who descended from Hezekiah—Josiah—was a good king. The others were idolatrous and evil, and so the Lord could no longer save Judah. The Lord will not force us to serve Him, and He cannot save us if we refuse to heed His Word and to obey the commandments.

The great prophet Jeremiah lived in the last days of Judah, and Zedekiah, the last king, even went so far as to consult him, but Jeremiah told him that the end of Judah was at hand. There always is an end to our opportunity to reform, although many people do not like to think so. The results of a bad life cannot be wiped out in a moment, and when we go into the other world, we remain what we have made ourselves by our daily choices here.

Judah was conquered by Babylon, and its royal household and all its able men were carried away, and Jerusalem and the temple were destroyed. But the "poor of the land"—who represent those who are humble in heart and recognize their own weakness and need of the Lord—were allowed to remain in their homes in the Holy Land.

---

## Primary

Even the little children should get the idea that the Lord cannot prosper people who turn against Him and refuse to obey Him. Teach the name *Jeremiah* as well as the names of the two kingdoms, Judah and Israel, and try to tell the story in such a way that Assyria will be connected in their minds with Israel and Babylon with Judah. The carrying off of the people and the fate of the great city of Jerusalem and of the temple should interest them. Tell the children who the Samaritans of Gospel days were.

Do you remember the names of the two great prophets whom the Lord sent to warn the people of Israel? They were Elijah and Elisha. Elisha cured a Syrian captain named Naaman of a terrible disease by telling him to wash seven times in the Jordan River. You would think that the people of Israel would have listened to the warnings of such a great prophet as Elisha, but they didn't. They went right on worshiping the golden calves and doing all sorts of wicked things, and so the Lord could not help them against their enemies. These enemies became more and more powerful, and finally the king of Assyria conquered Israel and carried all the people away captive and brought foreigners in to settle the land in their place.

The kingdom of Judah lasted longer than the kingdom of Israel.
This was because some of them worshiped the Lord in the temple.
But many of them worshiped idols instead.
Finally Judah, too, became so wicked that the Lord could not save it.
Who was the last king of Judah?
What nation had gained control there?
The great prophet Jeremiah tried to turn the people back to the worship of the Lord, but they would not listen.
What happened to most of the people?
Who were left in the land?
What happened to Jerusalem and the temple?

---

## Junior

Give this class as clear and detailed a view as possible of the story of the divided kingdom, dwelling on the individuals and nations concerned, their relation to each other and to earlier and later history, and the underlying causes of events. Our lessons on the prophets will be helped by this background. Show the class the location of Syria, Assyria, and Babylon on a map.

Assyria extended its power farther and farther westward, and Israel, because of its own wickedness, could not stand against it. The Lord cannot help us if we refuse to obey Him. So finally Israel was conquered and all its people were carried away into captivity. They never came back, and no one knows what became of their descendants. They are sometimes referred to as "the lost tribes of Israel." The king of Assyria brought in other people from the east to take their places. The descendants of these people were still living in the Holy Land when the Lord came on earth hundreds of years later. We know them as the Samaritans.

Judah, the southern kingdom, lasted longer than Israel. Some of the kings and many of the people followed the bad example of Solomon and worshiped idols as well as the Lord, but they did still have Jerusalem and the temple to remind them of what they ought to do, and several of their kings were good and tried hard to bring them back to obedience to the Lord. We have had lessons about three of these good kings: Asa, Hezekiah, and Josiah. Several great prophets also lived in Judah, notably Isaiah and Jeremiah.

But gradually idolatry and evil practices began to prevail in Judah also. The eastern nations, Assyria and Babylon, gained more and more control. Judah saved itself for a time by an alliance with Egypt and by paying tribute and giving up the treasures of the palace and then of the temple. But after the people of Israel were carried away, there was no protection on the north, and then Egypt became of no more help. See if you can find early in our first chapter for today the reason for this.

Who was the next to the last king of Judah?
Where was he taken when he was carried away?
What great nation finally took possession of the land?
Who was the last king of Judah?
To whom did he send messengers to inquire of the Lord?
What did the Lord tell them?
What happened to Zedekiah?
What classes of people were carried away with him?
Who were left in the land?
Why were they left?
What happened to the temple?
What happened to Jerusalem?

The prophet Jeremiah had advised the king to submit to Babylon. For this reason the king of Babylon allowed Jeremiah to remain in his home. After Jerusalem was destroyed, Jeremiah tried to persuade all the people who were left to settle down quietly and obey the king of Babylon. But some of them were afraid and decided to flee to Egypt, and they forced Jeremiah to go with them. So Jeremiah died in Egypt. The prophecies recorded in the book of

Lamentations are believed to have been given through him in Egypt before he died, as well as the last few chapters of the book of Jeremiah.

The last few verses of II Kings 25 tell how the king of Babylon finally took pity on Jehoiachin, Zedekiah's predecessor, in his captivity. From that time on the exiles had an easier time, and after seventy years the Lord "put it in the heart" of the king of Babylon to allow all who wanted to return to the Holy Land and rebuild Jerusalem and the temple. So the Jews who lived in the Holy Land when the Lord came on earth were descendants of the people of Judah.

---

### Intermediate

Stress the correspondence of Assyria and Babylon in connection with that of Israel and Judah, and point out Jeremiah's connection with the final decline and fall of Judah. The danger of trying to compromise with worldly ambitions is an important lesson for the Intermediates.

In time Syria was absorbed by Assyria, the great nation further east whose capital was Nineveh. Syria represents knowledges of good and truth. Assyria represents reasoning or the rational mind. In Isaiah 19:23-24 we read: "In that day shall there be a highway out of Egypt to Assyria, and the Assyrian shall come into Egypt, and the Egyptian into Assyria, and the Egyptians shall serve with the Assyrians. In that day shall Israel be the third with Egypt and with Assyria, even a blessing in the midst of the land." Egypt represents the natural plane of the mind in which memory-knowledges are stored up. Israel represents the mind of the spiritual person, the person of the church who has become to some extent at least regenerate. So the quotation from Isaiah shows us what our minds ought to be like, with our reasoning power acting freely in connection with our memory knowledge, but both enlightened and controlled by the spiritual understanding—Israel a blessing in the midst. When Israel ceased to worship the Lord, it surrendered its proper function and finally was captured by Assyria. That is, when the mind of a person of the church stops looking to the Word for its light and guidance, that person's reasoning power actually becomes an enemy of his spiritual life and eventually takes away his spiritual understanding and his freedom altogether. The people of Israel were carried away captive to Assyria and never came back. Foreigners were brought in from the east to take their places. Later, when we study the Gospel, we shall learn something about the descendants of these foreigners, who came to be called the Samaritans.

Assyria tried to capture Judah also, but was driven off by the power of the Lord. Because Judah continued the worship of the Lord in the temple at Jerusalem its history was different from that of Israel, even though many of its people and most of its kings also worshiped idols. Judah represents the heart or will. The heart of a person who has reached a state of regeneration clings to its good intentions even when the thinking has become worldly and the motives mixed. Mere worldly reasoning cannot change these good intentions. Assyria could not conquer Judah. We have had lessons about several of the good kings of Judah, individuals who tried to bring the people back to the sole worship of the Lord. A person who sees his good character slipping away may try again and again to "turn over a new leaf." But temptations continue, and without the support and protection of true spiritual principles in the mind the good will cannot hold its ground. After the people of Israel were carried away by Assyria, Judah was greatly weakened. Even its good kings were reduced to "buying off" their enemies with the treasures first of the king's house and finally of the temple itself. In the same way, one may compromise with falsity and evil little by little until he has nothing left.

During the latter years of its existence Judah relied on the support of Egypt. Our memory-knowledge of the truth seems to sustain us for a time. But finally a new and more powerful enemy took over Assyria and then Egypt, and Judah could no longer stand. This enemy was Babylon. Babylon represents the "love of dominion," which means the desire to be first and to make other people do what we want. We all know from our own experience how natural this desire is to us and how strong it is.

The history of the last years of Judah shows us how this selfish desire to have our own way gradually takes over in the heart, once we have let worldly reasoning take the place of the guidance of the Word in our minds. Notice that this very thing had been prophesied by Isaiah in the days of king Hezekiah (II Kings 20:16-18) not long after Israel was carried away captive by Assyria. You remember that Hezekiah had showed the messengers from the king of Babylon—who came to him ostensibly on a friendly mission—all his treasures. Now these treasures are gradually carried away to Babylon. The king of Babylon, Nebuchadnezzar, did not immediately destroy Judah. First he took away to Babylon some of the most promising of the young princes, among whom was Daniel. Then he surrounded Judah by getting control of Egypt. Then he besieged Jerusalem, and king Jehoiachin and his family gave themselves up voluntarily and were carried away to Babylon along with the "mighty men of valor" and the craftsmen and smiths. Nebuchadnezzar spared Jerusalem and the kingdom at this time and set up as puppet king an uncle of Jehoiachin, whose name—Mattaniah—he changed to Zedekiah. But when Zedekiah rebelled, Jerusalem was taken and burned and the temple destroyed. Zedekiah's eyes were put out, his sons were all killed, and all the remaining people were carried away to Babylon except the "poor of the land," who were left to be vinedressers and husbandmen. This teaches us how the heart gradually gives way to selfishness until it stops worshiping the Lord at all or trying to do right. The poor of the land are those who are humble and conscious of their own weakness and need of the Lord. If once we have started on the regenerate life, there are always some of these "poor" remnants left deep in our hearts to keep our spiritual life from being entirely destroyed.

This is where the prophet Jeremiah comes into the story. He of course represents the Word of the Lord trying to reach and guide us in this difficult state. Jeremiah had perhaps the hardest life of any of the prophets. When selfishness is getting control of our hearts, we do not like to listen to the teachings of the Word. Jeremiah was despised, plotted against, thrown into prison and into a pit partly full of water, beaten, put in the stocks, and almost starved to death; and finally he was carried away to Egypt against his will by some of the fugitives. Yet he spoke the Word of the Lord faithfully and boldly through it all. We learn all this from the book of Jeremiah and from Lamentations—believed to have been written through Jeremiah in Egypt—rather than from the books of Kings. We have assigned a chapter in Jeremiah with our lesson today to show how the books of the prophets often fill out the details of the historical story as well as point up the reason for what happened. Even in the last days of Judah, Zedekiah recognized Jeremiah as a prophet and sent messengers to him to inquire of the Lord. But even the Lord cannot help us against our will. If we persist in disregarding His commandments, He must let justice take its course. We notice, however, that the poor were left in the land, and we know that after seventy years some of the captives were allowed to come back and rebuild Jerusalem and the temple.

*Basic Correspondences*

| | | |
|---|---|---|
| Assyria | = | reasoning, or the rational mind |
| Babylon | = | the love of dominion from the love of self |
| the poor | = | the humble |

---

## Senior

The gradual taking over of Judah by Babylon, and the connection of the two great prophets Isaiah and Jeremiah with this period is the important study for the Seniors. The teacher should be prepared to give more details about Jeremiah than are given in the Senior notes. The Intermediate notes will be found helpful here.

Israel was finally conquered by Assyria—which represents worldly reasoning—and its people had been carried away captive, never to return. Assyria then threatened Judah, but Hezekiah, who had served the Lord faithfully, asked His help, and the Assyrian army was dispersed by a miracle and Judah saved for the time being. The heart of the person who has entered upon the regenerate life cannot be overcome by mere worldly ideas. But behind these worldly ideas there is a more powerful enemy which can overcome the good intentions of the heart. You remember that the king of Babylon sent messengers to Hezekiah, ostensibly to inquire as to his health, and that Hezekiah received them as friends and showed them all his treasures. Babylon represents the selfish love of dominion–that feeling that everyone ought to do what we want them to do. Isaiah told Hezekiah just what the result would be. Read II Kings 20:16-18. His prophecy was fulfilled. The king of Babylon, once Hezekiah had shown him the treasures of Jerusalem, did not rest until he made them his own. In our lesson for today he has captured all the countries surrounding Judah even as far as Egypt and is ready for the final attack.

This is characteristic of the selfish love of dominion. It creeps into the life by degrees until it reaches the heart. Deprived of a true understanding of the Lord and the Word, the heart has no stability. In its "well-meaning" states it still tries to do right, but when these states recede, it easily falls prey to selfishness, which has already invaded the mind and the daily life.

There was one good king in Judah after Hezekiah. This was his great-grandson Josiah, about whose sweeping reforms we recently learned. But Josiah's reforms did not last. The three kings who followed him were all evil. Josiah's son Jehoahaz was taken captive and carried into Egypt, and his brother Eliakim, called by the Egyptians Jehoiakim, was set up in his stead, paying tribute to Egypt. Presently he rebelled against Egypt, which had been driven back at this time by the king of Babylon. Jehoiakim's reign of eleven years was troubled by constant raids, and his son Jehoiachin held his throne only three months before Nebuchadnezzar, king of Babylon, attacked Jerusalem and carried away to Babylon "all the princes, and all the mighty men of valor, even ten thousand captives, and all the craftsmen and smiths," and the king, his family, and his officers, together with the treasures of the temple and of the king's house, leaving only the poorest of the people to care for the land.

Nebuchadnezzar set up Zedekiah, the king's uncle, as a puppet ruler, but after he had reigned nine years, he too rebelled. Then Nebuchadnezzar besieged Jerusalem and two years later captured and destroyed it. The punishment of Zedekiah is described in verses 6 and 7 of chapter 25. It pictures the destruction of all ability to see the genuine truth or to produce any spiritual development. Again Nebuchadnezzar set up a puppet ruler, a grandson of Josiah's scribe Shaphan, not as king this time but as governor. The people left behind finally overthrew him, and then, afraid to face the wrath of Babylon, they emigrated for refuge to Egypt.

This history is a picture of what may happen to anyone who once permits worldliness to enter his heart. Take, for example, the case of a young person brought up in any church today. When he leaves home and is separated from the associations of his home church, he still means to remain Christian. But many conditions surround him which make it easy for him to stop going to church on Sunday. If he has gone before just as a matter of habit and does not really understand what his church means and its importance in his life, he will make less and less effort to attend worship. Without regular worship, the duties and pleasures of his external life will gradually fill his mind. He will, however, still think of himself as a good person and a Christian, and what he wants to do will consequently seem to him to be right. His own will finally comes to be ruler in his heart in place of the Lord's will. "Babylon" has captured "Judah." The final step is the complete blinding of his mind to spiritual truth and the destruction of spiritual character with all its beauties. He has become a slave of worldly and selfish principles.

From the book of Jeremiah we learn how the Lord through the Word continues to warn and tries to guide such a person to a humbler state of mind. But the Lord cannot save anyone against his will. Justice must take its course if we refuse to obey the Lord. It is interesting that the original name of Zedekiah—*Mattaniah*—means "God's gift," and that *Zedekiah* means "the justice of God."

Chapter 25 marks the end of that portion of the consecutive history of the Old Testament which has an inner sense. But just at the close of a chapter we see the beginning of a development which was to lead to the return of a part of Judah to the Holy Land some seventy years later. For it is recorded there that Evil-merodach king of Babylon "did lift up the head of Jehoiachin king of Judah out of prison," changed his prison garments, and thereafter treated him as a favored ward.

We recognize in general that the taking captive of Judah by Babylon pictures the invasion of the heart of a well-intentioned person by selfishness and the love of dominion. This does not happen at once. The will to good reasserts itself many times before it is finally overcome. And even then the possibility of return is preserved by the Lord.

## Adult

The major discussion topic is the nature of the love of dominion and the insidious way in which it can enter the heart and gain control of it—particularly its manifestation in people of the church.

Because the Scriptures everywhere apply to us, the story of the fall of Israel and Judah should bring us some very sobering thoughts. Israel was conquered by Assyria. Its people were carried away captive and never returned, foreigners being brought in to take their places. Assyria was not allowed to extend its conquest to Judah, although for a time in Hezekiah's reign the Assyrian army threatened Jerusalem. But a century or more later Babylon came into control of both Assyria and Egypt and was able to destroy Jerusalem and carry off all the royal household and the men of might and ability, leaving only the poor of the land to tend the fields and vineyards. Seventy years later some of the people of Judah—all who so desired—were allowed to return and rebuild Jerusalem and the temple, but the Jewish nation never again served as the representative of the Lord's church among men. We may note in passing that it was the descendants of the returned captives of Judah and the descendants of the "poor of the land" not carried away who were the Jews in the Holy Land when the Lord was born, and that the Samaritans of the Gospels were the descendants of the foreigners brought in to take the place of the people of Israel.

Israel and Judah represent, respectively, the intellect and the will of the person of the church. Assyria represents the rational mind or reasoning in general, and Egypt represents the natural mind or the plane of memory-knowledge. The proper relationship of Israel to Egypt and Assyria is described in Isaiah 19:23-24: "In that day shall there be a highway out of Egypt to Assyria, and the Assyrian shall come into Egypt, and the Egyptian into Assyria, and the Egyptians shall serve with the Assyrians. In that day shall Israel be the third with Egypt and with Assyria, even a blessing in the midst of the land." That is, in the properly ordered mind there should be free interplay of reasoning and memory-knowledge, but the spiritual should stand as "a blessing in the midst." Israel sacrificed her opportunity to be such a blessing when she separated herself from Judah and substituted the worship of the golden calves for the worship of the Lord. Once the person of the church begins to entertain the thought that outward good works constitute religion, he is separated from the divine source of all power to do good. His intellect and reasoning are used more and more to exalt worldly learning above revelation, and his mind is finally carried away captive by the world outside the church.

Judah—the heart—also worshiped idols; but it maintained at the same time the worship of the Lord in the temple at Jerusalem. Consequently its people were kept reminded of their true God, and some of them remained faithful. Even several of the kings, as we have learned in other lessons, were true followers of the Lord and made strenuous efforts to destroy the idols and reform the people. The heart which has once experienced the happiness and peace of regenerate life cannot be subverted by worldly reasoning alone. Assyria could not conquer Judah.

There existed, however, another enemy which had been gathering strength over the centuries and now rose to take over Assyria and all the land tributary to Assyria. This was Babylon, "the land of Shinar," the land of the Chaldees, from which Abraham had been called so long before. Babylon represents the love of dominion, the old natural selfish will which prompts us to feel that what we want is right and that everyone and everything should be made to serve us. Swedenborg applies the meaning of Babylon specifically to the love of dominion through the misuse of religion, the setting up of the fiat of men above the Word of God as the authority for the church.

Shortly after the fall of Israel the king of Babylon sent messengers to Hezekiah king of Judah ostensibly to inquire for his health. Hezekiah was deceived, received the messengers as friends, and showed them all his treasures. Then Isaiah came to Hezekiah and told him that Babylon would one day carry off all the treasures of Judah and that Hezekiah's descendants would be servants in the court of Babylon. Our chapters for today describe the fulfillment of this prophecy. Once the insidious love of rule is admitted into the inner chambers of the heart of the person of the church, its control of his life follows. There is nothing which the Word and the writings more clearly and positively condemn than arrogance and the love of rule.

The great prophet of the last years of Judah was Jeremiah. The story of these last years is told very briefly in II Kings, but in much more fullness in the book of Jeremiah. For Jeremiah was recognized as the Lord's prophet by the last kings of Judah and was consulted by them even though they had no intention of obeying the Lord. Because of their wickedness they rejected Jeremiah's counsel again and again, and he himself was shamefully mistreated. People may and do go to the Word and study it in the hope of finding confirmation of their own will and opinion, but when they find that it obviously condemns them, they disparage and reject it.

When the Lord came into the world, He had to come in the Holy Land because of the correspondence of all its parts and places, long established by the letter of the Word. And He had to come where the Word was, since He was to fulfill it. Therefore some of the Jews, with the Word, had to be brought back to the Holy Land, and the temple had to be rebuilt. And there were a few good Jews left—the poor of the land, the humble—who would receive the Lord when He came. But, as we have pointed out, the Hebrew nation as a nation ceased to represent the Lord's church on earth when Judah was taken captive. The connection of the Lord with mankind was maintained for a time by the prophets of the captivity and restoration, and then for some four hundred years only by the few humble souls who still believed and obeyed the Law and the Prophets in simplicity. When this connection was threatened by the perverted teachings of the scribes and Pharisees, the Lord had to come into the world to restore it.

## From the Writings of Swedenborg

*Apocalypse Explained*, n. 1029: "From these passages in Daniel [parts of chapters 2-7] it can be seen that 'Babylon or Babel' means in the Word the love of dominion over the entire globe, likewise over heaven and over the Lord Himself; and that the church of the Lord successively becomes Babylon; and that as it becomes Babylon so it is devastated as to all the good of love and all the truth of faith; and that this is its end, that is, it is no longer a church; and when it is no longer a church it is reckoned among the idolatrous nations, except those in it who worship the Lord, regard the Word as holy, and admit instruction from it. . . . When, therefore, the sons of Israel wholly departed from the statutes which were representative of the spiritual things of the church, through which they had communication with heaven, they were all given into the hands of the king of Assyria . . . The same thing happened to the Jews [those of Judah]. When they had adulterated and profaned all the statutes, judgments, and laws that represented good and truth of faith, to the extent that there was no longer anything of good and truth left, and when their church thus became Babylon, then not only their kings and princes and the whole people, but also all the treasures of the house of Jehovah, and afterwards all its golden vessels, were given into the hand of Nebuchadnezzar, king of Babylon; and moreover the temple itself was burned . . . But since the Lord was to be born in that nation and make Himself manifest where the church then was and where His Word was, so that nation after a captivity of seventy years was brought back from Babylon, and the temple was rebuilt. And yet no other church remained with them except a church like that called

Babylon, as can be seen from many things which the Lord Himself said about that nation, and from the way they received Him; and for this reason Jerusalem was again destroyed, and the temple burnt with fire."

## Suggested Questions on the Lesson

J. What nation finally conquered Israel? *Assyria*

J. What happened to the people? *taken away forever*

J. Why was Judah able to hold out longer against its enemies? *faithful to David's line*

J. What did its good kings try to do? *reform*

P. What great nation finally conquered Judah? *Babylon*

J. What king of Judah first allowed messengers of Babylon to spy out the land? *Hezekiah*

J. What great prophet foretold what the result would be? *Isaiah*

P. Who was the last king of Judah? *Zedekiah*

P. To what prophet did he send to inquire of the Lord? *Jeremiah*

J. What did Jeremiah tell him? *Jerusalem would be destroyed*

J. What happened to Zedekiah? *blinded, taken to Babylon*

J. Who were carried away to Babylon? *princes, mighty men, craftsmen*

P. Who were left in the land? *the poor*

I. What do Israel and Judah represent? *mind and heart divided*

S. What does Assyria represent? *worldly reasoning*

I. What does Babylon represent? *love of dominion from love of self*

S. Who are pictured by "the poor of the land"? *those who are humbly conscious of their need of the Lord*

# THE BOOK OF PSALMS

*II Samuel 23:1-2; Psalm 1*

In connection with the study of Psalm 19, we shall deal in some detail with the history of the book of Psalms and with the use of the Psalms in the temple worship. There we shall emphasize rather the spiritual character of the book and the use of the Psalms in our personal life. In all classes the testimony of David in II Samuel 23:1-2 and of the Lord in Luke 24:44 should be read, and our use of the Psalms in our church service should also be pointed out.

---

## Doctrinal Points

*Happiness can come only as we look constantly to the Lord for guidance.*

*The first downward step is taken when we listen to the arguments of the ungodly.*

---

## Notes for Parents

The book of Psalms is without doubt the best loved and most generally read book in the Bible. We ought to be able to assume from this that it is the best known. But is it? How many of us read *all* the Psalms—in the course of a year, let us say? Do not most of us say we love the Psalms but actually know only the twenty-third by heart and a few others really well?

There is a reason for all this. Many of the Psalms were dictated to David by the Lord, as David himself testifies in II Samuel 23:1-2. David was a musician as well as a king, and the Psalms were given through him as songs to be sung, because music is an expression of the emotions and reaches the heart. What the Psalms give us are words from the Lord Himself to express adequately all the feelings we ought to have in the course of our lives about the Lord and about ourselves in relation to Him.

We all have times when we think about God. So we all find certain Psalms which mean something to us. The reason why the twenty-third Psalm is the best known and loved is that it brings comfort in the states of trouble and bereavement which come to all alike, and in which people are most likely to turn to the Lord.

But very few of us "walk with the Lord" in all our experiences. Most of us, when all is going well with us, are satisfied with things—including ourselves—as they are, and have no desire to look within to see whether all is really right there or not. And the Psalms probe deep. They point out our weaknesses and sins and steadily direct our thought to these and to our need of the Lord's correction and guidance every day, whatever our outward circumstances may be. Some do not like to be reminded of these things. So they "edit" the Psalms to suit themselves, picking out the "smooth" and comforting things and ignoring the rest.

This is not what the Lord tells us to do. In the very first Psalm He points out to us clearly that there is but one road to genuine and lasting happiness and that is to delight in the law of the Lord and to meditate in it day and night—in the times when all seems bright to us as well as in our dark and troubled states.

In the first verse we are told the particular temptations into which we are most likely to fall. How prone we all are to listen to the worldly advice of those who have no real belief in God and spiritual things! We let ourselves be influenced, we yield our principles here and there. We say, "everybody does it." This is the first step toward spiritual death. From this, as our verse shows us, we go on gradually to accept the way of the sinner as our own and finally give up our belief in God and the Word and sit "in the seat of the scornful." How shallow and short-sighted this course is, as the Lord tells us when He says that the ungodly are "like the chaff which the wind driveth away."

---

### Primary

The children should learn that the Psalms are songs, that David was chosen by the Lord to write many of them, that they were sung in the services of the tabernacle and temple in Jerusalem, and that we sometimes sing them in our services. Read the first Psalm to them and then talk to them about how our souls grow just as a tree does. You may even tell them that the Word is the river close to which our tree of life must grow. Tell them about the place of the book of Psalms in the Bible, and about what the Psalms give us.

The worship of ancient Israel was different in many ways from our worship in our churches today, but there was one part of it which we should have recognized if it had been translated from Hebrew into English, for they sang the very same Psalms which we sometimes sing today.

When David was king, he made Jerusalem his capital and brought the ark there, making a new tabernacle or tent to keep it in, and he wrote many psalms or songs to be sung in connection with the worship there. For David was a musician and a player on the harp as well as a king. Music was a very important part of their worship, and whole families were trained to sing and play on instruments.

Many of the Psalms were written by David.
Did David make them up himself?

Let us read what he says in II Samuel 23:1-2. You see the Lord put the words into David's mind. So the Psalms, as well as the rest of the Word, are the Lord speaking to us.

And the very first Psalm tells us how to be happy; for the Lord wants us all to be happy and He knows much better than we do what will give us happiness. You know sometimes we think we want something and then after we get it, we find we don't like it at all. Let us listen to what the Lord tells us in the first Psalm and think about what it means. The word *blessed* means "happy." Read Psalm 1.

In this Psalm the Lord Himself is telling us how we may be happy.
What does He say will delight the happy man?
To what does He compare him?
To what does He liken the ungodly man?
What does He say in the last verse about the way of the righteous and the way of the ungodly?

This means that the Lord can always be with us when we do right, but that when we do wrong, He cannot keep us safe.

---

## Junior

First cover briefly the position of the book of Psalms in the Word, the origin of the Psalms and their use in Hebrew worship, and the general character and purpose of the Psalms. Then take up the first Psalm verse by verse, explaining especially the meaning of the three prohibitions in the first verse. You will find these discussed in the Senior notes. Adapt your illustrations, however, to the experience of the Juniors.

Today we are taking up a book which is a book of the Word but which in its letter is neither history nor prophecy. The strictly historical books of the Word in the Old Testament (those with an inner sense) end with II Kings, and the strictly prophetical books begin with Isaiah. In between these in our Bible are ten books, only one of which has an inner sense. The other nine, like the book of Ruth, give us interesting pictures of the life of the times and some valuable historical details, but they are not part of the Word for the New Church.

The book of Psalms is sometimes called the book of David because the Lord gave so many of the Psalms through David.

Who was David?
How do we know that he did not make up the Psalms?
What is a psalm?
How many Psalms are there?

In the original Hebrew the Psalms are poems. In English they do not appear to be poetry, but they are meant to be sung and can be sung in chant form if we wish to sing them in church. They have always formed an important part of Jewish worship. They were sung in Solomon's temple by trained choirs to the accompaniment of various instruments. Several of these instruments are mentioned in Psalm 150.

The Psalms are given us by the Lord to help us express the feelings and thoughts we ought to have, and often do have, about Him and about our relations to Him. That is why people have always loved them and found help in them. We know that we all like to express our feelings, but we also know that many of our feelings from day to day are selfish and wrong, and these often "come out" when we do not really mean to show them. So it is especially good for us to read and sing the Psalms and try to bring our feelings into the pattern which they give us.

The very first Psalm gives us the basis for this pattern. Remember that *blessed* means "happy." We all know that sometimes things which we think are going to make us happy actually do just the opposite. So we need to listen to this teaching from the Lord. He really knows.

What is the first thing He tells us we must not do if we want to be happy?
What is the second?
What is the third?
What must we do instead?
To what does the Lord liken us if we take His advice?
What does He say the ungodly are like?

The last two verses tell us plainly that we cannot be happy if we do not try to learn about the Lord and live the kind of life He tells us is right. Can you see that the whole history of the Israelites as we have been studying it in the Word teaches us this same lesson?

---

### Intermediate

After a brief introduction about the book of Psalms as a whole, present the first Psalm as giving us the basis for a life that will turn out to be genuinely happy. Develop the correspondence of verse 3 and contrast it with the correspondence of chaff. Emphasize the need of daily reading of the Word.

In the twenty-fourth chapter of Luke we are told that after His resurrection the Lord opened the understanding of some of His disciples to understand the Scriptures, explaining many things which had puzzled them and which they had not been ready to understand before they saw Him pass through death and appear whole and alive afterward. In Luke 24:44 He says: "These are the words which I spake unto you, while I was yet with you, that all things must be fulfilled, which were written in the law of Moses, and in the prophets, and in the psalms, concerning me." For the Jews the law of Moses meant the first five books of the Old Testament as we have it today, the prophets meant the books of Joshua, Judges, Samuel, and Kings—which they called the "former prophets"—and the books of the Old Testament from Isaiah through Malachi, which they called the "latter prophets." They did not include in these the books of Lamentations and Daniel. These two, the book of Ruth, and the ten books between II Kings and Isaiah they did not consider to be of the same degree of inspiration as the rest, and they collected them in a separate group which they called the Kethubim or Sacred Writings.

As New Church young people, you should remember that what could be called the New Church *canon* of Scripture—the list of books considered to be the Word of God—is the same as the Jewish canon, plus the books of Psalms, Lamentations, and Daniel, and in the New Testament the four Gospels and the book of Revelation. For us a book is identified as a book of the Word by the possession of a continuous internal meaning relating to the Lord's life. This can be recognized if you know your correspondences. We shall treat of the books of Daniel and Lamentations later. In regard to the Psalms you should remember that the Lord Himself told His disciples that the Psalms treated of Him.

The Psalms are perhaps the most read and most loved part of the Bible. This is because we find in them the expression of all our states and needs in words better than any we could think of ourselves and also a clear statement of what the Lord can and should mean to us in these states. People do not read the Psalms when they are feeling proud and self-satisfied, but when they are realizing their weakness and need of the Lord.

The first Psalm tells us just this. *Blessed* means "happy." We cannot be happy if we listen to worldly advice, if we choose our associates from those who care nothing about the Lord, or if we set ourselves up and despise as ignorant those who disagree with us. We can be happy only if we look to the Lord for guidance in all things and read and "meditate" on the Word every day. For it is only as we study and obey the teachings of the Word that the Lord can enter our hearts and give us as our own the unselfish love which brings happiness.

Verse 3 is a beautiful picture of the life of a good man or woman. Trees picture general principles. A river pictures truth from the Lord flowing into our minds to make our principles sound and strong and our thinking sane. A man is like a strong tree planted by the rivers of water when his life is based on the principle of obedience to the Lord and nourished by a constant inflow of truth from the Word. The leaves of the tree are the true thoughts which come from the mind of such a man. They do not wither because his thoughts, being according to the Lord's truth, never have to be discarded or changed. The fruit of the tree is a useful life, a life of service to God and man.

The chaff to which the ungodly are likened is a picture of the foolish and worthless thoughts of those who imagine they know enough to live without the Lord. People who depend upon human intelligence are always finding themselves faced with the necessity of changing their ideas. You will hear people say, "What is true for one generation may not be true for another. There is no absolute truth." This is an "ungodly" state of mind and such people are blown away by every wind of changing human opinion. Our study of the Word should show us that there is one constant stream of truth to which we can go in every age and in every situation. We read in Isaiah 40:7-8: "The grass withereth, the flower fadeth: because the spirit of the Lord bloweth upon it: surely the people is grass. The grass withereth, the flower fadeth: but the word of our God shall stand for ever."

*Basic Correspondences*

a river = truth flowing from the Lord
leaves = thoughts growing out of principles
fruit = useful works
chaff = worthless thoughts

## Senior

Psalm 1 is one to which the Seniors should pay particular attention. Center the lesson around the warning in the first verse, and stress the fact that this warning is given us plainly by the Lord Himself in the form most likely to reach through our thought to our will.

Music is primarily an expression of the emotions. We often sing without using or even thinking of words, and we find satisfaction in humming or whistling. But when we do sing words, they impress us more and remain in our minds longer than if they were merely spoken. This is because our emotions are reached by music. So, although we may regularly read the Psalms, it is even better to sing them and we should make ourselves familiar with the rules of chanting so that we may have this satisfaction. The Psalms were intended for singing. David, through whom many of them were written, was a skilled musician. The Psalms were a regular part of the temple worship and certain families among the Levites were trained for singing them and for their accompaniment on various musical instruments. Read I Chronicles 15:16-22.

But, as we learn from David's "last words," David did not compose the words of the Psalms: they were put in his mouth by the Lord. Of the ten books which we find in our Bible between II Kings and Isaiah, only the book of Psalms has an inner sense. The ancient Hebrews placed all ten of these books, as well as the books of Ruth, Lamentations, and Daniel, in a third group, called the Kethubim or Sacred Writings, considered to be of a less degree of inspiration than the Law and the Prophets. Our New Church "canon" of Scripture is the same as the Hebrew canon with the addition of the Psalms, Lamentations, and Daniel. Our test is whether a book has an internal sense. In the case of the Psalms, the Lord Himself in Luke 24:44 tells us that they, together with the law and the prophets, treat of Him. Several Psalms even in their letter are prophetic of the Lord's life. Read Psalm 22:18.

In the Psalms we are taught plainly by the Lord what our relation to Him is, how we should recognize the weakness of our own natures, and how we should see His wisdom and power in all creation and in every experience of life, and look to Him constantly for guidance and strength.

The first Psalm sets our pattern for life. If we would be blessed, or happy, we must delight in the law of the Lord, and read and meditate upon the Word daily. Only when we do so can the Lord be always with us and prosper our way. The godly man is like a strong, fruitful tree, which can weather any storm. The ungodly man is "like the chaff which the wind driveth away." The promise of the Lord is sure.

But in the spirit of the familiar command, "Cease to do evil; learn to do well," the Psalm begins by telling us the things we must avoid if we would be happy. This is where we must all begin, and you who are just on the brink of your independent adult lives should think very seriously of the three prohibitions in verse 1. Notice the three positions involved: walking, standing, and sitting. You might picture it in this way: Suppose you meet on the street someone who is perhaps popular and attractive but whom you know to be a worldly and selfish person, with no interest in religion and no fixed good principles. You know he is a person with whom it can do you only harm to associate, but he invites you to walk along with him and, instead of refusing politely and going in the opposite direction, you go with him, listening to his worldly conversation. You reach his home and he invites you in. Instead of parting from him immediately, you stand there in a discussion with him. Finally you go into his house and sit down with him, committed to his companionship. Now for the person in the picture substitute any thought or suggestion which you know to be contrary to the principles of love to the Lord and the neighbor, and follow the story through, and you will understand what the first Psalm is really saying to you. One of the older poets expressed this temptation in these words: "First endure, then pity, then embrace."* One of the writers of the New Church, John Bigelow

*Alexander Pope (1688-1744), "Essay on Man," Epistle II, line 217. The verse from which this line is taken reads:

(1817-1911), was the author of a book which he called *Resist Beginnings*. It is a useful phrase to keep in mind, for one of our most common tendencies is to think we are strong enough to go a little way on a forbidden path and turn back before we become deeply involved. We need to study the Psalms to remind ourselves how weak we really are. Trusting in self instead of in the Lord is always a dangerous business.

---

## Adult

The Adults, who are more familiar with the Psalms than the children, will probably be most interested in discussing the reason for their popularity and the implications of this reason. The fact that the first Psalm presents our fundamental choice and tells us clearly the consequences involved in each alternative should make a deep impression. Point out our constant temptation to compromise, and our need to read and use all the Psalms as the Lord has given them to us instead of just picking out a Psalm or a few verses here and there which especially please us.

In approaching the study of the book of Psalms we should also be familiar with Luke 24:44. Although the Jews did not consider the book of Psalms of equal inspiration with the Law and the Prophets, we are given in the letter of Scripture the assurance first of David and then of the Lord Himself that the Psalms were divinely inspired and that they thus inmostly treat of the Lord's life. And we are familiar with the fact that some of them—notably the twenty-second—are literally prophetic of that life. We should all be familiar with our New Church "canon" of Scripture and the reasons behind it, because the inclusion of books with an inner sense and those without it side by side in both Old and New Testaments has been one of the fruitful sources of the confusion in men's minds concerning doctrinal authority.

Vice is a monster of so frightful mien,
As to be hated needs but to be seen;
Yet seen too oft, familiar with her face,
We first endure, then pity, then embrace. —*Ed.*

The ancient Hebrews were much more careful in this matter than the Christian Church has been. They at least kept the books of whose divine inspiration they were not absolutely sure in a separate collection—the Kethubim or sacred writings. They did not mean these when they spoke of the Law and the Prophets. They should have known from David that the Psalms were inspired, but their familiar use in the temple services apparently made them doubtful. They perhaps seemed to them what our hymn books are to us.

It was natural to the Israelites to express their feelings in song, and we know from Psalm 137 that their songs were famous even outside their own nation. I Chronicles 15:16-22 tells us that certain families of the Levites were specially trained as singers and musicians for the tabernacle and temple worship, and Psalm 150 names several of the instruments used to accompany the Psalms. We find particular groups of instruments called for by their Hebrew names in the titles of certain Psalms. The word *Selah*, which we come upon here and there throughout the Psalms, is thought to have been a musical notation. We should all learn to sing the Psalms. The rules for chanting are really very simple, and the chant form is the only one in which they can be sung without changing the wording in such a way that the divine order and sequence would be destroyed.

We know that the Psalms are different from every other part of the Word and that they are the most universally read and loved of all its books. There are several reasons for this. One is that they are direct expressions of the feeling and thought of the ordinary man—perfect expressions put upon our lips by the Lord. Another is that they cover the whole range of our inner experience, if we are sincere and religious people. Another is that they help us to recognize the Lord's hand in nature and His providence in all the events of life. And still another—the most important of all—is that they give us the feeling of close, personal contact with the Lord. When we read or sing the Psalms, we are talking with the Lord. In this sense every Psalm may be thought of as a prayer.

Let us come now to our special assignment for today—the first

Psalm. It should not be hard to see why it is the first, for it sets before us our fundamental choice: to believe in God and obey Him or to deny God and His Word. This choice is offered to each one of us and it is our own free choice. No one can make us either believe or disbelieve. We cannot say why we do one or the other—although after we have made our choice, we can find countless reasons to support it, whichever it is. The godly and the ungodly man are simply two men who have freely chosen to face in opposite directions. But the Lord leaves us in no doubt as to the outcome. The godly man will be happy and the ungodly man unhappy.

In this Psalm the "counsel of the ungodly" is set in direct contrast with the "law of the Lord." This is the phase of the problem which we perhaps need to see most clearly. In the Gospels the Lord tells us, "Ye cannot serve God and mammon." Our most subtle and persistent foe is the temptation to try to compromise between worldly reasoning and the law of the Lord. But our Psalm tells us plainly that if we let ourselves begin to walk in the counsel of the ungodly, we are all too liable to go the rest of the way—to find ourselves presently standing in the way of sinners and finally sitting in the seat of the scornful. AE 687[6] defines these steps for us (see below).

The beautiful picture of the godly man as a fruitful tree growing beside the river reminds us of the tree of life in the garden of Eden—there also contrasted with that other tree whose fruit was death—and of the same tree of life on the banks of the river of water of life in the Holy City New Jerusalem. And verse 2 brings to mind the first of Swedenborg's "Rules of Life": "Diligently to read and meditate on the Word of God."

The last verse of the first Psalm sets the key for the whole book: "For the Lord knoweth the way of the righteous: but the way of the ungodly shall perish." Throughout the Psalms the results of our fundamental choice of God or self are kept steadily before us. This is because the Lord knows our weakness and that we need to see both sides of the picture not once but often. The attempt to close our eyes to the dark side, to read out of the Word all the harsh condemnations of the evil is not delighting in the law of the Lord, but is walking in the counsel of the ungodly. The Lord wrote the Word. He knows us better than we know ourselves. When we read the Psalms, therefore, let us read them in all humility as He gave them to us. And let us not pick out only the ones we especially like. Let us read and meditate upon them all.

---

## From the Writings of Swedenborg

*Apocalypse Explained*, n. 687[6]: "Here [Psalm 1:1] the expressions 'to walk,' 'to stand,' and 'to sit,' are used as following one another, for 'to walk' pertains to the life of thought from intention, 'to stand' to the life of the intention from the will, and 'to sit' to the life of the will, thus it is life's being [*esse*]. Moreover, 'counsel,' of which 'walking' is predicated, has respect to thought, 'way,' of which 'standing' is predicated, has respect to the intention, and 'to sit in a seat' has respect to the will, which is the being [*esse*] of man's life."

---

## Suggested Questions on the Lesson

P. Who was the second of the three great kings before the division of the land? *David*

J. What special talent did David have? *musician and poet*

P. What book of the Bible was written in part through David? *Psalms*

J. What did David say about what he wrote? *it was the Word of the Lord*

P. What is a psalm? *a song*

P. How did the Jews use the Psalms? *hymns*

I. What did the Lord tell His disciples about them? *they were about Him*

J. Can you repeat the first Psalm? *"Blessed is the man . . ."*

P. What does *blessed* mean? *happy*

J. What three things are we told not to do if we want to be happy? *walk with ungodly, stand with sinners, sit with scornful*

J. What are we told to do? *delight in the law of the Lord*

P. To what is a good man likened in the first Psalm? *a tree*

P. To what is an ungodly man likened? *chaff*

I. What does the Lord do for us in the Psalms? *expresses our spiritual states and needs*

S. How does the first Psalm set the pattern for the whole book? *If we wish to be happy we should delight in the law of the Lord, and meditate daily on the Word.*

# THE BOOK OF PSALMS

*Psalm 19*

The teacher should read carefully the quotation from *Our Heavenly Father's Book* which forms the major part of the Adult notes. This gives a general background of information in regard to the book of Psalms as a whole, from which he may draw such facts as he thinks will interest his class. The point which should be stressed in all the classes is that the Psalms are songs inspired by the Lord to direct the expression of our feeling and thought about Him and our relation to Him. It will also be helpful to our church services if the older children, young people, and adults can be impressed with the rightness and power of singing the Psalms and the value of learning the chant form, which is the only way in which they can be sung without doing violence to the letter.

## Doctrinal Points

*It is the Lord who gives us all good things, and we must keep this fact always in mind.*

*The books between II Kings and Psalms do not have an inner sense.*

*It is truth from the Lord which turns us from our natural selfishness. "Fear of the Lord" does not mean fear of punishment.*

*Our hearts need cleansing as well as our thoughts and conduct.*

## Notes for Parents

The Psalms constitute perhaps the best known and best loved book in the Bible. Psalm 23, the "Shepherd Psalm," has probably been learned by more Christians than anything but the Lord's Prayer. This is because it speaks of the Lord's protection and comfort, and when we are in trouble or bereavement—as we all are at one time or another—we inevitably turn to the Lord for help. He is our Creator and knows our states and needs as no merely human friend can, and we feel instinctively that we need Him.

Even men who have professed not to believe in God at all have often been known to call upon Him in times of danger.

We should, however, look to the Lord for other things besides protection and comfort. We need Him just as much when our skies are bright and everything is easy for us. In fact those are the very times when we are most likely to forget Him and to let the "secret faults" and "presumptuous sins" of which Psalm 19 speaks gain dominion over us. We need the Lord's constant correction and guidance if we are to keep the words of our mouths and the meditation of our hearts acceptable in His sight. And this is, after all, the most important thing in life. What God thinks of us is much more important than what men think. The Psalms express for us all these needs of ours, and the more we read them the more deeply they will enter into our thought and life and the more the Lord can do for us through them.

When we look up at the stars at night and think of the wonderful order with which day and night follow each and the world is maintained without any effort or planning of ours, it should make all of us realize how great and wise our Creator is and want to learn more all the time of His ways so that we may order our own lives in harmony with them. All our troubles and unhappiness come from thinking of ourselves first and trying to run our own lives without the Lord's guidance and help. The more whole Psalms we know, the more help we can get from them.

---

## Primary

Connect the lesson with David and be sure the children know that the Psalms are meant to be sung and that the Lord gave us these songs to sing. Follow the notes and questions in the Primary notes as an outline. In talking of the meaning of Psalm 19 you can help the children to see that even at their age they can understand and use some of the Psalms.

Do you like to sing? Do you ever sing when you are unhappy? No, we sing when we are happy. We pour out our happiness in our singing, and then other people know we are happy and that helps to make them happy too.

Do you know that in the Bible there is a whole book of songs? It is called the book of Psalms, because a *psalm* means a song of praise. The Psalms are songs of praise to the Lord because He is so good to us. He made us all and He made the beautiful world for us to live in. He gives us our food and our clothing and our homes and every good thing we have. He wants us always to be happy; so He has given us His Word to teach us the way to happiness. We sometimes think that we would be happy if we could only have everything we want, but we ought to know better; for often when we get what we think we want, it does not make us happy at all.

The children of Israel loved to sing.
Do you remember how Moses sang after they crossed the Red Sea?
That was the way in which he naturally expressed his thanks to the Lord.
The Psalms were inspired in the minds of David and others by the Lord and then written down to become part of the Word.
David was called the "sweet psalmist of Israel."
The Psalm we have for today is titled "To the chief musician, a Psalm of David."
Perhaps the Lord had put the words into David's mind on some night when, as a young boy, he was sitting out under the stars guarding his father's sheep at Bethlehem.
When we think of the beautiful world the Lord has given us to live in, we can understand the words of this Psalm.
We know that the Lord's way is the right way.
Then we remember how many faults we have.
And then we can pray the last two verses.
Let us read the whole Psalm together.

---

## Junior

The background of the book as a whole, the difference between the Jewish canon of Scripture and the New Church canon, and the facts about the temple choirs and bands will interest the Juniors, but be sure to spend part of the lesson time on the outline of Psalm 19, so that they will feel that they understand it.

You will notice that in taking up the book of Psalms at this time, we are passing by several books in our Bible. All these books, from I Chronicles through Job, are interesting and useful books which you will want to read someday, but they do not have an inner sense. They, as well as the books of Psalms, Proverbs, Ecclesiastes, Song of Solomon, Lamentations, and Daniel, were placed by the Jews among the Kethubim or Hagiographa, meaning the Sacred Writings. The Hebrew Bible consists of the Law (the five books of Moses), the Former Prophets (Joshua through II Kings, except Ruth), the Latter Prophets (Isaiah, Jeremiah, Ezekiel, and Hosea through Malachi), and the Sacred Writings, which include all the other books of our Old Testament. The Sacred Writings were not considered to be directly inspired like the Law and the Prophets. The Lamentations of Jeremiah are actually a continuation of the book named for him and are of equal inspiration, and the Lord Himself, by several statements in the Gospels, restored the Psalms and Daniel to the inspired Scriptures. See Luke 24:44 and Matthew 24:15.

The Psalms were used in the temple worship. We are told that in the days of the temple four thousand of the tribe of Levi were assigned to carry on the musical part of the service. They were divided into twenty-four "courses" of skilled musicians, each course serving in turn for one month out of every two years. In each course some were singers and some played upon instruments. They sang in parts, and women's voices as well as men's were used. And they had many different kinds of instruments: wind instruments such as trumpets, cornets, and flutes; stringed instruments such as the harp and psaltery; and percussion instruments such as the timbrel or tambourine, cymbals, and triangle. Read Psalm 68:25. The music was much simpler than most of ours today and the instruments more crude, but as these musicians spent much of their lives in instruction and practice, we can imagine that their performance was relatively as perfect as that of our finest choirs and orchestras today.

It is quite probable that the Jews hesitated to include the Psalms among their most sacred books because they were their "hymn book." But seventy-three of the Psalms are directly attributed to David and many others are traditionally believed to have been written through him, and we must remember that David in his last words said: "The Spirit of the Lord spake by me, and his word was in my tongue." Read II Samuel 23:1-2. David was called "the sweet psalmist of Israel."

A psalm is a "song of praise." Music is an expression of our feelings. We know that we often hum or sing or whistle without thinking about words at all. And we know that when we listen to music, it is our emotions which are affected, for often we find that we cannot even express afterward what we have felt. The Psalms were inspired by the Lord to give us a true form for expressing the feelings which we ought to have about the Lord and our relation to Him. So they have come to be perhaps the most read, most used, and most loved part of our Bible. They cover the whole range of religious feeling: awe, adoration, gratitude, humility, penitence, and prayer.

Some of the Psalms cover this whole series of emotions in a single Psalm. Such a one is Psalm 19, which we have chosen for our special study today. It is titled, "To the chief Musician, A Psalm of David." This would indicate not only that it was written through David, but that it was written down by him for the "chief musician" to be included in the hymn book being prepared for the service of the new tabernacle which David erected after he brought the ark to Jerusalem. The words may have been put into David's mind by the Lord after David was anointed by Samuel (I Samuel 16:13) and while he was still in Bethlehem caring for his father's flock. We can imagine the young man, with the sheep all around him, lying out under the open sky looking up at the stars.

The Psalm expresses first our wonder at the perfection and order of the beautiful world the Lord has given us to live in. Day and night succeed each other without any planning or effort of ours, and everyone in the world sees these things and should be able to realize from this alone something of the greatness and glory of the Creator. Then with verse 7 we pass to the thought of all that the Lord's law, or truth, does in our souls and of how earnestly we should desire to know and to obey His judgments. And this brings us to a realization of how far short we fall of being what we ought to be, and to a desire to be shown our faults so that we can get rid or them.

The prayer in the last verse of the Psalm is one which we should all learn and repeat often. It is a prayer that we may be always true and good both inside and out in the sight of the Lord.

---

### Intermediate

The general purpose of the book of Psalms and the spiritual meaning and application of Psalm 19 are the points of emphasis for this class.

The books printed in our Bibles between II Kings and the Psalms are—like the book of Ruth, which we also omitted—interesting and valuable books, but not part of the New Church canon of the Word. The Jews do not consider the Psalms part of their most sacred literature either, but the Lord Himself gave them their place when He said that interiorly they treat of Him (Luke 24:44). It is this inmost connection with the Lord which makes a book part of the Word. The Jews probably hesitated to include the Psalms because they thought of them as their hymn book.

The Psalms are songs—songs of praise. Originally they were all sung. Many of them were written through David, who as we remember was called "the sweet psalmist of Israel." We remember also that he was known as a skillful player upon the harp or lyre. After David was anointed by Samuel (I Samuel 16:13) it is said, "The Spirit of the Lord came upon David"; and among David's last words (II Samuel 23:2) he said, "The Spirit of the Lord spake by me, and his word was in my tongue." He knew that the words of the Psalms he wrote were inspired in his mind by the Lord.

Music is an expression of the emotions, and we cannot always put our feelings into words. In the Psalms the Lord puts into words for us all the many and varied feelings and thoughts which we have concerning Him and our relation to Him. That is why the Psalms are so much loved and why many of them are so well known. Even the most self-confident and thoughtless people have experiences which make them realize their need of the Lord, and sometimes their hearts can be reached through the Psalms.

Psalm 19, which we have especially for our lesson today, is entitled "To the chief Musician, A Psalm of David." It is possible that the words of this Psalm came into David's mind from the Lord while he was still a young man in Bethlehem guarding his father's sheep. He had been called from his inconspicuous shepherd's life to be anointed by Samuel and had had the experience of being given strength to kill a lion and a bear (I Samuel 17:32-37). As he lay out under the stars at night, with the sheep all around him, we can imagine that he must often have thought about the wonderful things that had come to him through the spirit of the Lord. It is when we are thinking quietly about the meaning and purpose of our lives and our relation to the Lord that the Lord can come closest to us.

The natural heavens, with the sun, moon, and stars, do make us realize how great and wise and wonderful their Creator must be. But you remember from our lesson on the Creation story that the heavens picture the spiritual or heavenly plane of our minds, and that the sun, moon, and stars picture love to the Lord, faith in Him, and knowledges of heavenly things. It is these "heavens" within us which make us different from animals and able to come into the "image and likeness" of our heavenly Father. It is of these things—truths from the Lord through His Word—that the Psalm really speaks.

That is why, after apparently speaking of the sun of the natural heavens, the Psalm suddenly says, "The law of the Lord is perfect, converting the soul." It is the Lord's truth which converts or turns our souls away from selfishness and toward the Lord. The same law or commandment enlightens our eyes, that is, makes us able to understand the real meaning of life and of the things that happen to us.

What do you think the "fear of the Lord" is? It is certainly not the fear of punishment, for that would hardly be called "clean, enduring forever." The time when we are afraid of punishment is the time when we are doing wrong things, and it is not a happy time which we should wish to continue. And besides, we know that the Lord never punishes—evil punishes itself. No, the fear of the Lord of which the Psalm speaks is the holy fear of doing anything which would be against the Lord and the coming of His kingdom, anything that would separate us from Him. We can understand this from the way we feel toward our parents at different times. When we are in selfish, willful states, all we fear is punishment; but when we are in happy, unselfish states, we would do anything rather than hurt our parents because we love them so much. This is the good kind of fear we shall have even in heaven, which Psalm 111:10 tells us is "the beginning of wisdom." We are never wise except when we are good and loving. We know that. We often look back at our willful, selfish actions and wonder how we could have been so foolish.

Then in our Psalm (verses 10 and 11) we think how happy we are when we are good and obedient. In keeping the commandments "there is great reward." The Lord can give us all good things if only we will follow the way which He has showed us. But verses 12 and 13 remind us that we are naturally selfish and weak and need the Lord's help from day to day to search out the bad things in our hearts and minds and put them away from us. Verse 13 is a prayer for this help. We do not understand our own hearts very well. Sometimes we suddenly become willful and disagreeable without really knowing what started it, and afterward we cannot imagine why we behaved as we did. These are the "secret faults" and "presumptuous sins" which try to get control of us, and which we need to see and fight with the Lord's help.

The final verse of the Psalm is one which we should all learn and say often. It was the final prayer which the Lord put into David's mind after he had been meditating on all these things, and it is meant for us, too. If we think about it and say it often, it will help us to keep our hearts free from ugly, selfish feelings, and to keep our tongues from saying hasty, hurtful things. As you grow older, this Psalm will mean more and more to you and you will find many other Psalms which will help you in developing the heavenly character which the Lord wants you to have.

*Basic Correspondences*

| | | |
|---|---|---|
| the glory of the Lord | = | divine truth in its light |
| the sun | = | divine love |
| honey | = | enjoyments from good |
| honeycomb | = | pleasures from truth |

## Senior

After giving something of the general background of the book of Psalms, the teacher should concentrate on its use for our individual instruction and inspiration and in our worship, using Psalm 19 as an example and following Swedenborg's outline of its internal meaning.

We have been tracing the history of the children of Israel from their beginning with Abraham through their captivity in Egypt and return to the Holy Land to the height of their glory as a nation, and then their decline because of their own ingratitude and faithlessness until they were finally carried away captive.

Now we come to a book which has very little to do in its letter with the history of the Hebrew nation. Perhaps this is one reason why the Jews never ranked it with the Law and the Prophets, but classed it with the Hagiographa or Sacred Writings not directly inspired. Another reason probably is that the book of Psalms was the "hymn book" of the temple, not brought out to be read to the people, but in constant use in the musical part of the worship.

The Lord, however, said to His disciples after the resurrection that all things must be fulfilled "which were written in the law of Moses, and in the prophets, and in the psalms" concerning Him (Luke 24:44). He named the Psalms with the Law and the Prophets as containing a meaning which applied to His life in the world. A few Psalms in the letter contain evident prophecies concerning His life. Psalm 22, from which He quoted on the cross, is such a one. But inmostly all the Psalms treat of the Lord and of the various states through which He passed when He assumed our finite human nature. It is this inmost sense which is the final proof of divine inspiration.

In their internal sense the Psalms describe the states of men in their relation to the Lord. We can find in the Psalms adequate expression for all the emotions which the thought of God excites in us. For the Psalms are songs, and music is the expression of the emotions. That is why the Psalms are so universally known and loved. Everyone finds something in them which appeals particularly to him. With the exception of the Lord's Prayer, the twenty-third Psalm is certainly the best-known part of the Bible. This is because the most universal craving of the human soul is for protection and comfort. But we should look to the Lord for other things besides these. We should seek His guidance, His judgment, and His correction. The Psalms which express the sense of our own sins and inadequacy are not so popular, but we need to read them even more often. And we need to be very familiar with the Psalms which are specifically songs of praise and thanksgiving, because it is the Lord who gives us all the good things we have and we need to keep this fact always in mind in order to avoid self-praise.

The Psalm chosen for our special study today is not a long one, but it follows a complete pattern of worship. We find its general interpretation in Swedenborg's "Summaries of the internal sense of the Prophets and Psalms," one of the manuscripts found and published after his death. It was apparently an outline of a proposed longer work. We may wish that the work could have been completed, but the outline is extremely helpful. Of Psalm 19 we find the following explanation:

Verses 1-4. The Divine truth will go forth in every direction.
5-6. This truth will go forth from the Lord from the first things to the last things of heaven and the church.
7-11. This Divine truth perfects man, because it is wisdom.
12-13. There will be no pride.
14. Thus there will be what is pure and acceptable.

From this outline we see that divine truth in its effects on the individual life is the subject of this Psalm from beginning to end. What seems in the letter to be a quite natural recognition of the

Lord's handiwork in the order and beauty of the material universe is also a recognition of the universal application of divine truth. This understanding explains the apparently sudden shift of thought of our own weakness and inadequacy, so that the Psalm ends in a humble plea for the Lord's help in discovering and overcoming these weaknesses.

It is interesting to compare this Psalm with Psalm 111, which has a very similar pattern. We notice the same general thought throughout, but there is a difference in emphasis. In Psalm 19 we begin with the name *God* (Elohim) which, we remember, shows that the subject concerns divine wisdom, and, although in the rest of the Psalm the name *Lord* (Jehovah) is used, showing that divine love is the necessary motivating power, the Psalm is full of such "truth" words as speech, line, law, testimony, statutes, commandment. The Psalm begins with truth and carries through to love, "the meditation of my heart." In Psalm 111, on the other hand, the name Lord is used throughout and the striking words in that Psalm are "love" words such as works, righteousness, compassion, meat (food). This Psalm begins with love and carries through to truth, "a good understanding." This constant emphasis on the actual inseparability of good and truth is something to watch for in all our study of the Word. Good desires are helpless without truth by which to bring them into right expression and act, and truth without the desire to act according to it is turned to falsity.

Seventy-three of the Psalms are attributed by their titles to David, and many of the others are believed to have been given through him. Swedenborg always gives references to this book under the title of *David*. But many scholars attribute some of the Psalms to other writers, and we may note that Psalm 90 is entitled "A Prayer of Moses, the man of God," and that Swedenborg considered the titles of the Psalms inspired. However, he makes no direct allusion to this title in the writings. The book of Psalms is generally divided into five "books," each book closing with a doxology. The division is as follows: Psalms 1-41, 42-72, 73-89, 90-106, and 107-150. The first book was probably arranged under

David's supervision for use in the new tabernacle he erected after he brought the ark to Jerusalem. The second book is believed to have been collected and added under King Hezekiah, the third under King Josiah, and the fourth and fifth after the return from captivity.

---

## Adult

The background, history, and nature of the book of Psalms are the important subject for this class, touching briefly on the analysis of Psalm 19 by way of example. If there is time, it may be helpful at the end to ask each member of the class to tell what is his favorite Psalm and why.

In Luke 24:44 the Lord, after His resurrection, says to the assembled disciples, "These are the words which I spake unto you, while I was yet with you, that all things must be fulfilled, which were written in the law of Moses, and in the prophets, and in the psalms, concerning me." Thus the Lord Himself assigned to the Psalms the same degree of inspiration which the Law and the Prophets possessed. And we read in II Samuel 23:1-2: "Now these be the last words of David. David the son of Jesse said, and the man who was raised up on high, the anointed of the God of Jacob, and the sweet psalmist of Israel, said, The Spirit of the Lord spake by me, and his word was in my tongue." The ancient Hebrews, probably because the Psalms were their temple songs and were not specifically concerned with their history, did not class them with the Law and the Prophets, but with the Kethubim or sacred writings, and that is where they are placed in the Hebrew Bible of today. We might note that the books of Lamentations and Daniel were also so classed, and that with the exception of these three books the New Church canon of (Old Testament) Scripture and the Jewish canon are identical.

In the 1880s the New Church Board of Publication issued in several small volumes a *Manual of Religious Instruction* prepared under the direction of a committee of the American New-Church Sabbath School Association. Two volumes of this series, a brief outline of the history and general content of all the books of the Bible called *Our Heavenly Father's Book*, were written by the Rev. William B. Hayden. They are among the fine work of the past which we are in danger of losing through neglect. It would be hard to produce a more interesting brief statement concerning the book of Psalms than Mr. Hayden's; so it has seemed well to include in our present Sunday school material the bulk of his brief chapters on this book and on the "Music and Choirs of the Temple." Mr. Hayden says:

> This collection of inspired sacred poems is placed in the Bible as one book, and has been so regarded since the days of Nehemiah, probably, or four hundred and twenty-five years before Christ. The Hebrew title, Tehillim, means Praises, or Songs of Praise. Our word Psalms is derived from Psalmoi (Psalmos, originally, the twang of a stringed instrument), the Greek of the Septuagint version. The term Psalter comes also from the Greek, Psalterion, through the Latin, Psalterium. (Psaltery was primarily the name of a species of harp.) It may be looked upon as an inspired Hymn Book. There are one hundred and fifty of these hymns, of different styles and length. They include a wonderful diversity of subjects, expressing every phase of religious feeling and experience; and are adapted to all the wants of private devotion, as well as to the public worship of the Lord in the sanctuary. They were originally intended and arranged for musical performance, with instrumental accompaniment.
>
> The principal author is David, the King, "the sweet Psalmist of Israel"; and the whole book, as referred to in the New Testament, bears his name. Seventy-three psalms are ascribed to him in their titles; Asaph is named as the author of twelve; eleven are ascribed to the sons of Korah; to Solomon two (72 and 127); one to Ethan (89); and one to Moses (90). This last therefore is the oldest one in the collection, and in the original language bears every mark of being very ancient. The remaining fifty are anonymous; though it is highly probable that many of these also were written by David. They were all composed in close connection with the national sanctuary, and in the line of holy prophets and seers.
>
> In the Hebrew Bible the collection is divided into five books, each one closing with a doxology except the last, to which, as well as to the whole collection, the final Psalm serves as a doxology.
>
> The first book contains the first forty-one Psalms (1-41) and closes with the doxology, "Blessed be the Lord God of Israel from everlasting and to everlasting. Amen and Amen." Thirty-seven of these psalms bear

the name of David; while the other four are usually ascribed to him, and no doubt correctly. The psalms in this book are remarkable for the predominance of the Divine name Jehovah (Lord) over that of Elohim (God). As before explained, this shows that in these psalms the operations of the Lord's love, mercy, goodness, compassion, tenderness, and forgiveness are principally treated of; and thus that their appeal is primarily to the human heart.

In this no doubt we have the original Hebrew Hymn Book, the first collection made for the service of the Jewish Church. It was most probably arranged by David himself, after he became King at Jerusalem, or under his supervision and authority, about one thousand years before Christ. . . . Psalm 23 is presumed to have been composed by David, when, as a young man, he tended his father's flock at Bethlehem, as also 19. (It is believed by many that Ps. 2 was originally numbered 1, and that the psalm at present standing first, was prefixed as an introduction to the whole collection, at a much later date.)

The second book contains thirty-one psalms (42-72), ending with the doxology, "Blessed be the Lord God, the God of Israel, who only doeth wondrous things. And blessed be his glorious name forever: and let the whole earth be filled with his glory. Amen and Amen. The prayers of David, the son of Jesse, are ended." The first eight of these are ascribed to the sons of Korah; eighteen bear the name of David; one (50) that of Asaph. The last one (72) is sometimes attributed to Solomon, but seems rather to have been written for Solomon, perhaps a prayer and invocation at the time of his being anointed and proclaimed king by the command of David.

This book is believed to have been collected and added to the first in the reign of the good King Hezekiah, or about seven hundred years before the Christian era. In it the Divine name Elohim (God), greatly predominates over the name Jehovah: showing that in these psalms the operations of the Divine Wisdom and Truth are principally treated of, with His attributes of sovereignty, majesty, and power; while they appeal most directly to man's understanding and conscience.

The third book includes the next seventeen psalms (73-89). The first eleven are ascribed to Asaph; four to the sons of Korah; one to David (86); and one to Ethan the Ezrahite (89). In the psalms of Asaph the Divine name Elohim predominates, in the remainder of the book the name Jehovah. It closes with the doxology, "Blessed be Jehovah forevermore. Amen and Amen"; and is supposed to have been collected and added to the others in the reign of Josiah, about six hundred and twenty-five years before Christ.

The fourth book, opening with the prayer of Moses, Ps. 90, includes seventeen in all, to 106. Of these only three bear titles, 101 and 103 being ascribed to David. This book, therefore, is one emphatically of anonymous psalms, for the most part of a very general character, evidently arranged with reference to the service of song in the sanctuary, abounding in praise and thanksgiving. Throughout, the name Jehovah prevails; the name Elohim (God) being rarely used except in connection with a pronoun or some epithet, as *my God, God of Jacob*, etc. It is believed to have been compiled and added soon after the return from the Babylonish captivity, probably in the time of Ezra, and either by him or under the supervision of the great synagogue, a little more than four hundred and fifty years before Christ. It closes with the doxology, "Blessed be the Lord God of Israel from everlasting to everlasting; and let all the people say, Amen. Praise ye the Lord."

The fifth book contains the remaining forty-four psalms, 107 to 150. Ps. 107, the opening psalm of the return is supposed to have been sung at the first feast of tabernacles (Ezra 3). In this book are found the fifteen "Songs of Degrees," 120-134, presumed to belong to the period when the Jews under Nehemiah were repairing the walls of Jerusalem in the face of their enemies, and to have been sung by the workmen and guards while engaged in their duties. As Zerubbabel, and the prophets Haggai and Zechariah, were members of the great synagogue established by Ezra, the authorship of this book is mainly attributed to them. In the Septuagint, Vulgate, and Peshito versions, many of these psalms are ascribed to those prophets in their running titles. In this last collection the name Jehovah prevails almost exclusively. It is largely devoted to thanksgiving and praise, and closes with the ascription which has passed so widely into Christian usage, *Hallelujah*, "Praise ye the Lord. . . ."

In the original language several of the psalms are arranged in alphabetical order. Each verse usually begins with a letter of the Hebrew alphabet, till all are gone over. This may be seen exemplified in Ps. 25, which has twenty-two verses, the number of letters in the Hebrew alphabet. There are seven of these psalms, 25, 34, 37, 111, 112, 119, 145. But they do not all carry out the plan regularly or fully. In 111 and 112 every half verse begins with a different letter. In 37 every alternate verse has such a beginning; while Ps. 119 has twenty-two divisions or cantos, each one of which begins thus, and in our Bibles has the names of the respective Hebrew letters written over them. Every couplet also of this psalm contains some reference to the Word of the Lord, under the several appellations of Word, Law, Precepts, Testimonies, Commandments, Judgments, and Statutes. . . .

Several of the Hebrew words in the titles of some of the psalms refer to the musical performance. *Neginoth* means stringed instruments; *Nehiloth*, some wind instrument, like flutes. *Alamoth*, meaning *virgins*, probably denoted the treble voices. *Selah*, so frequent in the midst of psalms, is supposed by many to denote a pause or rest in the music; by others, however, with more probability, it is believed to have indicated the point at which the *instruments* were to *lift up*, joining in with the *voices*, which up to that place had been singing alone.

. . . . . . . . . . . . . . . . . . . . . . . .

We read in Exodus of the song of triumph that was sung at the deliverance at the Red Sea, with the accompaniment of music and dancing. After this we find frequent allusions to it [music]. As described in the Bible, it is in connection with its true and most proper use, of praise and thanksgiving to the Lord, and the public worship of the sanctuary. The cultivation of it by the Levites was a part of their official training; while in the schools of the prophets founded by Samuel, it received marked attention and reached a high degree of development. In the days of David and Solomon, when the psalms had come to be written, and especially after the temple service began, the arrangements in connection with it were very elaborate and complete.

Of the thirty-eight thousand men who composed the tribe of Levi in the reign of David, four thousand were set apart for this service. The three great divisions of the tribe had each a representative family in the choir, or band; Heman and his sons represented the Kohathites, Asaph the Gershonites, and Ethan (or Jeduthun) the Merarites. As the functions were hereditary, and the members had ample leisure for the pursuit and practice of the art, great proficiency and genius were developed in certain families.

Over this great body of musicians presided the sons of Asaph, Heman, and Jeduthun, twenty-four in number, as heads of the twenty-four courses of twelve each into which the skilled minstrels were divided. These skilled or "cunning" performers were two hundred and eighty-eight in number, each having a number of pupils, or sub-choir under his immediate supervision. Each "course," or full band would thus consist of one hundred and sixty-six musicians presided over by a body of twelve skilled players or leaders, with one of the sons of Asaph, Heman, or Jeduthun as chief conductor of the whole.

The instruments employed covered a wide range. What they all were is not now in every instance known. Great ingenuity however was summoned to devise every possible form; and we know that each of the three most general kinds was represented in great variety: 1. wind instruments,

> like the trumpet, cornet, and flute; 2. stringed instruments, like the harp and psaltery; 3. the instruments that are beaten, like the tambourine, cymbals, and triangle. The Hebrew names of many of these we still find written in the titles of our psalms.
>
> The singers were a separate body from the instrumental performers, and seem to have included female voices, and to have been distributed into *parts* . . . It is believed that children also were sometimes included. [See Psalm 68:25, Ezra 2:65, and I Chronicles 25:5-6, and also I Chronicles 16.]

When we think of the lifetime effort of these choirs, it should at least make us willing to put a little time ourselves into learning to sing the Psalms in the only way in which they can be sung, the chant form. Realizing that music is the expression of the heart, we should wish to sing as well as to read the Psalms.

One further point should be noted in regard to the Psalms in general, which Mr. Hayden does not mention. Our attention is called to it by the editor of Swedenborg's summary of the internal sense of the Psalms. He says: "The titles which appear in the common English Bibles at the head of many Psalms, in Roman type, are part of the sacred text, and contain an internal sense like every other portion of the Word of God, as is evident from their being referred to in these Summaries of the Internal Sense." This fact is seldom called to our attention.

The Psalm we read for our specific assignment today, Psalm 19, is, as Mr. Hayden has noted, one thought to have been composed by David in his youth when he was tending his father's flocks. The long night watches under the skies would set the current of divine inspiration in such a direction. Swedenborg's interpretation of it is as follows: "Verses 1-4 [the original Latin, following the Hebrew, says 1-5, counting the title as verse 1], The Divine truth will go forth in every direction. 5-6, This truth will go forth from the Lord from the first things to the last things of heaven and the church. 7-11, This Divine truth perfects man, because it is wisdom. 12-13, There will be no pride. 14, Thus there will be what is pure and acceptable." We notice that, although the subject of the Psalm is truth and its effects, only in the first verse is the name *God* (Elohim) used. Everywhere else it is *Lord* (Jehovah). This suggests that it is truth proceeding from love or good which has these effects in the human life. If we study this Psalm in the light of Swedenborg's brief interpretation of it, the familiar words will take on new and deeper significance for us. The last verse is a prayer we might all well say in the quiet moments before the opening of our church services.

## From the Writings of Swedenborg

*Arcana Coelestia*, n. 2826[13]: "There is indeed a fear within all worship, but under another appearance and another condition, and this is *holy fear*. But holy fear is not so much fear of hell and of damnation, as it is of doing or thinking anything against the Lord and against the neighbor, and thus anything against the good of love and the truth of faith. It is an aversion, which is the boundary of the holy of love and the holy of faith on the one side; and as it is not a fear of hell and damnation, as before said, those have it who are in the good of faith; but those have less of it who are in the good of love, that is, who are in the Lord."

## Suggested Questions on the Lesson

P. What book of the Bible are we studying today? *Psalms*
P. What is a psalm? *a song*
I. What did the Lord tell His disciples about the Psalms? *they told about Him*
P. Through whom were many of them written? *David*
J. How were they used by the Hebrews? *hymns*
J. What do they teach us? *ways of expressing our feelings about the Lord*
P. What is the first verse of Psalm 19? *"The heavens declare . . ."*
J. What do you think this means? *refers to our awareness of the perfection of creation*
I. What is said in this Psalm about the law of the Lord? *". . . perfect, converting the soul"*
S. What is meant by the "fear of the Lord"? *desire not to displease Him*
I. What is the last part of the Psalm about? *happiness in doing right, prayer to continue in this state*
S. What does that mean for us? *our need to ask the Lord's help to overcome our faults*

## TRUST IN THE LORD

*Psalm 91*

The lesson may be introduced by showing the position of the book of Psalms in the Bible—between the historical books and the Prophets—and this is a good opportunity to remind the younger children that all the books in our Bible are not part of the Word. Then point out that the Psalms were written not to portray any historical sequence but to express ever-recurring states of feeling and thought. All classes above the Primary should be told the belief of the Jews about the Psalms and why we know that they are a part of the Word.

### Doctrinal Points

*The Lord will take care of our souls if we trust in Him.*
*The book of Psalms is part of the New Church canon of the Word.*
*Faith in the Lord implies trust in His guidance.*
*If we are unselfish interiorly, we are really living in heaven while we are in this world.*

### Notes for Parents

Everyone loves the Psalms. This is because they are songs and songs touch our hearts, and because in the Psalms the Lord gives us beautiful words to express our hopes and our fears, our joyful states and our griefs, and above all our sense of our own weakness and need of Him. We are told that even the most hardened materialist will instinctively fall on his knees and pray in a time of great danger which he himself can do nothing to avert. In the bottom of our hearts we all know that there is a God and that we need His help. But we do not all admit that we know this.

We do not all take advantage of the privilege every man and woman has of living close to the Lord. We human beings have the power—which no animal has—of knowing the Lord, learning of

Him, and walking in the light of His truth. In fact it is this power which makes us human. What a tragedy it is that any man or woman should choose to live like a mere animal!

In Psalm 91 the Lord, as everywhere in the Word, is speaking of our souls—the real person—not of our bodies. It is our souls that can dwell "in the secret place of the most High" and the dangers against which the Lord can guard us are dangers to our souls. In Psalm 64 we read of the wicked that they "whet their tongue like a sword, and bend their bows to shoot their arrows, even bitter words." The things which really hurt us are the false thoughts that make their way into our minds and the selfish desires that eat away our good intentions. These are our temptations and some of them come upon us unawares, like the "pestilence that walketh in darkness," and some we see clearly, like the "arrow that flieth by day," but still are unwilling to oppose. The Lord wants to keep us safe from all of them, and our guardian angels are always at hand ready to help us, but we must make the choice ourselves.

If we turn to the Lord, acknowledge our need of His help, and try to learn and obey His truth, all the promises of this Psalm will be fulfilled. But we must make the effort to learn the truth which can protect us from falsity and evil. "His truth shall be thy shield and buckler."

---

### Primary

Be sure the children learn that a psalm is a song that we should sing the Psalms in church, and why they are sung differently from hymns. Stress the value of memorizing the Psalms and show the children how we can use them to help us to resist temptation, using Psalm 91 as an example.

You remember King David, don't you? He was the one who conquered all the enemies of Israel. And you remember that he brought the ark to Jerusalem, and that he sang and danced before it as it was carried into the city. David was a musician as well as a warrior. When he was a young man, he played the harp before King Saul to soothe Saul when he was unhappy.

So it was natural that the Lord should choose David to write down many of the Psalms. For the Psalms are songs. The Hebrew people sang them in their services in the temple and we sometimes sing them in our services in church. And we try to learn as many of them as we can so that we can say or sing them to ourselves when we are thinking about the Lord or when we are troubled about anything and need His help especially. For the words of the Psalms are given us by the Lord Himself.

What is our Psalm for today about?
In it the Lord tells us that if we will learn His truth and do as it teaches, we need never be afraid of anything.
Whatever may happen to our bodies, our souls will be safe.
The Lord's angels are always with us even though we cannot see them.

If we trust the Lord and try always to learn more and more about Him and to do what He shows us is right, nothing that may happen to us can really hurt us, and so we shall not need to be afraid of anything. Remember though that the first part of doing right while we are children is to obey our parents.

We should learn as many of the Psalms as we can, because in them the Lord teaches us how to say the things we ought to think and feel.

## Junior

This is a good lesson in which to introduce the Juniors to the basic fact that in the Word the Lord is always speaking to us of our souls rather than of our bodies. If the class shows interest in this idea, the teacher may take up one or two of the dangers mentioned in Psalm 91 and show what they mean spiritually. This information will be found in the Intermediate notes.

Our lesson for today is in the book of Psalms. A psalm is a song. As they are printed in our Bible [KJV] the Psalms look just like all the rest of the Word. They do not look like poetry. But in the Hebrew language they are poetry, and we sometimes sing them as part of our church service. Because the English version of the Psalms is not written in meter like most songs, we have to have a special kind of music, called chanting, to enable us to sing the Psalms.

The Jews sang the Psalms as part of their temple worship. Their singing was a form of chanting, too, and they had choirs trained for just this purpose. In fact, certain families of the Levites handed this duty down from one generation to another. So their singing was famous. One of the Psalms written about the captivity of the people of Judah shows us this. Read Psalm 137. Then read Psalm 126, which tells how they sang when they were allowed to go back to their own land. They sang these songs so much that they felt that the words were their own instead of the Lord's; so to this day the Jews do not consider the book of Psalms as sacred as some of their Scriptures. But we have means of knowing better. You know perhaps that many of the Psalms are attributed to King David, who was a skillful player on the harp (I Samuel 16:14-23), a musician as well as a warrior. But we read in II Samuel 23:1-2: "Now these be the last words of David. David the son of Jesse said, and the man who was raised up on high, the anointed of the God of Jacob, and the sweet psalmist of Israel, said, The Spirit of the Lord spake by me, and his word was in my tongue." David knew that the words of his Psalms were not his own, but were spoken through him by the Lord. And then we have another proof that the book of Psalms is part of the Word. When the Lord appeared to His disciples after His Resurrection, "He said unto them, These are the words which I spake unto you, while I was yet with you, that all things must be fulfilled, which were written in the law of Moses, and in the prophets, and in the psalms, concerning me." (Luke 24:44) The Psalms are songs written for us by the Lord to teach us about Himself and the feelings and thoughts we ought to have about Him, and to help us express those feelings and thoughts.

Our Psalm for today shows us what trust in the Lord can do for us as we go through life. To understand this Psalm we need to remember that it is our souls about which the Lord is talking to us. Our bodies are just a sort of clothing which we wear for a few years while we live in this world. What happens to our bodies is not really very important, although we should try to keep them in good condition so that we can be as useful as possible to our neighbors while we are here. But our souls are our real selves and they go on forever. It is our souls that feel love and hate, trust and fear, happiness and unhappiness. It is our souls that think. And it is our souls that act by means of our bodies. So what happens in our souls is very important. The person who in his soul wants to learn of the Lord and keep close to Him is "he that dwelleth in the secret place of the most High." He really lives with God. He knows that no matter what happens to him in the world—even if he has sickness and poverty and bereavement and disappointment—his soul is safe in the Lord's keeping. So he is not afraid of anything. It isn't what happens to our bodies that counts but the way our souls take what happens. We all admire brave people who can bear pain with a smile and stay friendly and cheerful instead of complaining of their troubles. We can all be like that if we try.

All the bad things that the Lord speaks of in this Psalm are really pictures of wrong thoughts and feelings which try to get into our hearts and minds and hurt us. But if we trust in the Lord—which means to know that He is always wise and right and therefore to do what He tells us to do—His angels will always be with us to help us fight off the ugly and harmful thoughts and feelings as they come. All these bad things come to us from the hells and we need the Lord and the angels to help us meet them. As you grow older, you will learn more and more about these enemies of our souls, but you need not be afraid of them if you begin now to deal with them as the Lord teaches us. One of the first and best ways is to learn as many verses from the Psalms as possible and use them when you are tempted. This is what is meant in verse 4 of Psalm 91 by the words, "His truth shall be thy shield and buckler." Each one of us is like a soldier fighting for the kingdom of God, and our armor is the Word, the Lord's truth.

---

### Intermediate

The correspondence of the various dangers mentioned makes a good study for this class. The teacher should think of simple illustrations of these dangers which will fall within the pupils' experience.

Psalms are songs, songs which were sung as part of the worship in the temple as well as at other times. The Jews did not consider them a part of the most sacred Scriptures, but the Lord, when He was talking to His disciples after His resurrection, named them with the Law and the Prophets and said they taught of Him (Luke 24:44). And when in His Second Coming He opened for us the inner meaning of the Scriptures, He enabled Swedenborg to see the spiritual sense of the Psalms.

Our lesson for today is Psalm 91. Many people know this Psalm by heart and many more know some verses from it. It is a very useful Psalm to learn because it reminds us that the Lord and the angels are always with us and that if we trust in the Lord and try to do right, nothing that happens to us can really hurt us. We are all often tempted to be afraid of various things and to worry when troubles come to us. If we think we have only ourselves to depend on, these fears and troubles will be too strong for us. But if we can remember that we are not alone at all, but that the Lord and the angels are always near us and ready to help us, we can face any trouble bravely. So if we have this Psalm in our minds and can say it to ourselves when we need help, it will always give us the courage we need.

Let us see what some of the dangers are from which the Lord can deliver us. We know that in the Word the Lord is telling us of spiritual rather than of material things. In verses 5 and 6 the dangers are divided into two classes: those that strike by day and those that come in the night. Day, when it is light, pictures the state when we see things plainly; night, when we cannot see very well, pictures a state of ignorance. We know that the things which are dangerous to our souls are evil and falsity. And if we think a little, we can see that there are some evils which creep into our hearts and some false ideas which we accept as true because we don't know any better. These are the "pestilence that walketh in darkness" and the "terror by night." Then there are other wrong desires which we know very well are wrong and yet we enjoy having them, and there are some falsities which we really know are false but like to believe just the same because they excuse the wrong things we are doing. These are the "destruction that wasteth as noonday" and the "arrow that flieth by day." The Lord can protect us against both these forms of evil and falsity if we try to keep close to Him by learning His truth and obeying it. "His truth shall be thy shield and buckler." Truth from the Word is the armor which can protect us.

Again, in verse 13, the lion and the young lion refer to the power of evil and the adder and the dragon to the power of falsity. We can remember this if we think how hateful feelings can tear us to pieces inside, and how false ideas can poison our minds. The "noisome pestilence" in verse 3 is the same evil which eats into our system, and the "snare of the fowler" the falsity which captures our thoughts.

Now let us think of verses 11 and 12. You have all been taught from childhood that guardian angels are always with us. Sometimes, however, we get hurt without any fault of our own and we may be tempted to ask why our guardian angels didn't take better care of us. Here again we must remember that it is our souls which are important—not our bodies—and that it is our souls which the angels are trying to protect. I wonder if you can see that to take these two verses literally would be a form of "falsification of truth"—see if you can remember what that is—and would turn them into a stone over which we might stumble. Do you remember the Gospel story of how the devil tempted the Lord in the wilderness? In the letter the devil quoted this very passage, but the Lord was not deceived. Read the story in Matthew 4:5-7.

The Lord answered the devil, "Thou shalt not tempt the Lord thy God." We tempt God when we try to see how far we can go in our selfish ways without getting into trouble, just as we tempt our parents sometimes until their patience with us is worn out. All the promises of our Psalm are made to those who dwell "in the secret place of the most High." We know that this cannot be said concerning our bodies. It is only with our souls that we can approach the Lord. Our bodies live in this material world in houses made with hands. But our real homes are where our souls are living, and each of us chooses where his soul shall live. If we let ourselves be selfish and just try to get our own way and look for excuses to do what we want to do, our souls are at home in hell, because selfishness and false reasonings are the life of the hells. But if we try to forget ourselves and to learn the Lord's ways and make other people happy, our souls are living in heaven even while we are in this world, and the Lord can protect and help us in everything we do.

The Psalm ends with the promise of long life. In the original Hebrew it says "length of days." When we remember what the day represents, we see that this means that our souls will be in the light of truth always.

*Basic Correspondences*

| | | |
|---|---|---|
| day | = | a state of understanding |
| night | = | a state of ignorance |
| shield and buckler | = | protection against falsities |
| stone | = | truth or falsity |

## Senior

This is a good lesson in which to urge the Seniors to begin a regular program of reading in the Word and the writings. No habit will stand them in better stead as they go out into their independent lives in the world. It is this habit, together with the habits of prayer and of church attendance, which will keep them in safety close to the Lord.

With the end of II Kings we have finished with the narrative history of the Jews as representing the spiritual church in the world. The ancient Hebrew church was only representative of a church, because its worship was wholly external, but so long as the people observed the laws and statutes given them at Sinai, the Lord could maintain His connection with men through the correspondence of those rites. When, however, the nation ceased to observe them, it could no longer be even a representative of a church. So it was carried away into captivity, and the rest of its history to the time of the Advent of the Lord is barely mentioned in the books of the Word. We get most of our knowledge of the return from Babylon and the rebuilding of Jerusalem and the temple from the books of Ezra and Nehemiah, which are not part of the Word which has an inner sense. However, we also learn from II Kings 25:12 that when Judah was taken captive some of the "poor of the land" were left as vinedressers and husbandmen. That is, there were still some individuals left in whom there was humility before the Lord—these are what is meant by the "poor" throughout the Word—and we also know that there were some who even in captivity still observed the prescribed Jewish rites. We shall see this when we study the book of Daniel.

The book of Psalms is of a different character from all the other books of the Word. We know that it is a book of the Word because the Lord Himself tells us so in Luke 24:44. Swedenborg interprets the general meaning of each of the Psalms in a summary form in his work *Prophets and Psalms*, and he gives us the meaning of many individual verses in the course of his writings. There are, for example, twenty-two places in the writings in which he quotes one or more verses of Psalm 91 and in many of them explains their spiritual meaning. But the book of Psalms in its letter does not tell the history of the Jews or even of men in general. It is a book of songs, and songs are the expression of emotion. That is why people have always loved the Psalms and why they are easy to memorize. Every religious person can find particular Psalms which say what he feels and which bring him help from the Lord in his states of anxiety. In their inmost meaning the Psalms are expressions of the states through which the Lord passed when He was in the world, and we know that in some of them even in the letter there are prophecies of events in the Lord's life on earth. For example, compare Psalm 22, verses 1, 7, 8, and 18 with Matthew 27:46, Matthew 27:39, Matthew 27:43, and John 19:23-24.

Psalm 91, on which this lesson is centered, is a good Psalm to learn. We all have troubles in our outward life—disappointments, sicknesses, bereavements—and we are liable to feel alone and discouraged in the face of them. When such times come, repeat this Psalm and realize that it is forever true. The Lord and the angels are always at hand to help us. The Lord does not always save us from outward dangers and troubles—we need them to show us our own weakness, to broaden our sympathies, and to develop our spiritual strength. The Lord in the Word is always speaking of our souls rather than of our bodies. The dangers mentioned in Psalm 91 are spiritual dangers, evils and falsities from the hells. Some of them comes upon us unawares; these are the dangers which are said to come in the night. Others are falsities and evils which we can clearly recognize but which we still want to think and do. These are the dangers which are said to attack by day. The Lord will save us from all these dangers if we dwell "in the secret place of the most High," that is, if in our inmost hearts we try to keep close to Him and trust His guidance.

But the Psalm also teaches us that there is more to this matter of trust in the Lord and our soul's safety than just a feeling. There is mental effort, too. "Under his wings shalt thou trust: his truth shall be thy shield and buckler." Wings in the Word picture spiritual truths. We must want truth from the Lord—more and more truth and deeper and deeper truth—to use in our daily lives. If we are brought up in the church and go to Sunday school regularly, we learn a certain amount of this truth, but that is only the beginning. We must continue all our lives not only to read the Word regularly but to study for ourselves the writings which the Lord has given us in His Second Coming to open the inner meaning of the Word to our understanding. In AC 4096 Swedenborg tells us that the understanding of spiritual truth in the Word can be given only to a mind "which has been instructed, and which perceives delight in the memory-knowledge of such things," and also that "The good which is of love and charity flows in from the Lord, and does so through angels who are with man; *but not into anything else in him than his knowledges*." You remember that we who live in the world today do not have a direct perception of the truth such as the people of the Most Ancient Church had, but that truth must be shown us in the knowledges which have entered our minds by an external way, as light from the sun reflected from the drops of water in the cloud makes the rainbow. Swedenborg says elsewhere, "The good love truth." We never in this world or in the next reach the point when we "know enough." The Lord can protect us in our temptations only as we seek to learn more and more of the Word and its meaning every day. "His truth shall be thy shield and buckler."

---

### Adult

Serious thought should be given in this class not only to the spiritual meaning of the dangers mentioned in the Psalm but to the fact that the promises are also spiritual and that they are made under the definite condition that we acquire and use the truth which the Lord gives us. Mental laziness gives the lie to good intention.

Let us begin by asking ourselves why the Psalms play so prominent a part in our public and private devotions. In the first place, the Psalms are songs, and music because it expresses the emotions has a very deep appeal. In the second place, the Psalms put into words—words inspired by the Lord—our inner states, those states of thought and feeling which we of ourselves find it so difficult to express. Finally, the Psalms throughout describe our relationship with the Lord, that highest privilege of man which distinguishes him from the animals. In their inmost sense the Psalms show us the inner states through which the Lord Himself passed while He was on earth, and because we are created in His image and after His likeness they show us in their spiritual sense states of every regenerating person.

The book begins with the clearly drawn contrast between the righteous person and the ungodly person, in the first Psalm, and throughout the book the need of the righteous for the help of the Lord in meeting the assaults of evil and falsity is a constant theme. The triumphant praise of the Lord with which the book closes is the result of experience of the Lord's saving power. The Introduction to the book of Psalms in the International Bible Commentary says: "No book in the Bible so completely unites the world's divided Christendom. Roman Catholic and Protestant, Anglican and

Non-Anglican, use it in public and private devotion. No book so completely expresses the varied needs of the human heart."

Psalm 91 is one which many people know by heart and in which many have found support and comfort. Even without a knowledge of the spiritual meaning one gets from it the feeling of the nearness of the Lord and the angels, the sense that one is not struggling alone and that in the end, as Paul says, "all things work together for good to them that love God." But there is and always has been a tendency to think that the promises of this Psalm concern salvation from external dangers, and to feel that when sickness and bereavement come to us, it must be because we do not have sufficient faith in the Lord. In fact, this is always the excuse offered by the faith healers when they fail to cure. Even from the literal sense of the Word we should know better than this, for it is in this obvious external sense that the devil quotes this Psalm in tempting the Lord in the wilderness (Matthew 4:5-7), and the Lord's reply indicates that the promise is not to be taken literally. In the New Church we know that in all the Word the Lord is speaking to our souls, and that the dangers from which He wishes to save us are spiritual dangers. In the interest of our spiritual growth the Lord permits many afflictions to come to our bodies.

In his summary of the internal sense of the Prophets and Psalms Swedenborg interprets Psalm 91 entirely in its relation to the Lord's states during His glorification. The summary is as follows:

1. Song in praise of the Father by the Lord, who is to be made one with Him.
2-6. Thus there will be protection from enemy attack.
7-9. Thus there will be no uprising of the hells,
10. not even against the church.
11-12. Thus heaven will serve Him.
13-16. There will be no fear from the hells, when the Divine has been made one with the Human.

And Swedenborg does not leave us without help in the understanding of this Psalm's meaning in our own lives. Scattered through the writings there are some twenty-two instances in which he quotes and often explains one or more verses from it. He says, for example: " 'To trust under his wings' signifies under truth known" (AE 283[6]); "The 'dread of night' denotes falsities of evil which are from hell; the 'arrow that flieth by day,' falsity which is openly taught, whereby good is destroyed; the 'death that wasteth at noonday,' evil which is lived in openly, whereby truth is destroyed" (AC 6000[9]); " 'The pestilence that creepeth in thick darkness' denotes the evil which vastates in secret; 'the death that wasteth at noonday' denotes the evil that vastates openly" (AC 7505); "To destroy the interior and exterior falsities that vastate the truths of the church is signified by 'treading upon the lion and adder'; and to destroy the interior and exterior falsities that vastate the goods of the church is signified by 'trampling on the lion and dragon' " (AE 714[24]).

We all know that we are constantly assailed by temptations, and we know from our doctrines that these temptations come from the hells. Some of the evils and falsities we see immediately in their true character. These are the dangers which are said to come "by day" and "at noonday." There are others which we do not immediately recognize because our thinking is obscure. These are the dangers that come "by night" and "in darkness." We know that although in general we mean to be good, we often yield even to the temptations which come "by day." We need help from above to reinforce our weak wills. And certainly we need the Lord's help to recognize and reject those evils and falsities which disguise themselves.

Our Psalm teaches us that this help is always available. But it also teaches us that if we would obtain it, there are conditions which we must fulfill. To imagine that we can go our own way and then when trouble comes call upon the Lord and be saved is merely wishful thinking. The Psalm is addressed to the person who "dwelleth in the secret place of the most High." That is not where we are dwelling when we live according to our natural thoughts and inclinations. The wings which we are to trust are spiritual truths, and it is faithfulness to truth which is to be our shield and buckler.

We cannot expect to have this security and protection if we neglect the daily reading of the Word and the study of its spiritual meaning as the Lord has opened it for us in His Second Coming. We read in AC 4096: "The good which is of love and charity flows in from the Lord, and does so through angels who are with man; *but not into anything else in him than his knowledges.*" We like to think that good intentions are all we need, but the writings tell us that good receives its quality from truth and exercises its power through truth. They tell us also that "the good love truth"; so we should keep in mind that the quality of our intentions is actually measured by the effort we are willing to make to learn the truth.

In AE 471[2] we read: "The expression 'to answer' frequently occurs in the Word, and it signifies, in reference to the Lord, influx, inspiration, perception, and information, likewise mercy and aid." The answers to our prayers for salvation from our troubles will not necessarily be preservation from any outward calamity, but will be an understanding of the reason why it is permitted to come to us and the strength to meet it and use it for our spiritual development.

## From the Writings of Swedenborg

*Arcana Coelestia*, n. 7102[10]: "Here the 'dread of night' denotes the falsity which is in secret; the 'arrow that flieth by day,' the falsity which is in the open; the 'pestilence that creepeth in thick darkness,' the evil which is in secret; the 'death that wasteth at noonday,' the evil which is in the open." [We need to know that Swedenborg made his own translation of the Hebrew—a very literal translation.]

*Arcana Coelestia*, n. 7505: "*A very grievous pestilence.* That this signifies a consumption in general, is evident from the signification of 'pestilence,' as being the vastation of truth. . . . [in Psalm 91:5, 6] 'the pestilence that creepeth in thick darkness' denotes the evil which vastates in secret; 'the death that wasteth at noonday' denotes the evil that vastates openly."

## Suggested Questions on the Lesson

P. In what book is our lesson today? *Psalms*

P. What is a psalm? *a song*

J. How do we know that the book of Psalms is part of the inspired Word? *Luke 24:44*
I. Why do you think everyone loves the Psalms? *appeal to heart*
J. In Psalm 91 what does the Lord promise the man who lives close to Him? *protection*
I. Of what two general classes of dangers does the Psalm speak? *of night, of day*
J. Is the Lord talking about dangers to our bodies? *no*
P. What does He say our armor against these dangers is? *obeying His Word*
P. What does He tell us about the angels? *will take care of us*
J. How can we use this Psalm to help us? *use against bad thoughts and feelings*
S. What is the difference between the dangers by day and those by night?
*"day" = deliberate evils*
*"night" = errors of ignorance*

## A PSALM ABOUT THE WORD

*Psalm 119*

The teachers of the older classes should look through all the notes from the Junior up to get a fuller background and be able to answer possible questions about the Psalms in general. The two major points in regard to Psalm 119—which are given in their simplest form in the Primary notes—are the center of the lesson.

### Doctrinal Points

*The Lord came to fulfill the Law and the Prophets and the Psalms.*

*Conjunction with the Lord and the heavens is by means of the Word.*

*Only knowledge of the Word can give us a true understanding and guide our lives aright.*

*Faith in the Lord is dependent upon knowledge of Him.*

*Good done from self is not charity.*

### Notes for Parents

Judah and Israel were overcome and carried away captive because they refused to obey the Lord in spite of all that He had done for them. They rejected or perverted the orderly worship in the temple and worshiped all manner of idols instead. In Christian countries like ours we have no temptation to make figures of wood or metal and worship them as gods, but many of us have our idols just the same. Anything we think of as more important for us than learning and doing the Lord's will is our idol. It may be money or success or pleasure. It may be husband or wife or children. It may be our own ideas. Or it may be simply physical ease and comfort. Think of all the excuses people have for not thinking about the Lord, not trying to obey Him, not reading the Word or going to church, and you are identifying their idols.

Our Psalm for today is in every verse a praise of the Word of the Lord. A psalm is a song of praise. The book of Psalms was the hymn-book of the temple. It is also often called the book of David, because King David wrote many of the Psalms and directed the organizing of certain families of the Levites into trained singers and musicians to sing and accompany the Psalms in the services of the temple. David was himself a skillful player upon the harp or lyre, and was called "the sweet psalmist of Israel." But David knew and declared that the words of the Psalms were not his own but were put into his mouth by inspiration from the Lord.

Psalm 119 points out to us very clearly and positively that it is from the Word of God alone that we get any understanding of God, of our own nature and relation to Him, and of the meaning and purpose of life. Without knowledge of the Word we stumble through life in darkness. Without obedience to the laws of the Lord as given us in the Word—which are the fundamental laws by which the whole universe is governed—we can have no lasting security, peace, or happiness.

Psalm 119 is an "alphabetical" Psalm. The Hebrew words which you find in some Bibles printed at the top of the sections are the names of the twenty-two letters of the Hebrew alphabet in their order. In the original Hebrew each one of the eight verses of any given section begins with the letter which heads the section.

## Primary

The children should know what a Psalm is, through whom many of the Psalms were written, and that they were used in the temple worship. The children should be helped to pick out the key words in each verse as the teacher reads the lesson from the Word.

From the very earliest times in the world people have liked to sing. It is usually when you are happy that you feel like singing, but sometimes, too, people express their sad feelings in song. Singing and playing on different kinds of instruments have always been ways in which people naturally expressed their gratitude to the Lord for all the wonderful things He gives us to keep us safe and happy.

Perhaps you remember that when Moses and the children of Israel were delivered by the Lord from their slavery in Egypt, after He had helped them to cross the Red Sea in such a wonderful way, Moses led them in a song of rejoicing and thanks. And then Miriam, the prophetess, who was the sister of Moses and Aaron, "took a timbrel in her hand; and all the women went out after her with timbrels and with dances. A timbrel is a musical instrument, one which continued to be a favorite with the Hebrew women all through the history of the Jews in the Old Testament.

In the Bible there is a whole book of songs. It is called "The Psalms." Many of the Psalms were given us by the Lord through King David, who was himself an expert player upon the harp or lyre, and was also called "the sweet psalmist of Israel."

The book of Psalms is a collection of the songs of worship which were sung in the temple.

There are altogether one hundred and fifty Psalms in the book.

The one we have for today is the longest of them.

There are two special things you should remember about this Psalm.

One is that it is an alphabetical Psalm.

That means that in the original Hebrew each of its twenty-two sections begins with a different letter of the alphabet, each verse in the section with the same letter.

The letters are in the correct order of the Hebrew alphabet.

The second thing is that every verse in the whole Psalm contains some word which refers to the Lord's truth as we find it in the Bible.

This word may be *law*, or *statutes*, or *way*, or *testimony*, or *commandments*, or *judgments*, or some other similar word.

Let us read part of this Psalm and see if you can pick out such a word in each verse. [Read Psalm 119:9-16.]

---

## Junior

A good many facts concerning the Psalms and their use by the ancient Hebrews have been given in the Junior notes, which should be of interest to the children. The alphabetical character of Psalm 119 should also interest them. But the principal thought to leave with them is that of the vital importance of the Word to our lives.

The Psalms are meant to be sung, and you know that we do at times sing them in church. We have an organ or piano for accompaniment. The ancient Hebrews, of course, did not have pianos. They did have an instruent that was called an "organ," but it was not at all like ours. We know only that it was a wind instrument, probably made of several pipes fastened together. In the Bible the word *organ* is used to cover all the wind instruments. It is mentioned first in Genesis 4:21. The Jews also had other instruments which were used to accompany the Psalms. If you will look through the headings of the Psalms, you will often find in some Bibles the Hebrew name of the type of instrument which was to be used with the Psalm—*Neginoth* means stringed instruments, *Nehiloth* wind instruments like the flute. Some of the words in these headings refer to the particular tune to which the Psalm was sung. For example, the heading of Psalm 22 gives *Aijelath Shahar*, which means "the hind of the morning." We learn from the book of Chronicles that four thousand men of the tribe of Levi were set apart to carry on the musical part of the worship. Three men, Heman, Asaph, and Ethan (or Juduthun) were the original leaders chosen in the time of David, and the same families continued to be brought up to be the singers and players. It was their life work. The women as well as the men took part. Read Psalm 68:25.

Many of the Psalms were certainly inspired through David, and the whole book is often called the book of David. King David, as you may perhaps remember, was a skillful player on the harp (lyre) and was also called "the sweet psalmist of Israel." But read II Samuel 23:1-2, and see that David himself knew and declared that the words of his Psalms were from the Lord and not from his own mind.

The Psalm we have for our lesson for today is the longest one of all. You will see that it has twenty-two sections of eight verses each, and that above each section (KJV) a strange word is printed. These words are the names of the twenty-two letters of the Hebrew alphabet in their order, and in the original Hebrew each of the eight verses of a section begins with the letter which heads the section.

So Psalm 119 is called an "alphabetical" Psalm. There are a few other Psalms of the alphabetical type, but none so clear and complete as this. The Jews felt that there was something holy about their alphabet, and there really was, for the Hebrew language was the one chosen by the Lord as best suited to His purpose in giving the Word of the Old Testament.

But there is another still more striking fact about Psalm 119. It is all about the Word: its origin, its power, and its effect upon our lives. If you read this Psalm attentively, you will find in every single verse some word or words which refer to the Lord's Word in one or another of these aspects: law, testimony, way, precepts, statutes, commandments, judgments, word. Many of the verses of this Psalm are familiar to us. We should repeat them to ourselves often and we should read and reread the whole Psalm, because it is given to impress upon us the importance of recognizing that the Word is the voice of the Lord speaking to us, that no part of it can change or fail, that we cannot have any real understanding of the Lord, of ourselves, or of the meaning of life without studying it, and that we cannot have any lasting happiness without obeying it. We should never forget that all the misery in the world comes and always has come from failure to learn and live the truth as the Lord has given it to us in His Word.

---

### Intermediate

The history of the ancient Hebrew nation should be rounded out for this class by telling them the reason for the return from exile. The teacher may then give as much of the history and position of the book of Psalms as he thinks will interest the class. But the major portion of the class period should be devoted to the nature and the lesson of Psalm 119.

Our lesson today is from the book of Psalms, which is often also called the book of David, who was called "the sweet psalmist of Israel." The book of Psalms was the hymn-book of the temple and for this reason, probably, the Jews did not include it with the Law and the Prophets as part of their most sacred Scriptures. But David himself attributed his Psalms to inspiration from the Lord, and the

Lord later placed them with the Law and the Prophets as part of the Word. Read II Samuel 23:1-2 and Luke 24:44.

Psalm 119, the longest of the Psalms, is an "alphabetical" Psalm. You will see in your Bible that it is divided into twenty-two sections of eight verses each, and that there is a strange word at the head of each section (KJV). These words are the names of the twenty-two letters of the Hebrew alphabet in their proper order, and in the original Hebrew each verse in a given section begins with the letter which heads that section. Swedenborg tells us that every letter of the Hebrew alphabet "signifies a thing in the spiritual world" and that "therefore David wrote the 119th Psalm, in order, according to the letters of the alphabet." The same thing is done in Psalm 111, but not so evidently, and there are five other Psalms which at least partially carry out this principle.

But there is another characteristic of Psalm 119 which makes it a particularly important one for us to study. It is throughout a Psalm about the Word—its origin, its power, and the place it ought to have in our lives. Every one of its hundred and seventy-six verses contains some word or words expressive of divine truth as it is given us in the Word of God: *law, testimonies, ways, precepts, commandments, judgments, statutes, word, faithfulness, ordinances, name.* Many of the verses of this Psalm are very familiar to us. We sometimes sing or read selections from it in church. And we should read and study it and give it a chance to make its deep impression upon us.

For the Word, as we know, is not only our instructor in all things concerning the Lord and our souls, but it is our only means of coming into contact with the Lord. All knowledge of the Divine which exists in the world anywhere has come originally from our Word or from the Ancient Word which preceded it. We cannot find out about God for ourselves. He has to reveal Himself to us, and He does so not independently to each one's heart, as some people like to think, but always through the verses of the Word which we have taken into our minds. Remember the covenant of the rainbow in the story of Noah. It is the raindrops of truth from the Word in our memories which reflect the pure white light of truth from God and bring it back to us in beautiful varied colors according to our states and needs.

Our Psalm tells us, "Thy word is a lamp unto my feet, and a light unto my path": the Word enlightens our minds and shows us the right way of life. It tells us, "Thou through thy commandments hast made me wiser than mine enemies: for they are ever with me": it shows us how to recognize and fight our temptations. It tells us, "For ever, O Lord, thy word is settled in heaven": the Word is the expression of the fundamental order of heaven; it does not change with earthly times. It tells us, "Great peace have they which love thy law: and nothing shall offend them" (the original meaning of *offend* is to cause to stumble, as in RSV): obedience to the Word enables us to live in inner peace and to be undisturbed by any of the adversities which come to us. Every verse of the Psalm gives us something important to think about, which helps us to come into the state of mind and endeavor expressed in verses 33 and 34: "Teach me, O Lord, the way of thy statutes; and I shall keep it unto the end. Give me understanding, and I shall keep thy law; yea, I shall observe it with my whole heart."

*Basic Correspondences*

| | | |
|---|---|---|
| lamp | = | divine truth |
| judgment | = | of truth |
| justice | = | of good |
| the undefiled (perfect) | = | one who speaks and does truth from charity |

## Senior

The vital importance of reading the Word regularly and guiding our thinking as well as our conduct according to its precepts is the important lesson for the Seniors. The skepticism and materialism which they will meet in the world needs this sane approach to life to balance it.

In Luke 24:44-45 we read that the Lord after His resurrection, in talking to the assembled Apostles, said: "These are the words which I spake unto you, while I was yet with you, that all things must be fulfilled, which were written in the law of Moses, and in the prophets, and in the psalms, concerning me. Then opened he their understanding, that they might understand the scriptures." This places the book of Psalms on an equal basis with the Law and the Prophets as part of the Old Testament Scriptures. David himself, to whom many of the Psalms are attributed—so that it is often called the book of David—declared that he received them by inspiration (II Samuel 23: 1-2). The Jews class the book of Psalms among the "Writings" which they do not hold to be equal in inspiration with the Law and the Prophets. This is probably because the Psalms were the hymn-book of the temple and were not kept with the Law and the Prophets.

The 119th Psalm is one of seven "alphabetical" Psalms in the book, the others being 25, 34, 37, 111, 112, and 145. The form is carried out more obviously and completely in Psalm 119 than in any of the others, and is an interesting study in itself. The Hebrew words printed above the sections of the Psalm (KJV) are the names of the twenty-two letters of the Hebrew alphabet in their proper order, and in the original Hebrew each of the eight verses in any given section begins with the letter which heads the section. This very old device of alphabetical form has a sound foundation, as you will see from the quotation from the *Apocalypse Revealed* at the end of this lesson.

But the spiritual meaning of the letters of the alphabet is beyond our present reach, and we are more immediately concerned with another phase of the Psalm. If you will read it carefully, you will find in every verse some word or words which refer to the Word of the Lord as the law or way of life. You will also find that many of its sections and many of its verses are very familiar to you. This is partly because in the New Church we sometimes sing or read selections from this Psalm, and partly because in it the Word is presented to us in such a variety of brief striking statements that its verses are often memorized and widely quoted. We find in it verses which adequately express our praise of the Lord, our consciousness of our own weakness and failures, our desire to be guided by the Lord, and our sense of rest and peace on coming into the order of the Word. It is a Psalm to which we can go with assurance when we are looking for a strong statement from the Word to help us in meeting some particular temptation. With this in mind read the first section of the Psalm and see how it sets forth the importance of the Word to our well-being and happiness, our constant need of it, and the happy result of learning and keeping its precepts.

In our modern world, into which you are going shortly to make your own way, you will find many who know almost nothing about the Bible and who have no sense of loss from their ignorance. They may seem successful and happy, but a longer acquaintance with them will reveal that their happiness is entirely dependent upon external conditions. Loss of dear ones, loss of money or position, illness, any untoward event may in a moment destroy their security and peace. Often they have no inner steadiness or vision.

This is because strength and peace come from the Lord alone, and our contact with the Lord is in the Word. The Lord is the Word in its inmost. Unless we know the Lord and our relation to Him, our lives are necessarily limited to the material plane, whose pleasures, while very real, are uncertain and fleeting. If we do read the Word and come to know the nature of God, His order, and the meaning and purpose of life, we can enjoy the pleasures of the natural world even more keenly because of our gratitude to Him for them, and we can accept our bereavements and adversities with equal serenity as opportunities to learn and to grow spiritually.

In the ninth verse of our Psalm we read: "Wherewithal shall a young man cleanse his way? by taking heed thereto according to thy word," and in the ninety-eighth verse: "Thou through thy commandments hast made me wiser than mine enemies: for they are ever with me." These are verses which every young person just starting out in the world should memorize and repeat to himself often, and there are many others in the Psalm which should be stored away in our memory for the Lord to call forth for us in time of need. Every one of us should so live and learn from the Word that we can say from experience: "Through thy precepts I get understanding: therefore I hate every false way."

---

## Adult

The reason why the Psalms should be sung in church is important for this class, as well as the facts noted concerning the New Church canon of Scripture. The two main points concerning the letter of Psalm 119 should be stated, and then the Psalm may be discussed in more detail than with the other classes, drawing on the knowledge of it which the members of the class have. Favorite verses will perhaps be suggested and compared.

Psalm 119, the longest of the Psalms, is one of the most interesting in the letter. In the first place it is the most completely worked out of the seven "alphabetical" Psalms, the other six being numbers 25, 34, 37, 111, 112, and 145. None of them, of course, is alphabetical in the translation, but Psalm 119 is printed in KJV Bibles with the names of the letters of the Hebrew alphabet in their order at the head of the sections, and we should know that in the original Hebrew every one of the eight verses in any given section begins with the letter which heads the section.

Another interesting fact—which is evident in the translation—is that each verse of the Psalm contains some word or words referring to the law of the Lord: *statutes, commandments, way,* etc. This makes it clear that the whole Psalm treats of the Word and its importance in our lives.

In Revelation 1:11 the Lord says to John at the beginning of his vision: "I am Alpha and Omega, the first and the last." We know that Alpha and Omega are the first and last letters of the Greek alphabet. It is in connection with the explanation of this verse that Swedenborg tells us in AR 38: "Since every letter signifies a thing in the spiritual world, and thence in the angelic language; therefore David wrote the 119th Psalm, in order, according to the letters of the alphabet." When we stop to think that the letters of our own alphabet are the symbols by means of which all our thoughts and feelings are expressed, communicated to others, and preserved for posterity, we can better understand why "every letter signifies a thing in the spiritual world," and how a Psalm composed in the complete alphabetical form is intended to impress upon us the whole range of its subject.

The Psalms are meant to be sung, and we know that music is the expression of the affections. We should remember this whenever we sing the selections in church. Sometimes people complain of the difficulty of singing the selections, and because of this some of our churches have even been reduced to the practice of reading instead of singing them, and often the singing of them is left to the choir. But this is a serious loss to all in the church. The Psalms cannot be sung to ordinary "tunes" without distorting the words of Scripture, and we should all be willing to make the effort to learn the few simple rules which govern the necessary chanting, and to practice until we can follow the chants easily. When we read the Psalms, they make a deep impression on our minds—as any part of the Word does—but when we sing them, our hearts are engaged. In the temple worship the Psalms were sung by families of the Levites set apart and trained from childhood for that particular service, and they were sung to the accompaniment of various instruments, both wind and strings. The women of the families also took part.

We are all familiar with many of the verses of Psalm 119. The opening section is a recognition of the fact that happiness can come only as we learn and obey the law of the Lord, and a prayer to be enabled to obey it. The next section begins with the often-quoted verse, "Wherewithal shall a young man cleanse his way? by taking heed thereto according to thy word," and suggests various ways in which this instruction may be carried out. Then follow sections which acknowledge our own weakness and need of the Lord's guidance and help. The temptations through which we must pass and our gratitude for strength received from the Word are followed by recognition of its supreme and impregnable position and expressions of our love for it, including verses which express our grief that everyone does not learn and keep the law and that our sincere efforts to convert them often fail. Perhaps the best-known sections are verses 97 to 112. From this point on the Psalm increases in intensity and devotion, and near the end is the beautiful verse (165): "Great peace have they which love thy law: and nothing shall offend them." *Offend* is here used in its original meaning of "turn aside" or "cause to stumble." But it is significant that after all this rejoicing in the knowledge and keeping of the law, the Psalm ends on a thoroughly humble note: "I have gone astray like a lost sheep; seek thy servant; for I do not forget thy commandments." So we find in this Psalm a complete pattern of life in which we are governed from childhood to old age by dependence upon the Lord as we find Him revealed in His Word.

The Lord Himself placed the book of Psalms with the Law and the Prophets as fully inspired Scripture (Luke 24:44), contrary to the tradition of the ancient Hebrews, who considered it as belonging among the "Writings," not of equal inspiration with the Law and the Prophets. The book of Psalms and the book of Daniel were excluded from the Jewish canon of Scripture, the former probably because it was in common use as a hymn-book, and the latter because they felt no prophet would be inspired outside the Holy Land. Ezekiel, it is true, prophesied in captivity, but he had been a priest and perhaps a prophet before he was taken captive, and also he recorded more than once that he was carried in the spirit to Jerusalem for his visions. For the same reason Judaism separated the Lamentations of Jeremiah, which were written in Egypt, from the body of his book and placed them also among the "Writings." The Lord refers to Daniel as a prophet in Matthew 24:15. The New Church canon of Old Testament Scripture is the Hebrew canon plus the Psalms, Daniel, and Lamentations.

The Lord said that the Psalms treated of Him. Psalm 119 has its internal senses throughout, and in *Prophets and Psalms* Swedenborg gives us the following very brief summary of its celestial sense: "The Lord fulfilled the Law, or the Word, from its firsts to its lasts, and therefore He was hated, and suffered temptations, and thus made the Human one with His Divine."

## From the Writings of Swedenborg

*Apocalypse Revealed*, n. 38: "Since every letter signifies a thing in the spiritual world, and thence in the angelic language; therefore David wrote the 119th Psalm, in order, according to the letters of the alphabet, beginning with Aleph and ending with Thau, as may appear from the initials of the verses there; the like appears in Psalm 111, but not so evidently. Therefore, also Abram was called Abraham, and Sarai was called Sarah; which was done for the reason that in heaven by Abraham and Sarah, they should not be understood, but the Divine, as is also the case; for the letter 'H' involves infinity, because it is only an aspirate."

*True Christian Religion*, n. 234: "There is conjunction with the Lord by means of the Word because He is the Word, that is, the essential Divine truth and good therein. This conjunction is effected by means of the sense of the letter, because the Word in that sense is in its fulness, in its holiness, and in its power . . . This conjunction is not apparent to man, but it exists in affection for truth and in the perception of truth. There is affiliation with the angels of heaven by means of the sense of the letter, because within that sense there is a spiritual and a celestial sense; and the angels are in these senses, the angels of the Lord's spiritual kingdom in the spiritual sense of the Word, and the angels of His celestial kingdom in the celestial sense. These two senses are evolved from the natural sense of the Word when it is read by a man who regards the Word as holy. The evolution is instantaneous; consequently the affiliation is also."

---

## Suggested Questions on the Lesson

P. What is a psalm? *a song*
P. How did the Jews use the book of Psalms? *hymnal*
P. Through whom were many of the Psalms written? *David*
J. What did David say about the Psalms? *inspired by God*
I. What did the Lord say about them? *prophesied about Him*
P. Which one is the longest of the Psalms? *119th*
J. What is peculiar about its structure? *"alphabetical"*
J. What is its general subject? *the Word*
J. How is this subject impressed upon us? *in every verse*
I. Why should we study the Word? *to learn how to live*
J. Why should we obey its precepts? *to find eternal happiness*
S. Why are some of the Psalms written in alphabetical order? *to show they contain a complete summary of a subject*
S. Where in the Word does its power rest? *letter or literal sense*